# FAMILY LEAVE POLICY

ISSUES IN WORK AND HUMAN RESOURCES

---

*Daniel J.B. Mitchell, Series Editor*

**BEYOND UNIONS AND COLLECTIVE BARGAINING**
*Leo Troy*

**CYBERUNION**
Empowering Labor Through Computer Technology
*Arthur B. Shostak*

**WORKING IN THE TWENTY-FIRST CENTURY**
Policies for Economic Growth Through Training,
Opportunity, and Education
*David L. Levine*

**INCOME INEQUALITY IN AMERICA**
An Analysis of Trends
*Paul Ryscavage*

**HARD LABOR**
Poor Women and Work in the Post-Welfare Era
*Joel F. Handler and Lucie White*

**NONUNION EMPLOYEE REPRESENTATION**
History, Contemporary Practice, and Policy
*Bruce E. Kaufman and Daphne Gottlieb Taras, editors*

**LABOR REGULATION IN A GLOBAL ECONOMY**
*George Tsogas*

**FAMILY LEAVE POLICY**
The Political Economy of Work and Family in America
*Steven K. Wisensale*

# FAMILY LEAVE POLICY

The Political Economy
of Work and Family
in America

## Steven K. Wisensale

*M.E. Sharpe*

Armonk, New York
London, England

**Library of Congress Cataloging-in-Publication Data**

Wisensale, Steven K., 1945–
    Family leave policy : the political economy of work and family in America / Steven K. Wisensale
    p. cm.—(Issues in work and human resources)
    Includes bibliographical references and index.
    ISBN 0-7656-0496-5 (alk. paper)
    1. Parental leave—United States. 2. Family policy—United States. I. Title. II. Series

HD6066.U5 W57 2001
33i.25′763—dc21                                                                00-046387

Printed in the United States of America

The paper used in this publication meets the minimum requirements of
American National Standard for Information Sciences
Permanence of Paper for Printed Library Materials,
ANSI Z 39.48-1984.

∞

BM (c)   10   9   8   7   6   5   4   3   2   1

To Nan—for her love, support, and good humor over the years.

# Contents

# List of Tables, Figures, and Map

**Tables**

**Figures**

**Map**

# Foreword

Public policy in the United States often proceeds on a piecemeal basis. Interrelated issues arise but are perceived as separate. In keeping with this tendency toward isolation, social policy toward the family and labor policy have traditionally been on separate tracks. Labor law, for example, deals with the problems of the individual at the workplace. Is he or she receiving the required minimum wage? Is he or she being adversely treated by the employer due to union activities? Is the individual subject to discrimination at the workplace due to race, sex, or other protected categories? For the most part, the relationship between the individual at work and issues of family support has not been clearly perceived. Family issues were not concerns of labor policy; they were the subject of social programs such as Social Security or welfare.

As Steven K. Wisensale shows in this volume, labor and employment cannot be separated from family concerns any more. Perhaps in the past, when males were seen as the sole breadwinner, such an approach was tenable. But the advent of greater female participation in the workforce, even within traditional families, suggests that the separation of labor policy and social policy is artificial. The growth of nontraditional families accentuates the need for change.

In fact, the kinds of benefit packages that employers had developed by the 1950s—the era of "Ozzie and Harriet"—already involved families, even if the employment model upon which they were based was that of the male breadwinner. Health insurance, for example, often covered dependents as well as the employee. Pensions were support mechanisms as much for the spouses of employees as for the employees themselves. Public policies that affected such benefits—such as the tax code—were de facto family policies as much as they were labor policies.

Similarly, changes in social attitudes (e.g., the growing conviction that welfare mothers should be working) meant that just as labor policy was becoming indirect social policy, so, too, was social policy intersecting with the traditional realm of labor policy. But the linkage between social policy toward families and labor policy became apparent when it was embodied in the issue of family leave—the major focus of Wisensale's policy analysis. Thus, it is quite appropriate that M.E. Sharpe include Wisensale's analysis in its publication series on work and human resources.

Family leave policy at the federal level was a key element of the Clinton administration's domestic agenda. In fact, the Family and Medical Leave Act was the first bill President Clinton signed into law. Thereafter, political candidates of both parties sought to depict themselves as advocates of family-friendly policies. Since the tendency toward more equal male/female workforce participation is continuing, and since more nontraditional family arrangements can be expected in the future, the linkage of social policy toward the family and labor policy will only become tighter. Wisensale's analysis of the continuing debate is an outstanding contribution toward our understanding of these trends.

Daniel J.B. Mitchell

# FAMILY
# LEAVE
# POLICY

# Introduction

# A Warm Rose Garden in February

While thinking about writing his book *Moral Politics: What Conservatives Know that Liberals Don't* (1996), George Lakoff asked his good friend, Paul Baum, if he could think of a single question the answer to which would be the best indicator of the difference between liberal and conservative attitudes. "Yes," Baum replied, "if your baby cries at night, do you pick him up?" Although somewhat simplistic perhaps, the exchange between Lakoff and Baum is symbolic of the division between liberals and conservatives with respect to social policy in the United States. It is the difference between demanding that self-reliance and individual responsibility flourish on one hand (those who would allow the baby to cry) and providing support and assistance to those who ask for help on the other (those who would pick up the crying baby in the dead of night).

To Lakoff, American social policy, and particularly family-oriented policy, can be divided into two camps: strict fathers (conservatives who often oppose government intervention) and nurturing parents (liberals who frequently favor such intervention). It is the difference between "strict father" Gary Bauer (1996) (*Our Hopes, Our Dreams: A Vision for America)* and "nurturing parent" Hillary Clinton (1993) (*It Takes a Village*). Or, it is the difference between George Bush's veto of the Family and Medical Leave Act (FMLA) (the strict father) and Bill Clinton's endorsement of it (the nurturing parent). It is precisely at this intersection where the private and public families have converged and where conservatives and liberals have drawn their respective lines in the sand. Put another way, one of the most pressing questions confronting policymakers in the new century will be this: Where do we draw the line between what the family is able and willing to do and what the government is expected to do? For George and Vicki Yandle of Marietta, Georgia, the answer to this question came far too late and at a price much too high.

Dixie Yandle had just turned eleven when she was diagnosed with synovial carcinoma, an extremely aggressive and incurable form of cancer that attacks the soft tissue surrounding joints. Within three weeks, one of her legs was amputated and she was placed on chemotherapy for the next two years. For her parents, Dixie's illness was emotionally and financially devastating. Home schooling had to be arranged, battles with the insurance company had to be fought, and many two-hour drives to and from the hospital had to be planned around busy work schedules. Despite the fact that George was an award-winning salesman at a local car dealership, his bosses grew impatient with his unpredictable schedule, questioned his loyalty to the firm, and raised concerns about their company's insurance premiums being raised to offset Dixie's costly medical treatments. Consequently, George was fired from his $80,000 a year job and remained unemployed for the next eighteen months.[1]

For Vicki, the home care demands of her daughter became so severe that she quit her job at a local furniture store to care for Dixie full time. George, on the other hand, eventually found a similar but lower-paying job at another local car dealership where his boss, who also had an ill child, was empathetic to his family situation and more open to a flexible work schedule. But with Vicki unemployed and George earning substantially less than before, the Yandles were struggling to survive on one-third their previous income. To avoid the bank's foreclosing on their home, they asked their adult children, who were also parents, to move in with them and pay room and board.[2]

But the Yandles were not suffering in silence, nor were they alone. As their story began to circulate beyond greater Atlanta, national television appearances and interviews were followed by testimony before legislative panels. No one should be forced to choose between their job and their family, they argued. The nation's families need and deserve a national family leave policy. However, despite their efforts and the efforts of other families who told similar stories, family leave was not looked upon favorably by everyone.[3] Just three days after the Yandles testified at a hearing in Washington in September of 1992, President George Bush vetoed the FMLA for the second time in his short tenure. But with the election of Bill Clinton two months later, the political landscape changed considerably. The new president-elect announced that he would sign the FMLA if Congress passed it one more time.

On February 4, 1993, six years after Dixie's initial diagnosis, the Yandles received a phone call from a White House aide requesting that they fly to Washington and participate in a bill signing ceremony the following morning in the Rose Garden. Perhaps even more impressive, Vicki was asked to introduce Bill Clinton who, having been inaugurated just two weeks earlier as the first Democratic president in twelve years, would sign the very first piece of legislation passed during his administration: the Family and Medical Leave Act. Introduced in 1985 and vetoed twice by George Bush, the FMLA was passed by the Senate (71–27) in the afternoon on February 4 and by the House (265–163) just before midnight.

It was an unusually warm and sunny day on February 5 as a small, enthusiastic crowd gathered in the Rose Garden. Present in the bipartisan audience were first lady Hillary Rodham Clinton; Tipper Gore, wife of the vice president; Marion Wright Edelman, director of the Children's Defense Fund; House Majority Leader Richard Gephardt (D-MO); Labor Secretary Robert Reich; Republican Senator Christopher (Kit) Bond of Missouri; Representative Patricia Schroeder (D-CO); Democratic Senator Bob Krueger of Texas; Health and Human Services Secretary Donna Shalala; and George Yandle, husband of Vicki.

Shortly after 9:30 A.M., President Clinton and Vice President Gore emerged from the White House, waved to the audience, and shook hands with a small group of legislators. The president then moved to a small wooden table where he signed the very first bill of his young administration. Using ten different pens to affix his signature, he distributed them to the bill's supporters standing nearby, including Vicki Yandle.[4] After completing his task, he rose from his chair and acknowledged the applause coming from the audience. Al Gore then moved to the podium. "Today marks the end of gridlock and a new beginning," stated the new vice president. "A decade of deadlock has ended" (C-SPAN Archives 1999). Gore then referred to the emotional and financial pressures his family faced after his young son was nearly killed by a car in 1989 in the parking lot at Baltimore's Memorial Stadium following a baseball game. "Many families all over this country know why this legislation is so critical," stated Gore. "Indeed, my wife Tipper and I met many families when we were with our son at Johns Hopkins Hospital who will benefit from this legislation. It is appropriate today for the president of the United States to be introduced by representatives of one of the American families that this bill is really designed to help, George and Vicki Yandle" (C-SPAN Archives 1999). He then turned the microphone over to Vicki Yandle.

Reading from a prepared statement, Mrs. Yandle thanked Congress for passing, and the president for signing, the FMLA. "Our family needed protection like what's provided in this law. Our family faced a terrible tragedy but this tragedy was made unnecessarily harder for us by the fact that George did not have job security during this time. In times of crisis," she continued, "people should not have to worry about keeping their jobs. They should not be forced to choose between their loved ones and the jobs they need. Thanks to President Clinton, other families will not have to make this terrible choice" (C-SPAN Archives 1999).

The president thanked Mrs. Yandle and reminded everyone that "it was America's families who have beaten the gridlock in Washington to pass family leave" (C-SPAN Archives 1999). He then thanked key Democrats who were standing behind him, including then Senate Majority Leader George Mitchell (D-ME), Senators Christopher Dodd (D-CT) and Ted Kennedy (D-MA), and Representatives William Ford (D-MI), Patricia Schroeder (D-CO), and William Clay (D-MO), and House Speaker Tom Foley (D-WA). In the spirit of bipartisanship, he praised Republican Senators Kit Bond (R-MO), George Jeffords (R-VT), and Dan Coats (R-IN), along with Congresswomen Marge Roukema (R-NJ) and Susan Molinari (R-NY) for their support of the legislation. "Family and medical leave is a matter of pure common sense and a matter of common decency," stated Clinton. "It will provide Americans with what they need most, peace of mind. Never again will parents have to fear losing their jobs because of their families" (C-SPAN Archives 1999).

The FMLA took effect six months later on August 5, 1993. It allows a worker to take up to twelve weeks of unpaid leave in any twelve-month period for the birth or adoption of a child, to care for a sick child, spouse, or parent with a serious health condition, or for the worker's own health condition. It guarantees job security in that an employee is entitled to return to the same or comparable job and requires the employer to maintain health benefits as if the employee never took leave. It prohibits a worker on leave from collecting unemployment or other forms of government compensation, and it only applies to companies with fifty or fewer workers and to workers who have been employed for at least one year or 1,250 hours. It also allows a company to deny leave to a salaried employee who falls within the highest 10 percent of the company's payroll if the worker's leave would create "substantial and grievous injury" to the business operations. It requires employees to notify their employers prior to taking leave and permits the employer to request medical opinions to justify the employee's absence. And, in the event a worker elects not to return to work after the leave expires, the employer may require the employee to repay all health care premiums that were paid during his or her absence.

When President Clinton signed the FMLA in 1993 he may have temporarily muffled those critics who reminded policymakers that the United States was one of two industrialized nations without such a policy on the books. However, and as will be discussed in greater detail in subsequent chapters, the law is quite limited in scope and does not apply to all family types, nor does it cover all caregiving scenarios. It only applies to about 6 percent of the nation's corporations and 60 percent of the work force. Because it is unpaid, most single parents cannot afford to take time off from work even if given the opportunity. Also, although the law is touted as an example of intergenerational policy making, it does not cover grandchildren who care for grandparents, nor does it cover in-law care. That is, a wife may care for her elderly mother or father but she cannot provide such care to her mother-in-law or father-in-law and be covered under the law. And further, the FMLA is totally insensitive to same-sex partners. Despite the fact that more than a thousand communities, corporations, nonprofit organizations, and universities have adopted domestic partnership policies that grant equal status to same-sex couples with respect to benefit coverage, the FMLA does not apply to this type of nontraditional family.

But nonetheless, the bill-signing ceremony in the Rose Garden marked the end of an eight-year struggle to adopt a family leave policy and represented the beginning of a new administration that promised change for America's families. "While the Republicans talk about family values, the Democrats show that they value families," proclaimed Clinton numerous times during the 1992 campaign.[5] But beyond that, the adoption of the FMLA also symbolized the federal government's recognition that both the family and the American workplace have changed considerably over the years. Therefore, appropriate policies were needed to address these changes. How far public policy has come on this issue and where it should go in the future is the subject of this book, which is divided into three major parts.

In Part I, the focus is on family and work amidst political and economic change. A brief historical overview of the American family will be presented in chapter 1. Is the family in a state of decline or is it merely in transition? Major demographic changes will be identified and their policy implications will be explored. Chapter 2 will examine the family from a political perspective by discussing in particular the emergence of family policy and tracing it through the administrations of four presidents: Carter, Reagan, Bush, and Clinton. A policy such as the FMLA can be better understood if it is first discussed within a broader political framework. Chapter 3 will cover the economics of family life, including the rise of the dual-earner couple and the demands placed upon both government and business for more family-oriented policies. And chapter 4 will address the relationship between work and family and explain how the private and public sectors have responded to this relatively new challenge.

Part II will be devoted entirely to family leave policy in the United States. Why was the United States slow in passing the FMLA compared to other industrialized countries and how does our policy differ from similar policies elsewhere? Chapter 5 will analyze state initiatives (thirty-two states adopted some form of leave policy prior to the federal FMLA in 1993), discuss their similarities and differences, and explain how actions at the state level influenced federal initiatives. In chapter 6 the formulation of the FMLA will be explored, with particular emphasis placed on how political and economic forces shaped the final version of the bill. Chapter 7 will discuss the implementation and evaluation of the FMLA. Included is a summary of a report on the law's impact, a review of the Department of Labor's monitoring activities during the first seven years of the FMLA's existence, and an analysis of more than 200 federal appellate court decisions related to the FMLA.

Part III of the volume looks to the future. Included is chapter 8, which identifies efforts put forth by the states and federal government to expand the FMLA, including a push to adopt paid leave. Chapter 9 is dedicated to a comparison of leave policy in the United States with models in the European Union. What, if any, lessons can be learned from Europe and applied to the United States? And the final chapter will draw important conclusions and offer specific options for policymakers as we continue to address the issue of work and family in America.

## Notes

1. The costs of Dixie Yandle's care exceeded $2 million over a six-year period. She died in April of 1993, slightly more than two months after President Clinton signed the FMLA and four months before it went into effect on August 5.

2. The Yandles' story was presented in a made-for-TV movie, *A Child's Wish*, which was aired January 21, 1997, on CBS. President Clinton's cameo appearance marked the first time a sitting president appeared in a popular film. According to Vicki Yandle in an interview with the author on October 7, 1999, the film was accurate in dramatizing the Yandles' experience with two exceptions. One, the main character in the film had leukemia and not the rare form of cancer that afflicted Dixie. And two, Dixie's character in the film meets President Clinton, a scene that never occurred in real life.

3. The National Partnership for Women and Families, formerly known as the Women's Legal Defense Fund, provides stories of a number of families who had experiences similar to the Yandles'. These stories can be accessed through the NPWF web site at www.nationalpartnership.org.

4. The signing ceremony was organized so quickly that the pens used by the president to sign the bill could not be embossed with specific information commemorating the event. See Ron Elving's (1995) *Conflict and Compromise: How Congress Makes the Law.*

5. This phrase or something similar was used repeatedly by the Clinton camp throughout the 1992 presidential campaign. For example, in response to a question from reporter Ann Compton during his first TV debate with President Bush, then Governor Clinton stated, "I think the president owes it to family values that he values America's families."

# Part I

## Family and Work Amidst Political and Economic Change

# Chapter 1

# The Changing American Family

In Neil Howe and Bill Strauss's *13th Gen: Abort, Retry, Ignore, Fail?* there is a cartoon depicting a confused teenager in a card shop asking the clerk a question: "Do you have a card for a half-sister's biological father's permanent companion?" (1993, 15). Though the authors' attempt to present a picture of family change may be labeled unrealistic, extreme, or even outrageous by some, the cartoon does grab one's attention and demands that at least some thought be devoted to the changing family as a new millennium begins. An excerpt from Judith Stacey's *In the Name of the Family: Rethinking Family Values in the Postmodern Age* (1996) produces a similar response. Her description of a wedding she attended in California's Silicon Valley in the 1980s is an animated version of Howe and Strauss's cartoon.

> Serving as the wedding photographer was the bride's former husband accompanied by his live-in lover, a Jewish divorcee who hoped to become his third wife. All of the wedding attendants were step-kin or step-in-laws to the groom. Two daughters from the bride's first marriage served as their mother's bride matrons; their brother joined one daughter's second husband as ushers for the groom; and the proud flower girl was a young granddaughter from the bride matron's first marriage. At least half the pews were filled with members of four generations from the confusing tangle of former, step, dual, and in-law relatives of this postmodern, divorce-extended family. (1996, 18)

Both of these portraits of family life in the 1990s, though admittedly extreme, are a far cry from those descriptions that dominated popular culture in the 1950s or even earlier.

**Family Change as Depicted in Popular Culture**

Family-oriented TV shows poured into millions of homes across the country in the 1950s and 1960s. *Ozzie and Harriet, Leave it to Beaver, Father Knows Best, The Donna Reed Show*, and others all revolved around several common themes: Dad worked and Mom did not; the kids were always well-behaved (even *Dennis the Menace* was tolerable) and, whatever conflicts arose among family members, they were minimal and short-lived. There was no evidence of, or reference to, divorce, child support, out-of-wedlock births, domestic violence, family counseling, single-motherhood (single fathers were acceptable, however, on *The Andy Griffith Show*, *My Three Sons*, and *Bonanza*), or drug and alcohol abuse. Human sexuality was suppressed to such a degree that even when the TV audience got a glimpse of the parents' sleeping quarters, they almost always saw two beds, not one.

In this idyllic black and white world, a world that was satirized almost a half century later in the film *Pleasantville*, producers and script writers ultimately agreed with Tolstoy's assessment that all happy families look the same but unhappy families are all different, each in their own way. For nearly two decades American TV viewers were saturated with nothing but happy families. Things would change considerably in the 1970s and 1980s when nontraditional families became more common. With few exceptions (*The Waltons* glorified the traditional extended family but it was set in the 1930s and 1940s), TV families included women who worked outside the home and children with only one parent. Personal conflicts were visible, and sexuality was no longer suppressed. When *Murphy Brown*, a fictitious character on a family sitcom, chose to become a single mother, she became the flash point for the family values debate in the 1992 presidential election. And, by the mid-1990s, the subject of dysfunctional families dominated TV talks shows. Today, most traditional nuclear families on TV are found in black and white reruns.

But television shows are not the only barometers for measuring changes in family life over time. Hollywood films are also helpful. Through the 1940s and 1950s most films focused on family unity, regardless if it was during the Great Depression (*The Grapes of Wrath*), World War II (*The Fighting Sullivans* and *Since You Went Away*), or the early years of the Cold War (*The Best Years of Our Lives, A Tree Grows in Brooklyn*, and *Father of the Bride*), when men came back from war and working women returned home to raise children. However, with films such as *Rebel Without a Cause*, which captured a troubled family dealing with teenage torment, and *A Raisin in the Sun*, which provided white America with a glimpse of black family life and the devastating effects of racism, the door was opened for filmmakers to explore the unexplored.

Whether or not art imitates life or vice versa has been a popular question that has challenged philosophers and social commentators for more than a century. However, films in the 1970s painted a series of family portraits that differed greatly from their predecessors. *Alice Doesn't Live Here Anymore, An Unmarried Woman*, and *Kramer vs. Kramer* represent a few examples that exposed dysfunctional families and bitter divorces, as well as the independence of women, and the trials of single parenthood. In the 1980s work and family issues emerged in such films as *Ordinary People, Baby Boom*, and *Parenthood*. And, as we approached the new millennium, films with family preservation as their theme began to emerge. Couples, despite being strained by affairs, substance abuse, and domestic violence, chose to "stick it out," not unlike the true-life story of the Clintons in the White House. Films such as *Flirting with Disaster, Something to Talk About, When a Man Loves a Woman*, and *Leaving Las Vegas* can be included in this category. So can Oscar winner *American Beauty*, a story about a dysfunctional family in modern suburbia where moral relativism prevails.[1] But meanwhile, as the changing American family was being depicted on the screen (accurately or not) over the last sixty years, family change was also being reflected in school textbooks.[2]

## Farewell to Dick and Jane: A Changing Family in School Textbooks

Between the 1930s and 1960s, 85 million children learned to read from *Dick and Jane*, a series of elementary reading books published by Scott, Foresman and Company that portrayed family life as always happy, stable, and carefree. Dad worked and Mom stayed home with the children, cooked all the meals, and never drove the family car. In their book, *Growing Up with Dick and Jane* (1996), Carole Kismaric and Marvin Heiferman remind us that whatever crises arose, they were limited to a lost toy, a missing pet, or a runaway wagon. During the Great Depression and World War II, Dick and Jane's charmed life was seen by children as a dream that may come true some day.

After the war, Dick and Jane's life in the storybooks closely resembled the lives of millions of kids who had moved to the suburbs. Between 1945 and 1955, 11 million of the 13 million new homes constructed were in suburbia. As Kismaric and Heiferman describe it, the trouble-free world of Dick and Jane was surrounded by a white picket fence in a very safe neighborhood. It was a world not too different from that of the carefree world of white suburban kids, the baby boomers, who were born after the war and knew little about the Great Depression or World War II. In essence, the fictitious characters and the real kids became mirror images of each other. And those images that were shaped and reinforced in the classroom during the day were fortified by television at night where very similar families appeared during prime time.

*Dick and Jane* slowly changed and eventually faded as the years passed. With the publication of Rudolf Flesch's *Why Johnny Can't Read* (1955), school boards were pressured to turn to phonics as the primary method for teaching reading. Interest groups also lobbied publishers to make major changes in the learning materials used to mold young minds, as diversity and multiculturalism eventually emerged as core issues. After all, *Dick and Jane* stories were anchored to a family structure of the 1920s in which the father worked and the mother stayed home with two or more children.

By the mid-1960s, "pressure groups wanted textbook publishers to show a mother going to work, and a father who did his fair share of housework and child care. Editors were told by teachers and school administrators that the characters had become stereotypes, not right for the time, not representative of the changing demographics of America, its ethnic and racial mix" (Kismaric and Heiferman 1996, 106).

In 1965 Dick and Jane said hello to new neighbors, a black family with three children: Mike, Pam, and Penny. "Mike is just like Dick. He's the same height, wears the same kind of clothes and runs around just as much" (Kismaric and Heiferman 1996, 98). The year 1965 was significant for another reason: Scott Foresman ceased publication of *Dick and Jane*, though it continued to sell the last edition through 1970. Times had changed and so had the American family.

In an effort to keep pace with a changing family amidst a rapidly changing society, school officials across the country sought learning materials that reflected the new family images which were emerging. There were kids who had single mothers, interracial parents, stepbrothers and sisters, multiple grandparents, and gay and lesbian relatives. Or, if their families were not like these, they knew kids who lived such lives. To address these changes, New York City public schools introduced the Rainbow Curriculum. Geared to elementary-age children learning to read, the curriculum consisted of a series of books that addressed multiculturalsim and family diversity. However, books such as *Heather Has Two Mommies*, *Daddy's Roommate*, and *Gloria Goes to Gay Pride Day* proved much too controversial for many parents. Within a year, school chancellor Joseph Fernandez had resigned, and Congress was considering a proposed bill that would cut federal funds from any public school that encouraged homosexuality "as a positive alternative lifestyle" through counseling, the curriculum, or the distribution of pamphlets.[3]

But the debate over whether school curricula merely reflected family change or contributed to the family's demise was not confined to the content of elementary school books. Concern was also raised about high school and college textbooks that focused on the American family. Paul C. Vitz of New York University published a report on the treatment of marriage in high school textbooks. In *The Course of True Love: Marriage in High School Textbooks* (1998), Vitz found that too many of the texts lumped marriage in with health-related subjects and avoided important issues associated with interpersonal interaction in marriage. His recommendation was to abandon such texts and rely instead on the great works of literature to teach the lessons of life, love, and marriage.

Similarly, several years after New York City's debacle with its Rainbow Curriculum, Norval Glenn, research director of the Institute of American Values's Council on Families, completed a study that assessed the portrayal of families and marriage in college textbooks. *Closed Hearts, Closed Minds: The Textbook Story of Marriage* (Glenn 1992) reported on twenty recently published undergraduate marriage and family textbooks and reached three major conclusions. First, current textbooks convey a predominantly negative view of marriage by presenting it as more of a problem than a solution. Second, the texts focus too much attention on adult relationships and, therefore, shortchange children. And third, argues Glenn, the texts are saturated with errors, distortions, and glaring examples of important omissions. "These textbooks are a national embarrassment," contends Glenn. "They are both a cause and a result of a society in which marriage as an institution is growing steadily weaker" (1997, 3).[4]

Popular culture's depiction of the family is one way to gauge changes in domestic life over time, as is the portrayal of family life in school textbooks. However, a more reliable and perhaps more respected source for at least identifying, if not explaining family change in America, is the United States Bureau of the Census.

## U.S. Census as Barometer of Family Change

The U.S. Bureau of the Census offers the most detailed statistics available on the American family. In gathering its information, the Bureau begins first with the definition of a *household*. A person within the household is then identified as the householder, or the person who owns, rents, or otherwise maintains the home. Households are then divided into *family households* and *nonfamily households*. A distinguishing characteristic between the two categories is that in a family household there resides at least one relative of the householder. A nonfamily household includes a person living alone or residing with nonrelatives, such as friends, roommates, or boarders.

The Bureau then divides family households even further, into families maintained by married couples and "other families" maintained by men or women with no spouse at home. In short, according to the Bureau, a family household is a group of two or more people living together who are related by birth, adoption, or marriage, thus constituting what is commonly referred to as the traditional nuclear family. However, a family household may also consist of a single parent with his or her child or children sharing a home, or it can be any combination of relatives with no spouse of the householder under the same roof.

In 1998, the Bureau of the Census reported that there were 102.5 million households in the United States. Of these, about 71 million, or 69 percent, are family households, compared to about 31 million or 31 percent nonfamily households (U.S. Bureau of the Census 1998). More important, however, is not so much what these numbers represent today, but how they have changed over time. For example, in 1940, 90 percent of all households were classified as family households. By 1970 that percentage had dropped to 81 percent, by 1980 to 74 percent, and by 1998 to 69 percent. There are other signs of family change, including the changing state of marriage, the rise of single parenthood, the increase of same-sex partners, smaller families, more dual-earner couples, and an aging population as a whole.

**Changing State of Marriage**

On July 1, 1999, the National Marriage Project at Rutgers University published *The State of Our Unions: The Social Health of Marriage in America*. Using national indicators related to marriage, the report presents important historical and statistical information about marriage over the last forty years. Marriage rates have fallen to a forty-year low. More couples are experiencing unhappiness in their marriage. Young women in particular are pessimistic about having a successful marriage. And teenagers are also pessimistic about the future of marriage, although they do recognize the importance of it. Two positive trends are that the rates of unwed births and divorce are in decline. These two developments coincide with a report issued by the Population Reference Bureau three years earlier. *The United States in Mid-Decade* (Population Reference Bureau 1996) concluded that although the family unit had undergone radical changes in the previous twenty-five years, it was beginning to stabilize and the major changes in family structure have probably passed.

Whether or not this assessment is accurate remains to be seen. However, in the meantime, some facts remain indisputable. For example, although marriage still dominates as the preferred choice for forming families, the rate of marriage has declined from 11 per 1,000 population in 1950, to 8 per 1,000 in 1995 (U.S. Bureau of the Census 1997). Running parallel to this trend is the decision by more young people to delay marriage. For example, between 1960 and 1980 the median age at first marriage increased from 22.8 to 24.7 years for men and from 20.3 to 22 years for women (U.S. Bureau of the Census 1998). By 1997, the age at first marriage had risen to twenty-six for men and to twenty-four for women (U.S. Bureau of the Census 1997). Correspondingly, the rate of nonmarital cohabitation has been on the rise over the last four decades. In 1960, according to the Bureau of the Census, there were 440,000 unmarried cohabiting couples. By 1997 there were over 4 million such couples and almost 36 percent of them had children under the age of fifteen (U.S. Bureau of the Census 1998).

Another major trend associated with marriage is the rate of divorce. In the 1950s and 1960s, the divorce rate ranged between 2.1 to 2.6 per 1,000 population. By the late 1970s the divorce rate reached 5.3 where it leveled off during the 1980s. By 1998 the rate had dropped some to 4.3 but still remained one of the highest in the world (Singh 1994). Furthermore, using current statistics, some predict that half of all marriages will end in divorce (U.S. Bureau of the Census 1998). However, some individuals will marry and divorce multiple times, thus adding to the number of divorces overall and increasing the percentage of stepfamilies. When broken down by race, about one-third of the white and Hispanic marriages end in divorce. For blacks, however, the rate is about 50 percent (Kamerman and Kahn 1997).

But divorce is not the end. In the United States in particular, remarriage has become quite common (Cherlin 1992; Norton and Miller 1992; Sweet and Bumpass 1987). About 75 percent of divorced men and 60 percent of divorced women choose to remarry and, therefore, increase the number of so-called blended families. Today, for example, 20 percent of married-couple families have at least one stepchild under age eighteen.[5]

## The Rise of Single Parenthood

The United States far outdistances other nations in the percentage of single parents (Wolff, Rutten, and Bayers 1992). A high divorce rate, combined with a steady rise in out-of-wedlock births, particularly among teenagers, has produced a major change in family composition over the last thirty years. For example, in 1970 about 11 percent of families were headed by single parents, mostly mothers. By 1997, that figure had risen to 28 percent. However, while the percentage of mother-headed households doubled over that same time period, the percentage of father-headed households tripled. Today, 23 percent of all families are headed by a single mother; 5 percent are single-father families (U.S. Bureau of the Census 1998). Consequently, today fewer children live with both parents and the percentage varies across racial and ethnic categories. In 1980 more than 80 percent of white children lived with both parents. By 1995 it had dropped to 75 percent. For Hispanic children the percentage dropped from 75 in 1980 to 62 in 1995, and for black children there was a decrease from 42 percent in 1980 to 33 percent in 1995 (U.S. Bureau of the Census 1997). But even more important, perhaps, is the overwhelming evidence that shows most single-parent families living either below or near the poverty line (McLanahan and Sandefur 1994). Household economics is a topic to be covered later.

## The Increase in Same-Sex Couples

Two dramatic events occurred within the gay community over the last thirty years that have had profound effects on the profile of the traditional American family. In 1969, a police raid of the Stonewall Inn, a gay bar in New York City, produced several nights of riots and galvanized the gay rights movement on a national level. Numerous demonstrations followed and specific demands were made of policymakers to grant equal status to gays and lesbians. A little more than a decade later, the AIDS epidemic produced more demands by gays who sought insurance coverage for their partners, demanded equal access to dying lovers in hospitals, and requested that their desired input in making funeral arrangements be recognized. This, in turn, produced what is commonly referred to as the domestic partnership policy. Today, more than 1,000 corporations, organizations, and universities offer such a policy to employees who request, in writing, that their same-sex partners be covered under the same benefits as those granted to married couples. In 2000, Vermont became the first state to adopt a domestic partnership policy. These developments have resulted in a marked increase in same-sex partners "coming out" and revealing their lifestyles to census takers. As a result, in 1997, according to the Bureau of the Census, 2 percent (about 132,000) of the nation's households that included two unrelated adults consisted of same-sex partners with children under fifteen years of age (U.S. Bureau of the Census 1998). Furthermore, a growing number of same-sex couples are choosing to form families through adoption or various methods of reproductive technologies.

## Smaller Families

What many view as a recent shift toward smaller families is actually a trend that began in the nineteenth century. Interrupted only briefly by the post–World War II baby boom generation (1946–1964), it picked up where it left off in the mid-1960s (Coontz 1992; Kamerman and Kahn 1997; South and

Tolnay 1992; Cherlin 1992). The fertility rate (the number of live births per 1,000 women of reproductive age, fifteen to forty-four years of age) increased considerably during the postwar baby boom and peaked at 118 births in 1960. By 1997, it had declined to 65.4 live births per 1,000 women. This trend obviously affected family size, and in 1970, the average family consisted of 3.58 individuals. By 1990 it had declined to 3.17 but then climbed back to 3.20 where it holds today (U.S. Bureau of the Census 1997). Put another way, between 1960 and 1990, families with three or more children dropped from 36 to 20 percent, while those with only one child increased from 32 to 42 percent (Kamerman and Kahn 1997). But more impressive, by 1996 the most common household type was that of a married couple with no children, representing 29 percent of all U.S. households. Either the couple had no children or they were no longer living at home. About 25 percent of all households consisted of married couples with children, and another 25 percent were individuals residing alone (U.S. Bureau of the Census 1997).

### More Dual-Earner Couples

Although the increase in the number of dual-earner couples will be discussed in greater detail in chapters 3 and 4, it has become such an important development in the last twenty years that it deserves some attention in this opening chapter. The family in which the father is the sole "breadwinner" and the mother stays home to raise children and "keep the house" has not been the norm since the 1970s. By 1997, and after three decades of married women steadily entering the labor force, this type of household represented only 18.7 percent of all married-couple families (U.S. Bureau of the Census 1998). For example, in 1960 only 32 percent of married women worked; by 1996 the percentage stood at 61 and continues to climb (Chadwick and Heaton 1999). More significantly, however, and a fact that will be discussed in some detail later, is the number of married mothers with young children who have entered the workforce. According to the Bureau of Labor Statistics of the U.S. Department of Labor, in 1997 there were 11.3 million married-couple families with children under six years of age. Of these families, 61.4 percent consisted of mothers who were in the labor force (U.S. Bureau of Labor Statistics 1998). This fact alone is loaded with serious policy implications that will be explored in depth in succeeding chapters.

### An Aging Population and the Future of Family Care

The number of persons aged sixty-five and older has increased substantially over the last thirty years (Manton and Stallard 1994). Just in the ten-year period between 1980 and 1990, the number of persons sixty-five or older increased from 25.5 million (11.3 percent of the total U.S. population) to 31 million (12.5 percent of the total population). Equally significant is the trend within the trend. That is, during that same time period, the population of those over eighty-five grew considerably, from 2.2 million in 1980 (about 1 percent of the U.S. population) to 3.0 million in 1990 (about 1.2 percent of the U.S. population) (U.S. Bureau of the Census 1996). This age group, with its multiple chronic illnesses, will place great demands on the healthcare system in general and family caregivers in particular. And, in terms of future population projections, there is no relief in sight.[6]

According to existing census data, moderate projections indicate that the population of people sixty-five and over who represented 12.5 percent of the total U.S. population in 1990, will increase to 13.3 percent by 2010 and reach as high as 20.4 percent by 2050. For the elderly minority the increase is even more rapid, rising from 13 percent of the elderly population in 1990, to 16 percent in 2000, to 22 percent in 2020, and to 33 percent by 2050 (U.S. Bureau of the Census 1996). By mid-century, the elderly population, like the U.S. population as a whole, will be very heterogeneous in race, ethnicity, and socioeconomic status. Clearly, with the baby-boom population aging, the demand for family care will increase and companies will be pressured by employees for release time to assist aging parents. Signs of this conflict are already visible on the horizon.

In a 1997 study of 1,509 people conducted for Metropolitan Life by the National Alliance for Caregivers and the American Association for Retired Persons (AARP), surveyors found that one in four families had at least one adult who had provided care for an elderly relative or friend in the previous twelve months. On average, the caregivers surveyed were forty-five years of age or older in 1996, and they provided about eight years of care (National Alliance for Caregiving and AARP 1997). In a follow-up study two years later, it was learned that 62 percent of fifty-five individuals surveyed indicated that they had asked supervisors, coworkers, or management for some kind of help or support with their caregiving responsibilities at home (MetLife 1999). However, only 23 percent of companies with 100 or more employees have programs in place to support elder care (Families and Work Institute 1997). "Elder care is to the twenty-first century what child care has been for the last few decades," contends Joyce Ruddock, head of the Long-Term Care Group at Metropolitan Life (*New York Times* 1999d, 1).

As has been presented here, families have undergone major changes during the past three decades: higher divorce rates, postponement of marriage, lower fertility, more dual-earner couples, and smaller families amidst an aging population. Historically, the families, particularly the women within those families, have played a key role in providing care and support for older, frail elderly relatives. Only 7 percent of such families rely exclusively on formal care arrangements (Wolf 1994; Soldo and Freedman 1994). Whether or not working women will be able and willing to provide informal care to the elderly in the future remains an unknown, as does the role that government will play in addressing both the current and future needs of family caregivers. How the government responds to this challenge may ultimately depend on the particular perspectives of those in power.

### Perspectives in Conflict: Is the Family in Decline or in Transition?

In 1859, an article appeared in the *Boston Quarterly Review* that concluded that "the family, in its old sense, is disappearing from our land, and not only our free institutions are threatened but the very existence of our society is endangered" (Lantz et al. 1976). Nearly 150 years later, these sentiments were echoed by George Will in an editorial, "As the Family Disintegrates So Does Our Society." Heralding the publication of James Q. Wilson's *The Moral Sense* (1993), Will blamed a steady decline in parental investment in children for many of society's problems. "A child's moral sense is at risk in a cold, erratic, disorderly family," stated Will. "The failure of families and work experiences to perform that shaping function has many consequences," he concluded (Will 1993, 14).

Others sounded similar alarm bells, including David Blankenhorn in *Fatherless America: Confronting Our Most Urgent Social Problem* (1995); Maggie Gallagher in *The Abolition of Marriage: How We Destroy Lasting Love* (1996) and also in *The Age of Unwed Mothers* (1999); Dana Mack's *The Assault on Parenthood: How Our Culture Undermines the Family* (1997); and Sylvia Ann Hewlett and Cornel West's *The War Against Parents: What We Can Do for America's Beleaguered Moms and Dads* (1998). The message is consistent and clear: The American family is unraveling because of major cultural and political failures, and drastic steps should be taken immediately to salvage it.

Such an assessment of the American family appears to coincide with the views of the American public. On August 1, 1999, the *New York Times* ran an article that covered nationwide Gallup polls over the last half century. For the first time in fifty years, in response to the question, "What do you think is the most important problem facing the country today?" the respondents named "family decline," along with ethics and morality, as the number-one challenge confronting the nation.[7] This finding is a far cry from previous "number one" concerns, such as peace and war, civil rights, the economy, and violent crime (*New York Times* 1999a, 4).

Even more recently, the July/August 1999 issue of *Society* devoted an entire symposium to "American Families in Crisis." Included were articles by Jean Bethke Elshtain (1999), Steven L. Nock (1999), David Popenoe (1999), and Frank F. Furstenburg, Jr. (1999). Elshtain, chair of the Council on Civil Society and a professor at the University of Chicago, contends that our major institutions, particularly the family, are not only in decline but intertwined. Our economic system and family values are like a pair of twins joined at the hip. "When, for example, we come to believe as employers and employees that relationships are typically short-term, that loyalty is outdated, and that 'me first' is the final rule, should it surprise or even concern us when these same principles come to dominate our understandings of marriage, parenthood, and civic life?" (Elshtain 1999, 18).

Although it may be tempting at this point to employ Mark Twain's famous quote ("The reports of my death are greatly exaggerated") to counter such doomsday assessments of the American family, there is general agreement among researchers, policymakers, and popular commentators alike that the family has been undergoing major changes. This is particularly true when the last fifty years are selected as the time frame for assessment. But, even then, attempts to reach consensus on the extent of family change, the speed at which it is occurring, whether or not a particular change is positive or negative, and to what degree the family shapes society and vice versa, can be a confusing and elusive process. Furthermore, highly visible but contradictory studies do not help matters any.

In 1996, the Population Reference Bureau (PRB) stated that increases in the number of two-parent households with children, decreases in the divorce rate, and other changes suggested that the American family was stabilizing, not declining. "It's true that the American family has undergone some very radical changes in the past 25 years," stated Carol De Vita of the PRB. "But what I want to emphasize is that the major changes in the family structure are probably passed" (Holmes 1996, A1).

Echoes of the Population Reference Bureau's Report were heard in Washington two years later. In the spring of 1998 Cable News Network (CNN) reported that the U.S. Census Bureau had issued findings from a study in which it was concluded that the trend of the shrinking, dysfunctional, and fragmented family that began in the 1950s has begun to stabilize in the 1990s. Both the divorce rates and the percentage of single-parent families leveled off in the 1990s. The divorce rate per 1,000 people was 4.1 in 1995, down from 4.7 in 1990 and 5.0 in 1985. With respect to single-parent families, in which the percentage of such households doubled between 1970 and 1990 from 6 to 12 percent, it increased less than two percentage points during the 1990s. However, other findings of the study indicated that certain trends were moving in the opposite direction. For example, births to single women continued to rise. In 1990, about 26 percent of births were to single mothers; by 1994 it had climbed to 33 percent. The proportion of single fathers also increased, from 14 percent in 1990 to 17 percent by 1995 (CNN, May 28, 1998).

One year later, on November 24, 1999, the National Opinion Research Center (NORC) at the University of Chicago issued a report that ran counter to the two studies referred to above. While recognizing that the family had undergone a major transformation over the last thirty years, the NORC study predicted even greater change for the coming century. Households will continue to move away from the traditional model of a stay-at-home mother, working father, and children. "Because of divorce, cohabitation and single parenthood, a majority of families rearing children in the next century will probably not include the children's original two parents," stated Tom W. Smith, author of the NORC report, *The Emerging 21st-Century American Family* (National Opinion Research Center 1999).

In discussing change in general and family change in particular, it is important to keep in mind that the survey methods, polling techniques, data-gathering strategies, and types of questions being asked by researchers about families often generate information that was never gathered before. Consequently, the exercise of comparing families of the present to those of the past may produce a very distorted picture. Stephanie Coontz, for example, argues in *The Way We Never Were* (1992) that it is difficult to draw any definitive conclusions about how families have changed and whether or not they are better or worse as a result.

Contrary to popular beliefs that today's families have abandoned extended-kinship networks, that there are more out-of-wedlock births than ever before, and that a rising divorce rate is dissolving the institution of marriage, Coontz argues that there were indeed other times in our history when families were seen as weak, fragmented, and unstable. Arguing that the family has always been vulnerable to social and economic change, she emphasizes that the 1950s represented the most atypical decade in the history of marriage and the family. "Taking the 1950s as the traditional norm overstates both the novelty of modern family life and the continuity of tradition," writes Coontz. "In some ways, today's families are closer to older patterns than were '50s families" (Coontz 1992, 41). Therefore, the family is not so much in decline, contends Coontz, as it is in a state of transition. Sam Roberts reached a similar conclusion, "What today is regarded longingly as traditional was always more idealized than real," he wrote in *Who We Are: A Portrait of America* (1993, 29).

Richard T. Gill would agree with Coontz and Roberts on several points.

In his *Posterity Lost: Progress, Ideology, and the Decline of the American Family* (1997), he concludes that the parents of today's baby boomers, not the boomers themselves, are the real revolutionaries. He cites three reasons why this is the case. First, the baby boomers' parents had more kids than the parents before them or since. A 2.2 fertility rate in 1940 climbed to 3.8 by 1957, just beyond the mid-point of the baby boom era (1946–1964). By 1976 it had fallen to the extremely low level of 1.7, or 55 percent below where it had been nineteen years before.

Second, the baby boomers' parents also divorced less than couples did before or since, breaking a trend that had risen steadily since the 1870s. Following the eighteen-year break of the baby-boom era, divorce again began to rise. And third, the mothers of baby boomers chose to stay home from work during this period, breaking another major trend that saw women entering the labor force at a steady clip from the turn of the century through World War II. However, the trend of women going to work resumed after 1964 when the baby-boom era concluded. In short, in terms of family demographics, the 1950s appear to be more of a freak accident of the past than a standard by which to measure social trends of today (Gill 1997).

David Popenoe, however, assumes a much different position with respect to families. In *Disturbing the Nest* (1988), he cites five major trends in families that may ultimately be destructive. First, individuals within families are becoming more autonomous, thus eroding family solidarity. Second, the family is becoming less capable of fulfilling its primary social functions: procreation, regulating sexual conduct, socializing children, and providing care to family members. Third, the family is losing its authority to other institutions, such as the state, schools, and media. Fourth, as families shrink in size and become less stable, their members are more inclined to leave the unit permanently. And fifth, the concept of "familism," the tradition of putting family needs above personal wants, is declining in comparison to other values, such as individualism and egalitarianism.

In a full-page essay that appeared in the April 14, 1993, issue of *The Chronicle of Higher Education*, Popenoe assailed what he considered to be the misguided optimism of Stephanie Coontz (1992), Judith Stacey (1990), Arlene Skolnick (1991), and other so-called family optimists who dismiss "family decline" as a myth and celebrate "alternative life styles." To them, the family is not necessarily in trouble nor is it the source of society's ills; it is merely adjusting to larger systemic changes. To Popenoe, however, the picture is very different. The American family is not simply "changing"; it is getting weaker. Family decline is responsible for some of our most pressing social problems, and the breakup of the two-parent household is at the very center of the problem. "In short," writes Popenoe, "the child-centered two-parent family shows growing signs of disintegration, reflected most clearly in the continued high rate of divorce and the steady growth in the number of unwed mothers" (1993, 48).

Popenoe is not alone in his perspective on the family. His allies, also alarmed at the state of America's families, include William Galston, former White House domestic policy advisor; Barbara Dafoe Whitehead, codirector of the National Marriage Project at Rutgers University (Popenoe is the other codirector); Mary Ann Glendon of Harvard Law School; Jean Bethke Elshtain of the University of Chicago; Sylvia Ann Hewlett, president of the National Parenting Association; and David Blankenhorn, president of the Institute of American Values. Founded in 1987, the Institute is a private organization devoted to research, publication, and public education on major issues of family well being and civil society. Among other things, the Institute supports the Council of Families in America, an interdisciplinary research organization composed of academics and family experts under the direction of David Popenoe.

If Blankenhorn is not a pessimist, he is, at the very least, an extremely restless sentinel. In *Rebuilding the Nest: A New Commitment to the American Family* (Blankenhorn et al. 1990), he identifies what he refers to as the "five key indicators of the deinstitutionalization of marriage in the U.S." These include the almost constant rise (until very recently) of out-of-wedlock births, the percentage of unmarried teen mothers, the steady rise in the divorce rate over the past twenty-five years, the increasing percentage of children living with one parent, and the decreasing percentage of adult life spent with a spouse and children. Inspired by Gramsci's "pessimism of the intellect, optimism of the will," Blankenhorn tends to side with the pessimists and their assessment of family life in America. "My own sense is that, in the final analysis, the pessimists have the better argument—that we as a society are increasingly unwilling, either through public behavior or private action, to value purposes larger than the self, and are especially unwilling to make those sacrifices necessary to foster good environments for children" (1990, 17).

Clearly, not everyone studying families in the United States, even when they share the same national census data, always agree on the pictures they see or the conclusions that are drawn. For example, in *Public and Private Families* (1996), Andrew Cherlin reminds us that the purpose of the family has changed. Originally designed to cope with scarcity, the family is now required to perform in an era of greater (though not necessarily equitable) prosperity. In a similar vein, Sheila Kamerman and Alfred Kahn (1997) contend that the two most powerful trends afoot with respect to America's families are the rise in the number of lone-mother families and the increase in the employment rates of wives. "Greater economic independence for women has led to higher numbers of lone mothers and the growth in divorce rates and out-of-wedlock births has led to a greater need for economic independence for women" (Kamerman and Kahn 1997, 406).

But regardless of one's perspective concerning the family, optimists and pessimists alike consistently find common ground on at least three issues. First, they agree that the statistical profile of the U.S. family has changed dramatically over the last twenty years. The divorce rate has increased sharply, single parenthood continues to rise, more mothers work, there are more non-traditional families than ever before in our history, and more couples delay marriage longer and have fewer children than previous cohorts.

Second, there is also general agreement that external forces, particularly economic change, have had a major impact on the family. This is especially true for young middle-class families. With many of today's younger couples unable to do as well financially as their parents' generation, and one wage earner unable to support a family on a sole income, the dual-earner couple has become commonplace. This development, in turn, has left less time for parents to be with children, created a strain between work and family, and produced a greater demand for family-oriented public policies.

And third, the U.S. population is aging and more people with chronic illnesses are projected to live longer than at any point in our history. Consequently, greater numbers of elderly and politicians alike will rely on a stable dependency ratio between employed young and unemployed old to protect Social Security and to provide less costly informal family care to those in need. These three emerging phenomena will affect both the structure and function of the family well into the twenty-first century. And clearly, the role that public policy should play with respect to the changing family will be at the core of future political debates.

## Policy Implications of Family Change

Historically, the family has served as society's fundamental social unit, producing and raising children, caring for the young, old, and disabled, and socializing its members in character development and general citizenship. Referred to as the "germ cell of civilization" by Sigmund Freud, the family's primary strength lies in its ability to perform its important functions (sometimes succeeding, sometimes failing), despite being subjected to major internal disruptions, including divorce, illness, and domestic violence. Its primary weakness, on the other hand, is its vulnerability to external forces such as social and economic change. If policymakers are reluctant to intervene in the former sphere (the so-called private family), pressure will mount to address the latter (external forces). How and to what extent new policy initiatives respond to the internal and external forces affecting today's households may ultimately determine the future health and well-being of America's families.

Among the social trends and external forces cited previously, one of the strongest and most persistent developments has been the steady flow of mothers into the work force. As early as 1987 the Congressional Research Service was informing policymakers that 65 percent of women with children aged three to five years were employed, a percentage that represented the fastest growing portion of the U.S. labor market. In 1987, 70 percent of all mothers with children aged six to seventeen were in the labor force, and a decade later, the percentage had increased and was still climbing. According to the Maternal and Child Health Bureau (1998), by 1997 about 78 percent of mothers with children between the ages of six and seventeen were employed. For mothers with children under the age of six, 65 percent were in the workforce. Not surprisingly, more families and the advocacy groups who represent them have demanded the enactment of appropriate child-care and family-leave policies.

Jane Flax (1983) predicted such an outcome years earlier. She and others strongly argued that the synergism between internal developments and external forces ultimately affects the internal functioning of the family unit. For example, in an unstable economy, such as during periods of high inflation and recession, the wife may feel compelled to take a paying job to support the family. This act, in turn, may result in a change in personal relations within the unit as well as place greater demands on the state to adopt policies that support such families. The wife, who may no longer be economically dependent on her husband but needs support in raising children or caring for elderly parents, will begin to demand child-care programs and family-leave benefits from her employer, the government, or both. Developments such as these, in which the private family went public with its demands, drove issues such as family leave policy onto the political agenda. An analysis of the formulation and implementation of the Family and Medical Leave Act of 1993 may shed some light on this question. But the FMLA has to be viewed within a much broader context by first exploring the history of family policy in the United States.

## Notes

1. A good source for capturing the changing American family on film from the 1930s through the 1980s is *Homeward Bound*, a sixty-minute video produced by Schaffer Productions for American Movie Classics in 1994.

2. The study of the family in popular culture does not have to end with films and TV sit-coms. In the May 2000 issue of the *Journal of Marriage and the Family*, an article by Ralph LaRossa and others chronicles 490 nationally syndicated cartoons

published between 1940 and 1990. The comic-strip families wrestled with the most controversial family issues of the twentieth century, including the role of women, the proper place of men in the family, and the contribution of fathers to the overall development of their children. See Ralph LaRossa, Charles Jaret, Malati Godgil, and G. Robert Wynn (2000), "The Changing Culture of Fatherhood in Comic Strip Families: A Six-Decade Analysis." *Journal of Marriage and the Family* 62, 2, 375–387.

3. Examples of so-called culture wars at the local level are included in Elaine B. Sharp's *Culture Wars and Local Politics* (1999), published by the University Press of Kansas.

4. On June 29, 2000, at the Smart Marriages conference in Denver, leaders of the marriage movement released a new joint statement: *The Marriage Movement: A Statement of Principles*. More than 100 prominent scholars and religious and civic leaders pledged that "in this decade we will turn the tide on marriage and reduce divorce and unmarried childbearing, so that each year more children will grow up protected by their own two happily married parents and more adults' marriage dreams will come true." Signers of the statement included Robert Bellah, William Galston, Amitai Etzioni, James Q. Wilson, Judith Wallerstein, Maggie Gallagher, Mary Pipher, and Mary Ann Glendon. Names of other signers and information about the Marriage Movement can be found at its web site at www.marriagemovement.org.

5. Included in the U.S. Census Bureau's category of "own children" are stepchildren, along with birth and adopted children.

6. A source for understanding the significance of a shifting dependency ratio amidst changing demographics is Richard Easterlin's "The Economic Impact of Prospective Population Changes in Advanced Industrial Countries: A Historical Perspective" (1991, 299–309). While there is a tendency to focus on the ratio of "old vs. young" in terms of the stability of Social Security, often overlooked is the dependency ratio between available family caregivers and frail elderly relatives in need of social support. However, Easterlin's prediction that women would return to the home in the 1980s proved inaccurate. See Janet Z. Giele's "Decline of the Family: Conservative, Liberal, and Feminist Views" (2000). In *Public and Private Families: A Reader*, ed. Andrew J. Cherlin. New York: McGraw Hill.

7. James Q. Wilson's *The Moral Sense* (1993) was one of many books published in the 1990s that raised questions about America's moral foundations and offered an analytical framework for understanding major changes in society. Other works included William J. Bennett's *The Index of Leading Cultural Indicators* (1994) and *The Death of Outrage: Bill Clinton and the Assault on American Ideals* (1998); Robert Bork's *Slouching Towards Gomorrah: Modern Liberalism and American Decline* (1996); Richard Gill's *Posterity Lost: Progress, Ideology, and the Decline of the American Family* (1997); Gertrude Himmelfarb's *One Nation, Two Cultures* (1999); and Christopher Wolfe's *The Family, Civil Society and the State* (1998). Standard references for grasping the status of the American family in the 1990s are Robert Bellah's *Habits of the Heart: Individualism and Commitment in American Life* (1996), and Christopher Lasch's *Haven in a Heartless World: The Family Beseiged* (1995).

# Chapter 2

# The Family and American Politics

Family policy, what government does to and for families, is a term that has been employed quite frequently in the recent past, despite the fact that those who use it have experienced some difficulty in defining it clearly. Mary Jo Bane (1980), for example, has argued that family policy in a formal sense simply does not exist in the United States. Gilbert Steiner, in *The Futility of Family Policy* (1981) took it a step further. Not only does family policy not exist in the United States, contends Steiner, the complexity of our political system will prevent it from ever assuming a form similar to what exists in Europe and Scandinavia. At best, if one argues from this perspective, family policy is more an academic discipline than a blueprint for government action.

Others, such as Cherlin (1988, 1996), Dempsey (1981), Edelman (1987), and Scanzoni (1991), have been less pessimistic and, therefore, more willing to at least view family policy as a dual image on a split screen. On one side are specific policies aimed at particular families; on the other side are more general policies that, to a greater or lesser degree, affect families in some way, indirectly. Kamerman and Kahn (1997) also see a split screen but choose instead to use the terms *implicit* and *explicit* family policy. "The United States has no explicit national, comprehensive family or child policy," they argue, "nor has there been any such policy or cluster of policies in the past" (1997, 307). What we have is a hodgepodge of social policy that sometimes is geared to families but often is not.

A portion of this chapter was published previously by the author in *The Policy Studies Review.* It is reprinted here with permission. Steven K. Wisensale, 1997, "The White House and Congress on Child Care and Family Leave Policy: From Carter to Clinton." *Policy Studies Journal* 25, 1: 75–86.

That said, where the family fits within the political landscape and why some policies are implicit and others are explicit can best be explained by first grasping the broader historical and political context within which the family has functioned during the past two centuries. This can be further explained by dividing U.S. social welfare policy into three distinct segments. Phase I represents the nation's formative years, from the colonial period to the Civil War, when individualism and self-reliance dominated social, political, and economic life. Phase II was the era of government intervention, which began with the Progressive Era at the turn of the century, and expanded during the New Deal of the 1930s and the Great Society of the 1960s. Phase III was and remains the age of retrenchment, when liberalism ended in the 1970s and Reagan's conservative agenda dominated American politics in the 1980s and into the 1990s. Each period is discussed below.

### Phase I—The Formative Years: Individualism and Self-Reliance—From the Colonial Period to the Civil War

For the first 150 years of the nation's history the family was considered to be a free and independent unit that was immune to interventions from the outside, particularly by the government. Operating under the "poor law" system it adopted from England in which the poorest and most deserving received assistance, the United States relied on local voluntary organizations, not government agencies, to provide support for needy families. Existing within an almost pure capitalistic system in which the government's laissez-faire policy toward private enterprise mirrored its approach to individuals and families, the early American family was indeed what John Demos (1970) referred to as a "little commonwealth." And, particularly when laissez-faire was fused with Social Darwinism in the post–Civil War era, it became clear that a given family's destiny to either succeed or fail depended on how well it perfected its skills of personal responsibility and self-reliance.

Another important development during this period was the fortification of states' rights and responsibilities. This held true particularly for policies related to families. Although the family is often presented as the cornerstone of American civilization, responsibility for its stability and general well-being was reserved for the states, not the federal government. Marriage and divorce laws, child custody decisions, adoption statutes, and child-support enforcement legislation, to cite but a few examples, were traditionally generated by state legislative bodies and clarified by state courts. Only recently have we witnessed a growing interest in family matters at the federal level.

With the exception of compulsory public education for children—which at best can be described as implicit family policy, and even that would be stretching it—there is little evidence of deliberate government intervention that was designed to improve the status of individuals or to address the needs of families, other than those in severe poverty. However, it was not always because government refused to provide such assistance. According to Kamerman and Kahn (1997), until the 1960s, most private social welfare agencies, such as settlement houses and family service organizations, refused public funds as a matter of principle. This practice, of course, changed drastically during the Great Society programs of Lyndon Johnson.

Equally important is the fact that it was during the nation's formative years when gender roles were clearly defined. The rise of the middle class at the end of the nineteenth century and the introduction of leisure as a new concept helped to separate work from home and identify women's "place" as being in the home, and not involved in *paid* work. This development, in turn, would coincide with the emergence of the "family wage" in which one earner or "breadwinner" in the family, usually the father, made enough money to support a wife and children. Thus, by the time the country recovered from the Depression of 1894, and just prior to the beginning of the Progressive Era around 1900 that would usher in government intervention as an acceptable tool for correcting economic and social injustices, the philosophical seeds of American social policy had been planted. Rooted deeply beneath the political landscape were the principles of individualism and self-reliance, personal responsibility, Social Darwinism, laissez-faire economics, states' rights, the family wage, and the women's "place." These and other principles would help shape the nation's social policy in general and determine the fate of family policy in particular for the next 100 years.

To summarize what has been stated so far, at least four points should be emphasized. First, our family policy is far more implicit than explicit. That is, as a result of incremental policymaking, a dominant characteristic of U.S. social policy, most families and children benefit from government action only if a large social-policy initiative produces some sort of beneficial by-product for them.

Second, our social-welfare policy in general has always focused on the individual and very rarely on the family. Daniel Patrick Moynihan reminded government officials in the 1960s of the important differences between policies focused on the individual and those concerned with families. "American social policy until now has been directed toward the individual," Moynihan stated in 1965. "Thus our employment statistics count as equally unemployed a father of nine children, a housewife coming back into the labor market in her forties, and a teenager looking for a part-time job after school" (Rainwater and Yancy 1967, 387). Moynihan concluded that the time had come to adopt a national family policy as early as 1967. However, with the exception of Richard Nixon's ill-fated welfare reform initiative, the Family Assistance Plan, the response to Moynihan's recommendation was lukewarm, to say the least.

Third, family policy, which often comes in the form of family law, has been generated primarily at the state level and not in Washington. Unlike many Scandinavian and European countries with centralized political systems that can formulate and implement social policy from the top down, the United States has, historically, engaged in an ongoing struggle between the rights and responsibilities of state and federal government.

And fourth, whether we like it or not, the government has been involved in family matters in some form and at some level of intensity over the last 100 years. Even inaction is policy. Although the government chose not to intervene in family matters during the nation's first 150 years, that is not to say that a policy toward families was nonexistent. There was indeed a family policy afoot in the nation prior to 1900. It encouraged personal responsibility and self-reliance among the nation's households and discouraged government intervention in family maters, except for assisting the poorest of the poor. This philosophy would change drastically, however, over the first six decades of the twentieth century.

## Phase II—Government Intervention: The Progressive Era, New Deal, and Great Society

In its purest form, the capitalistic system opposes government intervention of any sort. After all, according to Adam Smith (1776), the free market acts as an "invisible hand" that ultimately guides the economy toward a state of prosperity that is beneficial to all. Therefore, Andrew Cherlin concludes, "It is but a short extension to argue that, according to capitalist economic theory, the government should not intervene in family affairs" (1996, 163). However, by the end of the nineteenth century, concern was growing that wealthy industrialists were acting irresponsibly in their quest to accumulate even more riches. In doing so, they had put the most vulnerable members of society at risk.

Organizations formed that demanded government, both state and local, assume a more regulatory role and address issues related to health and safety, labor laws, and social services for the needy. Women demanded equal rights and voting privileges, and journalists, novelists, social activists, labor union leaders, and members of religious organizations were openly critical of the prevalence of poverty, child labor, poor housing conditions, and inadequate public health and sanitation practices. When politicians joined the reform movement and began to convert citizen demands into policy proposals, an important watershed in American history had occurred and the country would never be the same again (Cherlin 1996; Skocpol 1992). The Progressive Era produced an entirely new policy paradigm: Government should be held responsible for correcting wrongs and addressing inequities.

With government intervention on the horizon, and the days of laissez-faire economic policy numbered, a very significant phenomenon was about to occur. If government saw fit to intervene in the private affairs of business and end laissez-faire in its purest form, would it not also intervene in the private affairs of families to address their specific needs as well? For America's families, the first government venture into the "little commonwealth" came in the form of policies directed toward children. Kindergartens were created, as were juvenile courts, maternal and child health clinics, the U.S. Children's Bureau, widows' benefits, workers' compensation, and unemployment legislation (Kamerman and Kahn 1997; Skocpol 1992). There was also an increase in the creation of settlement houses and the construction of orphanages, as well as a rise in the use of foster care to protect children from harm. By the time President Theodore Roosevelt addressed the First International Congress in America on the Welfare of the Child in 1908, the nation began to witness a dramatic shift in twentieth-century social policy. This shift showed, at the very least, a greater concern for individuals within the family if not for the family unit as a whole. States passed maternal custody rights, enforced maternal care of infants, and enacted Mothers' Pension Laws, the precursors of Aid to Families with Dependent Children (AFDC) (Jacobs and Davies 1994). But even more government intervention would occur in the future.

## *The New Deal and America's Families*

When Franklin Delano Roosevelt was sworn into office in 1933 he inherited the worst depression in the nation's history. Convinced that the cause of the economic collapse was systemic and, therefore, its solution lay in an aggressive interventionist strategy designed and implemented by the federal government, Roosevelt put forth his New Deal. Consisting of a wide variety of social programs that included numerous public works projects that were introduced with a "hit or miss" attitude, the centerpiece of the New Deal was the Social Security Act of 1935. It, perhaps more than any piece of legislation ever enacted, established the foundation upon which government policies directed toward families would be built. One can draw this conclusion for at least three reasons.

First, the Social Security Act was structured under the family wage system. That is, the "breadwinner-homemaker" family, in which the husband worked and earned enough money to support his wife who stayed home to raise the kids, was not only recognized, it was rewarded.[1] Those who "earned" their pensions—at that time and until well into the 1960s that almost always meant men—benefited at retirement. As reported in the previous chapter, this traditional family type has been in steady decline over the last three decades. However, the division of labor between men and women that was shaped to a great degree by the family wage system and institutionalized by the Social Security Act is at the very heart of today's debate over work and family.[2]

Second, the Social Security Act also fortified women's dependence on men. Or, to be more precise, wives' dependence on husbands. If husbands died or were absent for other reasons, and the family's income fell below a certain level, wives, who were also mothers, were eligible for assistance under Aid to Families with Dependent Children (AFDC), a means-tested program for the poor that was incorporated in the original Social Security Act. In 1939, Congress extended the Social Security Act even further by establishing widows' benefits. Survivor benefits for eligible children would be added as well in subsequent years. Not to be overlooked is the fact that the family of the 1930s, to which the Social Security and AFDC applied, differed greatly from the American family of the 1990s. New Deal policymakers simply did not envision large numbers of women becoming eligible for Social Security or AFDC by getting divorced, having children out of wedlock, or working outside the home (Cherlin 1996; Carlson 1986).

And third, the Social Security Act of 1935 and the passage of Medicare and Medicaid thirty years later were instrumental in providing greater financial independence for the elderly and more autonomy for their adult children who would no longer have to support them. The convergence of these two developments, among other societal changes, ultimately contributed to the steady decline of the extended family. With its slow decline, the government intervened in family matters even further by eventually funding in-home health services and subsidizing nursing home care for the aged and other dependents.

### The GI Bill: America's First and Only Family Policy?

If the Social Security Act represents one of the most important pieces of social welfare policy to be enacted, the GI Bill cannot be far behind. To some, it is considered one of the best examples of family policy the nation ever produced, even though "family" is not in its title nor is it visible in the language of the bill itself. Passed in 1944, the bill had two primary objectives. One, it was viewed by liberals in particular as an opportunity to resume the social reforms of the New Deal that were interrupted by World War II. And two, forced onto the national agenda by the American Legion, the GI Bill was designed to appease returning veterans in search of jobs and offer them other rewards for the service they provided to their country. Congress had not forgotten the unrest created by dissatisfied veterans returning from World War I.

More importantly, the GI Bill produced two significant outcomes that had a direct impact on the well-being of America's families. One, it subsidized higher education, and two, it made buying a home easier for the average citizen. In 1940, only one in nine Americans was a high school graduate. However in 1947, just three years after the bill's passage and two years after the end of World War II, almost half (49 percent) of the 1.6 million students enrolled in colleges and universities were veterans. By 1956, when the program ended, 2.2 million veterans had gone on to higher education and college had become a middle-class expectation. With respect to housing, in 1940, two out of every three Americans were renters. By 1950, just six years after the passage of the GI Bill, more than 60 percent were homeowners with low-interest loans. Suburbia and the new middle class were off and running, and so was the American economy (Skocpol 1992).

Writing in her book *Protecting Soldiers and Mothers: The Political Origins of Social Policy in the United States* (1992), Theda Skocpol contends that the GI Bill broke the mold of previous U.S. social policies. Prior to the 1930s, government-sponsored social policies were primarily directed toward aging men (Union veterans of the Civil War), widows, and children. Even the Social Security Act of 1935 was geared toward retirees, not younger wage earners in their prime. "By contrast," writes Skocpol, "the GI Bill authorized massive federal investments in young men right at the start of their lives as workers and providers for families" (1996, 68). The use of "young men" and "providers for families" in the same sentence clearly smacks of language that is often used in support of the traditional family wage system. Therefore, and not surprisingly, the GI Bill had a history of strong bipartisan support throughout its existence.

"With the GI Bill," writes conservative columnist George Will, "social policy sent strong cues to young Americans, telling them to stay in school, grind out good grades, defer marriage past the teenage years, defer children until the family income has begun to rise" (1997, 82). The GI Bill, which cost $14.5 billion, also solidified the family wage system for at least the next two decades. While veterans returned from abroad and received subsidies for housing and education, many women who held jobs during the war returned to the home.[3]

However, more than fifty years after its enactment, President Clinton still heralded its accomplishments. In April 1995 at FDR's Warm Spring retreat, and on the fiftieth anniversary of Roosevelt's death, President Clinton, who had witnessed the loss of both houses of Congress to conservative Republicans just a few months earlier, gave an address in which he referred to the GI Bill as Roosevelt's "most enduring legacy." It "gave generations of veterans a chance to get an education, to build strong families and good lives, and to build the nation's strongest economy ever, to change the face of America" (Skocpol 1996, 66). On at least two occasions during his State of the Union messages, Clinton called for the resurrection of the GI Bill, though not on as grand a scale as the original.

## *The Great Society*

Without question, the Social Security Act and the GI Bill stand tall as monuments dedicated to successful interventionist policy by big government. However, each law was geared primarily toward men and both laws recognized and fortified the traditional "breadwinner/homemaker" household under the family wage system. But the seeds for change were planted in the early 1960s with the emergence of Lyndon Johnson's Great Society program and the beginning of the second feminist movement of the century.

Following in the philosophical footsteps of Franklin Roosevelt, President Johnson moved to expand the role of the federal government well beyond the borders established by the New Deal. On May 22, 1964, during a commencement address at the University of Michigan, Johnson presented his dream for a Great Society. He promised to establish working groups on cities, the environment, education, and poverty. Almost immediately, fourteen separate task forces were created to address many of the nation's problems. Eight months later, he outlined the new program during his State of the Union address on January 7, 1965. Within two years, he witnessed the passage of the Elementary and Secondary Education Act, the Higher Education Act, Medicare, Medicaid, Model Cities, the Voting Rights Act, and Head Start. Although it was big government's finest hour since the New Deal, it was also its last hurrah. Big government would slowly vaporize in less than two decades.

But the expansion of government's role in addressing social problems was not the only major development during the 1960s. Seeds for social change were also planted with the publication of Betty Friedan's *The Feminine Mystique* (1963) and the passage of the Civil Rights Act in 1964. Friedan's book, which argued strongly that a woman's independence is lost in the traditional breadwinner/homemaker household, helped launch the modern feminist movement. One year later, the Civil Rights Act was passed. Unable to defeat the bill on racial grounds, southern segregationists made a last-ditch effort to make the bill unpalatable to a predominantly male Congress by inserting a small clause outlawing gender-based discrimination. When their tactic failed and the bill was enacted, it opened the door for major federal court decisions that banned discriminatory practices against women in hiring, wages, career advancement, and sports. As more women entered the workplace, the jewel in the crown of the family wage system, the breadwinner/homemaker household, began to slowly tarnish. Subsequently, the pressure to adopt appropriate policies to address the needs of this new dual-earner family increased and Lyndon Johnson was not oblivious to this development.

On June 4, 1965, one year after his University of Michigan address in which he announced plans for his Great Society, Johnson delivered the commencement address at Howard University in Washington, DC. "Unless we work to strengthen the family," he stated, "to create conditions under which most parents will stay together, all the rest: schools, and playgrounds, and public assistance, and private concern, will never be enough to cut completely the circle of despair and deprivation" (Domestic Policy Council 1986, 1). Model Cities, Head Start, Medicare and Medicaid, all products of the Johnson years, were designed to address the needs of the less fortunate. They also represent examples of *indirect* family policy. Even Richard Nixon's attempt to overhaul AFDC with his Family Assistance Plan in 1969 and 1970 was limited to two specific types of families: the very poor and the working poor. He, like his predecessors, saw no need to assist middle-class American families with broad-based universal (as opposed to means-tested) policies. Indeed, in vetoing the 1970 Comprehensive Child Development Act, Nixon emphasized that he did not believe Americans should be taxed to support babysitting programs for the middle class. This perspective on government's role in relation to families would change over time, thanks in no small measure to the efforts of Jimmy Carter.

### Jimmy Carter and American Family Policy

While Presidents Roosevelt through Ford supported the federal government's role in strengthening poor families, including Lyndon Johnson, who was particularly concerned about the declining status of black families, and Richard Nixon, who tried unsuccessfully to eliminate the existing AFDC program through his innovative Family Assistance Plan, Jimmy Carter "was the first President to address the family cause generally without class or race qualifiers" (Steiner 1981, 15). "There can be no more urgent priority for the next administration," Carter stated in 1976, three months before his election, "than to see that every decision our government makes is designed to honor, support, and strengthen the American family" (Steiner 1981, 14). Two months later, he would echo this point and spell out the possible consequences if his advice were to go unheeded. "I believe that government ought to do everything it can to strengthen the American family because weak families mean more government" (Carter 1976, 1012). Thus began a journey of American family policy that would span more than two decades, ten congressional elections, and five presidential campaigns, and include four different occupants of the White House: Carter, Reagan, Bush, and Clinton.

During the 1976 presidential campaign, candidate Jimmy Carter spoke openly about the need for a national family policy. "It is clear that the national government should have a strong pro-family policy, but the fact is that our government has no family policy, and that is the same as an anti-family policy. Because of confusion or insensitivity, our government's policies have often actually weakened our families, or even destroyed them" (United States Government Printing Office 1978, 1).

The statement above was quickly followed by the issuance of his "Nine Point Plan for the Family," a collection of campaign promises that included (1) welfare reform to encourage families to stay together (an attempt to end AFDC's "man-in-the-house rule"); (2) stricter child support laws; (3) more sensitive transfer policies for armed forces families; (4) pro-family tax reform; (5) retention of tax exemptions for dependent children; (6) federally funded day care for working mothers; (7) discouraging the construction of freeways that displace families; (8) instituting a family impact statement; and (9) insuring that government actions be sensitive to the needs of families. The plan did not include a call for a family leave policy (Steiner 1981).

With respect to the ultimate fate of specific proposals put forth in the nine-point plan, many were introduced and defeated in the 95th and 96th sessions of Congress. These defeats included efforts at major tax reform, stricter child support laws, a federal day-care policy, and the family impact statement. The call for more sensitive transfer policies was converted to an executive order that resulted in fewer transfers and longer assignments for military personnel. The ninth point of the plan called for government actions to be more sensitive to the needs of families. To some extent, this item in particular was addressed by Carter during his last year in office, when he became the first president in American history to call for a national conference on families.

Held just months before Carter's loss to Ronald Reagan in the 1980 election, the first and only White House Conference on Families is still viewed by many as one of the major watersheds in the developmental history of family policy (Dempsey 1981; Steiner 1981; and Cherlin 1996). More than a thousand delegates met in three separate cities (Baltimore, Minneapolis, and Los Angeles) during the summer of 1980 to address a variety of family-oriented issues and, ultimately, to present to the President a checklist of policy recommendations and legislative proposals designed to strengthen and support the nation's families. While some consensus was reached on proposed solutions to problems confronting the aged and handicapped, there was little agreement on other family-oriented issues such as teen pregnancy prevention, the Equal Rights Amendment, and abortion. All told, thirty-four of sixty-two proposals were eventually adopted, but only seven were supported by more than 90 percent of the conference delegates (Dempsey 1981).

In the end, the contentious conference gatherings produced little in terms of significant policy initiatives that were eventually enacted into law. However, in addition to providing a glimpse into the future of the "family values debate," the conference did produce at least two important outcomes. First, for the first time in history, the family had been placed on the national agenda and a new policy question was posed: Where should the line be drawn between what the family is expected to do and what government has been created to do? And second, perhaps equally significant, the WHCF raised the consciousness of America, forcing many people to think beyond policy proposals geared primarily to individuals, and to consider instead the general health and well-being of our families. Almost immediately after the closing session of the conference, an onslaught of books and articles on family policy began and has continued for more than twenty years. Works by Anderson and Hula (1991), Cherlin (1996), Dempsey (1981), Diamond (1983), Genovese (1984), Kamerman and Kahn (1997), Levy and Michael (1991), Moynihan (1986), Peden and Glahe (1986), Steiner (1981), Wisensale (1989a, 1990, 1991), and Zimmerman (1988, 1992) are but a few examples.[4]

Although Jimmy Carter deserves much credit for initiating various policies directed toward families, and it was during his term that a national dialogue on American families began, few proposals were enacted and those that were hardly resembled those produced by the New Deal or the Great Society. Theodore Lowi's (1969) famous pronouncement that "the end of liberalism" had occurred appeared to ring true, certainly in 1980. By the time Jimmy Carter's four-year term came to an end and Ronald Reagan was sworn in as president in January 1981, it was clear that major political change was on the horizon. For the next twelve years, Republicans would occupy the White House, and Americans would bear witness to a different attitude toward the role of government. Whether the Reagan presidency should be described as a "revolution," as some have done so, or as "a significant imprint," as others have labeled it, the fact remains that it clearly marked the end of liberalism in American politics.

## Phase III—Retrenchment: The Reagan Revolution and Conservative Politics

In the Ronald Reagan Presidential Library in Simi Valley, California, there is a display labeled "The Reagan Revolution." On the left side, quite appropriately, is a statement beneath a photo of Franklin Roosevelt. Dated October 12, 1937, it reads, "Americans do not look on government as their interloper in their affairs. On the contrary, they regard it as the most effective form of self-help." On the right side, also appropriately, beneath a photo of Ronald

Reagan is also a statement. It reads, "In this present crisis government is not the solution to our problems; government is the problem." Dated January 20, 1981, this statement represents one of Reagan's most memorable lines from his first inaugural address. It set a tone for shaping public policy that remains operative to this day.

By the time Reagan assumed the presidency in 1981, the family had made its way onto the national political agenda. However, with the new occupant of the White House viewing government as an obstacle and not a facilitator, whatever hope there was for a national family policy, which may have been generated by the White House Conference on Families, soon vanished. New federalism (now known as devolution), deregulation, and privatization would dominate American domestic policy for the next eight years and beyond. The responsibility for the health and well-being of the nation's families would either rest with the fifty states, as had been the policy in the past for the most part, or be shouldered by the families themselves.

Strongly endorsed by the conservative wing of the Republican party, the New Christian Right, and other advocates of the so-called pro-family movement, Reagan differed significantly from his immediate predecessor in conceptualizing family policy (Cherlin 1983; Goettsch 1986; Hadden 1983; McNamara 1985; and Pankhurst and Houseknecht 1983). This can best be exemplified by referring in particular to three documents that were produced during the Reagan presidency: *The Family: Preserving America's Future*, Executive Order 12606, and the Family Support Act of 1988.

### The Family: Preserving America's Future

Issued on December 2, 1986, *The Family: Preserving America's Future*, was a fifty-two-page report issued by the White House Working Group on the Family. Chaired by Gary Bauer, who later would lead the conservative Family Research Council and seek the presidency in 2000, the Working Group consisted of twenty-one members who represented a variety of federal agencies and departments. Included on the panel was Clarence Thomas, then chairman of the Equal Opportunity Commission and now a member of the U.S. Supreme Court.

Four major themes dominated the report. First, unnecessary government intervention can be harmful to families. Second, big government has stripped the family of its power and influence. That is, "[t]he family has paid too much. It has lost too much of its authority to courts and rule-writers, too much of its voice in education and social policy, too much of its resources to public officials at all levels" (Domestic Policy Council 1986, 3). Third, private choices sometimes create public burdens. In other words, American taxpayers must cover the costs of fighting drug abuse, caring for abandoned spouses and abused children, and supporting fatherless children. And fourth, the report presents a strong argument for raising children at home and avoiding professional child-care. "Families who choose to have children are making a desirable decision. Mothers and fathers who then decide to spend a good deal of time raising those children themselves rather than leaving it to others are demonstrably doing a good job. They are the bedrock of our society" (1986, 3).

Critics of the report attacked early. For example, according to Arthur T. Johnson, the Working Group was uncompromising. It defined the family in the traditional manner: two parents, married, with the father working and the mother at home. "There is no hint that the Working Group would accept any other definition. It would make divorce more difficult to obtain, end legalized abortion, permit in-home education as opposed to compulsory school attendance, and do away with child care external to the home" (1987, 281). In short, the Reagan administration strongly endorsed the traditional breadwinner/homemaker model under the family wage system.

### Executive Order 12606: The Family Impact Statement

Although Jimmy Carter was the first president to raise the idea of a family impact statement when he included it in his nine-point plan on the family, it first originated in Scandinavia in the 1960s (Kamerman and Kahn 1978). With its primary objective being to protect families from the harmful interventions of government, both its design and purpose closely parallel that of the environmental impact statement that has been employed since the early 1970s. That is, prior to the passage of legislation or the actions of a given agency, an assessment is made to determine the extent of damage that could be inflicted by government on a particular ecological unit, be it the Mississippi River or the American family.

First suggested in the United States by anthropologist Margaret Mead and child psychologist Edward Zigler in a 1973 hearing before the Senate Labor and Public Welfare Subcommittee, the family impact statement was adopted by a large majority of the delegates at the 1980 White House conference on Families (Dempsey 1981). Although the White House Working Group on the Family also recommended its adoption, it was not until seven years after the WHCF and fourteen years after Mead and Zigler testified on its behalf that it was officially implemented.

On September 3, 1987, President Ronald Reagan issued Executive Order 12606; which required executive departments and agencies to "identify proposed regulatory and statutory provisions that may have significant potential negative impact on the family's well-being and provide adequate rationale on why such a proposal should be submitted" (Domestic Policy Council 1986, 1). The order included criteria in the form of seven questions to which department or agency heads were required to respond in writing. For example, does this action by government strengthen or erode the stability of the family? Does this action strengthen or erode the authority and rights of parents? Can this activity be carried out by a lower level of government or by the family itself? And what message does this policy send to young people concerning the relationship between their behavior, their personal responsibility, and the norms of American society?

The dominant themes that emerge from such impact criteria are obvious: Government is viewed as a potentially dangerous intrusion. Parental authority should never be eroded by government action. And, problems associated with the family are best resolved at the state and local level, not in Washington, DC. To implement Executive Order 12606, the U.S. Office of Management and Budget was designated as overseer of family impact analysis, and the Office of Policy Development was required to submit an annual report on the impact process to the president through the Domestic Policy Council. As a policy tool, however, the Family Impact Statement faded by the end of Reagan's second term.[5]

### *The Family Support Act of 1988*

Sometimes forgotten is the fact that the "welfare reform debates" of the past usually centered on the amount of benefits to be increased, not reduced. For example, in 1950, Congress deliberately increased the benefit levels of AFDC recipients in an effort to allow poor mothers to stay home with their children. This approach coincided with the dominant policy theme of the day: the breadwinner/homemaker household, also referred to as the family wage system, should be preserved regardless of its economic status. The Family Support Act of 1988 and its subsequent offspring, the Personal Responsibility and Work Opportunity Act of 1996, were both designed to produce a completely opposite effect: poor mothers were to leave the welfare rolls for work while their children were placed in child-care programs. Meanwhile, the working poor and middle-class families were denied child-care benefits by the same politicians who supported it for AFDC families.

Several factors contributed to the growing demand for welfare reform in the 1980s and 1990s that were not as visible when Nixon tackled the issue in the early 1970s.[6] First, the 1970s and 1980s produced the women's movement that resulted in more than 50 percent of women entering the labor market and shattering the traditional family wage system. Thus, as Cherlin (1996) argues, it did not appear so punitive for welfare reformers to demand that AFDC mothers also enter the labor market. In short, conservatives skillfully managed to stand liberal feminists on their heads.

Second, the characteristics of the welfare recipients had changed. More were younger, never-married single mothers, not the poor dependent widows for whom the AFDC program was originally designed. Therefore, the growing perception of uncontrollable and irresponsible sexual behavior on the part of welfare recipients (whom some referred to as "welfare queens") resulted in women, for the first time perhaps, being placed in the category of "the undeserving poor." Previously, such a label was reserved for able-bodied unemployed males.

Third, the welfare rolls included more black recipients over the years. If George Ball is correct when he states that a program just for the poor eventually becomes a poor program, then it is even more the case if the poor program, AFDC, includes a disproportional number of minorities. And finally, the language of welfare reform changed considerably. That is, the instigators for reform came from both the left and the right side of the political spectrum but found common ground through the use of similar language. Charles Murray (1984), of the conservative Manhattan Institute, and David Ellwood (1988), a liberal from Harvard who later would become one of the key players in the battle over the 1996 welfare reform law, both spoke in terms of "dependence," "responsibility," and the "need to become self-sufficient."

Consisting of much complexity that was deeply embedded in a series of compromises, the Family Support Act of 1988 sent forth one central message that was very clear: even poor parents must take responsibility for the financial support of their dependent children and themselves. That is, fathers must contribute child support, and mothers, except those with very young children, need to be trained for jobs and seek employment. Further, two-parent households became eligible for AFDC in all states in an effort to slow the dissolution of poor families. Clearly, the Family Support Act and the Reagan administration's support of it exemplified what Scanzoni (1991) refers to as "the use of the family as vehicle for social change" (1991, 591).

But the passage of the FSA is significant for at least two other reasons. One, it served as a political stalking horse for a much more aggressive welfare reform bill that would follow eight years later. The decades-long logjam had been broken. And two, liberals and conservatives found common ground that would provide firm footing for future debates about other family issues, such as child care and family leave. For example, with the FSA, conservatives got the reduction in AFDC benefits they sought and the work requirement they desired. Liberals, on the other hand, accepted a jobs program for moms because it increased their autonomy, gnawed away at the traditional family wage system, and forced conservatives to recognize the importance of child-care programs for working mothers.

It should be emphasized that during the Reagan years neither a child-care bill nor a family-leave bill ever reached his desk. A reluctant Congress, a divided coalition of child and family advocates that was forced to lobby two important bills simultaneously, a president who was adamantly opposed to both proposals, and well-organized opposition by business all combined to kill both initiatives before George Bush was elected president in November 1988. Each would rise again and be enacted by two different administrations, united by the common experience of being pressured by rapidly changing demographics in the workplace and at home.

## The Bush Years and the American Family

When *Time* magazine (1991) named George Bush its "Man of the Year," it indicated that there were two presidents, and that the "foreign President Bush" was much different from the "domestic President Bush." In foreign affairs, Bush's approval ratings soared to over 90 percent during the collapse of the Soviet Union, the reunification of East and West Germany, and the United Nations' victory in the Gulf War for which he received much of the credit. His repeated reference to America's role in a "new-world order" was well received by the general public (Barrileaux and Stuckey 1992).

Domestic policy, however, was quite another matter. Some have argued, for example, that "Bush had the most limited domestic agenda of any president since Hoover" (Thompson and Scavo 1992, 150). He began his presidency with the themes of a "kinder, gentler nation" and "a thousand points of light," and ended it by defending a sluggish economy that his opponent described in a campaign sound bite as "it's the economy, stupid." When he agreed to the 1990 budget deal, which included tax increases, he reneged on his promise of "Read my lips, no new taxes," and alienated the right wing of his party. Like Reagan, Bush saw little or no role for government in addressing many of the nation's domestic challenges. "He had an almost nineteenth-century approach to social ills. The answer is not government, but the kindness of individuals" (McDaniel and Thomas 1991, 20).

The explanation for Bush's limited domestic policy, other than the passage of the Americans with Disabilities Act, may extend well beyond his preference for limited government involvement in addressing the nation's social problems. Upon entering the White House in 1989, he was confronted immediately with a political reality that would haunt him for the next four years. Although he won the presidency, his party lost ground in Congress, primarily because many Bush voters split their tickets and voted for Democratic congressional candidates. Consequently, Bush ran behind the winning ticket in 85 percent of the House districts (Cohen 1989). If weak under the 101st Congress, he became even weaker after the 1990 off-year elections and the formation of the 102nd Congress. With his party already down eighty-five seats in the House and ten in the Senate, Bush and the Republicans lost additional seats.

Faced with an aggressive Democratic Congress, Bush's legislative strategy on domestic issues during the 101st and 102nd Congresses was more reactive than proactive. This approach produced twenty-five vetoes in his first three years in office; Congress overrode only one veto during his four-year term (Kolb 1994). Both the veto and the threat of veto were employed by Bush very effectively to defeat family leave and shape child-care legislation during his brief tenure.

During the 1988 presidential campaign, a Gallup poll in May and a *New York Times* survey in July reported that over half the respondents desired an increase in federal day-care spending (Berry 1993). With opponent Michael Dukakis supporting the Democratic version of the child-care bill (commonly referred to as the ABC bill) and family leave, candidate George Bush responded by proposing a tax credit program to support day care. He also argued that corporations should adopt family-leave policies voluntarily rather than have such a measure be mandated by government.

When Congress reconvened in 1989, however, it soon became clear that the adoption of child-care legislation would not be easy. House and Senate Republicans introduced the Bush version of the child-care bill, believing that the real problem was not the regulation or supply of child care, but rather that working families needed more income. They pushed for a "toddler tax credit" of $1,000 for families with up to two children under age five and called for a "parental choice" model of child care—whether it was a relative, a neighbor, or a private organization providing the service. The Democrats, on the other hand, continued to support the original child-care bill introduced during the Reagan years that called for a large block-grant approach (Johnson 1989).

Following a year of debate, gridlock, and eventual compromise, the Child Care and Development Block Grant was signed into law by President Bush in October 1990 as part of the Omnibus Budget Reconciliation Act. It allocated $732 million that was distributed to states, a tax credit that applied to children under age thirteen whose family incomes did not exceed 75 percent of the state median income, and the expansion of Head Start to provide full workday and full calendar-year service. It included religious organizations as providers but excluded public schools. Standards on health and safety were to be created and enforced by the states, not the federal government.

While the child care bill succeeded in the 102nd Congress, family leave remained stalled for years. By May 1990, the original bill introduced by Representative Patricia Schroeder (D-CO) five years earlier had been modified to cover only businesses with fifty or more employees. It provided twelve weeks of unpaid leave and included a job guarantee. After passing by a 237–187 vote in the House and by a voice vote in the Senate, President Bush vetoed the measure on June 14, 1990. A House effort to override his veto failed eleven days later. The bill reemerged two years later in the midst of the 1992 presidential election and Bush vetoed it for a second time—just weeks before the November election. His opponent, Governor William Jefferson Clinton of Arkansas, would use that veto against Bush in the 1992 election and again in 1996 against Bob Dole (R-KS), who led the fight against both Democratic override attempts in the Senate. Clinton, like Bush, Reagan, and Carter, would also address family issues during his years in the White House.

### Clinton's Family Policy

During the 1992 election, Bill Clinton reminded voters that he was a "New Democrat." As founder and leader of the moderate Democratic Leadership Council, Clinton separated himself from the orthodox big-government liberalism of his party and sought instead to establish a "New Covenant" between the American people and their government. Often borrowing Republican rhetoric to distance himself from traditional "tax-and-spend" liberals, the focal point of Clinton's domestic strategy, both during the 1992 campaign and the first two years of his presidency, was economic policy.

Confronted with an unemployment rate of 7 percent, a federal deficit of $290 billion, and a $3 trillion national debt when he entered the White House, Clinton responded with the 1993 Budget Resolution and Stimulus Package, which barely passed Congress. His other early successes (besides the Family and Medical Leave Act) included the "Motor Voter Law" that simplified voter registration, the National Service Program that granted scholarships to students who performed volunteer community service, and the "Brady bill" which required a five-day waiting period for the purchase of a handgun (Quirk and Hinchliffe 1996). His effort to eliminate the ban against homosexuals serving in the military was reduced to a watered-down policy of "Don't ask, don't tell," and his national healthcare initiative engineered by Hillary Clinton failed miserably. Throughout most of his two-term presidency he was confronted with a Republican-controlled Congress.

With respect to Clinton's family policy, a defining moment occurred in the spring of 1992 after vice-presidential candidate Dan Quayle attacked Murphy Brown, the fictitious TV character who chose to have a child out of wedlock. Quayle's verbal assault came on the heels of a riot in South Central Los Angeles after several policemen had been acquitted in the Rodney King beating case. In early May, approximately two weeks after Dan Quayle's attack on Murphy Brown, Clinton delivered a speech in Cleveland, Ohio, in which he outlined his "eight-point plan on the American family."[7] It included an intense media campaign to combat teen pregnancy, an $800-per-child tax credit for preschool children, an expansion of the Earned Income Tax Credit, a greater emphasis on child support, a call for more child-sensitive divorce laws, more parental responsibility, greater emphasis on family preservation programs, and the adoption of a family leave policy (Marshall and Schram 1993).

Two months later, the Republicans devoted an entire evening to "family values" at their nominating convention, while a Democratic Congress pressed Bush to sign the FMLA. Bush responded by proposing a family-leave bill based on tax incentives for corporations. This proposal was rejected quickly by Congress, prompting Bush to veto the FMLA for the second time in two years. Once again Congress was unable to override his veto, but in November, Bill Clinton became the first Democrat to be elected president in twelve years.

With the Democrats' victory, the 103rd Congress underwent a major transformation. The 1992 elections produced 110 new House members and thirteen new senators, including unprecedented numbers of women and minorities. The number of women in the Senate grew from two to six, and in the House, the number of women representatives grew from twenty-nine to forty-eight. Blacks increased their numbers from twenty-six to thirty-nine in the lower chamber, and Hispanics added six to their previous total of thirteen. The newcomers did little to change the partisan composition of the two legislative bodies. The Democrats' 57–43 advantage in the Senate was identical to that of the 102nd Congress, and their 258–176–1 House edge represented a loss of only ten seats. Not unlike the Reagan-Bush era, there were discussions about the number of votes necessary to override presidential vetoes, but now such talk was in the Republican camp (*Congressional Quarterly Almanac* 1994). Due perhaps to the near doubling of females in Congress, family-oriented issues in general and the family leave bill in particular received increased attention even before Clinton was sworn into office. The child-care bill was not on Clinton's agenda because Bush had signed it two years earlier.

Whatever political influence Clinton had when he signed the Family and Medical Leave Act on February 5, 1993, he and the Democrats saw it vaporize on November 8, 1994, when the American voters gave control of both houses of Congress to the Republicans for the first time in forty years (Campbell and Rockman 1996). Instead of pushing forward with his domestic agenda, Clinton found himself in a defensive mode for the next two years.

He fought House Speaker Newt Gingrich (R-GA), Senate Majority Leader Bob Dole (R-KS), and the *Contract with America*, a checklist of ten legislative proposals that a Republican Congress introduced and debated during its first 100 days.

With the Republican bombardment of the White House in 1996, Clinton found himself cornered on two issues in particular as the election neared: welfare reform and gay rights. Passed by a conservative Congress that was determined to win control of the Oval Office, the Personal Responsibility and Work Opportunity Reconciliation Act of 1996 (welfare reform) was designed to reduce federal spending by $54 billion over six years and to end "welfare as we know it." AFDC (Aid to Families with Dependent Children) was replaced by TANF (Temporary Aid for Needy Families), a block-grant program that required states to establish time limits for welfare recipients of five years or less, and provided bonuses for states that were most successful in reducing caseloads. The new law also reduced spending in a variety of means-tested programs, including food stamps, Supplemental Security Income (SSI), school lunch and other child nutrition programs, and foster care. It established a work requirement for welfare recipients, offered incentives to reduce out-of-wedlock births, funded a new program to provide abstinence education, included stiff child-support enforcement measures, and provided child care for those who left welfare for work.

Clinton had vetoed similar bills twice. However, despite being informed by key advisers that one in five families with children would see their income fall by $1,350 per year, and reduced caseloads would not necessarily reduce poverty, Clinton signed the legislation. Any potential attack from the right that would have painted him as "soft on welfare" during the 1996 presidential campaign was skillfully avoided. According to David T. Ellwood, one of three top White House advisors who resigned in protest after Clinton signed the bill, the battle for moderate welfare reform ended when the Democrats lost both houses of Congress in the 1994 elections. "If it had not been for the 1994 elections, we could have had thoughtful and progressive reform legislation. We got hit by a freight train, in part, because our own train moved too sluggishly" (Ellwood 1996, 13).

The president also skillfully avoided another controversial issue raised by the Republicans in 1996: the Defense of Marriage Act (DOMA). Driven through Congress by Republicans in the middle of the campaign, DOMA gave states the right not to recognize same-sex marriages (such marriages were illegal anyway, but Hawaii was moving closer to adopting such legislation). Because Clinton had supported gay and lesbian rights in the past, Republicans assumed he would veto the bill and embarrass himself in an election year. Instead, he signed it. But unlike the Rose Garden signing ceremony for the FMLA in 1993, Clinton signed the Defense of Marriage Act alone in the oval office at midnight, less than six weeks before the election.

But not all of Clinton's responses during the 1996 campaign were defensive. What worked for the Democrats in the 1992 election was employed again in 1996: the family. Choosing "Families First" as their campaign theme, the Democrats captured, at least temporarily, what Steiner (1981) refers to as "the higher moral ground" on family values. Not only did Clinton remind voters that the FMLA was the first bill he ever signed as president, he also reminded them that his opponent, Robert Dole, had voted against it twice and had engineered two filibusters on the Senate floor designed to prevent its adoption. Clinton also reminded voters that he had expanded the Earned Income Tax Credit (EITC) during his first term and promised to expand it further if reelected. The EITC, which can be traced to the Carter administration, has received much bipartisan support over the years. It is geared to lower-income intact families and will be discussed in greater detail in the next chapter.

## Family Policy in Historic Perspective

Historically, the United States has, at best, practiced implicit rather than explicit family policy. Slowly disengaging from the early roots of self-reliance, individualism, and laissez-faire economics, the nation called for, and accepted, more government intervention to address society's ills. The Progressive Era, the New Deal, and the Great Society all stand as important benchmarks for understanding the development of American social welfare policy. But even during these eras of great government expansion and intervention, social-policy initiatives focused primarily on the needs of individuals rather than families. And, equally significant, whatever family-oriented policies were adopted were done so at the state, not the federal level. Two distinct exceptions to this were the passage of the Social Security Act in 1935 and the GI Bill in 1944. However, both pieces of legislation fortified the family wage system and the traditional breadwinner/homemaker household.

The passage of the 1964 Civil Rights Act, which excluded discrimination based on gender, the movement of more women into the workforce and the rise of the feminist movement pushed family issues onto the political agenda in the mid-1970s. Jimmy Carter's nine-point plan on the family and the White House Conference on Families represented the first time in American history that a president addressed family concerns without race or class criteria. However, whatever energy was generated by the Carter administration in pushing family policy onto the national agenda was quickly diffused by Ronald Reagan, who saw government as the problem, not the solution. But still, passage of the Family Support Act near the end of Reagan's second term, the signing of the nation's first child-care bill by George Bush in 1990, and the discovery of the Earned Income Tax Credit by both liberals and conservatives as fertile soil for political compromise all illustrate that Washington was not completely dominated by political gridlock on family matters during the Reagan-Bush years.

By the time Bill Clinton assumed the presidency in 1993, the Family and Medical Leave Act was waiting in the wings for his signature. Decades of political and social change produced a climate in which the traditional family wage system that had been represented by the breadwinner/homemaker household was, for the most part, replaced by middle-class, dual-earner couples or single parents who demanded more government intervention to address family needs. Therefore, few political observers were surprised when, just six years after its enactment, Clinton proposed that the FMLA be expanded to provide paid leave. After all, he, perhaps more than any president to precede him (as ironic as it may sound when considering his personal escapades that spawned an impeachment trial), understood how to employ family values within a political context.

## Notes

1. Three years prior to the passage of the Social Security Act, the 1932 Economic Act stipulated that in the case of layoffs, when husbands and wives both worked for the government, wives were to be fired first. This was eventually repealed during World War II when many women took jobs in the war industry.

2. A good source for understanding the relationship between men and women in the workplace during this period in history is Laura Hapke's *Daughters of the Great Depression: Women, Work, and Fiction in the American 1930s* (1995), published by the University of Georgia Press. The debates of the 1930s between traditionalists who promoted the "back-to-the-home" movement and the radicals who sought to support mothers in the workplace carried over to the post–World War II era and continues today.

3. In both his 1994 and 1995 State of the Union addresses, President Clinton called for a "GI Bill for America's workers."

4. The impact of the White House Conference on Families deserves some comment. Within six years, special family-policy task forces and commissions were created in twenty-four states, prominent think tanks began to devote more time and energy to family-policy issues, and foundations showed a greater willingness to fund research projects and programs devoted to families. All of these developments occurred after 1980.

5. The Family Impact Statement is rarely used today. In its place is the Family Impact Seminar, which pulls together policymakers, researchers, and practitioners who focus on a given issue prior to a legislative session. Model bills are then prepared, introduced, and monitored. See the article by Karen Bogenschneider, Jonathan Olson, Kirsten Linney, and Jessica Mills, "Connecting Research and Policymaking:

Implications for Theory and Practice from the Family Impact Seminars," in *Family Relations* (2000), 49, 13, 327–339. Also see S. Wisensale's "Partnering with the State Legislature: The Connecticut Family Impact Seminar," in Tom Chibucor and Richard Lerner's *Serving Children and Families Through Community-University Partnerships: Success Stories* (1999a).

6. An excellent source for capturing Nixon's attempt to reform the welfare system is Burkes' *Nixon's Good Deed* (1974).

7. A more detailed explanation of Clinton's family policy is available in Peter Navarro's *Bill Clinton's Agenda for America* (1993), published by Williams. Refer to chapter 6 on children and families. Other stimulating works on Clinton's domestic policy in general are Lammers and Genovese's *The Presidency and Domestic Policy: Comparing Leadership Styles, FDR to Clinton* (2000). Also see Stoesz's *Small Change: Domestic Policy Under the Clinton Presidency* (1996) and Burns and Sorenson's *Dead Center: Clinton-Gore Leadership and Perils of Moderation* (1999).

# Chapter 3

# The Economics of Family Life

When American economist Paul Samuelson, winner of the 1970 Nobel Prize, was asked to name the most influential economists in history, people were not surprised to hear the names of Smith, Mill, Walras, and Keynes. However, when Samuelson included Knut Wicksell (1851–1926) on his list, an obscure Swedish economist, eyebrows were raised and so were questions. Undaunted, Samuelson went on to explain that not only would he include Wicksell in his top ten, but he would even place him in the top four, along with Adam Smith, Leo Walras, and John Maynard Keynes. But who was Knut Wicksell and why was he afforded so much respect by one of his peers? In brief, he was, in the minds of many people, the grandfather of family economics.

Born in Sweden in 1851, he was educated at Upsala University where he studied math and physics before becoming an economist and assuming a teaching position at the University of Lund. It was during his formative years in academia that he developed his economic theory on gender wage differentials. By the turn of the century, he would be hailed as Sweden's leading economist and honored 100 years later as the "forerunner and radical in the area of gender and the family" (Persson and Jonung 1997, 3).

Wicksell's contribution to economics was revived in the summer of 1995 in Rungsted, Denmark, at the 15th Arne Ryde Symposium on "Economics of Gender and the Family." With over 100 economists in attendance, more than forty papers were presented that included such titles as "Women's Hours of Work and Marriage Market Imbalances," "Childcare, Human Capital and Economic Efficiency," and "Intra-household Distribution of Resources and Labor Market Participation Decisions." But of all the presentations, perhaps the most interesting was the joint keynote address by Inga Persson and Christina Jonung (1997), who, during their talk on Anna and Knut Wicksell, revealed the contract the couple had agreed to during their "wedding" ceremony in Paris in July of 1889.

The contract is interesting in a number of respects. First, Wicksell and Bugge chose a common-law marriage over the traditional union that was so popular in 1889, concluding perhaps that their version of "marriage" would provide greater independence for both. The third item in their contract, for example, allows for either party to dissolve the marriage—a form of no-fault divorce eighty years ahead of its time. Such autonomy for a woman within a marriage was particularly unique and unheard of in 1889.

Second, this clearly was not a traditional breadwinner/homemaker household. Anna, for example, played a major role in Knut's career, assisting him with research and in the preparation of lectures. However, despite being a mother, she also carved out a career for herself and worked hard to further the cause of women's rights in Sweden. At age forty-eight she completed her law degree and specialized in international legal problems.

And third, the contract clearly established parameters within which economic rights and responsibilities are combined with parental obligations and expectations, even if their union was to dissolve. In the 1800s, marriage at its very worst often meant slavery for women; marriage at its best frequently meant complete lifelong dependence on a man. "If she inherits nothing from her parents, she will probably become just one more poverty-stricken seamstress, working hard to buy food for the morrow and ignored by all honorable wealthy admirers," stated Wicksell (Gardlund 1990, 39). But his marriage to Anna Bugge, as illustrated in the contract they signed in 1889, was to "become a free and tender union between equal citizens" (Persson and Jonung 1997, 4). In reality, it was a common law cohabitation agreement between two consenting adults.

## From Knut Wicksell to Gary Becker

If, as some have argued, Knut Wicksell is the founder of family economics, Gary Becker can be credited for extending the field far beyond anyone's expectations. Born in Pottsville, Pennsylvania, in 1930, Becker received his B.A. from Princeton University in 1951 and both his master's and Ph.D. from the University of Chicago. Years later, he was hired by his alma mater and, in 1992, he was awarded the Nobel Prize in economics. He was specifically honored for extending "the domain of microeconomic analysis to a wide range of human behavior and interaction, including non-market behavior" (Becker 1993, 385).

In essence, Becker won the Nobel Prize because of his successful efforts in applying classical and neoclassical economic theory to various aspects of human behavior that were traditionally the territory of other social science disciplines, such as sociology, criminology, and demography. As a result, he encouraged other economists to do what his mentor and associate, Milton Friedman, had encouraged him to do: use economics as a tool for understanding human behavior and solving social problems. In delivering his lecture as part of the Nobel Prize award ceremony in 1992, Becker emphasized the four areas he focused on throughout his career: the development and accumulation of human capital, crime and punishment, discrimination against minorities, and the structure and economic functioning of families.

Becker's economic model is based on the belief that units, be they corporations, agencies, individuals, or households, all respond rationally to various economic stimuli in an effort to improve their conditions. Many believe his major contribution in the field has been in the area of human capital. Although the theory of human capital was developed years before Becker's work, his application of microeconomic analysis to it explained, among other things, why investments in education result in higher earnings. His book *Human Capital* (1964) also offers theoretical explanations for why some nations are more successful in international trade than others. According to Becker, differences in the supply and skill of human capital among nations are more powerful in explaining the respective trade histories of countries than the differences found in the supply and quality of their real capital.

Becker's extension of economic theory to human behavior has also included work in crime and punishment, his second area of expertise. In *Essays in the Economics of Crime and Punishment* (Becker and Landes 1974), he concluded that criminality is actually rational behavior and should be analyzed as such. It is not, he argued, the result of psychological problems or socioeconomic status. A criminal, like everyone else, responds to cost-benefit calculations performed in his head prior to committing a crime. Therefore, he will act in a very predictable and rational way.

A third focal point of Becker's research has been in the area of discrimination. In *The Economics of Discrimination* (1971), he argues that an individual, such as an employer, is willing to absorb a cost in order to avoid hiring (or "entering into an economic contract") with a potential employee because the employee has traits (sex, race, age, and so on) other than those of the employer. This behavior drives what Becker refers to as a "tax wedge" between social and private economic returns. Consequently, according to Becker, discrimination will be detrimental not only to the victims (the employees not hired) but also to those practicing the discrimination (the employers). Therefore, eventually the market should and will take corrective action; the "invisible hand" will perform appropriately. Not surprisingly,

Becker is a staunch opponent of affirmative action and similar civil rights legislation. "Civil rights legislation contributed to the decline in discrimination, but we argue that quotas and other rigid affirmative action programs have done more harm than good," he and his wife wrote in *The Economics of Life* (Becker and Becker 1997, 115).

But perhaps Becker's most radical venture in economic theory has been his analysis of the behavior of individuals outside the traditional market system, particularly with respect to the economic functioning of the family. In *A Treatise on the Family* (1981), a book that he worked on for six years and one that he describes as his most difficult challenge, Becker acknowledges that "economists hardly noticed the family prior to the 1950s, when they began to recognize spouses, children, and other family members" (1981, 2). The early work of Jacob Mincer (1962) and Clarence Long (1958) concluded that the labor-force participation of women depends not only on their potential ability to earn money, but also on their husband's income, the number of children they have, their housing costs, and other family expenses. But it was Becker who took family economics into a terrain that was relatively unexplored.

The crux of his rational-choice based theory is that a household acts as a small factory. Therefore, employees of the factory, the husband and wife, for example, will each perform those particular tasks they are most skilled in more efficiently. Thus, if the mother is more skilled in raising children and keeping house and the father's talents lie outside the home where he is rewarded with a very good salary and regular promotions, then the "factory" is operating efficiently and in the best interests of all parties concerned. It would be both irrational and inefficient for the couple to reverse their respective roles. Consequently, argues Becker, in the "marriage market," women will seek husbands who will be good income producers while men will seek wives who will be successful mothers and homemakers. He, like other family economists, such as Gronau (1973) and Chiappori (1992), assume decisions made within the family are Pareto-efficient. That is, no family member can be made better off without making another worse off.

Two ideas in particular best illustrate Becker's household economic theory. The first is *time*. As explained in his essay, "A Theory of the Allocation of Time" (1965), time is the household's most scarce resource. "Economic and medical progress have greatly increased length of life, but not the physical flow of time itself, which always restricts everyone to twenty-four hours per day" (Becker 1993, 386). In exploring the allocation of time among members of the household in the performance of various tasks, Becker moved beyond previous analyses that simply focused on the dichotomy between work and leisure.

The second idea that is a key component of Becker's household economic theory is *human capital*. "Human capital in the form of good work habits or addiction to drinking has major positive or negative effects on productivity in both market and non-market sectors" (Becker 1993, 2). In short, people within the family (a nonmarket setting) are seen as assets or durables as are those in the labor force (a market setting). His 1986 article, "Human Capital and the Rise and Fall of Families," which he co-authored with Tomes, explains the interaction between market and non-market forces. For example, a rise in real wages outside the household may allow for the substitution of in-home labor (usually performed by the wife) by hiring someone to perform such work. Thus, when it is no longer economical for one member of the family to remain at home and specialize in housework, there will probably be a shift of family functions to employment outside the home in corporations, government agencies, schools, and other assorted work sites. This revaluation of human capital on the part of family members in relation to housework, contends Becker, explains the increase in married women's participation in the workforce and the rise in divorce rates.[1]

Also associated with Becker's theories on the allocation of time and the distribution of human capital within households is his work on fertility. An early essay, "An Economic Analysis of Fertility" (Becker 1960), explains how parents decide both the number of children they choose to have and the educational level the children will achieve. The amount of time and other resources that parents invest in their children's human capital becomes a function of income and prices. That is, as wages rise, parents will tend to increase the investment in their human capital (their children) and elect to have fewer offspring. According to Becker and others, this explains the consistent decline in fertility rates among industrialized countries, and helps social scientists understand the variation in fertility rates not only among different countries, but also between urban and rural areas.

Writing in his *A Treatise on the Family*, in a chapter entitled "The Evolution of the Family," Becker presents in one paragraph what is, in essence, his major thesis on the economics of family life.

> As female earning power continues to grow and fertility continues to fall, the time spent in child care is sufficiently reduced to permit married women to spend appreciable time in the labor force prior to their first child and after their last child has entered school. The expectation of greater participation at older ages encourages girls and young women to invest more in market-oriented human capital, which further increases earning power and participation, and further reduces fertility. Consequently, the increase in labor force participation and the decline in fertility eventually accelerate

even when the growth in female earning power does not. Moreover, these two factors accelerate the increase in the divorce rate because the decline in the gain from marriage also accelerates. Furthermore, a growth in the divorce rate itself eventually encourages additional divorces; divorced persons become less stigmatized and can more readily find other divorcees to marry. (1981, 251)[2]

Although Becker recognizes the importance of the women's movement in changing the family, he places even greater emphasis on an expanding welfare state as the culprit. Social Security, unemployment compensation, Medicare and Medicaid, food stamps, housing subsidies and other government programs have all played a roll in disrupting the pattern of economic interdependence and emotional support among family members, or so he argues. That is not to say that he opposes all of these programs, but rather that they have expanded beyond their original purposes. Fifteen years after the publication of his *Treatise*, Becker and Becker, in *The Economics of Life* (1997), continued the assault on government intervention by attacking legislative proposals that called for child-care and family-leave policies.

Agreeing that the most dramatic change in the U.S. labor market this century is the large increase in married women in the workforce, he also recognizes that many women have been subjected to discrimination, in terms of both access to careers and pay equity. However, argues Becker, it is precisely because more women are seeking careers and entering the labor market that the gap between men and women's pay is steadily decreasing. The market has taken corrective action. "The growth in the employment and earnings of women over time is explained mostly by market forces rather than by civil rights legislation, affirmative action programs, or the women's movement" (Becker and Becker 1997, 132).

He argues relentlessly that free market systems are more efficient than those subjected to heavy government regulation and believes that the effects of a free-market system on individual behavior may be even greater over the long term. "That's why economists and many other defenders of a free-market system in the nineteenth century often emphasized the system's effect on values rather than on efficiency," he and his wife conclude in *The Economics of Life* (Becker and Becker 1997, 94). However, when it comes to divorce laws, Becker would prefer greater government intervention to make it more difficult to terminate a marriage. Specifically, he contends, the right to a unilateral divorce without cause is precisely what drives women into the workforce and keeps them there. "No-fault divorce laws discourage married women from leaving the work force for several years to care for their young children, because they realize that they will need good jobs if their husbands ditch them. Under mutual consent, women would be more able to stay home for a spell after having children, if they wanted to, because they would then have much less reason to fear being left in a financial bind" (Becker and Becker 1997, 99). In a 1985 article in *Business Week*, he called for the use of marriage contracts as a means of protecting women who stay home to raise children.[3]

Becker reminds us in his *Treatise on the Family* and other works that although household production is an important component of the output of all nations, it is not included in the Gross National Product (GDP). "After all," he states, "when a family hires someone to care for the children, clean the house, and cook, that work is counted in the Gross Domestic Product (GDP) figures. When a parent does it, it is not" (Becker and Becker 1997, 127). The failure to include household labor in a nation's GDP distorts any measures of economic growth, Becker concludes. Continuing his argument, he believes the movement of women into the workforce and the substitution of market production for household production explains the rapid expansion of the child-care industry in the United States. "Working women reduced the time they spent caring for their own children by hiring other women to do it for them. Women cared for one another's children" (Becker and Becker 1997, 128).

Not surprisingly, Becker is equally critical of government-mandated family leave policies. Such an approach interferes with the natural functioning of the free market and the basic laws of supply and demand. Not only is government intervention uncalled for and economically inefficient, it discriminates. Writing in 1991, a year after George Bush's first veto of the FMLA, and two year's before Bill Clinton's signature made it a national law, Becker warned that the enactment of such legislation, even if unpaid, is "only a first step toward the Swedish system of requiring full pay for employees on child-care leave. Forcing business to provide leave is both inefficient and unjust. It in effect discriminates against single persons and against married women and men with no children or with grown children. It's one thing to call for a gender-neutral productivity test for pay hikes and promotions, but another to make business give preference to persons with young children" (Becker and Becker 1997, 130).

## Critics of Becker

One cannot explore new territories of economic theory and venture repeatedly into controversial terrain as Becker has done over the years without drawing heavy fire from skeptics. Some critics, such as Bergmann (1987), are quite blatant in their attacks. His (Becker's) model "explains, justifies, and even glorifies role differences by sex" (1987, 46). In an article published in *Feminist Economics*, Bergmann refers to Becker's theory on the family as "preposterous." "Becker's method of thinking about the family leads, as does almost all neoclassical theory, to a conclusion that the institutions depicted are benign, and that government intervention would be useless at best and probably harmful" (Bergmann 1995, 149). Others are critical of Becker but present their arguments in slightly different terms and from a variety of perspectives. In short, unlike Becker, they tend not to see the free market as family friendly.

For example, some economists speak in terms of "production for use value" and "production for exchange value" in discussing the economics of the household. Production for use value occurs when a member of the family, usually the wife or mother, performs various household tasks for which she is not paid in the traditional manner. Washing clothes, cleaning house, shopping, cooking, and raising children are a few examples. Production for exchange value, on the other hand, is usually performed by the husband or father in which he engages in employment outside the home for which he is paid, either by the hour or by an agreed upon salary.

Some economists—feminists in particular—have argued that the individual within the household who produces for exchange value (usually the husband) holds more power over his wife who produces for use value (Firestone 1971; Humphries 1977; Millett 1970). What's worse, according to some neo-Marxists, is that such an arrangement also benefits the capitalists in at least two ways: One, the housework completed by women enables employers to pay their male employees less. Otherwise, if the wife did not assume the homemaker role, employees would demand higher wages to cover the cost of such in-home services as housecleaning, cooking, and child care (Zaretsky 1986). Two, the psychological support provided by the housewife enables her husband to survive in the boring but cutthroat world of big business, a world that provides high profits for the capitalists (Goode 1963). Therefore, to continue this neo-Marxian line of logic, the corporate structure will favor the traditional breadwinner/homemaker household.

Such reasoning coincides with the work of Friedrich Engels, who argued a century and a half ago that the division of labor within the household between men and women not only benefited the capitalists, but it also produced the gender inequities that became magnified by society as a whole. Under socialism, however, child care provided by the state will enable women to enter the workforce and male supremacy at home *and* at work will ultimately vanish. "The supremacy of the man in marriage is the simple consequence of his economic supremacy, and with the abolition of the latter will disappear of itself" (Engels 1972, 145).

Although Engels's dream for a socialist society never came true in the

United States, a combination of forces contributed to the increase of women entering the workforce. The massive shift from an agrarian to an industrial society, spurred on by World War II, brought many women into the labor force. The civil rights movement in the 1960s, the rise of feminism in the 1970s, and the decline of manual labor and the expansion of the service sector also contributed to the increase in women entering the job market. Equally important, according to Rubin and Riney, wives' labor force participation expanded most rapidly from the early 1970s through the 1980s. "Rising prices combined with wage stagnation for male workers generated a period of transition for families. Many wives worked to implement desired lifestyles and to finance higher housing costs" (Rubin and Riney 1995, 16). By the 1980s, more women chose to attend college, postpone marriage, and have fewer children than their mothers. Simply put, by the 1980s, better-educated women were entering the labor market and choosing to stay longer. This desire to remain attached to the job market, even after childbirth, eventually spawned a variety of advocacy groups that pressured government to provide state-sponsored child-care and family-leave programs (Cohen and Katzenstein 1988).

But still, other critics of Becker are more specific in their attacks and contend that his theory is based on several assumptions that have very weak underpinnings (Cherlin 1996). First, Becker assumes that women are more efficient at providing child care and keeping house than men. However, there is little, if any, evidence offered to support this assumption. Second, Becker also assumes that men will earn more outside the home than women. While this may be true, there appears to be limited interest on Becker's part in explaining why a wage gap exists in the first place and how the free market will correct such a discrepancy if called upon to do so. And third, Becker and his followers assume that the husband and wife are always in complete agreement when they assume their particular roles within the household, or decide how to distribute the family's income. In reality, this single "utility function" (the economist's term for identical preferences), in which the family is a unit of cooperation and consensus, rarely occurs.

Skeptical of Becker's approach, McElroy and Honey (1981) and Manser and Brown (1980) have explored alternative theories to household decision-making, which include what they refer to as "threat points." Under such a model, disagreements are recognized and, depending on the options available outside the marriage and the size of individual assets, divorce may be a rational act. According to Del Boca (1997), the availability of threat points "shifts the attention from resource-pooling to the control of resources" (1997, 66). In fact, the emotional stress produced by disagreements over the division of labor and control of resources within the household, a characteristic not uncommon in the modern family, may be counterproductive and, therefore, undermine the "small factory's" efficiency.

Becker is also open to criticism for assuming that mate selection is rational and the marriage market is balanced. David Buss's (1975) multigenerational study on mate selection, for example, concluded that while women did place greater emphasis on the earning potential of their spouses-to-be, men, on the other hand, focused more on the physical attractiveness of their mates than on their homemaker skills. Grossbard-Shectman and Neideffer (1997), though not necessarily opponents of Becker, offer a different theory of labor and marriage by exploring marriage market imbalances and the changing patterns of family formation.

With respect to imbalances, they theorize that in marriage markets with high male/female sex ratios, women in particular will receive more income from spousal labor and, consequently, will supply less labor outside the home. Marriage market imbalances have also been explored extensively by prominent sociologists, including William Julius Wilson (1987) and Lichter, LeClere, and McLaughlin (1991). According to Wilson, the disappearance of traditional industrial jobs from the inner city has left many African American men unemployed and unemployable. Therefore, African American women who are seeking men to marry have a continuously decreasing pool of men from which to choose. "As the disappearance of work has become a characteristic feature of the inner-city ghetto, so too has the disappearance of the traditional married-couple family," writes Wilson (1996, 31). Lichter, LeClere, and McLaughlin (1991) also found that marriage rates among women decline where unemployment among men is high.

Clearly, the financial health and general well-being of the nation's families depends on a number of factors. Until fairly recently, however, the family was ignored as a unit of economic analysis. Today, due in part to changing demographics, political pressures, and economic forces, more attention is being devoted to understanding how families form and dissolve, the functions they perform, and the economic decisions they make. Kurt Wicksell, Gary Becker, Barbara Bergman, and others have created a variety of frameworks for analyzing the family as an economic unit and for explaining the choices made by its members. Not to be overlooked is the effect external influences have on the internal functioning of the family. One important outside influence in particular that demands close scrutiny is U.S. tax policy and the extent to which it affects the economic status of America's families.

### Taxes and the Family

The income tax was passed in the United States in 1913. More than thirty years later, in 1942, it underwent major reform in which the original tax structure was dismantled and a high-income-based tax was replaced by one that was more broad based. With the primary purpose of the reform being to create and maintain tax equity, three major tax principles were put in place. First, the tax should be progressive so tax rates increase with income. Second, the system should be fair. Households with equal incomes and similar demographic profiles should pay the same amount in taxes. And third, the marriage neutrality that is embedded in the system should be preserved. Marriage neutrality means that the act of marriage should not change the tax burden of two individuals after they repeat their wedding vows (Bittker 1975). However, according to Levitan et al. (1988) and Rosen (1992), these three principles are often in conflict with each other. This observation offers at least one explanation (well-organized and tenacious pressure groups being another) as to why legislators find it so difficult to reform the American tax system (Hefferen 1982; Rubin and Riney 1995).

But, despite the difficulties, we have witnessed several successful attempts at tax reform. For example, one of the more significant developments occurred in 1948 when marital neutrality and income splitting were introduced. Under income splitting, a married couple's tax liability is determined by doubling half of what their joint income is. However, this reform, unfortunately, was particularly unfair to single individuals who could pay 40 percent more in taxes than a married couple who generated the same amount of income (Rosen 1987; Rubin and Riney 1995). This built-in inequity was labeled the "singles penalty."

When Congress moved on tax reform again in 1969, it addressed the "singles penalty" but, in doing so, created the "marriage penalty." In its simplest terms, some couples found themselves paying higher taxes after getting married than they did before as single individuals. However, the discrepancy embedded in the 1969 tax reform initiative is far more complicated than that, and the controversy surrounding it strikes at the very heart of the family values debate. Borrowing from Edward McCaffery's illustration in his *Taxing Women* (1997), let us assume that there are two married couples with identical total incomes. Mr. and Mrs. Traditional earn $50,000 in total income, but Mr. Traditional works full-time while Mrs. Traditional chooses to be a homemaker and stay home with their two children. On the other hand, Mr. and Mrs. Equal also have two children and bring in a total of $50,000, but both of them work full-time. However, the Equals could pay almost $3,000 more in taxes than the Traditionals.

According to McCaffery, such a policy blatantly represents "secondary-earner bias" and it harbors two components. First, he argues, "the rate structure encourages families to think in terms of a primary and secondary worker." The second component is not far behind. "There are strong disincentives against second earners working in the paid workforce at all, " he continues, "because they enter it at high marginal tax rates"(1997, 20). Because wives are usually viewed as the second earner in dual-earner couples, women are expected to leave the labor market before men. In short, accountants may be inclined to encourage Mrs. Equal to quit her job, stay home, and avoid the bias. And that outcome, argue feminists and liberals alike, is precisely what conservatives desire and the tax code reinforces. It is understandable, therefore, that tax reform has become a major topic of political debate in recent years and, occasionally, it has been entwined with family values (Steurle 1995; Mattox 1998).

Over a period of almost twenty years, beginning in 1981, six major tax reform measures were adopted. The famous Reagan tax cut in 1981, the Economic Recovery Tax Act (ERTA), was followed by two major tax increases, the Tax Equity and Fiscal Responsibility Act of 1982 (TEFRA), and the Deficit Reduction Act of 1984 (DEFRA). These acts in turn were followed by Bush and Clinton tax hikes, the Omnibus Budget Reconciliation Acts (OBRA) of 1990 and 1993, respectively. The 1997 Taxpayer Relief Act was passed only a few months after Clinton began his second term. Throughout this period, the dual-earner couple became the focal point of tax reformers, and numerous efforts were made to correct the so-called marriage penalty.

The 1981 tax reform initiative reduced liability for two-earner families and increased child-care credits up to $2,400 per child for dual-earner couples who earned less than $10,000. In 1982, dual-earner couples gained additional ground when they were permitted a 5 percent deduction for the spouse with the lowest income up to $30,000 a year, but with the maximum deduction not to exceed $1,500. The maximum deduction was doubled to $3,000 in 1983 but was then repealed by the Tax Reform Act of 1986.

Some argue that the 1986 Tax Reform Act was the most successful attempt to reform the tax system since 1948. Conceived and adopted during the Reagan administration, the Act dramatically reduced the marginal tax rates to 15, 28, and 33 percent of taxable income. All told, and by the time the act went into effect five years after Reagan assumed the presidency, the top marginal tax rate fell from 70 percent to 28 percent. Although the 1986 Tax Reform Act did not remove or even change the tax credit for child and dependent care that was incorporated in the 1981 reforms and was a benefit to the dual-earner couple with children, it did, however, eliminate the two-earner deduction. When signing the legislation, President Reagan did not forgo the opportunity to remind the public of one of the Act's primary objectives: to encourage women to return to the home. "With inflation and bracket creep also eroding incomes," he stated, "many spouses who would rather stay home with their children have been forced to go looking for jobs" (McCaffrey 1997, 210).[4]

Whether or not the 1986 act produced the desired outcome Reagan alluded to above is clouded by the fact that those with higher incomes (often dual-earner couples) ultimately benefited from the lower marginal tax rates (Aaron 1987; Rubin and Riney 1995). However, the marriage penalty remained, particularly for higher-income couples. "The exact effect depended on the deductions allowed, or the number of dependents, and on the relative incomes earned by the two spouses," state Rubin and Riney. "Spouses with widely divergent incomes received a marriage subsidy, while those with fairly equal incomes were penalized with a marriage tax" (Rubin and Riney 1995, 44). But in the end, it appears that any attempt to use the tax code to manipulate women's behavior in the job market was ineffective for two reasons: One, women are working *despite*, not *because of* taxes (McCaffery 1997). That is, the economic elasticities (a willingness to work at various jobs across a broad wage range) of women are much higher than the elasticities for men (Boskin and Sheshinski 1983; Killingworth and Heckman 1986; Triest 1990). And two, despite conservative wishes to the contrary, many women really want to work, to establish their own careers, and to be as independent as possible (Hochschild 1989, 1997). That is, their interests and desires run parallel to those of men.

Throughout the 1990s, whatever additional tax reform efforts were put forth coincided with the major themes characteristic of the 1986 Tax Reform Act. For example, the 1990 Omnibus Budget Reconciliation Act made additional adjustments in the tax code dealing with personal exemptions and deductions, but still did not address the marriage penalty that existed for some dual-earner households. Nor was it addressed in the 1993 and 1997 reforms. Instead, and once again, policymakers chose to play on the margins by appeasing families with adjustments in three programs in particular: the Earned Income Tax Credit, child and dependent care credits, and education tax credits. Each of these is discussed below.

**Earned Income Tax Credit**

As discussed briefly in the previous chapter, the Earned Income Tax Credit (EITC) has become a popular tool for politicians to address the concerns of the working poor. First enacted in 1976 near the end of the Ford administration, the EITC was greatly expanded in the 1980s and later became a key component of Clinton's tax strategy. Not coincidentally, because it is geared to the working poor, its popularity increased during a time when "workfare" became more appealing to welfare reformers. Unlike the child-care credit, the EITC is refundable. That is, the federal government, as well as state governments that have created their own versions of the act, will send a check to anyone whose credit is greater than the amount of the tax owed. However, an unfortunate drawback is that the credit is so complicated that many who are eligible never file a claim (McCaffery 1997).

Under the EITC, single or married workers, including dual-earner couples who earned less than $30,580 during the previous year and are raising "qualified" children in their homes, can receive a credit up to $3,816. For workers who earned less than $26,928 and were raising only one child, the potential EITC is $2,321. Single or married workers at least twenty-five and under age sixty-five, who are not raising kids in their homes and who earned less than $10,200 last year, are eligible for $347 under the EITC.[5]

Until fairly recently, the EITC has been conspicuously absent from discussions related to the marriage penalty. But the structure of the credit is insensitive to dual-earner couples. In essence, married couples are treated as single taxpayers. According to McCaffery (1997), this discrepancy is exacerbated by at least two other factors: one, the class issue, and two, the tendency to focus on the marriage penalty rather than on secondary-earner bias.

With respect to the first factor, when marriage penalties affect the upper-income families there is outrage. When poor families are affected, there is relatively little interest. Regarding the second factor, secondary-earner bias in the tax code represents a society unwilling to accept women in the workforce. "We should care about the secondary-earner bias, not the marriage penalty, at middle to upper levels of income, because decisions to marry or not are unlikely to be affected by tax factors, but decisions for women to work or not are affected. It is exactly the opposite among the poor. Decisions to work or not are matters of economic necessity; what can give way is the decision to marry or stay married. Addressing the marriage penalty among the poor will alleviate the secondary-earner bias as well, but perhaps the most pressing concern is the pressure on two-earner families themselves" (McCaffery 1997, 83–84).

## Child and Dependent Care Credits

Pro-family tax relief is not new, nor is it new to focus on children as a means for providing such relief. For example, in 1986, the White House Working Group's report, *The Family: Preserving America's Future* (discussed in the previous chapter), recommended doubling the tax exemption for children. Four years later, the Progressive Policy Institute, the think tank for the National Leadership Council, and an organization established by reform Democrats under the leadership of then Governor Bill Clinton, also recommended that the tax exemption for children be doubled. In 1991, the bipartisan Commission on Children went beyond tax exemptions and called for a $1,000 tax credit. Unlike a deduction, which reduces the amount on which one is taxed, a tax credit reduces the amount of the tax itself. When the conservatives under Newt Gingrich issued their *Contract with America* in 1994, they recommended a $500 tax credit for children. With such bipartisan support emerging, the debate no longer focused on the idea of a child credit, but rather on its amount.

In 1997, the child tax credit was a major component of the Taxpayer Relief Act. Initially set at $400 for each child age sixteen or under, it rose to $500 by 1999. Under such a plan, a family with four eligible children is entitled to a $2,000 credit per year. However, the policy is not universal. The credit is phased out for couples with income above $110,000 and for single parents who make more than $75,000 annually. Furthermore, the credit is not available to many lower-income families because it can only be used to offset income taxes, not payroll taxes. Payroll taxes tend to be the dominant form of federal taxes paid by poorer families (Center on Budget and Policy Priorities 1999). Consequently, it is estimated that only about 57 percent of all families with dependent children are eligible for even a partial credit. But, if the allowable child tax credit exceeds the amount of income tax owed, the family may be eligible for a refund based on a special formula.[6]

Another important component of the Taxpayer Relief Act of 1997 was the child and dependent care credit. The amount of the credit is determined by a number of factors: the number of children or dependents being cared for, the family's income for the previous year, and the amount of money spent for care during that year. Families with one child or dependent cannot claim more than $2,400 in expenses, and those with more than one child or dependent cannot claim more than $4,800. With eligible families receiving a credit that ranges between 20 and 30 percent of these expenses, the amount of the award can be as much as $720 for families with one child or dependent and $1,440 for families with more than one child or dependent.

**Education Tax Credits**

A third component of the pro-family tax initiative was the Hope Scholarship Credit. Available to first- and second-year, full-time undergraduate students, the college aid program provides a tax credit of 100 percent of the first $1,000 and 50 percent of the second $1,000 for a total of $1,500. Minus other grants, scholarships, and tax-free assistance, it covers tuition and fees. Based on a sliding scale, the Hope Scholarship is gradually reduced as the parents' income increases—between $80,000 and $100,000 for married taxpayers filing jointly. Those with incomes above these levels may not claim the credit.

Also, as of July 1, 1998, taxpayers may be eligible for the Lifetime Learning Credit. If a student is enrolled in at least one postsecondary course at a qualifying institution, students or parents may claim a 20 percent tax credit for the first $5,000 of tuition and fees paid each year. This credit, as with the Hope Scholarship, applies to *all* students in the family. Geared primarily to middle-class families, the education credits are generally unavailable to lower-income families.

In 1998, the White House issued a brief report, "The Balanced Budget Delivers a Mainstream, Middle Class Tax Cut." It included four scenarios of various family types with an explanation as to how each family would fare in 1999 after applying selected provisions from the 1997 Taxpayer Relief Act. The White House document is recreated below. All figures are based on the 1999 tax year.

### How Typical American Families Fared Under the 1997 Tax Act

#### Example #1

Consider a family of four with an income of $40,000 a year. The father is a carpenter who makes $25,000, and the mother works at a local department store and makes $15,000. They have two children, a son who is fourteen and a freshman in high school and a daughter enrolled full-time in her first year at a state university. Her tuition is $5,999 a year.

This family benefits from the tax cut in at least two ways. They will receive a child tax credit of $500 for their son, plus a Hope Scholarship of $1,500 for their daughter. In total, they will receive a $2,000 tax cut.

### Tax Cut

Family of four with two children aged fourteen and eighteen and $40,000 income:

| | |
|---|---|
| Child Tax Credit for fourteen-year-old | $500 |
| Hope Scholarship for eighteen-year-old | $1,500 |
| **Total Tax Cut:** | **$2,000** |

#### Example #2

Consider a family of three making $55,000 a year. The father has a degree in accounting and works for a local business in the accounting department. The mother works part-time at the local library. They have one daughter aged seven. The father would like to return to school to prepare for his CPA examination. He is going to attend the local liberal arts college. He has signed up for two courses with total tuition of $4,000.

This family will receive a $500 child tax credit for their daughter and an $800 tuition tax credit to help pay for the father's course work.

## Tax Cut

Family of three with one child aged seven and $55,000 income:

| | |
|---|---|
| Child Tax Credit for seven-year-old | $500 |
| Tuition Tax Credit | $800 |
| **Total Tax Cut** | **$1,300** |

### Example #3

Consider a family of three making $80,000 combined. They have a daughter who is seventeen years old and is trying to decide where to go to college. She is leaning toward a private liberal arts school. Her parents are staring at tuition payments in excess of $10,000 a year for four school years and wondering how they will pay for it.

This tax cut will help. Their daughter will be eligible for a $1,500 Hope Scholarship in each of her first two years in college. During her junior and senior years, she will be eligible for a tuition tax credit of $1,000 (because four school years fall across five tax years she will be eligible for another $1,000 in the fifth year).

| Year | Tuition | Tax Credits |
|---|---|---|
| 1998 | $1,500 | Hope Scholarship |
| 1999 | $1,500 | Hope Scholarship |
| 2000 | $1,000 | Tuition Tax Credit |
| 2001 | $1,000 | Tuition Tax Credit |
| 2002 | $1,000 | Tuition Tax Credit |

**Cumulative Tax Cut to Help Pay for Daughter's Education   $6,000**

### Example #4

A single mother lives with her six-year-old daughter in California. She's been working as a bank teller for several years and her pay is now $20,000 a year. Working toward becoming a loan officer, she is taking one course a semester toward a bachelor's degree. Her tuition is $1,000. This family will receive a $500 child tax credit for the daughter and a $200 tuition tax credit.

## Tax Cut

Family of two with one child aged six and $20,000 income:

| | |
|---|---|
| Child Tax Credit for six-year-old | $500 |
| Tuition Tax Credit | $200 |
| **Total Tax Cut:** | **$700** |

But despite the efforts of the 1997 Taxpayer Relief Act to give tax breaks to families, an analysis of the final outcome provides a different picture. According to Citizens for Tax Justice, a nonpartisan tax research group based in Washington, the 1997 act "was a disaster for the goal of fair, simple, and adequate taxation" (1998, 1). For example, of the 80 percent of tax filers who made less than $59,000 in 1997, only one in seventeen got a tax cut, and that cut only averaged $6. For the 15 percent of tax filers who made between $59,000 and $112,000, less than one in five received a tax cut, with the average being slightly above $81. The remaining 5 percent of Americans got 81 percent of the give-back. Even more striking, the top 1 percent of the "best-off" Americans, who had average incomes of $666,000 in 1997, consumed almost 68 percent of all the tax cuts granted, an average of $7,135 each. "President Clinton and the GOP-led Congress touted the 1997 tax act as middle-income tax relief, but the reality is far different," stated Robert S. McIntyre, director of Citizens for Tax Justice (1998, 1).

A more recent attempt to reform the tax code came in 1999 with the proposed Taxpayer Refund/Relief Act. Designed initially to provide $792 billion in tax refunds and relief over ten years, it was touted as the largest tax cut since Reagan's in 1981. Had it been enacted in its original form, not only would income tax rates have been reduced by 1 percent across the board over a period of years (2001 to 2005), but the marriage penalty would have been completely eliminated as well through a phase-out program between 2005 and 2008. It was also to include an expansion of the adoption credit and an increase in the dependent-care credit. However, this effort at reform was diverted by the battle between Congress and Clinton over the future funding of Social Security and Medicare. Consequently, the president vetoed the bill. In the end, the only tax bill to be adopted in 1999 was an extension of some smaller provisions from previous reforms that were set to expire in 2000.

## Other Taxes

Historically, in most of the debates over tax reform, the focus of discussion has been on personal income tax, not payroll taxes earmarked for Social Security and Medicare or state and local taxes, such as the property tax. But clearly, the financial status of families has been, and will continue to be, affected by these taxes. For example, both Social Security and Medicare taxes have increased considerably since the mid-1970s, due in large measure to the adoption of cost-of-living adjustments (COLAs) for Social Security, and the soaring healthcare costs of a growing aging population afflicted with chronic illnesses who need long-term care. Consequently, 73 percent of working families pay more Social Security payroll taxes than personal income taxes (Berlau 1998). Although aware of this problem amidst ongoing concerns about the allocation of resources across generations, politicians have been reluctant to tackle the issue. After all, the elderly have the best voting record of any age group and they are represented by the largest lobbying group in the world. The American Association of Retired Persons (AARP) has a membership in excess of 38 million people.[7]

Often overlooked in discussions about the economic status of families, particularly in relation to tax policy, is the effect state and local taxes have on various types of households. According to a report completed by economist J. Scott Moody (1999) of the Tax Foundation, property taxes hit an all-time high in 1999. It is estimated that state and local governments collected approximately $11 billion and $220 billion in property taxes, respectively. With the exception of the 1970s which witnessed tax revolts that were spurred on by Proposition 13 in California and Prop 2½ in Massachusetts, property tax collections have risen steadily since 1950 and particularly since 1981, having increased by 69 percent over the last two decades. When all state and local taxes are combined and then viewed from the perspective of a per capita tax burden, the three highest states in 1999 were New York ($4,914), Connecticut ($4,744), and New Jersey ($4,253). The three states with the lowest state and local per capita taxes in 1999 were Wyoming ($1,755), Alaska ($1,989), and North Dakota ($2,223). Placed in the context of family expenses, Americans spent more money per capita on taxes in 1999 than on food ($2,693), clothing ($1,404), and shelter ($5,833) combined (Fleenor 1999).

## The Changing Economic Status of America's Families: Why the Demand for Family Leave

As discussed in previous chapters, the family has changed considerably in both form and function over the years. Consequently, it has become the subject of heated political debates, including those during presidential campaigns. Equally important, the family has, at times, also been the focal point of major economic policy initiatives, particularly with respect to tax policy. The Earned Income Tax Credit, the Child and Dependent Care Tax Credit, Hope Scholarships, and various efforts to address the so-called marriage penalty are important examples that have been discussed here in some detail. But whether or not such policies have had a positive or negative impact on America's families may depend on at least two factors: one, what material you may be reading, and two, over what timeframe the analysis is being conducted.

On September 30, 1999, an Associated Press story entitled "Household Incomes Rise, 4th Straight Year" appeared in the *New York Times* (1999b). Comparing household incomes in 1998 to the 1989 pre-recession high, the story reported that the median household income (half earned more and half earned less) rose by 3.5 percent, or about $1,300, to a high of $38,900. This percentage increase outdistanced the 1989 pre-recession income by 2.6 percent. Alaska was the only state where the median household income declined from the previous year. It was also reported that poverty fell from 13.3 percent to 12.7 percent between 1997 and 1998, that the poverty rate for children fell below 20 percent for the first time since 1980, that the gap between the wealthiest and poorest Americans remained the same between 1997 and 1998, and that the difference between men's and women's earnings changed very little, with women earning 73 cents for every dollar earned by men. "The best news is that these gains finally are being shared with all groups, from the wealthiest to the poorest," stated President Clinton in reference to the annual report that was issued by the U.S. Census Bureau (*New York Times* 1999a, 1). Not everyone would agree with the president's statement.

To examine the economic status of families over four years is one matter. To look at the financial well-being of households over a longer time span is quite another. A view from a broader perspective may not only produce a much different picture, but it may explain the growing demand for child-care and family-leave policies. Writing in their book *The Economic Future of American Families* (1991), Frank Levy and Richard Michel divided more than forty years of economic change into two distinct segments: (1) 1945 to 1972, the years of economic growth, and (2) 1973 to 1986, the years of stagnation.

While family incomes doubled between 1947 and 1973, they grew by only 6 percent between 1973 and 1986. Young families in particular were hurt by the period of stagnation. A young man of thirty in 1986 earned about 15 percent less than his father did in 1973. And, what wasn't earned on the job was lost in housing costs. In the 1950s and 1960s, between 15 and 18 percent of a family's income (usually a one-earner household) was devoted to paying the mortgage. By 1973, the percentage was 20 percent, but by 1983, it had doubled to 40 percent.

Meanwhile, there were signs that the gap between rich and poor was widening. In 1947, for example, the richest fifth of families received $8.60 for every dollar received by the poorest fifth. By 1969, the gap had narrowed and the ratio stood at $7.25 to $1. But after 1969, the year in which the gap between rich and poor was one of the smallest in the nation's history, class divisions grew. This was particularly true during the 1980s when small gullies became large canyons. Consequently, both the higher- and lower-income classes expanded in size and the middle class began to shrink. Thanks to cost-of-living adjustments being attached to Social Security in 1972, many elderly people were able to escape poverty. In doing so they swapped places with one of the fastest-growing poverty groups in the nation, single mothers. By 1999, for every $11.25 received by the upper fifth, $1 was received by the bottom fifth.

But the widening income gap may not be as simple to explain as originally thought. The growth in family diversity and its impact on income distribution cannot be ignored. With more families headed by single mothers at one end of the income continuum and more dual-earner couples at the other, an increase in the divergence in income between the top and bottom fifths should not be surprising. However, whether or not the income gap will grow or shrink in the years ahead will ultimately depend on election results and political compromises.

In short, the forty years of economic change resulted in a widening of inequality, between both generations and among families. Younger families were hit harder than older families, and black families were hit harder than white families. "Because of these developments, income inequality among families with children has increased far more rapidly than income inequality among all families" (Levy and Michel 1991, 4). This fact is especially acute among female-headed households. But equally significant, Levy and Michel emphasize that from 1973 to 1986, the period of stagnation, the proportion of children in two-parent families declined. However, the increase in mothers' labor-force participation increased so rapidly that the proportion of children in *two-earner* families actually rose. Confronted with economic stagnation that resulted in fewer jobs, lower-paying jobs, higher taxes, rising inflation, and higher interest rates for mortgages, it is hardly surprising that women would leave what Demos refers to as "the little commonwealth" and Becker calls "the small factory," and venture into the labor market. Nor should it be surprising to anyone that demands for child-care and family-leave policies would follow.

### Explaining Income Disparities and Facing Tough Questions. Is Family Leave One More Example of Tinkering at the Margins?

The findings put forth by Levy and Michel coincided with the works of Kevin Philips in *The Politics of Rich and Poor* (1990) and *Boiling Point* (1993); Donald Barlett and James Steele in *America: Who Really Pays the Taxes?* (1994); and Stanley Greenberg in *Middle Class Dreams: The Politics and Power of the New American Majority* (1995). Similar conclusions were reached in more recent works, including Mishel, Bernstein, and Schmitt's *The State of Working America: 1989–99* (1999); Collins, Lonegar-Wright, and Sklar's *Shifting Fortunes: The Perils of the Growing American Wealth*

*Gap* (1999); Miringoff and Miringoff's *The Social Health of the Nation: How America Is Really Doing* (1999); and Theda Skocpol's *The Missing Middle* (2000). Three dominant themes emerge from all of these writings: One, Americans are working longer for less. Two, family income growth is slow despite a booming economy. And three, the gap between rich and poor continues to grow as the middle class gets squeezed financially and becomes what Skocpol (2000) calls "the missing middle."

There are numerous works, such as those cited above, that paint a fairly pessimistic overview of the economic progress of America's families over the last four decades. However, there are also books that either present a different view or offer a unique methodology for explaining the wealth gap as it presently exists. For example, Paul Ryscavage's *Income Inequality in America* (1998) not only recognizes the widening gap between rich and poor, but also finds common ground between economists' views and popular conceptions of the problem. More important, Ryscavage offers specific measures to both illustrate and explain income disparity in the United States.

On the other hand, W. Michael Cox and Richard Alm's *The Myths of Rich and Poor: Why We're Better Off Than We Think* (1999) lauds the successes of Reagan's supply-side economics and criticizes the conclusions of the pessimists. Although the authors recognize the negative impact economic stagnation has had on society at various times, they hasten to emphasize, however, that workers have been benefiting from the economy for many years. Pointing specifically to the consumption patterns of Americans, the authors conclude that such items as microwave ovens, air conditioners, and color television sets so prevalent in today's homes would have been classified as luxury items in the 1970s.

But, as Frank Levy argues in his *Harvard Business Review* article in which he compares *The State of Working America* to *The Myths of Rich and Poor*, "with so many different numbers available, an analyst has a lot of discretion in deciding how to spin them" (Levy 1999, 164). According to the "spin" of Mishel, Bernstein, and Schmitt (1999), the typical married couple family worked 247 more hours per year in 1999 than in 1996, an increase of more than six weeks on the job. By 2000, the United States passed Japan in the number of hours on the job by an average worker. The total in the United States is 1,966 hours per year per worker compared to Japan's 1,886.

However, the living standards of most working families still have not recovered from the recession of the early 1990s. Despite a major upswing in the stock market, the typical middle-class family had 3 percent less wealth in 1997 than it did in 1989. The Economic Policy Institute reported that "between 1947 and 1973, median family income grew from $20,102 to $40,979, or by 104 percent. This growth rate worked out to 2.8 percent a year on average, or a doubling in income every 25 years. After 1973, however, the growth rate slowed markedly. Over the twenty-four years from 1973 to 1997, median family income rose an average of 0.35 percent a years. At this rate, it will take 198 years for family income to double" (Economic Policy Institute 1999, 2). In short, the typical American family in the 1990s is working longer hours for stagnant or falling income in insecure jobs that offer limited benefits.[8]

With respect to income inequalities, a study by Collins, Hartman, and Sklar (1999) of United for a Fair Economy reports that the current gap between the rich and poor parallels that which existed in the 1920s. The top 1 percent of the household has more wealth than the entire bottom 95 percent combined. According to calculations completed by the Center on Budget and Policy Priorities (1999) and summarized in Table 3.1, between 1977 and 1999 the top fifth of households saw their annual income increase by 38.2 percent after federal taxes. The next fifth, those earning between $42,600 and $45,100 a year, gained nearly 6 percent in annual income. However, the bottom three-fifths all lost real income between 1977 and 1999, with the lowest one-fifth being hurt the most with a loss of 12 percent.

But meanwhile, the top 1 percent of households gained 115 percent. Put another way, in 1989 the United States had 66 billionaires and 31.5 million people in poverty. Ten years later, there were 268 billionaires and 34.5 million living below the poverty line ($13,880 for a family of three and $16,700 for a family of four in 1999). Or, in 1995, the richest 1 percent of households owned about a third of all net worth; the next richest 10 percent also owned approximately one-third, and the remaining households (89 percent) owned the remaining third. Or, still another way to capture the differences between income groups is to consider the fact that the wealthiest 2.7 million have as much to spend as the poorest 100 million (*New York Times* 1999b, 14). "The rising tide has lifted the yachts to tremendous heights, but many Americans are still bailing out their boats after decades of sinking real wages and wealth. Average workers are earning less, adjusting for inflation, than they did a quarter century ago" (Collins, Hartman, and Sklar 1999, 1). Table 3.1 illustrates the income disparity that currently exists within the United States.

Often put forth as a possible solution to the growing gap between the rich and poor is an increase in the minimum wage. First established in 1938 during Roosevelt's New Deal, its purpose was to ensure that workers were fairly compensated for a day's work. Historically, however, proposals to increase the minimum wage have been opposed by conservatives because, in their minds, it will either retard the hiring of workers, increase unemployment, or both.[9] Proponents, on the other hand, argue that a higher minimum wage will reduce employee turnover and absenteeism, lower recruitment and training costs, increase productivity, and increase morale and commitment to the com-

Table 3.1

**Growing Income Disparity** (1977–1999)

| Household groups | Share of All Income (%) | | Average After-Tax Income | | Change |
|---|---|---|---|---|---|
| | 1977 | 1999 | 1977 | 1999 | |
| One-fifth with lowest income | 5.7 | 4.2 | $10,000 | $8,800 | −12.0 |
| Next lowest one-fifth | 11.5 | 9.7 | 22,100 | 20,000 | −9.5 |
| Middle one-fifth | 16.4 | 14.7 | 32,400 | 31,400 | −3.1 |
| Next highest one-fifth | 22.8 | 21.3 | 42,600 | 45,100 | +5.9 |
| One-fifth with highest income | 44.2 | 50.4 | 74,000 | 102,000 | +38.2 |
| One percent with highest income | 7.3 | 12.9 | 234,700 | 515,600 | +119.7 |

*Source:* Congressional Budget Office data analyzed by the Center on Budget and Policy Priorities. Presented in the *New York Times*, September 15, 1999, p. 14.

*Note:* Figures do not add to 100 due to rounding.

pany. Supporters also argue that with a low minimum wage it is the American taxpayer who subsidizes the employers. Because employees do not earn enough to support their families, they must rely on public assistance programs such as food stamps, housing subsidies, and medical assistance (United for a Fair Economy 1999). The American taxpayer pays for these programs, thus subsidizing corporations.

Congress voted to increase the minimum wage by fifty cents in 1996 to $4.75, and again in 1997 by forty cents to $5.15. The most recent proposal in 1999 called for an increase of fifty cents an hour in January 2000 and again in January 2001. Under the current minimum wage, a worker can be fully employed at forty hours a week and still find himself or herself below the poverty level. According to United for a Fair Economy, the value of the minimum wage has slipped considerably in the last thirty years. For example, in 1968, the federal minimum wage represented 86 percent of the income necessary for lifting a worker and his family above the poverty line; by 2000 it represented only 64 percent. According to the Department of Labor, the real value of the minimum wage in 1968 was $7.49 an hour, almost $2.50 higher than the current wage of $5.15 an hour. The Department of Labor also estimates that 50 percent of the workers who would be most affected by an increase in the minimum wage are black and another 18 percent are Hispanic. Also, almost 7 million women, or about 60 percent of all workers to be affected by an increase in the minimum wage, would benefit the most (Poirer 1999).

As presented earlier in this chapter, despite a booming economy in the 1990s, the economic picture over the long term indicates that many American families have found it very difficult to keep pace economically. Therefore, in order to compensate for a steady decline in real income over the last thirty years, the traditional breadwinner/homemaker household gave way to the dual-earner couple. In some cases this adjustment is still not sufficient and "keeping pace" is even more difficult for the single-parent household.[10] These economic forces, combined with a civil rights movement that included gender equity as an issue and a desire on the part of women to gain financial independence while establishing their own careers, produced demands for government intervention and more calls for child-care and family-leave policies.

But despite the skills of the economists and the sophistication of the analytical tools they employ, we may still be haunted by two very challenging questions posed by Shirley Burggraf in *The Feminine Economy and Economic Man*. First, "How can society get women's work done when women no longer volunteer for their traditional jobs?" And second, "Now that the opportunity cost of women's productivity in alternative tasks is becoming increasingly and explicitly expensive, who is going to pay the costs?"[11] (Burggraf 1997, 26).

At least one other question can be added to Burggraf's. That is, in light of the economic landscape that was just painted, how far can programs such as child care and family leave take us in our efforts to level the playing field? Are we merely tinkering at the margins, or is the solution to the work and family dilemma the gateway to gender equity and greater income equality? The interaction between work and family and how both the private and public sectors have responded to this fairly recent phenomenon will be discussed in subsequent chapters.

## Notes

1. Becker's interest in the formation of families and the causes of family instability is visible throughout his writings. See chapter 10 in his *Treatise on the Family* where he explores "imperfect information, marriage, and divorce." Also refer to his work with Landes and Michael in 1977: "An Economic Analysis of Marital Instability," *Journal of Political Economy* 85, 6, 1141–1187. In 1973 and 1974, he published a two-part series on marriage. See "A Theory of Marriage: Part I" *Journal of Political Economy* 81, 4, 813–846, published in 1973, and "A Theory of Marriage: Part II," *Journal of Political Economy* 82, 2, 11–26, published in 1974. In his 1988 piece, "The Family and the State," *Journal of Law and Economics* 31, 1, 1988, 1–18, he discusses under what circumstances government intervention contributes to family efficiency. For example, government may subsidize schools to help poorer children, but it should also require parental consent for early marriage and other actions taken by minors. There should also be laws that limit access to divorce.

2. Becker has called for the end of no-fault divorce and the use of strict marriage contracts that limit access to divorce. In 1998, the state of Louisiana, concerned about its rising divorce rate, passed the Covenant Marriage Law. Prior to marriage, a couple may choose a "covenant marriage" over traditional marriage if they wish to make it more difficult to get a divorce. Included in the law is mandatory counseling prior to filing for divorce.

3. The 1985 *Business Week* article is reprinted in Becker and Becker's *The Economics of Life* (1997). He attacks unilateral divorce and calls for marriage contracts and mutual-consent divorce. "Contracts that increase the security of wives could even reduce the number of divorces by encouraging women who are not interested in pursuing a career to have children earlier and withdraw from the labor force longer while caring for young children" (1997, 105).

4. An excellent case study of the 1986 Tax Reform Act is Jeffrey Birnbaum and Alan Murray's *Showdown at Gucci Gulch: Lawmakers, Lobbyists, and the Unlikely Triumph of Tax Reform* (1987). Referring to Bismarck's famous quote that two things one should never watch being made are laws and sausage, the authors conclude that "compared to the Tax Reform Act of 1986, a sausage factory is tidy and orderly" (xvi).

The marriage penalty issue heated up in the spring and summer of 2000 when Republicans attempted to reform it by combining it with a tax cut of $292 billion over ten years, Clinton found it too severe and threatened a veto. That aside, a study by the Treasury Department found that of 51.4 million tax returns in 1999 from couples filing jointly, 24.8 million, or 48 percent, had a marriage penalty, averaging $1,141 (see "The Fight over Tax Changes: The Marriage Penalty and More" in the *New York Times*, July 23, 2000, p. 14).

5. "Qualified children" include sons, daughters, stepchildren, grandchildren, and adopted children, as long as they lived with the taxpayer for more than half the year. Nieces, nephews, children of a friend, or foster children can be "qualifying" children if they lived with the taxpayer all year and were cared for as members of the family. Qualifying children must be under age nineteen, or under age twenty-four if they are full-time students. Totally and permanently disabled children of any age are also considered "qualifying children."

6. The child tax credit also covers adoptions. According to the legislation, the term "qualified adoption expenses" means reasonable and necessary adoption fees, court costs, attorney's fees, and other expenses. There are some limitations. For special-needs children the maximum tax credit is $6,000. It does not apply to a step-adoption situation where the taxpayer is adopting the child of his/her spouse. Nor does it apply to a surrogate parenting situation where an adoption occurs.

7. Social Security has long been referred to as the "third rail of American politics." That is, if politicians go too far in reforming it, they will pay a price in the next election. Since the early 1980s, much has been written about the so-called generational wars. In 1994, Gary Becker published an article in *Business Week* entitled "Cut the Graybeards a Smaller Slice of the Pie" (reprinted in Becker and Becker, *The Economics* of Life [1997]). "I believe that the young eventually rebel against tax and other burdens," he wrote. "They will demand restraints on transfers to the elderly and, possibly, even major modifications in age-discrimination and retirement legislation." Other sources to consult on this topic include John B. Williamson et al., *The Generation Equity Debate*, New York: Columbia University Press, 1999; Ken Dychtwald's *Age Power: How the 21st Century Will Be Ruled by the New Old*, New York: Putnam: 1999; Robert Hudson's *The Future of Aged-Based Policy*, Baltimore: Johns Hopkins

University Press, 1997; Philip Longman's *Born to Pay: The New Politics of Aging America*, Boston: Houghton-Mifflin, 1987; and Harry Moody's *Ethics in an Aging Society*, Baltimore: John Hopkins University Press, 1992.

8. Measuring "insecure jobs" is open to question. However, according to Mishel, Bernstein, and Schmitt (1999), jobs have grown more insecure in the 1990s as the share of workers in "long-term jobs" (those lasting at least ten years) fell from 41 percent in 1979 to 35.4 percent in 1996, with the worst deterioration having taken place since the 1980s. Another measure can be found in political humor. There was a story circulating in Washington about a waiter who was delivering food during a banquet while President Clinton was giving a speech. "This administration has created more than three million new jobs," said the president. "Yeah," said the waiter sarcastically, "and I got three of them."

9. A recent challenge to the conventional wisdom that the minimum wage contributes to unemployment is David Card and Alan Krueger's *Myth and Measurement: The New Economics of the Minimum Wage* (Princeton University Press, 1998). Card and Kreuger's five-year empirical study of fast-food restaurants in New Jersey concluded that the minimum wage does not necessarily mean a loss of jobs and can sometimes help create new jobs. The two researchers surveyed about 400 employers both shortly before and several months after New Jersey increased its state minimum wage from $4.25 to $5.05 an hour. When compared with fast-food restaurants in Pennsylvania, a state that did not increase its minimum wage during the same time period, they found that employment at the fast-food restaurants actually expanded following the pay increase.

10. Three recent books in particular that challenge conventional economic theory and question the widespread belief that the economic boom of the 1990s benefited everyone are Thomas Palley's *Plenty of Nothing: The Downsizing of the American Dream and the Case for Structural Keynesianism*, Princeton University Press, 1998; Ruth Colker's *American Law in the Age of Hypercapitalism: The Worker, the Family, and the State*, New York: New York University Press, 1998; and Frank Levy's *The New Dollars and Dreams: American Incomes and Economic Change*, New York: Russell Sage, 1998 (revised edition of 1988).

11. These two questions posed by Shirley Burggraf should not be alien to Gary Becker or to others who are concerned about work and family issues. Nor should they be unfamiliar with the possible consequences if these go unanswered. At the very end of Becker's article, "Human Capital, Effort, and the Sexual Division of Labor," which was published in the *Journal of Labor Economics* 3 in 1985, there is the very last footnote, number 13. It reads, "Dustin Hoffman lost his job in *Kramer vs. Kramer* after he became responsible for the care of his child."

# Chapter 4

# The Changing Workplace:
# When Work and Family Converge

In 1993, Houston Oilers offensive tackle David Williams missed a football game against the New England Patriots when he decided to remain in Houston with his wife for the birth of their child. Despite endless pleas from his teammates and coaches, Williams stood by his decision because he was particularly concerned about his wife's health condition. "My family comes first," he stated. "That's the way I've always been, and that's the way I always will be, long after I'm finished being a football player" (*New York Times* 1993, 22). As a result of his actions, Williams was fined one week's salary ($111,111) and threatened with a suspension. Covered under the Family and Medical Leave Act (FMLA), he challenged the Oilers actions while his attorney threatened to file a grievance against the team if they did not withdraw their fine.[1]

Similarly, several years later, a Maryland state trooper requested a four- to eight-week leave of absence to care for his wife, who had just survived a complicated and life-threatening childbirth experience. When Mr. Knussman was denied his request and offered only two weeks instead, he sued the state of Maryland on the grounds of sex discrimination under the 1993 FMLA. When Knussman won $375,000 in 1998, it marked the first time the FMLA had been employed in a sex discrimination case and it was also a first for a monetary award under that particular law.

Predictably, both cases received national media attention. But contrary to popular impressions that are often left with the public following such sensational news coverage, the challenge of balancing work and family is not new. On January 5, 1914, Henry Ford initiated what many consider the greatest experiment in welfare capitalism: the $5 daily wage and the eight-hour day (Foner 1982). With it came a profit-sharing program and more leisure for workers, but not without strings attached. Also a part of Ford's initiative was the creation of a Sociology Department. Consisting of 100 employees hired by Ford himself, the Department was responsible for overseeing the employees' spending patterns, their use of free time, and whether or not they were meeting their family obligations. Any smoking, drinking, and gambling habits were identified and monitored. Unacceptable behavior was not tolerated. The homes of all assembly line workers were visited regularly to "ensure conformity of workers' home life to company standards of order, cleanliness, and temperance" (Ferber and O'Farrell 1991, 22).

Failure to comply with company rules could result in the withholding of an employee's wages until the deficiencies were corrected (Meyer 1984). Furthermore, profit sharing, which represented a large portion of the $5 wage program, was not available to young men who had no dependents, family men living alone, or men who were divorcing (Foner 1982). Therefore, to Henry Ford, efficiency "meant both the creation of a stable, disciplined labor force on the job and the reproduction of that work force through family life" (Foner 1982, 10). What some described as "benevolent paternalism," the Ford sociological program also helped to prevent, at least temporarily, the likelihood of his workers joining labor unions. That ended, however, when World War I arrived, and brought with it inflation, the devaluation of the $5 day, the rise of unions, and the use of strikes more frequently.

Ford's Sociology Department was dismantled in 1921. However, the reasons for its creation and the functions it served should not be dismissed lightly. Despite being called a "traitor to his class" by his fellow industrialists and being denounced by the *Wall Street Journal* for committing an "economic crime," Ford still stands as an example of a corporate head who at least understood the importance of the relationship between work and family (Foner 1982). While scholars continue to debate Ford's motives, be they humanitarian, paternalistic, or economic, the point to be emphasized here is that work and family constitute a very complex and dynamic relationship. At the very least, Henry Ford understood that. But to complicate matters further, while Ford's focus was on *men* during their hours of leisure, today's focus is on *both* men and women on the job and at home. How these two sets of responsibilities are balanced (some prefer to use the word *integrated*) is the subject of this chapter. More specifically, the primary focus here will be on women and how they have affected the relationship between work and family.[2]

## A Historical Perspective of Women Moving into the Workforce

The steady growth of women's participation in the American workforce, particularly during the last three decades, is considered to be one of the most dramatic developments of the twentieth century. But contrary to what many may believe, the attachment of women to the workplace is not necessarily new. What is new, however, is the attachment of *mothers* to the workplace. In order to understand this development, it is helpful if the movement of women (particularly mothers) into paid work is placed in its proper context and discussed within a framework of three distinct historical segments: preindustrial, industrial, and postindustrial society.

First, during the preindustrial age (1700–1850), agricultural activity dominated the economy. A strong patriarchal model both at home and in society at large denied women basic political, legal, economic, and personal rights. For most women, marriage meant the end of whatever individual rights they possessed. "A woman ceased to exist if she married, for she and her spouse became one flesh and the flesh was his" (Foner 1979, 11). Within the household economic unit, married women were responsible for sewing the family's clothing, preparing its meals, producing soap and candles, caring for children, growing certain types of crops for food, and performing other household tasks. These tasks often ranged from cleaning house, to teaching reading, writing, and arithmetic, to serving as a nurse in times of illness (Marshall and Paulin 1987). In short, domestic life was practically indistinguishable from economic life. It was indeed the era of the family economy, or what Demos calls the "little commonwealth" and Becker refers to as the "small factory."

With respect to the second historical segment, the industrial age (1850–1940), it was an era in which manufacturing was transferred from the home to the factory. Employers began to replace many skilled employees with machines and/or low-skilled workers, including women and children. As thousands of single women poured into the textile mills of New England, the canneries of coastal California, and the garment district of New York City, two concerns in particular were raised by skilled craftsmen. One, they feared they may be replaced by women at lower wages. And two, if not replaced by female workers, many men were convinced that, as more women entered skilled trades, their own wages would drop considerably (Marshall and Paulin 1987). Foner (1979) reports that such fears produced labor union strategies that clearly discriminated against female employees. For example, in 1907 the Molders Union threatened to fine any male union member $50 who gave instructions and assistance to female workers.

Despite major reforms at the turn of the century that targeted large monopolies and facilitated the creation and growth of labor unions in the early years of the Progressive Era, women were often discouraged from entering the labor force. When they did find employment, the wages were low and the working conditions were intolerable. But even in the face of such obstacles, the proportion of women entering the labor market nearly doubled from almost 10 percent in 1870 to 20 percent by 1940.

According to Marshall and Paulin (1987), the U.S. Bureau of Labor Statistics (1948), and Farnham (1939), other factors contributed to the increase in the labor-force participation of women as well. These included mandatory schooling for young children, which allowed women to work outside the home during school hours; increased use of contraception, which produced a decline in fertility rates and freed up more women to work; and limited job opportunities for men at adequate wages. However, according to Rebecca Farnham, the primary factor contributing to the migration of women into the paid labor market was "the inadequacy of men's earnings in modern times, when most workers have no land or home industry to support wages" (Farnham 1939, 8).

The third historical period is represented by the emergence of the postindustrial society, from 1940 to the present. It was during these six decades of American history that two extremely significant social developments occurred: the movement of married mothers into paid work and the transformation of the American family. Wedged involuntarily between these two trends was, and still is, American business. If our past is our future, then the lessons learned over these past sixty years should prove helpful as America's families and businesses continue to adjust to a constantly changing society.

Without question, a major catalyst for changes in the home and at work was the onslaught of World War II. It was during the war years that many men were shipped overseas to fight and women were called upon to work in defense plants and other war-related industries. Between 1940 and 1944, the number of women in the workforce increased by more than 6 million, to total 20.6 million, a 50 percent increase (Pidgeon 1954). In 1944, for the first time in American history, there were more married women (44 percent) in the work force than single women (43 percent). The remainder of the female workers (13 percent) were either widowed or divorced (Koziara, Moskow, and Tanner 1987). By the end of the war in 1945, the number of women employed grew to almost 20 million, or 36 percent of the total labor force (Gregory 1974). Given jobs that were previously off limits to them, they became welders, plumbers, metal workers, and machine operators. They built ships, planes, and tanks and manufactured ammunition, parachutes, and medical supplies. Numerous books, articles, and films, including *The Life and Times of Rosie the Riveter*, have chronicled the wartime accomplishments of America's "production soldiers."[3]

Although women proved they could handle what were generally considered to be male jobs, two facts in particular still distinguished them from their male coworkers. One, despite performing identical tasks, women tended to be paid lower wages than men at first. This changed in 1942 when the War Labor

Board adopted the principle of "equal pay for equal work" and applied it to the war industries. And two, another significant difference between male and female workers during the war years was the responsibility many women had for taking care of children and performing other household tasks. While some female employees were provided with on-site day care, assistance with shopping, laundry services, and food services that included take-home meals for the entire family, others lacked access to such programs.

Despite the passage of the Lanham Act in 1941, which provided federal funds to states for child-care programs, there were, in contrast to popular belief, major shortages of child-care facilities throughout the country. The first child-care projects on a large scale were not initiated until late spring of 1943. By the end of the war, more than 2,000 employer-based child-care centers were created to address the needs of working mothers, but many more were needed (Auerbach 1988). Without the centers, some factories, such as aircraft plants in Los Angeles, were greatly disrupted by high rates of female absenteeism. Aware of this problem, the West Coast Aircraft Production Council issued a statement indicating that one child-care center alone would allow forty mothers to work full shifts, totaling 8,000 worker-hours per month. The time gained would be enough to build one four-engine bomber in ten weeks. However, without the twenty-five child-care centers that were needed, the cost would equal one less bomber manufactured per month (Gregory 1974). What an interesting example of cost-benefit analysis!

With the conclusion of the war in 1945, three things happened. First, defense spending was slashed, women were laid off, and many either took lower-paying jobs or returned to their homes. Second, whatever pay equity policy existed in defense plants during the war quickly vaporized as the nation returned to a peacetime economy. And third, funding for child care disappeared as women were expected to raise their children at home in the traditional setting of the homemaker/male-breadwinner household. Each of these postwar developments is discussed below.

## Demobilization and Reconversion After the War: Where Did the Jobs Go?

Although women were greatly appreciated for the effort they put forth during the war, speculation grew as to what role they would assume once "the boys came home." Vice President Harry Truman raised the issue as early as 1943, just two years before the end of the war. "The last war put women into offices and they never left them," he said. "This war has put them into factories. Let no one imagine that women will permit themselves to be shunted out of these jobs which they have demonstrated so well their capacity to do"

(Kesselman 1990, 92). Standing in sharp contrast to Truman's comments, however, was a report published by the Brookings Institution in the same year. It concluded "women would of course be among the first to be demobilized when the war ends." Therefore, continued the report, "it would be difficult to argue that provision of permanent employment for this group is a paramount national obligation" (Schlotterbeck 1943, 13).

By 1945, the battle line concerning women's role in the labor market was clearly drawn. On one side stood various advocacy groups such as the Women's Bureau that produced studies indicating that 86 percent of women surveyed wanted to remain in the same occupational group in which they worked during the war. On the other side stood the traditionalists who called for women to return to their homes and resume their household responsibilities. Even when a survey conducted by the *Ladies Home Journal* concluded that almost 80 percent of the female respondents reported they enjoyed working more than staying home, the *Journal* put its own spin on the findings. "Jobs are more enjoyable, but homes are more important," concluded the authors (Giles 1944, 22).

It was not long after the war, however, that reality began to set in, as the number of women in the workforce declined from 19.3 million in 1945 to 15.8 million in 1947. The new jobs taken by women as they attempted to enter the labor market were often the very jobs they had avoided in the previous six months (Anderson 1951). "The unwillingness of women to take traditionally female low-paid jobs in the years after the end of the war suggests that for a while women workers resisted the process by which they were being forced to re-enter the female ghetto in the job market" (Kesselman 1990, 107). This observation coincides with the work of Lisa Anderson and Sheila Tobias. In *What Really Happened to Rosie the Riveter?* (1974), Anderson and Tobias strongly disagree with the common belief that women left their industrial jobs willingly after the end of the war. To them, because of severe peacetime discriminatory practices aimed at women, the Rosies of the world had few choices other than to take low-paying jobs or return to their homes.[4]

### Family Matters After the War

In August 1945 the Federal Works Agency, which was responsible for administering federal funding for child care centers, announced that because the war had ended and women were no longer needed in defense industries, all funding for child-care programs would be terminated by October 1945. Opponents of this policy only succeeded in extending Lanham Act funding until March 1, 1946. In recommending the extension, President Truman emphasized that the Federal Works Project Child-Care Program would continue temporarily in order to allow states and local communities to seek their own funding for such programs. This policy was implemented despite the fact that reports from child-care centers revealed that only one-third of the women using the centers were either soldiers' wives or war widows, indicating that the demand for such services went far beyond the war effort (Kesselman 1990). But because most state and local governments were unprepared to continue the funding, and due to only lukewarm support from labor unions and the child-welfare lobby, most child-care programs that existed during the war disappeared by 1947 (Dratch 1974).

The reluctance of the labor movement to support child care may be rooted in their desire to "take care of the boys" first. After all, child-care programs made it easier for women to either enter or remain in the labor force, thus placing them in direct competition with men for a limited number of jobs in an economy that was in transition from the manufacture of war supplies to the production of consumer goods. Trying to explain the reluctance of the child-welfare establishment to support the expansion of child-care programs after the war is quite another matter. However, at the time there was a general consensus among child development experts that young children would benefit greatly if they were in the care of their own mothers rather than in the hands of professionals in communal settings. A dominant theme in the research literature during the postwar era was that "mothers of infants up to age three should be barred from factory work" (Levy 1945, 152). It was a theme that would influence the child-care debate for the next fifty years. Perhaps we should remind ourselves that it was not until 1971 that the first serious attempt at national child-care legislation was made and it was not until 1990 that it succeeded, though very limited in scope.

For the United States, the Great Depression and World War II are perhaps the two most significant events of the twentieth century. The latter event in particular produced a major reassessment of women's role in the economy. "The fact that a woman could step into a man's shoes and wear them rather comfortably posed an implicit challenge to traditional notions about femininity and female limitations," writes Maureen Honey (1984, 1). But, continues Honey, "how did the strong figure of Rosie the Riveter become transformed into the naive, dependent, childlike, self-abnegating model of femininity in the late 1940s and 1950s?" (1984, 2).

The impact the war had on women in particular and on the long-term relationship between work and family in general remains a topic for debate. Some argue that the war is responsible for the rapid movement of married women in particular into the labor force (Chafe 1972). Others contend that the war had very little impact on the participation rate of women in the labor force (Rupp 1978), and still others believe that although women moved into the labor market, their overall economic status changed little (Anderson 1981). For Susan Hartman (1982), the role of women in World War II became the springboard for the next wave of feminism. But Betty Friedan's explanation of what happened to women in postwar America is perhaps the most frequently quoted. In short, after a Great Depression and a World War, an entire nation desired to shield its eyes from cruelty and seek out stability. Friedan offered her explanation in *The Feminine Mystique* (1963). "The American spirit fell into a strange sleep; men as well as women, scared liberals, disillusioned radicals, conservatives bewildered and frustrated by change—the whole nation stopped growing up. All of us went back into the warm brightness of home, the way it was when we were children and slept peaceful upstairs while our parents read, or played bridge in the living room, or rocked on the front porch in the summer evening in our home towns" (Friedan 1963, 186). It was not a terminal sleep, however. By the mid-1960s, major changes were afoot in the nation, and soon women would be returning to the labor force. By 1970, work and family pressures would spawn legislative debates on child care. Not far behind and waiting in the wings was the debate over family leave.

## The Ongoing Conflict Between Work and Family

Clearly, one of the most significant developments since the end of World War II has been the steady, if not dramatic, increase in the number of women entering the workforce. In 1940, nearly 86 percent of married women were full-time homemakers (Goldin 1990). By 1996, however, 61 percent were in the paid labor force (Institute for Women's Policy Research 1996). However, as illustrated in Figure 4.1, the most impressive period of growth for married female workers occurred between 1960 and 1996 when the rate practically doubled, climbing from 32 percent in 1960 to 61 percent in 1996.

Even more significant has been the rise in the number of mothers entering the labor market during this time period. As presented in Figure 4.2, working mothers of children under six have increased from about 37 percent in 1975 to 63 percent in 1996 (Tauber 1996). Today, mothers represent the fastest growing sector of the entire U.S. workforce (Grundy and Firestein 1997). Women with children have a higher employment rate than women overall (67.7 percent to 56.8 percent), and even women with children under age six are employed at a higher rate (59.7 percent) than women overall (56.8 percent) (Institute for Women's Policy Research 1996). On one hand, this is not surprising, as women's child-rearing years also tend to be the peak years of their earning potential. On the other hand, this phenomenon of working moth-

Figure 4.1 **Labor Force Participation Rates of Married Women, 1960–1996**

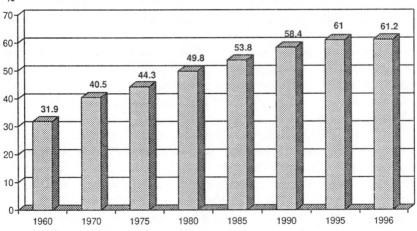

*Source:* Compiled from data in Cynthia M. Tauber's *Statistical Handbook on Women in America* (1996), 2nd ed. Phoenix: Oryx Press.

Figure 4.2 **Labor Force Participation of Married Women by Age of Child, 1975–1996**

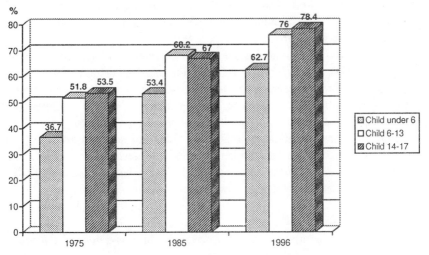

*Source:* Compiled from data in Cynthia M. Tauber's *Statistical Handbook on Women in America* (1996), 2nd ed. Phoenix: Oryx Press.

ers is indeed remarkable in that many American women are working without the support system (child care and family leave) commonly available to women in other countries.

Why more women have entered the labor market can be traced to at least four major developments that occurred during the 1960s and 1970s. First, the Civil Rights Movement of the 1960s produced the Civil Rights Act of 1964. Included in the Act was a provision that banned discrimination against women in hiring and in wages. This not only weakened the traditional family wage system, but it also permitted more women to challenge occupational segregation. As a result, numerous court decisions were handed down which clarified women's rights in the workplace. Second, the feminist movement that was spurred on by the works of Friedan (1963), Greer (1971), Brownmiller (1975), Steinem (1983), and Eisenstein (1983) encouraged women to seek financial independence from males and to establish their own careers outside the home. Third, the 1970s in particular, as was discussed in the preceding chapter, produced a major economic downturn that resulted in stagflation. Due to both high unemployment and inflation, men's earnings fell. Consequently, many women sought jobs in an effort to supplement family income. In fact, between 1960 and 1990, it was the decade of the 1970s that witnessed the highest increase in the percentage of mothers entering the workforce. The fourth development, the passage of the Pregnancy Discrimination Act of 1978, mandated that pregnant employees be treated the same as employees with any temporary disability, and that women who are unable to work because of pregnancy are eligible for leaves. In many respects this act provided the legal foundation upon which the Family and Medical Leave Act would be constructed.

But as more women entered the workforce, the debate over this development intensified. More specifically, four issues in particular emerged. One, has the dual-earner couple been putting too much time into work and neglecting its family responsibilities? Two, in the new economy of working mothers, are fathers equally sharing in household tasks or are women still doing most of the housework? Three, should corporations provide a special "mommy track" for women who are less career-minded and desire to devote more time to their families? And four, does the employment of mothers have a detrimental effect on infant development? Each of these issues is discussed below.[5]

## The Time Factor

With respect to the first issue, the time factor, there is a general consensus among many researchers that employees are putting in more hours at work and fewer at home. In *The Overworked American: The Unexpected Decline of Leisure* (1993), Juliet B. Schorr contends that employees today work more hours than they did twenty-five years ago, producing about an extra month of work per year. Arlie Hochschild in *The Second Shift: Working Parents and the Revolution at Home* (1989) and *The Time Bind* (1997) reached similar conclusions. It was Hochschild who identified the three shifts of the working family: first shift is at work, second shift is at home, and the third shift is the time and energy consumed by parents who feel guilty about spending less time on the second shift. Hochschild also created controversy when she concluded that work is an "escape valve" for some individuals who feel trapped in a bad marriage.

Whether or not Hochschild is correct remains open for debate. However, according to a recent study completed by the Families and Work Institute (1997), mothers' time at work outside the home has increased by five hours per week in the last twenty years, compared to an increase of 3.1 hours for men. Accordingly, the percentage of employees who would like to work less (63 percent) increased by 17 percentage points since 1992.

In a study based on the Current Population Survey, researchers concluded that between 1969 and 1996, both married-couple and single-parent families spent more time in paid work. While mothers' time devoted to child care decreased from ten to nine hours per week, fathers did not compensate for the difference, as their child-care responsibilities remained about 2.6 hours per week. When measured in terms of household chores, men have increased the time they spend on housework but it does not make up for the reduction by women (Robinson and Godbey 1997). This so-called time crunch is "best illustrated by the fact that in any single year, employed women spend over one third less time on child care and household tasks than women without paid jobs" (Council of Economic Advisers 1999, 12).

To put such statistics in perspective, the United States has acquired the dubious distinction of becoming the number one country in the world in hours worked per employee each year (1,966), followed by Japan (1,889), Canada (1,732), Britain (1,731), and Norway (1,399). On average, Americans work 350 hours more per year (almost nine full workweeks) than Europeans. By the end of 1999, almost 20 percent of Americans reported working more than forty-nine hours a week, up from 16 percent in 1985. "Nowadays you go to a social gathering and you see a lot of people wearing beepers, and at a baseball game you see all these people with their cell phones, in many cases still connected to work," states Princeton University labor economist Alan Krueger. "It's gotten far more difficult to measure where work ends and leisure begins" (Greenhouse 1999, 1).

## The Role of Fathers

Concerning the second issue, whether or not fathers are equally sharing in household tasks, research findings have been both contradictory and controversial. Despite major changes at home and at work, many top executives continue to expect their male employees to be loyal to the firm, put in long hours, and leave family matters to their wives. To many corporate managers, reducing work hours for family reasons is indicative of a weak job commitment and poor motivation. Such assessments are usually directed toward male employees. And, to some researchers, such an attitude may explain why, despite women's expanded role in the workforce, men's roles at home have not changed. Seven out of ten women surveyed indicated that they are disappointed in their husbands' contributions to household chores. Still, for 53 percent of women, the ideal kind of marriage is one of shared responsibility, in which both partners work and share housekeeping responsibilities (Townsend and O'Neil 1990).

Presenting a different view on the sharing of household tasks is Joseph Pleck (1993), who argues that men's contributions to household work and child care are greater than commonly believed. Contending that time spent in family roles has continued to increase for men over the last twenty years, Pleck cites a series of studies to justify his claim (Robinson 1988; U.S. Bureau of the Census 1990). He is particularly critical of Hochschild (1989) for measuring fathers' contributions to household chores only on *workdays*. He also contends that men use flextime at a rate comparable to women, and husbands also experience work-family stress on a scale equal to their wives. Therefore, and contrary to conventional beliefs, Pleck argues that men are also struggling to balance work and family responsibilities.

According to *The 1997 National Study of the Changing Workforce* (Families and Work Institute 1997), fathers spend about 2.3 hours per workday caring for and interacting with their children, an increase of thirty minutes per workday since 1977. Mothers on the other hand, spend nearly one hour more than fathers (3.2 hours compared to 2.3 hours per day) with their children on workdays, but the total time spent did not change much between 1977 and 1997. With respect to household chores, the Families and Work Institute (1997) identified a similar pattern. That is, mothers' workday time devoted to household tasks decreased by thirty-six minutes per day, while men's time increased by one hour between 1977 and 1997.

Complicating matters further, a more recent study conducted by the Working Women Department of the AFL-CIO (2000) reported that many couples work different shifts. Forty-six percent of women who are married or cohabiting with someone report that they work a different schedule than their spouse or partner. Among married women with children under eighteen, the figure is even greater, with 51 percent working a different schedule from their husbands. University of Maryland researcher Harriet Presser (2000) reached a similar conclusion. She found that 40 percent of all employed Americans work mostly during the evenings or nights, on rotating shifts and/or weekends. For the typical two-earner couple, the prevalence of nonstandard work schedules is particularly high. For example, of those with children under age fourteen in the household, 31.1 percent work evening, night, or rotating schedules, and 46.8 percent work weekends. This emerging pattern, argues Presser, is producing significantly higher separation and divorce rates among couples with different work schedules than those with spouses working only fixed daytime jobs or shift workers without children.

## The Role of Corporations

Regarding the third issue, whether or not corporations should accommodate employees who are struggling to balance work and family obligations, Felice Schwartz considerably changed the parameters of the debate by suggesting that a special "mommy track" be created. As founder and president of Catalyst, an organization that consults with corporations on the development of women managers, Schwartz published her suggestion in the *Harvard Business Review* (1989). In "Management Women and the New Facts of Life," Schwartz argued that the work and family conflict could be solved by permitting professional women to choose a career track from one of two distinct categories: career primary and career and family. Under the former category, businesses would apply "equal treatment" to those women who choose to place a career before family. The latter group, which came to be labeled the "mommy track" (a term that was never used by Schwartz), would be given lenient treatment by their corporate bosses so that they could facilitate their family lives. This choice, however, would result in lower pay raises and fewer promotions.[6]

The "mommy track" became a front-page story in the *New York Times*, *USA Today*, and *Business Week*. However, the most aggressive assault on Schwartz's two-track proposal came from Barbara Ehrenreich and Deirdre English. Venting their anger in a *Ms.* magazine (1989) article entitled "Blowing the Whistle on the 'Mommy Track,' " Ehrenreich and English attacked Schwartz for reinforcing sex discrimination rather than trying to solve the problem. How, they asked, would employers sort out the "breeders" from the "strivers," and what if some women chose to alternate between the two tracks as their family profiles changed and their career goals were modified? The solution, they argued, could be found in getting men to do more household chores and demanding that they become more involved in child rearing. To Ehrenreich and English, Schwartz's article was "a tortured muddle of feminist perceptions and sexist assumptions, good intentions, and dangerous suggestions" (1989, 87).

## The Effect on Children

The fourth issue commonly associated with work and family conflict is whether or not mothers' participation in the workforce is detrimental to the development of young children. Of all the issues, however, this one may be the most complicated and confusing. Depending on which study one reads, the types of questions that were used to collect the data, and which variables were analyzed, the results will differ. For example, while some research concludes that employed mothers spend more quality time with their children, others produce opposite results, that nonemployed mothers spend more quality time with their children. Examples of two studies are presented here to illustrate this point.

On one side are Jay Belsky and David Eggebeen (1991), who argue that maternal employment during a child's infancy can have negative effects on the child's social and behavioral development. For example, Belsky (1988) concludes that children who are in nonparental care for twenty or more hours per week during their first year are at risk of developing insecure attachments to their mothers. They are also more prone to be disobedient toward adults and aggressive toward peers as they reach age three. However, Belsky reminds us that his study and many others do not include measures for determining the quality of care children receive. Mary Monica (1993) has assumed a similar position. Adopting John Bowlby's attachment theory, Monica concludes that babies are psychologically at risk if separated from their mothers for twenty or more hours per week during their first year of life.

On the other side stands the work of K. Alison Clarke-Stewart (1991) and Kristin Droege (1995). Clarke-Stewart contends that children who attend child-care centers are more socially and intellectually advanced than children who are cared for at home. In a study of 150 preschool children aged two to four, Clarke-Stewart compared six different child-care arrangements. The determining factors in explaining the difference in children's development included the quality of education provided, opportunities to practice skills and follow rules with their peers, and the degree to which they were encouraged to be independent. In most cases, the home cannot provide all of these opportunities. Therefore, she argues, the major question is not whether daily separation from mother impairs a child's progress, but rather, which type of child care is best for a child's cognitive and social development? Droege piggybacks Clarke-Stewart's conclusion by arguing that the government should inform working parents about child care options and subsidize high-quality day care that emphasizes education and development rather than custodial care.

In a 1997 study by Clark, Hyde, Essex, and Klein, researchers assessed the association between the length of maternity leave and the quality of mother-infant interactions among nearly 200 employed mothers of four-month-old infants. They concluded that there is an association between length of leave and quality of mother-infant interactions. The longer the leave, the better for both. Therefore, they argue, the FMLA should be accessible to more parents and the duration of leave extended beyond twelve weeks. But research on the importance of "quality time" during the interaction between parent and child need not be confined to infancy.

Related to this same topic, a unique approach was taken by Ellen Galinsky in her book, *Ask the Children: What America's Children Really Think About Working Parents* (1999). Based on a survey of 605 working parents and 1,023 children ages eight to eighteen, Galinksy found that the dominant wish expressed by the children interviewed was that their parents be less stressed out and tired at the end of the workday so they could spend more time together. It is advertised as the first book to ask children what they really think about work, family, and many other topics. Among its contents are twelve important tips for raising children well, particular recommendations for navigating the transitions from home to work and from work to home, and specific tips for talking to children about work and family life. But while government has debated the issue of work and family over the years, and families strive to cope with the increased stress generated in both venues, the private sector has not exactly ignored the issue.

## The Response of the Private Sector

According to researcher Lotte Bailyn (1996), the phrase "work and family" first appeared in the *Wall Street Journal* in 1980 with a report that the New England Merchants Bank had called upon a university professor to run lunchtime seminars for working parents called "Balancing Work and Family Life." The next mention of the phrase by the *Journal* was nine years later when it was reported that more corporate managers and their spouses were seeking counseling because of work and family conflicts. Two years later in 1991, Sue Shellenberger began her regular column in the *Journal* on "work and family" issues. However, when she elected to have children herself, she found an unsympathetic employer that forced her to make too many compromises, prompting her to temporarily leave the newspaper to tend to her family's needs. Drawing attention to her own personal conflict with work and family when she returned to the paper, Shellenberger's articles became so popular the *Journal* requested that her one short piece every three weeks be expanded to a weekly column. Other publications began to cover work and family issues as well.

Beyond coverage in the mainstream press and serving as a focal point for academic researchers, the topic "work and family" also attracted the attention of practitioners who developed a specialty in the subject and served as consultants to businesses and labor unions. For example, in 1983 Work/Family

Directions was created. The Boston-based consulting firm continues to provide a variety of work and family services to corporations nationwide. In 1988, a newsletter, *The National Report on Work and Family*, was begun and continues to be published twice a month. It covers legislation, litigation, and employee-employer issues. A year later, Dana Friedman and Ellen Galinksy formed the Families and Work Institute, which has been extremely productive in preparing and disseminating reports on this topic. Other centers and institutes were created during this same time period and continue to specialize in work and family issues. These include Boston College's Center for Work and Family that was created by Brad Googins (1991), the Radcliffe Public Policy Institute at Harvard, and the Center for Working Families at the University of California at Berkeley. The Institute of Women's Policy Research and the National Partnership for Women and Families, both of which are based in Washington, DC, also focus on work and family issues. Examples of for-profit organizations that specialize in work/life matters are Hewitt Associates and Great Place to Work Institute (refer to Appendix B for additional resources). Still lagging behind, however, on family and work issues are American business schools.[7]

Meanwhile, throughout the 1980s in particular there were stirrings in both the labor and management camps concerning the issue of work and family. In 1986, for example, the AFL-CIO Executive Council issued a resolution confirming its commitment to America's working families. "The family is the key to social stability, community progress, and national strength. To strengthen the family is at the heart of the labor movement's long struggle to raise wages and living standards" (AFL-CIO 1992, 10). In 1988, the Coalition of Labor Union Women (CLUW), which was founded in 1974 for the sole purpose of moving work and family issues to the top of collective bargaining agendas, organized a national demonstration. "The American Family Celebration" brought together 40,000 union members and their families to lobby for the "American Family Bill of Rights," which included job security, healthcare, education, and equal opportunity (Grundy and Firestein 1997). The CLUW also created a special guide, *Bargaining for Family Benefits* (1991) that was designed to help negotiate work and family benefits in union work sites.

For many years one of organized labor's pet causes was the "family wage," the concept that each worker should earn a sufficient amount of money to support a family. Although feminists in particular were suspicious of the unions' goal because it appeared to apply only to men and echoed the traditional homemaker/male breadwinner household, this view changed over the years. Today the term "living wage," rather than "family wage," is used most frequently by labor unions and is directly linked to efforts to increase the minimum wage for workers. "Living wage regulations often require any employer receiving public funds to pay wages that provide a basic, decent standard of living for all workers and their families" (Grundy and Firestein 1997). Other pro-family causes taken up by labor include high-quality child care, family and medical leave, healthcare insurance, free public education, and the thirty-five-hour workweek, to name a few. By 1997, the Labor Project for Working Families compiled a database consisting of more than 450 examples of union contracts that included work and family benefits (U.S. Department of Labor 1992, 10).

While labor unions and other organizations have been in the forefront on work and family issues, many businesses have been reluctant to join the march. Historically, the private sector has always shielded itself against unnecessary costs and excessive government regulations. To some, the work and family issue represents the latest version of the Trojan Horse that would allow big government to intervene in corporate personnel matters. However, this perception was not held by every component of the business community. A term that emerged fairly recently and is now quite common in both the research literature and the mainstream media is the "family-friendly corporation." It can be found in the works of Galinsky et al. (1993), Harker (1996), and Googins (1991), among others. It is also visible in such popular publications as *Business Week*, *Fortune*, and *Working Mother*. A number of organizations and publications have developed criteria for judging "family friendliness" among corporations and have produced annual "best company" ratings.[8]

Perhaps the most popular and well-known set of criteria that is used to identify family-friendly corporations is found in the annual survey conducted by *Working Mother* magazine. Using more than thirty different categories that include paid parental leave, adoption aid, lactation programs, flextime, child care, elder care, the percentage of female employees in management, the prevalence of resource and referral programs, and wage scales, the survey has been completed in each of the last fourteen years. In 1986, when the annual study began, only thirty companies were honored as "family friendly." By 1999, *Working Mother* was naming (not ranking) its top 100 companies for family friendliness. While companies in 1986 were given special recognition for providing lactation programs, adoption assistance, and backup care, such policies are now common practices among the "top 100."[9] *Working Mother*'s 1999 list of the top 100 is presented in Appendix A.

The methodology employed by *Working Mother* is multifaceted and is refined regularly. Eligible companies include private or public corporations of any size. Not included in the surveys are government agencies, divisions of larger companies, or firms in the work/life or child-care business. The comprehensive questionnaire that is used consists of queries about a company's culture, employee demographics, specific policies on work and family life, and women's advancement. Participating companies are also required to submit supporting documents, including written personnel policies, handbooks on employee benefit programs, results of employee surveys, and, if applicable, reports of special in-house task forces or advisory committees. The methodology has been designed and is monitored by some of the nation's leading experts on employer-employee relations. For example, Norman D. Costa is an industrial and research psychologist who is the president and founder of Expert Survey Systems (ESS) in Brewster, New York. Lynn Martin is the former secretary of labor and an expert on women's advancement in corporations. And John Pepper is a trailblazer on work and family issues and former CEO of Procter & Gamble, a consistent "100 Best Company" (*Working Mother* 1999).

The responses to the questionnaire are organized under six major categories, with each category consisting of eight to ten subcategories. First, there is leave for new parents. This includes paid leave, lactation programs, paternity leave, and adoption aid. Second is the category of flexibility. Included is the availability of flextime, permission to work at home, and a compressed workweek (percentage of employees who put in forty-hour workweeks in under five days). The third category is child care, which includes on-site or nearby centers, a dependent care fund, and a resource and referral service, among other benefits. Fourth is work/life. Is managers' pay tied to employee satisfaction? Are employee surveys and task forces used to gauge worker satisfaction or to generate new ideas related to work/life matters? And is there a resource and referral service for elder care? The fifth category concerns the advancement of women within the firm. Measures include the total percentage of female employees, the percentage of female senior executives, and the opportunities for women to advance. The sixth and final category is pay. Does the company offer average or high pay and is there at least one (preferably more than one) savings option, such as profit sharing, a stock-purchase plan, a company-paid pension, and so forth?

The responses to the questionnaire are compiled, analyzed, and verified. Companies are then written up and rated on a scale of one to five (five the highest, one the lowest) under each of the six categories described above. For those companies that applied but failed to make the top 100 list, *Working Mother* provides feedback that identifies specific areas of weakness that demand attention.

By 1999, survey results indicated that the most progressive companies on the list were dominating the work/life (*Working Mother* prefers this term rather than work/family) movement in three distinct areas. First, they understand the importance of a flexible work schedule. Every company on the list of 100 offers flextime and sixty-nine of them are training managers on how to implement alternative work schedules. Second, the top 100 are willing to listen to their employees and even seek out their advice. No less than 95 percent have surveyed their employees on work/life issues and 88 percent have created work/life task forces. And third, the best companies communicate well with their employees. Rather than simply including obligatory family-friendly language in their employee manuals, good companies provide appropriate informational web sites, high-tech bulletin boards, and chat rooms devoted to personnel issues.

Although *Working Mother* elects not to rank its top 100 companies, it does maintain a "top ten" list of corporations that have appeared on the magazine's list most frequently during the last fourteen years. Presented in Table 4.1 are the ten companies that were listed in the 1999 edition of the magazine.

IBM has, for good reason, made the top 100 list each of the fourteen years the survey has been completed. Emphasizing its mission to become "the premier global employer for working mothers," the company remains unmatched for its policy on leave for childbirth, which gives parents (mothers *and* fathers) three years of job-guaranteed leave. If necessary, parents may be required to return to work after only one year. It maintains an $8.3 million dependent-care fund and supports forty-seven near-site centers where IBM employees are given priority in placement, and 2,610 family child-care homes. In 1998, the firm initiated new programs in New York and North Carolina that screen nannies for those employees who prefer in-home care for their children. It also hosted its first ever conference for Women in Technology, drawing 500 women from twenty-nine different countries (*Working Mother* 1999).

Besides IBM, other companies have moved forward on work/life issues as well. At Bristol-Meyers Squibb, employees can request that free baby formula be mailed to them in installments during their infant's first year. Chase Manhattan Bank provides back-up child-care service as a safety net for working parents whose babysitter may fail to show up on time or call in sick. Similarly, Eastman Kodak of Rochester, New York, offers backup elder care as well as free in-home assessments of elderly dependents. Rockwell added lactation rooms, Autodesk expanded its eligibility requirements for its child-care subsidies, and American Express, in response to employee concerns, created a new flextime policy.

As was the case with Henry Ford's Sociology Department, the motivations of family-friendly companies are not solely altruistic. Bottom-line benefits are visible. For example, Prudential estimates that its resource and referral program, designed to assist workers in finding appropriate services to meet their personal and family needs, has saved the company $7 million in reduced absenteeism and turnover. CIGNA, one of the nation's largest insur-

Table 4.1

**The Ten Companies that Appeared Most Frequently on *Working Mother*'s Annual List of "Top 100" Family-Friendly Companies** (1986–2000)

| Companies | Years on the list |
| --- | --- |
| IBM Corporation | 14 |
| Lincoln Financial | 13 |
| Bank of America | 11 |
| Prudential | 10 |
| Lotus Development | 9 |
| CIGNA Corporation | 8 |
| Fannie Mae | 6 |
| Ely Lilly and Company | 5 |
| First Tennessee | 5 |
| Deutsche Bank | 4 |

ance companies, contends that its lactation program has reduced new moms' absences by 27 percent. The Benjamin Group, a small company of only seventy-two employees headed by a female CEO, provides on-site child care and twenty-four-week maternity leave, which help reduce the employee turnover rate. According to company founder Sheri Benjamin, the money to fund its family-friendly policies is generated by avoiding the use of expensive headhunters to fill job vacancies—an average of $20,000 per position filled (*Working Mother* 1999).

Other positive reports about the financial benefits that are generated by a family-friendly workplace can also be found in mainstream pro-corporate publications, including *Business Week* (1996). In a feature article entitled "Balancing Work and Family: Big Returns for Companies Willing to Give Family Strategies a Chance," readers learned about First Tennessee National Bank. Efforts to balance work and family resulted in an improved employee retention rate that converted to a $106 million profit gain over two years. Aetna Life and Casualty Company cut its resignations in half by extending its unpaid parental leave to six months, saving it $1 million a year in hiring and training expenses. Other companies, such as Du Pont, Eddie Bauer, Marriott, Motorola, and Unum Life Insurance, offer comparable family-friendly benefits that produce similar results.

Not to be overlooked when discussing cost issues, a daily visit to *Working Mother*'s web site reveals that the top 100 companies do as well or better on the stock market when compared to less family-friendly corporations. The performance of the top 100 companies are monitored and reported every day, and graphs illustrating performances over the long term are provided as well. Also, each company's profile, based on the six major categories discussed above, is available at *Working Mother*'s web site at www.workingmother.com.

However, not everyone is in agreement with *Working Mother*'s approach or the efforts by other organizations to classify certain companies as "family friendly." In the April/May 2000 issue of *Ms.* magazine Betty Holcomb (2000) concludes that "family-friendly" policies are anchored to a strong class bias. That is, argues Holcomb, low-wage workers are half as likely as managers and professionals to have flextime, less likely to have on-site child care, more likely to lose a day's pay when they must stay home to care for a sick child, and three times less likely to get company-sponsored tax breaks to help pay for child care. Unfortunately, Holcomb contends, such practices take place within many of the companies that appear in the top 100 of *Working Mother*'s annual listing.

Similarly, Anita Garey also sees class bias in the manner in which *Working Mother* presents itself to the general public. Featured on the cover of almost every issue is a "mother-of-the-month." However, from 1993 through 1998 the mothers on the covers have held the following occupations: actor, astronaut, attorney, broadcast journalist, college administrator, concert violinist, corporate executive, engineer, entrepreneur, fitness expert, opera director, photographer, professor, and radio producer. "Waitresses, sales-clerks, secretaries, and nurses are still the invisible working mothers," writes Garey (1999, 4).

But still, according to a study completed by the Families and Work Institute (Galinsky and Bond 1998), the struggle to balance and integrate work and family life continues. This is despite the fact that at least 100 companies can be identified each year as family-friendly and others seek to be included on the list. While surveys show that nearly 90 percent of companies permit employees to take time off to attend school events, and half let workers stay home with mildly ill children without using vacation or sick days, relatively few companies go beyond this stage. For example, a mere 9 percent of companies offer child care at or near the workplace, only 33 percent offer maternity leaves of more than thirteen weeks, and less than a quarter (23 percent) of the nation's corporations offer elder-care resources and referral services. By the time the federal Family and Medical Leave Act was passed in 1993, less than 6 percent of the companies provided such a benefit for their employees.

Facts such as these prompted Netsy Firestein, executive director of the Labor Project for Working Families (1996), to create *The Work and Family Bill of Rights* a document that consists of five major principles:

1. The right to paid family and medical leave.
2. The right to have control over work hours through flexible scheduling, a shorter workweek with no loss of pay, and no mandatory overtime.
3. The right to quality child care and elder care that is affordable and accessible, and that provides living wages for the care provider.

4. The right to a living wage, including equal pay for work of equal value.
5. The right to adequate healthcare coverage for families and work.

Such a document is indicative of the position in which much of corporate America finds itself today. As part of a national political culture that nurtures a split personality of family obligations on one side and government responsibilities on the other, corporations often find themselves trapped in the middle. It is within this context that liberal politicians in particular point to examples from *Working Mother*'s top 100 and argue that family-friendly policies are both affordable and profitable. Therefore, continues the argument, government mandates such as the FMLA are not only harmless to firms, they may even ultimately prove to be a benefit by improving productivity and increasing profits. The business community, however, often responds by also referring to examples from *Working Mother*'s top 100 list, stating that such a list is solid proof that government intervention is unnecessary. "We're already doing what you want us to do," they contend. Besides, they continue, in the end the choice should be that of the private, not the public sector.

The arguments put forth by both sides on the issue of who is responsible for family-friendly policies are quite familiar but worth repeating here. Proponents of government intervention argue that family-oriented policies allow parents to bond with their children and yet still hold their jobs. Arguing more from an ethical position instead of an economic one, advocates contend that such policies ultimately strengthen families, reduce stress, improve worker morale, and reduce employee turnover.

Arguing from an economic perspective, opponents, such as Laurie Grossman (1993) of the *Wall Street Journal*, believe that parents should raise their children at home and that government mandated programs such as family leave are intrusive and create unnecessary costs for businesses. Such policies geared to employees with children discriminate against childless workers who may have to "cover" for absent colleagues. According to Elinor Burkett (2000), the backlash by childless couples has already begun and will grow in the years ahead. Besides, argue opponents, there is little if any evidence that family policies in other industrialized countries have strengthened families. That said, and as will be discussed in subsequent chapters, the extent to which work and family becomes a political issue will depend a great deal on who holds political power at any particular time.

## The Clinton White House Responds

The Clinton administration in particular, unlike the two administrations preceding it, has been very aggressive in pushing work and family issues to the top of the political agenda. In May 1999 the Council of Economic Advisers issued a special report, *Families and the Labor Market, 1969–1999: Analyzing the "Time Crunch."* Emphasizing the fact that the American family underwent drastic change over the previous three decades, the report drew six major conclusions. Each is summarized briefly below.

First, because of the unprecedented shift of mothers' time from household chores (unpaid work) to the market economy (paid employment), the hours American parents devote to paid jobs increased dramatically over thirty years. For example, in 1969 nearly 38 percent of mothers worked outside the home for pay. By 1999 the percentage had increased to almost 70 percent.

Second, coinciding with women entering the labor force and parents spending more time at work, the report concluded that there has been a significant reduction in both the amount of time available to parents and time they've spent caring for their children. More specifically, between 1969 and 1996 families on average witnessed a 14 percent decrease (twenty-two hours a week) in time available to spend with their children.

Third, with parents spending more time in paid work today compared to thirty years ago, the so-called time crunch has become a burden for working mothers in particular. According to the Council's report, these women spend more than one-third less time on child care and assorted household chores than women who are not in the labor force. While the total annual hours of paid work by wives increased by an average of 576 hours, or by 93 percent, husbands' total hours of annual paid work decreased slightly between 1969 and 1996.

Fourth, although at first glance the average American family is financially better off today than it was thirty years ago, this is not true for all households. As was discussed in the previous chapter, while the top quarter of families gained economically, the lower quarter lost, and the middle quarters remained very much the same when measured by per capita income and adjusted for inflation. Not surprisingly, with three quarters of the nation's families either experiencing stagnation or financial decline during the last thirty years, there has been a corresponding increase in the number of dual-earner households. This development, in turn, has generated demands for more family-friendly policies.

A fifth conclusion of the Council of Economic Advisers' report is a reminder that with the growth of single-parent households during the past three decades, we have witnessed a significant increase in the proportion of families that are "cash trapped" and "time poor." Consequently, not only do single-parent families have half as much total time as two-parent families, but they also tend to have less than half as much income. Therefore, single-parent families in particular find family-support policies to be especially helpful.

And finally, the Council's special report concluded that due to the ongoing changes in both the family and the workplace, more policy options need to be considered in order to better integrate the demands of work with family responsibilities. Such options include flexibility in work hours, family-leave opportunities, access to quality child care that is affordable, financial support for struggling families, and efforts to encourage more two-parent families to form and remain intact.

Slightly more than six months after the Council of Economic Advisers issued its special report, President Clinton delivered his eighth and final State of the Union address. "We need a twenty-first century revolution to reward work and strengthen families," he said, "by giving every parent the tools to succeed at work and at the most important work of all, raising children" (Office of the Press Secretary 2000). Almost seven years to the day that he signed the Family and Medical Leave Act into law, the president went on to identify specific initiatives that he would put forth to address the needs of America's families. Included in his wish list was the expansion of the Earned Income Tax Credit, the adoption of a $21.7 billion child-care plan, a tax credit for family caregivers of the elderly, pay equity for women in the workplace, and more funding for the Children's Health Insurance Program (CHIP).

A little more than two weeks after his State of the Union message, President Clinton continued to emphasize the importance of balancing work and family when he delivered his weekly radio address on Saturday, February 12, 2000. After reminding the audience that the seventh anniversary of signing the FMLA had occurred only a week earlier, the president emphasized that "no American should have to choose between the job they need and the parent or child they love" (Office of the Press Secretary 2000). He then announced that he was proposing that $20 million in new competitive grant funds be set aside to help states develop new approaches for providing paid family leave for workers. He also asked Congress to expand the existing law to give parents time off for teacher-parent conferences and for trips to the doctor, and called for an extension of FMLA benefits to employees of smaller companies.

But despite years of debate, and even after a number of family-friendly policies have been adopted, including child care and family leave, the basic public policy questions remain essentially the same. That is, whose responsibility is it to assist dual-earner couples, single parents, and nontraditional families to balance work and family obligations? What if the employers choose not to act? Is it then the responsibility of government to intervene in the affairs of the private sector and require corporations to adopt family-oriented policies? If so, which policies will be most helpful to families and cost effective for corporations? And, equally important, will an increase in family-friendly policies encourage more parents to enter the workforce and remain longer, thus taking more time away from raising their children?

These questions are similar to those that were posed in the 1980s. Proponents of family leave policy at that time were confronted with at least three obstacles they had to overcome. One, the private sector was reluctant to adopt family-friendly policies at the workplace. Two, a pair of conservative Republican presidents in the White House successfully repelled any family-leave initiatives for twelve years. And three, a Congress that had drifted toward the political right was slow to embrace family issues (beyond "family values" rhetoric) with any enthusiasm. Consequently, proponents of family leave diverted much of their attention away from Washington and concentrated instead on the states. How the states responded to the issue of work and family is the subject of the next chapter.

## Notes

1. Particularly upset over Williams's actions was Houston Oilers head coach Bob Young, who immediately created a sports-war analogy. "This is like World War II, when guys were going to war and something would come up but they had to go," stated Young. In fact, Williams had not planned to miss the game at all. He and his wife had planned an induced pregnancy for the day *after* the game. However, when complications arose before game day, he decided to stay in Houston, a world war on the horizon or not. See Mindy Fried's *Taking Time: Parental Leave Policy and Corporate Culture* (1998), p. 16.

2. A modern-day version of Henry Ford's welfare capitalism surfaced on February 3, 2000, when Ford Motor Company announced it was providing a free Hewlett-Packard computer and Internet access at $5 a month to all of its 350,000 global employees. One day later, Delta Air Lines announced that its 72,000 employees worldwide would be given a computer and Internet access at $12 a month for thirty-six months. A primary objective of both of these programs is to help employees become more comfortable with using technology in their daily lives and, therefore, more inclined to transfer their new and improved skills to the workplace.

3. Other sources chronicling women working in the war industries include Sherna Gluck's *Rosie the Riveter Revisited: Women, the War, and Social Change* (1987) and Maureen Honey's *Creating Rosie the Riveter: Class, Gender, and Propaganda during World War II* (1984).

4. In 1975, the Union for Radical Political Economics issued a small booklet, *Separated and Unequal: Discrimination Against Women Workers After World War II.* It chronicles the failure of unions in particular to combat discrimination against women after World War II. The booklet is part of the Susan C. Schneider Collection at the Joseph P. Healey Library, University of Massachusetts at Boston.

5. Although four areas of concern are identified and discussed in this chapter (time, the role of fathers, the "mommy track," and the effect that the work and family conflict has on children), an emerging concern that may grow into "category five" is the building resentment of childless employees toward coworkers who have so-called family benefits. See Elinor Burkett's *The Baby Boon: How Family-Friendly America*

*Cheats the Childless* (2000), published by The Free Press. A similar "backlash perspective" is offered by Brian Robertson's *There's No Place Like Work: How Business, Government, and Our Obsession with Work Have Driven Parents from Home*, 2000, Dallas: Spence. An excellent source for acquiring a broad understanding of the conflict between work and family is Gary Bowen and Joe Pittman's *The Work and Family Interface: Toward a Contextual Effects Perspective* (1995), published by the National Council on Family Relations (Minneapolis, MN). Included are articles by Gary Bowen ("Corporate Supports for the Family Lives of Employees: A Conceptual Model for Program Planning and Evaluation"); R.L. McNeely and Barbe A. Fogarty ("Balancing Parenthood and Employment: Factors Affecting Company Receptiveness to Family-Related Innovations in the Workplace"); and Dennis Orthner and Joe Pittman ("Family Contributions to Work Commitment").

6. The Clinton administration, concerned about women's status in corporate America, created the Glass Ceiling Commission in 1995 which, in turn, issued two reports, *A Solid Investment: Making Full Use of the Nation's Human Capital* and *Good for Business: Making Full Use of the Nation's Human Capital*. The Commission presented recommendations for improving corporate policies in the promotion of women in the workplace (Washington, DC: U.S. Government Printing Office, 1995). See also *Equal Pay for Working Families*, a 1999 report produced jointly by the AFL-CIO and the Institute for Women's Policy Research (1999). The ongoing work of IWPR's "Working Group on Social Indicators of Women's Status" can be accessed at its web site: www.iwpr.org.

7. An area yet to be fully explored is the role of business schools within the context of work and family issues. Following a review of MBA programs and undergraduate curricula at the top twenty business schools in the country, this author concluded that the topic is barely visible. Apparently, students who are interested in the issue must seek out appropriate courses in other schools and departments. Why are there not courses in business schools on the costs and benefits of family-friendly policies, for example? Such a finding spawns an unsettling question: Will the modern American corporation be competitive in the global economy if the trained MBAs who lead them do not understand the significance of the relationship between work and family? However, in 2000 the Harvard Business School Press released its *Harvard Business Review on Work and Life Balance*, Boston: Harvard Business School Press. It is the sixth time it has been published (with updates) since 1980.

8. In addition to *Working Mother*'s annual top 100, several other sets of criteria have been created to measure the "family-friendliness" of corporations. Refer to the works of Harker (1996), Holt and Thaulow (1996) and the Families and Work Institute (1991). In its *Reference Guide for Work-Family Programs*, the Families and Work Institute identifes four major stages in the evolution of a corporate work-family agenda. In stage one, the company's primary focus is on child-care and family issues. In stage two, the corporation creates special task forces and completes employee-needs assessments related to family and work issues. In stage three, companies tend to change their terminology from "work-family" to "work-life" or "work-personal life," and they pay more attention to the needs of nontraditional families. And at stage four, which is the most difficult level to reach, corporations will reengineer the work process to better address family needs. This is the stage in which work and family are *integrated* (Bailyn 1996). Both *Fortune* (1999) and *Business Week* (1996) have devised sets of criteria to determine "best companies to work for in America," as have the Great Place to Work Institute of San Francisco and Hewitt Associates.

9. The Marriott Corporation, which consistently makes "best companies" lists, created a Department of Work and Family Life in 1989. Located at the company's headquarters in Bethesda, Maryland, the Department oversees its 206,000 employees, half of whom are women. Among the company's offerings are a resource and referral program, a child-care discount program, a family-care spending account, and regularly scheduled work and family seminars. Each quarter it publishes *The Balance*, a quarterly newsletter on work and family issues. Marriott, however, also was the target of criticism in Betty Holcomb's (2000) article, "Family Friendly for Whose Family?" which appeared in the April/May 2000 issue of *Ms.* magazine. Holcomb contends that employees who work nontraditional shifts for Marriott do not have equal access to its family-friendly services.

# Part II

## Family Leave Policy in the United States

# Chapter 5

# State Initiatives in Family Leave Policy

As discussed in chapters 3 and 4, the last thirty years have witnessed more women of childbearing age entering the labor force and staying longer than ever before in our history. Economic pressures induced more households to shift from the traditional male breadwinner/mother-at-home model to the dual-earner couple, and a feminist movement that called for greater equality and autonomy for women pushed new legal questions into the courts and onto legislative agendas. Slowly, both the public and private sectors responded to the demand for balancing work and family and, subsequently, the issue of family leave became a focal point of discussion by the mid-1980s. How the states responded to this issue is the topic of this chapter; the federal government's response is addressed in chapter 6.

The concepts of maternity benefits and family leave are not new. Bismarck first established maternity benefits in Germany in the 1880s. Britain, France, and Italy adopted similar initiatives prior to 1919, and almost all of the Western industrialized nations had such policies in place by World War II. By 1985, the year in which Congresswoman Patricia Schroeder (D-CO) introduced the nation's first family-leave bill, 135 countries had already established maternity-leave benefit programs and, of these, all but 10 mandated paid maternity leave.

Why the United States, compared to European countries, has been a laggard in developing a leave policy is, of course, open to speculation. Kamerman, Kahn, and Kingston (1983) attribute the discrepancy between U.S. and European policies to differences in political ideology, a decentralized American political system, and the power and influence of European labor unions in securing such benefits. Gauthier (1996) and Baker (1995) have drawn similar conclusions more recently. But often overlooked in many discussions are the legal roots of maternity- and parental-leave policies that run deep in American history. Such information is essential in understanding and explaining the evolution of family-leave policy as we know it today.

## The Legal Roots

Historically, men and women have been treated differently, primarily because men were responsible for productive (paid) labor and women assumed the reproductive role. As a result, much of the legal framework was shaped by the dominant social norms that prevailed during the nation's early years. By the end of the eighteenth century, for example, a woman's legal standing was fused with that of her husband's on her wedding day. Two had become one and he was the one (Williams 1984). Consequently, women could not own property, sign contracts, keep any wages earned, vote, sit on juries, or even smoke in some cases. But as industrialization brought more women into the world of work, two significant developments occurred. One, by the middle of the nineteenth century there was growing interest in giving women more legal recognition. Therefore, states began passing property-rights laws for married women. And two, concerned about the effect productive labor would have on women's reproductive capacities, many states began to pass protective labor legislation (Williams 1984; Piccirillo 1988).

Convinced that women needed special treatment because of their maternal role, state legislators excluded them from night shifts, prohibited them from doing "hazardous work," and created minimum wages that were almost always below those of men (Rothman 1978). Some state laws prohibited women from working during a period before and after the birth of a child, and many declared women ineligible for unemployment insurance if they were pregnant or had recently given birth (Piccirillo 1988). In 1867, Wisconsin passed the first state policy related to maternity and employment, restricting the hours on the job for women (Kamerman et al. 1983). By the turn of the century, many states had followed suit.

Rather than being protective, however, such laws tended to perpetuate inequality between the sexes. Women were limited to "women's work," which usually translated into less desirable, lower-paying jobs with no opportunity for advancement. Beneath the veil of what many considered to be progressive legislation was the belief that women's most appropriate role was motherhood—a job that was best performed in the home. Thus, as motherhood became a liability in the workplace, women were confronted with very few career options. But more important, advocates for women's rights found themselves in a very awkward position and confronted with a difficult question: Should they support special treatment or equal treatment for women in the workplace? This dilemma would surface most dramatically in the early 1900s in a pair of Supreme Court rulings and become the focal point of a famous legal brief prepared by a future justice. These developments would help shape state maternity-leave policies for more than seven decades.

### Lochner, Muller, and the Brandeis Brief

Joseph Lochner, the owner of a nonunion bakery in Utica, New York, violated an 1896 state law that limited work hours in bakeries and confectioneries to no more than ten hours a day and sixty hours per week. Despite being upheld three times by state courts that declared baking an unhealthy occupation that causes serious respiratory ailments, the law was challenged again by Lochner when he appealed his case to the U.S. Supreme Court in 1905. In a 5–4 ruling, the Court struck down New York's ten-hour day for bakery employees, all of whom were men, on the grounds that the law arbitrarily violated freedom of contract. Justice Rufus W. Peckham wrote the majority opinion for the court. "Clean and wholesome bread does not depend upon whether the baker works but ten hours per day or only sixty hours a week. . . . Statutes of the nature under review, limiting the hours in which grown and intelligent men may labor to earn their living, are mere meddlesome interferences with the rights of individuals" (*Lochner v. New York* 1905, 45). In short, the *Lochner* majority concluded that the New York law was not a health and safety law but rather an illegal labor law that interfered with the free enterprise system.

The significance of the *Lochner* decision in relation to the development of family-leave policy in the United States is worth emphasizing for several reasons. First, it illustrates how difficult it was to employ the power of government to protect *men* from dangerous and unhealthy working conditions. The protection of women in the workplace would be addressed by the Court three years later. And second, in offering a dissenting opinion, Justice John Marshall Harlan cited numerous authorities in arguing that long hours of labor in bakeries was detrimental to employees' health. This approach, which was most unusual, set a precedent for the now famous "Brandeis brief," in which social science research was employed to influence a U.S. Supreme Court decision in 1908.

In September 1905, the state of Oregon launched criminal charges against Curt Muller, the owner of the Grand Laundry in Portland. Several weeks earlier, on Labor Day, one of Muller's supervisors at the laundry required a female employee, Emma Gotcher, to work overtime. This act was in violation of Oregon's ten-hour law that passed in 1903. Following two losses in state courts, Muller appealed to the U.S. Supreme Court in 1908, following a pattern similar to Lochner's. On the other side was the National Consumer League, led by Florence Kelley. Kelly drafted the Illinois maximum-hours law of 1893, led a group of women advocates to enact it, and served as the head inspector of a group of twelve who were appointed to enforce it (Woloch 1996). As an attorney, she also filed a brief defending the Illinois statute when it was attacked, arguing that excessive work damaged women's reproductive organs.

But the main character to emerge from the Muller case was none of the aforementioned individuals; it was Louis D. Brandeis. A graduate of Harvard Law School in 1875 and a financially successful attorney for major corporate clients, Brandeis gravitated toward cases that concerned the public interest. Joining a group of outspoken lawyers that included other future Supreme Court justices, such as Oliver Wendell Holmes Jr. and Felix Frankfurter, Brandeis began to practice what he and the group referred to as "sociological jurisprudence" or "legal realism." That is, laws should be viewed from the perspective of their origins.[1] Who desires the passage and enforcement of certain laws and what benefits do they derive from them? Often working pro bono for the public interest, Brandeis even repaid his own firm for the time he devoted to public issues. Among other causes, he challenged corrupt streetcar franchises, fought for lower utility costs, attacked insurance companies, and called for bank reform (Woloch 1996).

When asked by Florence Kelley and the National Consumer League to take the Muller case, Brandeis agreed and immediately made it clear that he faced two options, both of which were risky. One, he could take on *Lochner* directly and argue that all jobs, regardless if they were hazardous or not, endangered all workers' health (men *and* women) if they exceeded ten hours per day. Or two, he could take a less risky approach and try to squeeze through a small opening that was left by the *Lochner* ruling. That is, he could try to convince the Court that Oregon's ten-hour law did not interfere with the "freedom of contract" because it affected *only women* (Babcock 1978). Brandeis's decision to choose option two, and therefore distinguish the case of the women laundry workers from the male bakers, had a major impact on future legislation concerning women, work, and maternity leave.

In arguing before the U.S. Supreme Court in 1908 on behalf of laundress Emma Gotcher and Florence Kelley's National Consumer League, Brandeis presented his famous brief that blended legal arguments with social science data. Numerous references were made to studies in professional journals. In a section entitled "The World's Experience," the brief emphasized the dangers of long hours and the benefits of shorter hours. Overwork, argued

Brandeis, does more damage to women than men not because of "the speed and hazard of modern industry," but primarily because of women's "special physical organization." Too much work, he contended, would affect "childbirth and female functions" and lead to menstrual problems, miscarriages, premature births, an increase in infant mortality, and a rise in the number of enfeebled offspring (Brandeis and Goldmark 1908, 47).

Although the brief was effective in convincing the Supreme Court to unanimously rule against Muller in 1908, both the brief and the majority opinion handed down by Justice David Brewer were subjected to much criticism years later for a variety of reasons. For one thing, social science was new and the studies cited by Brandeis were never really challenged until much later when numerous flaws were identified. Also, although the brief focused on overworked women, it could have been applied to overworked men just as easily. But the main objection to the brief was the very argument upon which it hinged: sexual differences. "The brief treats all women as mothers or potential mothers," writes Nancy Woloch, "it either conflates the needs of families and society with those of women or prefers the former to the latter; and it depicts women as weak and defective" (Woloch 1996, 32). Or, put another way by Nancy Erickson (1982), the brief emphasized the vulnerabilities of the workers rather than the hazards of the work.

Brewer's opinion was moored to the dominant belief at the time that physical and social differences between the sexes justified different treatment with respect to labor contracts. Women, argued Brewer, were very dependent by nature, and even legal rights, including voting (still eleven years away), would not change their status. Therefore, continued Justice Brewer's logic, compensatory laws were needed to allow women some degree of equality under certain circumstances. However, while protective laws may be appropriate for women, such is not the case for men (Strum 1984). Thus, by striking down *Muller* but upholding *Lochner* the Justice had, in essence, codified the Brandeis brief. In short, Brewer's opinion conveyed the conventional wisdom of the day that women were unequal and inferior to men. Consequently, whether or not there should be special or equal treatment accorded to women who work became a part of the family-leave debate seventy-five years later.

Because of the demands of maternity, women were often viewed as little more than temporary workers, and married women in particular were vulnerable to discrimination. For example, during the Great Depression of the 1930s, many state legislatures considered bills that limited the employment of women (Gladstone et al. 1985). In subsequent years, females were denied access to professional schools such as law and medicine because it was assumed they would not use their degrees after graduation. Instead, continued the logic, they would surely choose motherhood before a career. So why admit them to the university and allow them to take a seat and, ultimately, a career from a man? With the exception of the World War II era, during which time many women not only entered the job market but assumed positions previously reserved for men, most females continued to receive two very strong messages: One, they were not supposed to work when pregnant. And two, it became increasingly clear that childbearing and employment were inherently incompatible in this society (Piccirillo 1988).

By the 1960s, however, the feminist movement began to attack employers' policies related to pregnancy. An important legal vehicle that was employed during this period to address sex discrimination was Title VII of the 1964 Civil Rights Act. It was designed to prohibit the practice of sex discrimination in employment through the creation of the Equal Employment Opportunity Commission (EEOC). However, it was not clear whether or not a corporate decision based on the pregnancy of an employee constituted discrimination. But, in 1972 the EEOC issued special guidelines concerning pregnancy in the workplace. One statement in particular was quite clear. An "employment policy or practice which excludes from employment applicants or employees because of pregnancy is in prima facie violation of Title VII" (*Guidelines on Discrimination Because of Sex* 1972).

Despite the strong wording in the regulations, many employers refused to abide by the guidelines, spawning numerous court cases. By 1976, the issue had reached the U.S. Supreme Court in *General Electric v. Gilbert.* Concluding that pregnancy was an "additional risk unique to women," the Court determined that male needs and risks would be considered the norm. "Only females who did not differ from this same set of needs and risks—nonpregnant females—would be given the same protection as men" (Piccirillo 1988, 302). In handing down its ruling in *Gilbert*, the Court dismissed previous EEOC interpretations of Title VII, overturned rulings in seven federal appellate courts, and also rejected eighteen federal district court decisions (Kamerman et al. 1983).

Concerned about the Court's ruling in the case, Congress moved to overturn the ruling by passing a law: the Pregnancy Discrimination Act of 1978. This initiative and a key court case that followed would set the stage for the passage of maternity- and family-leave legislation in the states during the 1980s.

### The Pregnancy Discrimination Act of 1978

The Pregnancy Discrimination Act (PDA) of 1978 (Public Law [P.L.] 95–555) was an amendment to Title VII of the 1964 Civil Rights Act. The Act mandates that "women affected by pregnancy, childbirth, or related medical conditions shall be treated the same for all employment-related purposes . . .

as other persons not so affected but similar in their inability to work" (Radigan 1988). Simply put, the PDA established the legal principle that men and women had to be treated equally when they were unable to work because of medical reasons. However, the law also contained at least two major loopholes. One, if employers chose not to provide disability benefits for their employees as a whole, regardless of the gender mix of their workforce, they were not required to offer such benefits to pregnant women. And two, the Act did not require employers to acknowledge workers' needs and obligations beyond the workplace that could affect their labor-force participation (Jacobs and Davies 1994).

Typical of most legislation, the PDA, in addition to the obvious loopholes identified above, also contained a sufficient amount of ambiguous language that prompted the EEOC to issue written interpretations and encouraged both employers and employees to sue in court. For example, shortly after the law's implementation, a series of court cases surfaced that centered on the right of employers to place women on mandatory leave as soon as their pregnancy was detected. This was the case in several suits involving airlines in which the courts ruled consistently that a pregnant flight attendant "put passengers in danger" and, therefore, it was the airlines' right to ground her as soon as the pregnancy was revealed (Piccirillo 1988).

Although the PDA did not address the issue of balancing work and family, it at least created a more equitable environment in the workplace by assuring women that employers could not discriminate against them because of a pregnancy. Moreover, the passage of the Pregnancy Discrimination Act of 1978 prompted some states to enact similar legislation. By the early 1980s, nine states adopted laws that mandated benefits for workers on maternity leave. Several states, California included, even offered as much as four months of unpaid leave. However, such laws were soon subjected to legal challenges because the benefits they afforded women were not available to men. One of the most celebrated cases falling within this category was *California Federal Savings and Loan (Cal Fed) v. Guerra*, popularly known as the *Garland* case. It, like the Pregnancy Discrimination Act of 1978, established some important legal underpinnings upon which state and federal family-leave legislation would be constructed (Jacobs and Davies 1994).

## The *Garland* Case

In 1982, Lillian Garland, while employed as a receptionist at the Cal Fed Bank in West Los Angeles, gave birth to a child. Because of a complicated pregnancy and delivery, her doctor recommended that she take a three-month leave from work to recover. However, when she returned to work following her recuperation, she was informed that her position had been filled. Garland then filed suit against Cal Fed, based on a 1978 California statute which stated that a company with fifteen or more employees must offer up to four months of unpaid leave to pregnant women and guarantee them the same or a comparable job when they return to work. Cal Fed, however, challenged the California law in federal court, arguing that it violated the 1978 Pregnancy Discrimination Act because the law benefited only women, not men. When the U.S. District Court for the Central District of California handed down its ruling in favor of Cal Fed in 1984, it stated its rationale in clear language. "California employers who comply with state law are subject to reverse discrimination suits under Title VII of the Civil Rights Act, by temporarily disabled males who do not receive the same treatment as female employees disabled by pregnancy" (U.S. Supreme Court Reports 1986, 115).

Outraged by the decision, a group of feminists and other activists in support of Garland quickly filed an appeal in the U.S. Court of Appeals. However, *Garland* was haunted by *Muller*'s ghosts in that the dilemma of "special treatment" vs. "equal treatment" emerged once again. While feminist organizations and labor groups such as the Coalition for Reproductive Equality in the Workplace (CREW) and 9 to 5 National Association of Working Women attacked the assumption that the law discriminated against men, other women's organizations saw it somewhat differently. For example, the National Organization for Women (NOW) and the Women's Legal Defense Fund (WLDF), now known as the National Partnership for Women and Families (NPWF), opposed the "special treatment" strategy of CREW and 9 to 5 and, instead, staunchly supported "equal treatment" for women. Under no circumstances, they argued, should females be viewed as a protected class. To them the historical record was clear. The use of protective legislation for women only spawned discrimination against female workers. Furthermore, continued the argument, extended-leave policies should not just be reserved for women in a maternal state, but rather be available to *all* workers, male *and* female, regardless of the cause of their disability (Elving 1995).

Two years later, the U.S. Court of Appeals handed down its decision, reversing the District Court's ruling. The Appeals Court emphasized that the Pregnancy Discrimination Act "does not demand that state law be blind to pregnancy's existence." The primary objective of Congress in designing the law was "to construct a floor beneath which pregnancy disability benefits may not drop—not a ceiling above which they may not rise" (*Cal Fed v. Guerra* 1985, 19). As anticipated, Cal Fed appealed the ruling to the U.S. Supreme Court, which ruled in 1987 by a six-to-three vote that the California law was valid. According to the decision, the California law was not in violation of federal law nor did it discriminate against men. What the law did do, however, was promote equal employment opportunity. Equally important, the Court concluded that the California statute did not mandate that employers must treat pregnant workers better than other disabled employees, but it created a minimum standard of benefits for pregnant workers that employers must meet (Jacobs and Davies 1994).

The significance of the Supreme Court's ruling in the *Garland* case should not be dismissed lightly. While the formulation of the Family and Medical Leave Act at the federal level is the focus of attention in the next chapter, a brief summary statement concerning the issue of "special treatment" vs. "equal treatment" is appropriate at this time. Shortly after the *Garland* case entered the appeals court circuit, U.S. Representative Howard Berman (D-CA), who, as a state legislator, had sponsored the California statute in question, was encouraged by one group of feminists to introduce federal legislation designed to protect female workers. This "special treatment" strategy was quickly countered by a Washington-based coalition that favored an "equal treatment" approach. It was this latter group that proposed legislation to establish "universal, non-gender-based parenting leave based on the principles of equal rights" (Jacobs and Davies 1994, 97). Selecting Patricia Schroeder (D-CO) as the sponsor of the bill, the group was instrumental in seeing that H.R. 2020, "The Parental and Disability Act," was introduced during the 99th Congress in April 1985 (Elving 1995). In subsequent years, the language would change from "maternity" to "parental" to "family," and from "disability" to "medical," until it eventually became the Family and Medical Leave Act. But most important, by the mid-1980s the "equal treatment" advocates had triumphed over the "special treatment" forces, at least at the federal level.

### The Emergence of State Maternity- and Family-Leave Initiatives

As discussed in chapter 2, whatever political momentum was generated for a national family policy during the latter part of the Carter administration was quickly dashed in the early years of the Reagan presidency. If government was indeed the problem and not the solution, Ronald Reagan made it extremely clear early on that "the problem" would be shrugged off by Washington and shifted to the states. In short, if any family-oriented policies were to emerge at all, they would be produced by state legislatures, not the United States Congress. So, despite Pat Schroeder's heroic attempt to push the first family-leave bill onto the floor of the House of Representatives in 1985, an effort that proved futile, similar legislation experienced more success in the states. By the time Bill Clinton affixed his signature to the 1993 Family and Medical Leave Act, about a third of the state legislatures had already adopted some form of leave policy, with some producing comparable or stronger legislation than the Clinton version.[2] Those states are identified in Map 5.1.

117

Map 5.1 **State Maternity/Family Leave Laws** (1993)

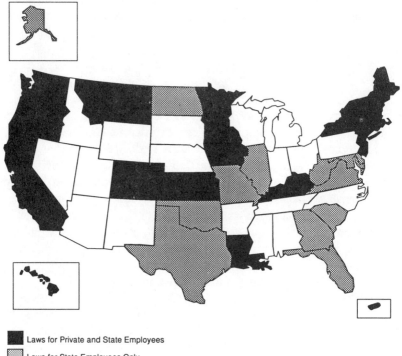

Laws for Private and State Employees

Laws for State Employees Only

No Laws

*Source:* Women's Bureau, U.S. Department of Labor. *State Maternity/Family Leave Law*. Washington, DC, 1993.

As illustrated in Map 5.1, there was some variation among the states with respect to the structure and function of their leave policies. Twenty-three states covered both private and state employees; eleven states applied their policies to state employees only. Nineteen of the states gave time off only for childbirth and pregnancy while fifteen states had adopted broader types of legislation, permitting leaves for more general family responsibilities. There was also much variation among the states in duration of leave and the size of companies to which the law applied. Illinois, for example, provided the longest leave period, one full year, but only state employees were eligible. Minnesota allowed six weeks for childbirth or adoption, but provided an additional sixteen hours to parents for school conferences. South Carolina offered six months off for pregnancy, but only eight days to care for ill family members. And perhaps Wisconsin had the most complicated model of all. Six weeks were covered for childbirth and adoption, two weeks for the employee's own illness, two weeks for the illness of a family member or legal defendant, but no more than ten weeks could be used for any combination of reasons for leave.

With respect to company size, that too varied. Although most state laws exempted employers with fewer than fifty employees, three states had a 100-employee cutoff and a few state laws applied to employers with only one employee. However, one area in which states found much commonality was that of eligibility. Almost all states required an employee to work full-time (thirty-five to forty hours) for one year prior to taking leave.

Somewhat interesting, though not necessarily easy to explain, is the geographic clustering by region of those states that had no leave policy on the books when Clinton signed the FMLA. Most were in the West, South, or Midwest. However, for states that had enacted some sort of leave legislation by 1993, their particular selection of a "special treatment" approach versus an "equal treatment" strategy depended on a number of factors that were also at the center of the debate in Washington between 1985 and 1993.

When the Schroeder bill was introduced in the House of Representatives in 1985, few, if any states, had a similar initiative in their legislative pipelines. Whatever laws were on the books concerning pregnancy and work tended to fall under four distinct categories. First, there were antidiscrimination statutes similar to the Pregnancy Discrimination Act that some states had enacted. Second, a few states provided some protection through access to unemployment insurance. Third, five states had extended their temporary disability insurance laws to cover pregnancy. And fourth, a number of states that did not necessarily fall under any of the categories identified above passed week mandates that provided minimum protection for employed pregnant women. Though not perfect by any means, it was a far cry from 1960 when thirty-five states explicitly declared women, who were otherwise eligible for benefits, ineligible if they were pregnant (Piccirillo 1988).

## Temporary Disability Insurance (TDI)

Prior to 1985, and long before the enactment of the Pregnancy Disability Act of 1978 and the *Garland* decision, five states addressed the issue of pregnancy in the workplace head on. In the 1940s, Rhode Island (1942), California (1946), New Jersey (1948), and New York (1949) enacted nonoccupational disability laws that included pregnancy and childbirth in the definition of disability. Puerto Rico followed in 1968 and Hawaii adopted its law in 1969. Companies in these Temporary Disability Insurance (TDI) states are required to offer paid leave to new mothers, just as it would be offered to other employees who are ill or temporarily disabled (Meyers 1995). The specific characteristics of each of these TDI programs are presented in Table 5.1.

Table 5.1

**State Temporary Disability Insurance Policies** (1999)

| | California | Hawaii | New Jersey | New York | Rhode Island |
|---|---|---|---|---|---|
| Number of employees in workforce (excluding unemployed) | 14,965,492 | 554,134 | 3,978,185 | 8,242,623 | 478,357 |
| Total annual benefits paid | $1,741 million | $38 million | $325 million | $562 million | $99 million |
| Eligibility requirements | Employees unable to work because of non-work-related physical or mental condition, including pregnancy and childbirth | Employees who suffer non-work-related physical illnesses or injuries, including pregnancy and childbirth | Employees unable to work because of any accident or sickness, including pregnancy, that does not arise out of employment | Employees unable to work because of any injury or sickness, including pregnancy and childbirth, that does not arise out of employment | Employees who suffer non-work-related physical illnesses or injuries, including pregnancy and childbirth |
| Maximum/average annual length of benefits | 52 weeks/12.6 weeks weeks (July 1996–June 1997) | 26 weeks / 4.6 weeks | 26 weeks / 9.6 weeks | 26 weeks / 4.9 weeks | 30 weeks / 11.6 |
| Maximum/average weekly benefits | $336 / $229 | $352 / $275 | $364 / $273 | $170 / $142.04 | $463 (1998) / $253.55 |

120

| | | | | |
|---|---|---|---|---|
| Annual employer contributions | None under state disability insurance plan; may share cost with employees under voluntary private plan; employees' contributions limited as below | Employers can assume full cost or can impose cost on employees; monthly average of $12.09 per employee paid by employers in 1997; employees' contributions limited as below | Individual employers' rates determined annually, based on statutory table (0.1–0.75% of employees' TDI-taxable wages in 1996) | Employers can assume full cost or can impose cost on employees; employees' contributions limited as below | None |
| Annual employee contributions | Annually determined percentage of annually determined wage ceiling; in 1997 employees contributed 0.5% of first $31,767 of earnings under state disability insurance plan (maximum contribution of $13.18 per month; same cap applies to contributions to voluntary plan) | If employees contribute, they pay half of cost of premiums or .5% of annually determined wage ceiling, whichever is less; in 1998, wage ceiling was first $614.62 in weekly earnings (maximum contribution of $13.30 per month) | 0.5% of annually determined wage ceiling; in 1998, wage ceiling was first $19,300 in annual earnings (maximum contribution of $8.04 per month) | Contributions range from $0 to .5% of first $120 in weekly earnings (maximum contribution of $2.60 per month) | Annually determined percentage of annually determined wage ceiling; in 1998, employees contributed 1.2% of first $38,000 in earnings (maximum contribution of $38 per month) |
| Mechanism | Both private and state plans | Private plans, self-insurance, or collective bargaining agreement | Both private (15.8% of all claims) and state plans | Private plans, self-insurance, and state plan | State plan only |

*Source:* National Partnership for Women & Families (1999), Washington, DC. Reprinted with permission.
*Note:* A detailed explanation of this data is available from the NPWF (www.nationalpartnership.org)

Employers are offered three options for running their TDI systems: a state-run program, a private insurance plan, or a self-insurance model. Employees in companies with one or more workers are covered, but this does not usually cover certain types of jobs, such as domestic laborers (Hartmann et al. 1995). As indicated in Table 5.1, there is much variation, both in the funding mechanisms used and amount of benefits provided. For example, in three states (Hawaii, New Jersey, and New York), employee and employer contributions, though not necessarily equal, support the TDI trust funds. In two states (Rhode Island and California), the employers make no contributions. With respect to the amount of benefits available to workers who take leave, there is also much variation among the five models. The wage replacement levels start at about 50 percent of an employee's salary in New York and climb to about 66 percent in Hawaii. However, all states maintain a maximum weekly cap calculated on the basis of average wages, but no state's maximum benefit per worker per week exceeds $400. The length of leave also varies by state, with the highest being California at fifty-two weeks. The other states set a maximum length of twenty-six weeks, with the exception of Rhode Island's policy, which is determined by individual physicians on a case-by-case basis. Coverage is limited, however, to thirty weeks.

At least three points should be emphasized in relation to the use of TDI programs by these five states as a means of addressing the issue of wage replacement during maternity leave. First, in many respects, the TDI model falls under the "special treatment" model. That is, although both men and women may take leave in these states under TDI, men cannot get pregnant. It is for this reason that some feminists and even nonfeminists prefer not to view childbirth as a disability and thus avoid the "special treatment" stigma altogether.

Second, the TDI policies are also quite narrow in that they apply to *maternity* and *not* to paternity or other family demands. Massachusetts did attempt to adopt a TDI program in the mid-1980s that would have allowed employees to take paid leave to care for family members (not just newborns), but that proposal died in legislative committee. More recently, several of the original five TDI states have proposed extending their programs to include "family needs," thus making it intergenerational. This issue will be fully discussed in a later chapter.

A third point deserving some attention is the peculiar fact that many years ago, five states adopted TDI programs that cover maternity leave. However, in more than fifty years, not one of those states chose to abandon its program because it was too expensive or administratively unmanageable. Nor, quite remarkably, have any states followed in the footsteps of these five states and adopted similar TDI models; the only exception being Massachusetts's failed attempt to adopt a similar but broader program in the mid-1980s. But what is less peculiar is the fact that pregnancy and childbirth claims in these five states account for only between 12 and 22 percent of total TDI claims, depending of course on the variability of fertility rates over time. And, the average length of pregnancy leave has averaged less than twelve weeks (Wever 1996).[3] Such facts clearly beg the question: If the program is not costly for employers or abused by employees, why has it not been replicated elsewhere? Herein lies a research puzzle for any intellectually curious policy analyst to ponder (Wisensale 1991a).

## Family Leave Policy in the States

In 1987, just two years after Pat Schroeder introduced the first federal family-leave bill on the floor of the House of Representatives, a number of state legislatures began to take up the issue. Confronted with growing constituent concerns about work and family pressures, and realizing that the Reagan administration's emphasis on New Federalism (now referred to as devolution) would shift more domestic policy to the states, legislatures in twenty-eight states introduced and debated parental- and family-leave bills. By the end of 1987, four states (Connecticut, Minnesota, Oregon, and Rhode Island) were successful in passing parental- and family-leave bills.[4] They are summarized in Table 5.2 according to type (family or parental), the size of companies to which the policy applied, and the length of leave permitted.

There was much variation across all four states with respect to specific provisions, such as length of leave, the size of companies to which it applied, coverage of employee benefits, and whether or not child care and elder care should be included in the same package. However, they also had at least three things in common. One, all the bills were initiated by Democrats who had control of both Houses of the legislature in each of the four states. Two, all four states adopted leave bills that did not include any kind of wage replacement. And three, all four states concluded that mandatory action by government and not voluntary efforts by business was the most realistic road to travel in addressing the conflict between family and work.

It should be emphasized, however, that Connecticut's approach was somewhat unique in at least two respects. First, not only was it the very first state in the nation to pass a family-leave bill, it also produced the first piece of legislation of its kind that was intergenerational in structure. That is, an employee could take time off to care for a child or an elderly parent. The other three states confined their coverage to child care only. And second, choosing an incremental route, the 1987 Connecticut bill only applied to state employees, unlike the other three states that included both the public and private sectors in their legislation. Connecticut eventually adopted a bill geared to the private sector two years later (Wisensale 1989a).

Table 5.2

**First Successful State Initiatives in Leave Policy** (1987)

| State | Type of leave | Size of company | Length of leave |
|-------|---------------|-----------------|-----------------|
| Connecticut | Family | State employees only | 24 weeks over 2 years |
| Minnesota | Parental | 21+ | 6 weeks |
| Oregon | Parental | 25+ | 12 weeks |
| Rhode Island | Parental | 50+ | 13 weeks |

Not to be overlooked is the fact that out of the original family- and parental-leave legislation produced in these four states emerges a composite sketch of the 1993 federal Family and Medical Leave Act. That is, the FMLA's application to both the public and private sector is borrowed from Minnesota, Oregon, and Rhode Island. The company size of fifty or more employees was in the original Rhode Island bill. The FMLA's provision of twelve weeks of leave was a component of the Oregon bill, and the intergenerational aspect of the federal bill, which clearly distinguished it from maternity or parental leave (equal treatment, not special treatment), was a key ingredient of Connecticut's 1987 law. Of course, the most obvious characteristic common to all state laws as well as the federal bill was the absence of paid leave. As previously mentioned, Massachusetts's effort in 1987 to create a Temporary Disability Insurance model that included family leave (a major expansion beyond the five TDI states that included maternity leave only) fell short (Wisensale 1989b). The issue of paid leave would not surface again until Bill Clinton raised it in 1999. This will be discussed in greater detail in chapter 8.

The issues raised and the compromises reached in shaping leave policy in these four states would, in many respects, be replicated in similar debates in Washington several years later. In several studies of state-initiated parental and family leave policies, Wisensale (1988, 1989, 1991) isolated eight issues that were addressed by legislators in their attempt to shape policy first in the states and later in Washington. For example, issue one raises the question as to whether any leave policy should be a matter of government responsibility or a private sector choice. In short, should the government (state or federal) simply mandate that companies provide family leave, or should corporations be encouraged to adopt such measures through political jawboning and the use of tax incentives? This very question became one of the major focal points of the debate over the federal FMLA and, ultimately, became a clear line in the sand between proponents and opponents of the legislation.

A second issue, though not debated with any intensity prior to 1999, concerned paid vs. unpaid leave. As discussed previously, five states do provide some form of wage replacement under Temporary Disability Insurance. However, during the formulation of state policy, with the exception of Massachusetts, the issue was never raised. Nor did it surface during debates at the federal level until President Clinton, in the latter part of his second term, suggested that states consider using Unemployment Insurance trust funds to cover family leave.

The third issue centered on the scope of the leave. That is, should it apply only to mothers of newborns or also include the care of older children who become ill? Should spousal care and the care of an elderly parent also be included? Interestingly, by the time the FMLA is adopted, very few of the thirty-two states that had adopted leave policies of some sort included an intergenerational care provision. In Washington, DC, however, in an effort to build a broad coalition that included the powerful American Association of Retired Persons (AARP), the intergenerational component was included. Also, it is probably more than coincidence that Senator Chris Dodd (D-CT), whom many consider to be the primary architect of the final version of the FMLA, came from Connecticut, the state that introduced and passed the nation's first intergenerational family-leave bill.

Perhaps one of the most contested issues to emerge from the family-leave debate at the state and federal levels was the length of the leave. Of the thirty-two states that had adopted a leave policy prior to 1993, the length of leave ranged from a low of four weeks in Hawaii to a high of twenty-four weeks in Connecticut (public sector) and sixteen weeks (private sector) over a two-year period. Twenty-two of the thirty-two states had established a twelve-week leave period, matching the federal FMLA's provision. But this issue in particular, despite whatever evidence was brought forth by experts in child psychology and parental attachment theory that called for as much as one year off to care for newborns, was very vulnerable to compromise. In order for proponents of the legislation to capture more votes from the opposition camp, as will be discussed in the next chapter on the formulation of the FMLA, the number of weeks had to be reduced. In short, political expediency trumped child development theory.

The fifth issue, and one that was also particularly vulnerable to political compromise, was company size. The size of the firm to which a leave policy should be applied became an important question for two reasons. One, by limiting the size to six employees, which was Massachusetts's original proposal, or 100 workers, which was Tennessee's model, policymakers can determine how many people within the state workforce will be eligible under a given leave policy.[5] And two, women, who are usually the primary caregivers, often work in smaller firms that are not covered by the policy. This became a focal point of a heated debate in Rhode Island where, for example, small jewelry-making companies dominated by female workers, do not fall under the 50+ employee cutoff (Wisensale 1989b).

But unlike the length of leave, which tended to be bargained down in order to win more votes, the size of the company was bargained upward during legislative debates. That is, the more employees needed for coverage to be mandated, the fewer companies would be held accountable under the law. Thus, with the FMLA applying to fifty or more employees, only 6 percent of the corporations are affected by the law, and just 60 percent of the workforce are eligible to use it. It should therefore come as no surprise, that the bipartisan Commission on Leave (1996) reported that the federal law was having little financial or administrative impact on the private sector.

Issue six concerned the matter of gender. This was particularly true in debates at the state level. During the first three years, from 1987 to 1990, in which more than thirty parental and family leave bills were proposed, ten states introduced legislation that tied leave benefits solely to female workers. Eight of those ten states were in a more conservative South. That is, the legislation crafted was "maternity," not "parental," and certainly not "family" or "intergenerational" in scope. This issue can become especially problematic when it is linked to the length of the leave, such as whether or not allotted time off can or should be shared by a married couple or applied individually. By simply employing the term "maternal" instead of "parental," the number of all eligible caregivers under a given leave law is probably cut in half.

The seventh issue concerned job security and benefit coverage. At least five questions emerged during state legislative debates that were related to benefits. First, should health and pension benefits be covered during the leave? If so, who should pay? Second, how should length of service with the firm and seniority be calculated for those who may develop a disjointed work history due to taking leave? Third, what impact should taking leave have on promotions and pay increases? Fourth, what guarantee is there that the employee on leave can or will return to the same job? And finally, who should answer these questions? Should the private sector make such decisions within individual company headquarters, or should the answers be produced by government and applied to corporations?

For the most part, state policies included benefit coverage during time off with the same funding mechanism that was in place when the leave period began. This was certainly the policy followed under the FMLA. Regarding questions two and three, the individual company's personnel polices were given priority over government mandates. But, concerning question four, in all family and parental leave bills at the state or federal levels, job security was guaranteed. In short, employees were given the same or comparable job upon their return to work (Wisensale 1989b, 1994).

The eighth and perhaps most volatile issue that confronted state legislators in shaping family-leave policy was that of cost. Opponents of leave policy argued that replacement workers would increase the cost and ultimately drive up the prices on consumer goods; that American products, due to higher prices, will no longer be competitive with goods of foreign competitors; and that, ultimately, small businesses will be destroyed by such a policy. Supporters of leave policy countered by stating that the absence of such a policy forces employees to hire caregivers while they continue working, or lose income while they take leave, not to mention the decline in worker morale and subsequent loss in worker productivity if the policy is not available. The Institute of Women's Policy Research (1988) put this argument in terms of dollars and cents. In its special report, *Unnecessary Losses: Costs to Americans for the Lack of Family and Medical Leave*, the IWPR concluded that dollars lost by female employees who have no maternity leave far exceed the costs of unpaid leave shouldered by corporations.

Based on its study of 7,000 families, the IWPR found that all women in the workforce who have babies lose earnings in the birth year as well as subsequent years. But because women without maternity leave also lose their jobs, they bear a total salary loss of $607 million annually (1988 figures). In addition, taxpayers must provide another $108 million in federal income assistance in the form of public welfare programs to cover periods of unemployment for some workers. All told, according to the IWPR, because both the public and private sector fail to provide adequate leave policies, the annual cost to families and taxpayers in 1988 exceeded $715 million. In all fairness to corporations, however (and particularly since the publication of *A Workable Balance* by the Commission on Leave, in which costs were categorized as "minimal"), representatives for the private sector have contended that leave policy has had a negative financial impact on corporations. One disturbing trend they point to in particular is the decline in morale among single or childless employees who feel discriminated against when they are asked to cover the workload of employees who have privileged access to family leave (Burkett 2000). But the cost issue once again emerged after President Clinton recommended that states use Unemployment Insurance to provide paid leave. This will be discussed in greater detail in chapter 8.

By the time the 1993 FMLA was signed into law, thirty-two states had adopted some sort of leave policy. Ten states had implemented the broadbased intergenerational family leave model similar to the FMLA. The other twenty-four states produced an assortment of more limited leave policies. Some states only allowed time off from work for childbirth and adoption.

Other states were even less generous, restricting their policies to school visitations by parents. One state allowed no time off except for bone marrow donors.

But a more important point to emphasize here is the number of states that adopted leave laws that are more generous than the Family and Medical Leave Act of 1993. The National Partnership for Women and Families (1998) identified seventeen states that provide additional benefits. However, this does not necessarily mean that all seventeen states have policies that extend beyond the FMLA in all categories. It does mean that certain states are more generous under certain conditions than federal policy. This information is summarized in Table 5.3.

Of the seventeen states, thirteen of them have policies that apply to companies of fewer than fifty employees. For example, Vermont's law offers leaves for childbirth or adoption to those in companies of ten or more employees. In Oregon, the cutoff is twenty-five employees. However, both of these states also have other provisions in their leave laws that are more comprehensive than the FMLA. There are eleven other states that allow leave to employees in companies of fewer than fifty workers, but their coverage is more narrow than the federal law. Kentucky, for example, allows time off for the adoption of a child under age seven regardless of company size, but no leave is granted for other reasons. Montana's law applies to one or more employees but, similar to Kentucky's statute, the leave is restricted to maternity. In Connecticut, workers in companies of three or fewer employees are eligible for maternity leave, as are employees in California and Iowa where the employee cutoff is five and four, respectively. In Massachusetts and New Hampshire, companies with six or more employees must provide maternity leave to their employees. The Maine law is comprehensive in that it includes family and medical leave, and it is also more generous than the FMLA in that it applies to fifteen or fewer employees. However, it allows only ten weeks of leave over a two-year period, compared to the FMLA's provision of thirteen weeks during a twelve-month period. Both Minnesota (twenty-one workers or more) and Louisiana (twenty-five workers or more) apply their laws to smaller companies than what is required under the federal FMLA.

Six states provide longer periods of leave than the FMLA. These include California, which allows twelve weeks of family leave plus four months maternity disability leave, for a combined total of twenty-eight weeks a year. Connecticut provides sixteen weeks of leave over two years for family leave, Louisiana permits four months for maternity reasons, Oregon allows twelve weeks of family leave plus another twelve weeks of maternity leave per year. Rhode Island's law provides thirteen weeks a year, and Tennessee's policy covers four months for maternity leave.

As presented in Table 5.3, there are two states that cover leave for family medical needs that are not included in the Family and Medical Leave Act. For example, Massachusetts allows for twenty-four hours of leave per twelve-month period for accompanying a child, spouse, or elderly relative to routine professional medical appointments such as physical, dental, and eye exams. Vermont's law is similar to the Massachusetts statute but more specific. It provides twenty-four hours of leave for any twelve-month period for addressing the emergency medical needs of a child, spouse, parent, or parent-in-law, but no more than four hours in any thirty-day period can be used for this purpose. These "family assistance" provisions were among the early recommendations put forth by President Clinton near the end of his first term to expand the FMLA.

Another of the President's recommendations called for an expansion of the federal law to allow parents to participate in more of their children's school activities. As was the case with the family assistance recommendations, the President's effort to include school visits in the FMLA was not adopted by Congress. However, seven states did include leave time in the laws for parental participation in children's educational activities. California, for example, permits forty hours a year but no more than eight hours per month. Vermont allows for twenty-four hours a year but no more than four hours in any month. Similarly, but far more restrictive, Illinois provides for eight hours a year for school visits but no one visit can exceed four hours a day. Massachusetts allocates twenty-four hours a year for school visits, and both Minnesota and Louisiana each permit sixteen hours. An interesting model is Nevada. Rather than stipulating a particular time limitation, Nevada prohibits terminating employees who attend school conferences or respond to their children's emergencies.

One other category in which a clear difference can be determined between federal and state family-leave law is in the definition of "family" itself. Under the federal FMLA, an employee may take time off for an elderly parent but not for a parent-in-law. That is, a wife may take leave to care for her ill elderly mother but not for her husband's mother. Further, the FMLA does not allow time off to care for a grandparent. It should be noted also that same-sex partners, even under a legal domestic partnership agreement, of which there are many today, are not eligible for leave under the FMLA. However, three states have adopted legislation that expands the meaning of "family care," though not one recognizes same-sex partners. The three states include Hawaii (the state that came very close to legalizing same-sex marriages in 1998), which covers care for in-laws, grandparents, and grandparents-in-law, and Oregon and Vermont, both of which include the spouse's parent.

Table 5.3

## State Leave Policies that Exceed Federal FMLA Provisions (2000)

| State | Company size | Length of leave | Special medical needs | For school activities | Defines family more broadly |
|---|---|---|---|---|---|
| California | 5 or more workers | 12 weeks family + 4 months maternity | | 40 hrs/year but no more than 18 mo. | |
| Connecticut | 3+ workers for maternity | 16 weeks over 2 years | | | |
| Hawaii | 1 worker for maternity | | | | In-laws, grandparents, |
| Illinois | | | | 8 hrs/year | |
| Iowa | 4+ workers (maternity) | | | | |
| Kentucky | All workers for adoption | | | | |
| Louisiana | 25 workers for maternity | 4 months maternity | | 16 hrs/year | |
| Maine | 15+ workers | | | | |

130

| State | Eligibility | Family/maternity leave | Family medical leave | Hours/year | Notes |
|---|---|---|---|---|---|
| Massachusetts | 6+ workers for maternity | | 24 hrs/year for family med appts. | 24 hrs/year | |
| Minnesota | 21+ workers, birth/adoption | | | 16 hrs/year | |
| Montana | 1+ worker maternity | | | | |
| Nevada | | | | No limit and prevents termination | |
| New Hampshire | 6+ workers for maternity | | | | |
| Oregon | 25+ workers | 12 weeks family + 12 weeks maternity/yr | | | Includes spouse's parent |
| Rhode Island | | 13 weeks/yr | | | |
| Tennessee | | 4 months maternity | | | |
| Vermont | 10+ for child, 15 + for family | | 24 hrs/year for family but no more than 4+hrs every 30 days | 24 hrs/year up to 4 hrs a month | Includes spouse's parent |

*Source:* Table was compiled from data made available by the National Partnership for Women and Families.

131

Why particular states chose to extend their leave benefits beyond the federal law is, of course, open to question and begs for further research.[6] But more important than searching for some sort of theoretical framework to explain why family-leave laws were adopted by some states and not others, is the realization that whatever legislative activity occurred in the states also influenced the design of the federal FMLA in Washington. That is, while several family-leave bills were being debated before a reluctant Congress and a hostile White House between 1985 and 1992, state initiatives kept the issue alive. The lessons learned from the formulation and implementation of thirty-two different versions of leave policy within the states' "laboratories of democracy" (Osborne 1988) helped shape the final version of the Family and Medical Leave Act of 1993. From the size of companies to which it applied (50 or more employees), to the length of the leave (twelve weeks), to whether or not it would become "maternity," "parental," or "family" leave in its final form, can be traced back to many of the debates that emerged from state legislatures. How the FMLA was formulated and who the key actors were in designing it is the focus of discussion in the next chapter.[7]

## Notes

1. The Legal Realism practiced by Brandeis and Holmes at the turn of the century became the foundation for today's Critical Legal Studies (CLS). Officially created in 1977 during a national conference at the University of Wisconsin in Madison, CLS's original organizers were veterans of Vietnam War protests and the Civil Rights Movement. Proponents of CLS theory believe that law grows out of society's power relationship. The basic principle of CLS is that the law *is* politics and is neither neutral nor value free. Therefore, more attention should be devoted to the social context of the law. Subgroups within CLS include feminist legal theorists, who examine the role of gender in law, and critical race theorists (CRT), who are concerned with the role of race in the formulation and implementation of laws. Noted CLS theorists include Roberto Mangabeira Unger, Robert W. Gordon, Morton J. Horwitz, Duncun Kenney, and Katharine MacKinnon.

A good start for anyone interested in pursuing this topic of economic forces influencing or determining political outcomes or legal structures is Charles Beard's [1935] classic work, *An Economic Interpretation of the Constitution of the United States*, (1986), published by The Free Press.

2. The U.S. Department of Labor has always reported that there were thirty-four states with leave laws prior to the passage of the FMLA in 1993. However, the number can vary depending on how leave policy is defined. Also, the DOL includes the District of Columbia and Puerto Rico in its total of thirty-four states.

3. One of the concerns raised by opponents of paid leave is that it will be abused by unscrupulous employees who simply want time off from work with pay. However, even when leave is paid, as is the case under the five TDI programs, the average length of the leave taken has been consistently less than the maximum amount of weeks allotted. The Commission on Leave (1996) also found that leave-takers on average did

not take the maximum amount of time available to them. However, that leave, of course, was unpaid.

4. In 1987, when the first four states adopted family/parental leave policies, twenty-four other states failed to pass such a law, including California, Massachusetts, New Jersey, and Wisconsin. Wisconsin produced an interesting story in that the business community split over the proposed bill. The Wisconsin Manufacturers and Commerce Association supported it while the National Federation of Independent Business opposed the proposal. This may represent the only example of such a split in the business community over government-mandated family leave policy. See Wisensale's "Family Leave Legislation: State and Federal Initiatives."(1989b) *Family Relations*, 38: 182–189.

5. Efforts to cover more workers under the FMLA continue. However, in a 1997 study by the National Partnership for Women and Families, it was learned that even if the FMLA were expanded to cover more mid-sized companies, the vast majority of employers will not be covered, and nearly a third of the labor force will not have access to the law. Specifically, by setting the exemption at twenty-five workers in a company instead of its current level of fifty employees, the percentage of employers covered would increase from about 6 percent to slightly more than 11 percent. For employees, however, the 60 percent covered under the current law would rise to only slightly more than 70 percent.

6. One frame of reference worth exploring for explaining state action (or inaction) on family leave policy can be found in Daniel Elazar's work on political culture. In his classic work, *American Federalism: A View from the States* (1984), Elazar identifies three types of political culture that help explain why states with particular characteristics reject or adopt certain policies. For example, in a moralistic state, government is viewed in a positive light and there is a general willingness to practice redistributive policies and spend money on public welfare programs. Individualistic states, on the other hand, tend to distrust government, rely more on market forces to solve problems, and are reluctant to employ redistributive policies as a means of addressing social problems. Under Elazar's third category, the traditionalistic state, the role of government is to maintain the existing order, not reform it. A work that employs Elazar's model, and specifically explores political culture in shaping family policy in the states, is Shirley Zimmerman's *Family Policies and Family Well-being: The Role of Political Culture* (1992), published by Sage.

7. A good article that captures both state and federal initiatives during the late 1980s and early 1990s is Anya Bernstein's "Inside or Outside? The Politics of Family and Medical Leave" (1997) in the *Policy Studies Journal* 25, 1: 87–99. Bernstein looks at the formulation of the federal FMLA as well as the development of leave policy in three states (Connecticut, Tennessee, and Massachusetts). Particular attention is devoted to the role of interest groups.

# Chapter 6

# Federal Initiatives in Family Leave Policy: Formulation of the FMLA

As a California state legislator representing suburban constituents in the San Fernando Valley, a liberal stronghold northwest of Los Angeles, Democrat Howard Berman had risen to majority floor leader by his second term and prior to this thirty-fifth birthday. It was his legislative leadership position that enabled him to engineer a bill through the General Assembly in 1978 that provided a four-month disability leave for new mothers. Four years later, in 1982, while Berman was running for a U.S congressional seat, the California Federal Savings and Loan refused to reinstate Lillian Garland when she returned to work following the birth of her child. It was one of 300 cases filed by employees that year, claiming that their employers had violated the 1978 act. Cal Fed, however, was the only corporation to file a lawsuit in federal court, arguing that the law violated the company's basic right to design, implement, and monitor its own personnel policies (Elving 1995).

Incorporating the Garland case into his congressional campaign, Berman promised voters that, if elected, he would introduce a similar bill in Washington. Having won his congressional seat easily, Berman was in the second year of his first term when the Federal District Court ruled against his maternity leave law in California. The statute violated federal laws, stated the Court,

---

A portion of this chapter was published previously in *The New England Journal of Public Policy.* A short segment of that article is published here with permission. Steven K. Wisensale, 1999, "Family Values and Presidential Elections: The Use and Abuse of the Family and Medical Leave Act in the 1992 and 1996 Campaigns." *New England Journal of Public Policy* 15, 1: 35–50.

particularly the gender equity clause of the 1964 Civil Rights Act, because it did not permit men to take maternity leave. Echoes from *Lochner, Muller, Gilbert*, and the Pregnancy Disability Act could be heard in the distance. The issue of special treatment versus equal treatment had surfaced once again and feminists found themselves split on the issue. On one side were advocacy groups such as 9 to 5 and the Coalition for Reproductive Equality in the Workplace who were outraged by the District Court's ruling (Radigan 1988). On the other side stood the National Organization for Women (NOW) and the Women's Legal Defense Fund (WLDF) which strongly supported equal rights for women and opposed any "special treatment" approach for new or expectant moms (Jacobs and Davies 1994; Kantrowitz and Wingert 1986). Therefore, the Federal District Court's ruling in 1982 represents an extremely significant benchmark in the developmental history of the Family and Medical Leave Act. It forced the issue of equal vs. special treatment onto center stage, and women's groups had to wrestle with it prior to formulating any kind of leave policy.

As Berman moved to introduce his legislation at the federal level, he was shocked to learn that those he had counted as allies had become his opponents. "Berman did not need to be helped," writes Ron Elving in *Conflict and Compromise: How Congress Makes the Law*, "he had to be stopped" (Elving 1995, 20). Fearing that a narrow focus on maternity leave would be perceived as "special treatment," advocates for a national leave policy made their first important strategic move in their long march toward legislative success. Any bill introduced would have at its core a commitment to "equal treatment" for those seeking time off from work. Therefore, from 1985 when the first leave bill was introduced until 1993 when it was finally enacted into law, during which time it went through four major name changes and was subjected to at least twenty-three specific compromises, the proponents' devotion and loyalty to "equal treatment" never wavered.

In analyzing and explaining the formulation of the Family and Medical Leave Act of 1993, one may select from a variety of prisms through which to view its development and ultimate passage. There is, of course, the view from the White House, Capitol Hill, special interest groups, and key actors, not to mention the perspectives of political analysts and commentators. There are also multiple political theories from which to choose, as there are numerous sociological and economic explanations that could be utilized. However, the analytical framework to be employed here is somewhat unique in that it attempts to capture the important developmental states of the FMLA's evolution over an eight-year period. Simply stated, the legislation will be traced through its four major name changes. It is the author's belief that this approach, more than any other, captures the essence of what could be termed the "legislative DNA" of the Family and Medical Leave Act of 1993. By referring to specific titles that were used for the bill, and combining that information with the political climate that prevailed within each stage of development, one can paint a fairly clear picture of how and why the final version of the bill came to be. The four distinct periods as depicted by the bill's names are presented below. A chronology that traces leave policy in the United States in general is presented in Appendix B.

## The Family Employment Security Act of 1984

Often forgotten in discussions concerning the history of the FMLA is the fact that the initial bill was created to provide job security. It was also designed to address the issue of "special treatment" versus "equal treatment." In response to Representative Berman's efforts to apply his California law to the nation, a group of parental-leave advocates convened in Washington to not only divert Berman from his "special treatment" strategy, but to produce a bill of their own that was anchored to the principle of "equal treatment." The group included representatives from the Women's Legal Defense Fund (WLDF), the National Organization for Women (NOW), the Junior League, the National Council of Jewish Women (NCJW), and the Women's Equity Action League (WEAL).

Led by Donna Lenhoff, a young attorney from the Women's Legal Defense Fund (now known as the National Partnership for Women and Families), the group had at least three objectives. One, to stop Berman in his tracks and offer instead a completely new paradigm shift. That is, to craft model legislation with a focus on equal rather than special treatment. Two, to influence the legislative process that had already begun, particularly within key committees responsible for issues concerning children and families. And three, to decide whether or not any newly proposed legislation should be patterned after European leave policies that include a wage replacement.

Lenhoff, who is often referred to as the architect of the original family-leave bill, drafted a model statute and titled it the Family Employment Security Act. Its underlying strategy was fundamentally consistent with objective one of the newly formed working group. It was a "new bill aimed not at maternity leaves alone but at a broad and ambitious array of employee rights all rooted in the principle of equal treatment" (Elving 1995, 22). Written so that all workers could benefit, the proposed bill extended beyond the demands of motherhood. The insertion of the word "family" in the proposed bill should not be taken lightly. It meant that pregnancy, a child's illness, and a spouse's disability, regardless of gender, would be covered. Equally important, with the inclusion of "employment security" in the bill's title, it was clear that one's job would be guaranteed at the conclusion of the leave period. So although the FESA was never formally introduced in its original form, its two underlying principles of "family care" and "job security" would remain key components of proposed legislation, and ultimately be incorporated in the final version of the Family and Medical Leave Act of 1993. But perhaps most important, by simply creating the FESA (as primitive as it was), legislators were given an option much different from Berman's. Therefore, the focus of the debate changed considerably.

However, neutralizing Berman's strategy was only one piece of the puzzle. There was already a movement within Congress to at least get leave legislation on the agenda. George Miller, a liberal Democrat from California, had just created the new Committee on Children Youth and Families in the House, which he chaired. Although select committees have limited powers (they cannot propose legislation, amend existing laws, or take new proposals to the floor), they can raise the level of awareness among other legislators, seek and obtain media coverage, and push their issues into the public arena. Former Congressman Claude Pepper (D-FL), for example, was very successful in raising issues related to the nation's elderly when he chaired the House Select Committee on Aging. Miller's strategy was similar, except he focused most of his attention on child care. However, following a series of hearings in which several key witnesses broadened their comments on child care to include parental leave, Miller's interest slightly shifted. He and other members of his committee had to be persuaded by Lenhoff and her supporters that any leave legislation needed to be broad-based and constructed on a foundation of "equal treatment," not "special treatment." This became particularly problematic because Miller and Berman were both from California and had become close friends ( Elving 1995; Jacobs and Davies 1994).

By the early fall of 1984, important strategic decisions concerning the future of leave policy had been made. Miller and Berman had backed off on their "special treatment" approach and turned the issue over to the Congressional Caucus on Women's Issues (CCWI). This proved to be a significant development for two reasons. First, the CCWI was led by Patricia Schroeder, a liberal from Colorado who was the most senior Democratic congresswoman on Capital Hill and a champion of children's issues. Not only was Schroeder the co-chair of the CCWI, she was also a member of Miller's Select Committee on Children Youth and Families and held a seat on the all-important Education and Labor Committee as well. It was the latter committee that would most likely serve as the legislative incubator for a new leave bill. And second, Schroeder, the CCWI, and other family-leave advocates were in full agreement with the original FESA supporters that any proposed leave legislation should be broad-based in coverage. It was also decided that the first leave bill in the nation's history would be introduced in 1985. But at least one more important decision had to be finalized before the legislative strategy could be implemented.

The third objective of the FESA group was to decide to what extent any proposed legislation should be modeled after current European policies, specifically as it relates to some sort of wage replacement. Simply put, should the proposed bill include a provision for paid leave? Confronted with a conservative president in Ronald Reagan and a Congress that was growing more conservative with each passing election, the early supporters of family leave policy chose to avoid, as much as possible, a legislative battle that focused on the cost of a new entitlement program. By choosing the incremental course instead, Lenhoff, Schroeder, and other supporters attempted to defuse the opposition early on by not including a paid-leave provision in the original proposal. As a result, strong opposition on a large scale from such groups as the U.S. Chamber of Commerce and the National Association of Manufacturers was delayed until several years later when the cost issue would become an important part of the debate.[1]

### The Parental and Disability Leave Act of 1985

In 1984, Ronald Reagan was swept into office in a landslide victory that was even larger than his initial win against Jimmy Carter in 1980. Despite the fact that his first term was tainted by a sluggish economy, and the gain of thirty-four House seats in 1980 was practically eliminated in the 1982 congressional elections, the Republicans maintained their majority in the Senate in 1984, and gained even more seats in the House. For traditional Democrats, the writing was on the wall and the party was in disarray. In short, the political soil in Washington was not fertile for cultivating liberal ideas such as child care and family leave. Following Reagan's State of the Union Address in January 1985, Governor Bill Clinton of Arkansas offered a televised Democratic response. As founder and head of the Democratic Leadership Council, a group of moderate Democrats, Clinton called for a new Democratic Party with ideas very different from the past. "The 1984 election seemed to have cost the Democrats far more than just four years," wrote Ron Elving. "It seemed to have cost the party its hope" (1995, 37). It was within this political climate in which a popular Republican president, who was convinced that "government is not the solution but the problem," and a Congress, that was eager to cut existing programs rather than create new ones in an effort to erase a major budget deficit, that the first federal family-leave bill in the country's history was introduced.

On April 4, 1985, Pat Schroeder introduced the Parental and Disability

Leave Act on the floor of the House of Representatives of the 99th Congress. It had at least three distinct characteristics. First, the title itself indicated that Berman and the proponents of "special treatment" legislation had been silenced and advocates for "equal treatment" had prevailed. The use of the term "parental" instead of "maternal" clearly eliminated any gender differences, and the use of the word "disability" extended the coverage beyond childbirth. Second, the bill number assigned to it, 2020, was indicative of a House leadership that did not give leave legislation a high priority. The lower the number assigned to a bill, the more likely it will pass during a legislative session. A 2020 number offered little hope. And third, and perhaps most surprising, in her haste to compose the proposed bill, Schroeder failed to recruit any cosponsors. Born to a single mother in an institution dominated by males, HR 2020 was destined to experience an early childhood filled with neglect and abuse (Radigan 1988).

In its original form, the bill required all businesses to provide at least eighteen weeks of unpaid leave for mothers or fathers of newborn or newly adopted children. For those with temporary disabilities that were not related to work and for employees who had ill children, twenty-six weeks of unpaid leave were mandated. In addition to these provisions, health insurance and other personal benefits would be continued during the employee's absence, and one's job would be guaranteed upon returning to work. It did not specify the size of companies to which the law would apply, nor did it provide for paid leave. However, the bill called for the creation of a special study commission to explore the possible options available for providing some sort of wage replacement. Compared to similar policies already adopted by countries in Europe and Scandinavia, this proposal was extremely limited. And yet, despite that, it still received a cold reception from Congress.

After being introduced, the Schroeder bill was quickly assigned to two committees, Education and Labor being one, and the Post Office and Civil Service Committee being the other. From each of these committees it was then assigned to appropriate subcommittees, a total of four in all. The former body, of which Schroeder was a member, was dominated by old-guard male Democrats who were not particularly sensitive to work and family issues at the time and viewed such legislation as "yuppie bills" (Jacobs and Davies 1994). However, it was generally believed that to be successful, HR 2020 would need strong support from Education and Labor. With respect to the Post Office and Civil Service Committee, 2020 would receive a much warmer reception because Schroeder served as the chair of one of its subcommittees. And indeed, on October 17, 1985, after months of delays and repeated efforts to get HR 2020 on the legislative calendar, the Colorado congresswoman held the first hearing on a federal leave bill in history—though the room was practically empty and the witness list was short (Elving 1995). However, it eventually moved successfully through two subcommittees before stalling in the summer of 1986.

The reasons underlying the bill's problems are not difficult to identify. There had been four hearings on HR 2020 by December 1985, but the substance of the bill had not been fully debated. Although forty members had eventually signed on as cosponsors, conspicuously absent were some key women legislators and the chairmen of the two committees called upon to usher the bill through Congress. When Schroeder voted against a plant-closing bill that had become the pet project of the Education and Labor Committee, she alienated the very legislators she needed to engineer her proposal through the committee process and onto the floor of the House. Consequently, advocates outside Congress but inside the beltway began to question whether or not she was becoming a liability. And finally, not to be overlooked was the glaring fact that no one in the Senate had produced a companion bill (Elving 1995). But at least a bill had been proposed in the House that was beginning to generate some interest on Capitol Hill and even in the media.

Meanwhile, about the time HR 2020 was being born, other relevant events were unfolding. In April 1985, the U.S. Ninth Circuit Court of Appeals in San Francisco overruled the 1984 decision of the Federal District Court that declared Berman's maternity-leave bill unconstitutional. However, and most important for the "equal treatment" advocates, the Appeals Court did not disagree with the lower court's emphasis on equal treatment; it opposed the decision that confined the concept of equality solely to pregnancy. That is, stated the Court, it was the intent of Congress in passing the Pregnancy Discrimination Act "to construct a floor beneath which pregnancy disability benefits may not drop, not a ceiling above which they may not rise" (*California Federal Savings and Loan Association v. Guerra* 1985, 11). For people like Schroeder, Lenhoff, and other advocates of broad-based leave legislation, the Ninth Circuit's ruling merely fortified their position on equal treatment.

Another significant event occurred several months later about the time a revised leave bill was being crafted and introduced in Congress. In January 1987, the U.S. Supreme Court, after hearing a final appeal from Cal Fed, upheld the California statute (the Berman law) by a 6 to 3 vote. Ruling that the California law neither violated federal law nor discriminated against men, the majority of the Court concluded that by recognizing pregnancy, California's pregnancy disability-leave law permits women as well as men to support their families without losing their jobs. In other words, the "statute does not compel California employers to treat pregnant workers better than other disabled employees, but merely establishes the benefits that employers must, at a minimum, provide to pregnant workers" (Jacobs and Davies 1994, 97). Once again an important court ruling provided an impetus for those who supported a broad-based leave policy. And, as will be learned later, a bill with expanded coverage will attract more supporters. This occurred after a newer version of the original Schroeder bill was introduced in 1987.

## Parental and Medical Leave Act of 1986

With doubts growing about Schroeder's ability to maneuver a leave bill through an unfriendly Education and Labor Committee, supporters of the legislation sought out another lead sponsor in the House and searched for a senator willing to offer a companion bill in the other chamber. Selected to assist Schroeder was Representative William Clay, who chaired one of the four subcommittees (Labor Management) to which HR 2020 was originally assigned in 1985. Clay was one of the early cosponsors of the bill and was respected by his colleagues. Secure in his district, he felt comfortable in assuming a leadership role and pushing an issue that he knew would eventually draw strong opposition from conservative legislators. Clay and his staff adopted a different title and drafted new paragraphs designed to address concerns that were ignored in the original Schroeder bill.

Because some advocates of the handicapped found the use of the term "disability" in HR 2020 to be offensive, the title of the bill was changed from the Parental and Disability Leave Act to the Parental and Medical Leave Act. As a result, the handicapped were no longer offended by the language, the use of the term "medical" appealed to an even broader audience, and by maintaining the word "parental" in the title, gender differences and the "special treatment" issue were neutralized. Other important decisions were made as well. The wording on job security was clarified to satisfy the concerns of labor unions. The question of whether or not women could use leave time to have abortions was handled by addressing it in a committee report but not including such language in the bill itself. Proponents feared that such a provision would only serve as a lightning rod and distort the debate. After all, the U.S. Catholic Conference was a very influential ally that the parental leave coalition could not afford to lose (Elving 1995; Jacobs and Davies 1994; Radigan 1988). And because the word "medical" had been inserted in the title of the revised bill, the language of the proposed legislation had to be reconstructed to more clearly define the meaning of the term "serious health condition," an allowable reason for missing work. As will be discussed in the succeeding chapter, this term has become quite contentious and the focal point of numerous court battles (Wisensale 1999d).

But while the House version of the bill was undergoing a major renova-

141

tion, a process that was successful in attracting more cosponsors, movement in the Senate was slow at first. However, Senator Christopher Dodd, a Democrat from Connecticut, willingly volunteered to introduce a companion bill. As a member of the Labor and Human Resources Committee and the ranking member of the Subcommittee on Children, Family, Drugs, and Alcohol, Dodd had become a strong advocate for children's issues in general and for a national child-care program in particular. He was familiar with the "child and family" coalition that had formed on Capitol Hill over the years, and was enthusiastic about supporting them on family leave. When Clay and Schroeder introduced their bill, HR 4300, in the House on March 4, 1986, Dodd followed with an almost identical bill (S 2278) in the Senate on April 6.

Over the next eight to nine months, as each of the bills worked their way through the complicated committee system, at least three significant developments occurred. First, both bills attracted much bipartisan support, clearly a good sign for the proponents. In the House, liberal to moderate Republicans such as Hamilton Fish and Bill Green of New York, Silvio Conte of Massachusetts, and Stewart McKinney of Connecticut signed on early. Others, including some conservatives, would gradually follow. In the Senate, only one Republican, Arlen Specter of Pennsylvania, joined Democratic Senators Dodd, Kennedy, and Moynihan as a cosponsor early on. But as was the case in the House, other Republicans would slowly move to the other side as important compromises were struck and a revised bill not only became more appealing to them, but also offered them political cover in upcoming elections. That is, once key Republicans moved to support the bill, others could more easily follow without paying the ultimate price at the polls on election day.

A second development that occurred after the Parental and Medical Leave Act was introduced in both houses was the series of debates that took place over particular provisions in the bill. Specifically, Marge Roukema (R-NJ), a ranking member of the all-important Education and Labor Committee, led the charge in the House by demanding that major changes be made in the bill. She argued that the twenty-six week medical leave provision should be reduced to thirteen weeks, and the eighteen-week parental leave option be cut to just eight weeks. She also called for a predetermined employment period that employees had to complete prior to being declared eligible for leave benefits. And, perhaps most important, she demanded that the bill apply to only those companies with fifty or more employees. The original HR 2020 applied to all companies regardless of size. HR 4300 established a cutoff at five employees. If her demands were met, Roukema argued, more Republicans could be recruited and the chances of the bill's being passed would improve greatly. By the time the FMLA was signed into law in 1993, almost two dozen important compromises had been made. Remarkably, almost all of Roukema's demands were included in the final version.

The third important development to occur during this stage was the awakening of the business community. In the early months of 1986 the U.S. Chamber of Commerce distributed a letter to each of its members informing them that a coalition in opposition to the parental leave bill had formed and they were encouraged to join the battle. Similar actions were taken by the National Federation of Independent Business (NFIB) and the National Association of Manufacturers (NAM). The NFIB even ran an ongoing poll among its 600,000 members to both remind them that the leave bill was still alive and well in Congress and to monitor their views on the proposed legislation. From 1986 to 1992, the NFIB consistently reported that 85 percent of its members opposed a government-mandated parental leave policy. Clearly, the die had been cast and the question of cost had entered the debate. And, quite predictably, as the bill moved closer to passage the cost issue rose in importance.

By mid-June of 1986 the proponents of HR 4300 were under pressure, not only to produce a favorable vote out of the Education and Labor Committee but to make certain there was evidence of strong bipartisan support for the proposal. The concerns raised by Marge Roukema were addressed directly. The company size was increased from five employees to fifteen (Roukema had wanted a cut-off at fifty employees). Eligibility for leave was set at 500 hours or three months, and the total time allocated for either medical or parental leave was set at thirty-six weeks over two years. However, perhaps the most significant adjustment was to make the bill intergenerational. That is, a worker could take time off to care for a child, teenager, spouse, or elderly parent. This recommendation prompted the fourth and final name change. From this point forward, the title of the bill in the House would be the Family and Medical Leave Act. In the Senate, the title (Parental and Medical Leave Act) would remain the same for another year or two.

The difference in the two titles was indicative of a potentially serious rift that was emerging within the proleave coalition. The Children's Defense Fund and the Junior League preferred "Parental" primarily because it implied care of children. Both groups were in the midst of a battle for a national child-care bill and needed Congress to think in terms of children rather than "family." Also, a narrower "parental" focus would be less expensive because fewer workers would need time off from work. Two other groups, the American Association of Retired Persons and the U.S. Catholic Conference, preferred "family" in the title because it recognized the importance of the extended family and multigenerational relationships. Besides, they contended, a bill with a broader focus would attract more supporters. It should be noted that Senator Dodd wrestled with this issue for several years before eventually adopting "family," a decision that disappointed Marian Wright Edelman, director of the Children's Defense Fund (Elving 1995).[2]

## The Family and Medical Leave Act of 1987

As the 99th Congress came to a close and members returned to their home districts to campaign for the 1986 elections, the newly named Family and Medical Leave Act met its predicted fate. Despite major changes, the bill emerged from the Education and Labor Committee with a favorable but partisan vote. By September, the Democratic leadership in the House concluded that the bill was not ready for a floor vote and suggested that it be introduced again in 1987. The companion bill in the Senate experienced even less success. However, in the November elections the Democrats reclaimed power. As a result, Ted Kennedy (D-MA) replaced Republican Orrin Hatch as the chair of the Labor and Human Services Committee, and Chris Dodd assumed the chair of an important subcommittee (Children, Family, Drugs, and Alcoholism) that was previously held by Republican Strom Thurmond of South Carolina. Thus, as the 100th session of Congress convened in January 1987, supporters of family leave had at least two reasons for feeling optimistic: Democrats controlled both houses and Ronald Reagan had only two years remaining in his term.

The provisions of the FMLA in the House (HR 925) and Senate (249) versions were quite similar. However, each followed a path that was noticeably different. In the House, the opposition from business organizations intensified, with the U.S. Chamber of Commerce referring to it as a "mandated benefit" (Rovner 1987). But the most serious threat came from Marge Roukema (R-NJ), who was relentless in her effort to soften the bill, arguing that the cutoff for company size should be set at 100 employees and the duration of the leave should be considerably reduced. Roukema, who introduced her own bill (HR 284), also insisted employers be permitted to exempt any employee from the law who was in the top 10 percent of the firm's salary bracket (*National NOW Times* 1987). Following a series of meetings among key actors, a compromise was struck that set the company size at fifty, reduced family leave from eighteen to ten weeks (every two years), and shortened medical leave from twenty-six weeks to fifteen over a one-year period.

Although the new configuration of the bill did not appease the business community (forty-three groups made up the anti-FMLA coalition by this time), it did appeal to such Republicans as Olympia Snowe (R-ME), Nancy Johnson (R-CT), and James Jeffords (R-VT) (Jacobs and Davies 1994; Radigan 1988). But perhaps most important, on November 10, 1987, Bill Clay, Pat Schroeder, and Marge Roukema held a joint news conference in which they expressed their belief that the revised bill (Roukema's bill) would pass the House. Although it received a favorable bipartisan 21–11 vote in the Education and Labor Committee in November, and passed through the Post

Office Committee in February, it never reached the House floor. Legislators were gearing up for the 1988 election, and because there appeared to be little movement on the bill in the Senate, House members saw no need to vote on it before the election. "My colleagues want to support the bill but don't want to vote on it," quipped Norm Mineta (D-CA), who headed up a special "whip task force" that was assigned to the FMLA (Elving 1995, 105).

Meanwhile, in the Senate, Dodd's Parental and Medical Leave Act had moved slowly. Although the Connecticut senator was not opposed to broadening the language of the bill so as to include care for elderly parents and spouses, he was concerned that such a step may result in children being shortchanged. After all, it was Dodd who was also trying to maneuver a child-care bill through the Senate at the same time he was arguing for parental leave. Not only was the child-care coalition forced to divide its lobbying efforts between the two legislative initiatives, but Dodd found himself wedged in the middle. Concerned about the status of his leave bill, he replaced "parental" with "family" in the title, reworked it during the summer, and saw that it was assigned a new number (HR 2488). Like the House version, Dodd's revamped bill allowed ten weeks for family leave but offered less (only thirteen weeks) for an employee's own illness. On the other hand, its coverage was broader than the House version because it applied to all businesses with twenty or more employees, compared to the fifty-worker cutoff under HR 925.

Dodd's strategy paid off. In the fall of 1988, and just prior to the elections, he moved it quickly through his subcommittee and then on to Ted Kennedy's Senate Education and Labor Committee where it received a favorable vote before being sent to the floor for debate. However, such rapid progress was not possible without a price. To address the concerns of his opponents, Dodd lowered the thirteen-week period for an employee's own illness to ten and increased the employee cutoff from twenty to fifty. In doing so, he achieved two important objectives at once. First, he brought his bill in line with the House version. It is always desirable to have two similar, if not identical, bills moving through Congress simultaneously. And second, it was Dodd who took the cost issue head on. When the U.S. Chamber of Commerce claimed the FMLA would cost at least $2 billion and perhaps as much as $16 billion, it was Dodd who called for a fiscal impact study from the General Accounting Office (GAO), which proved that the COC had inflated its numbers.[3] The GAO reported that the annual cost under the fifty-employee cutoff provision would be between $188 and $236 million, a far cry from the Chamber of Commerce's estimate. (United States General Accounting Office 1988). But despite such major compromises, actions that threatened to destroy a once solid family-leave coalition, the bill still met resistance from Senate Republicans who frustrated Dodd and other advocates by introducing controversial amendments and orchestrating a procedural filibuster (Jacobs and Davies 1994). By October 7, 1988, Senate Majority Leader Robert Byrd (D-WV) accused Republicans of being antifamily and pulled the bill from the floor (Morehouse 1988).

After the votes were counted in the 1988 election, Vice President George Bush had defeated Democratic opponent Michael Dukakis of Massachusetts. But although the Republicans retained control of the White House, the Democrats still controlled the House and Senate. And while the proposed child-care bill showed early signs of passing during the 101st Congress, less optimism was expressed about the future of the Family and Medical Leave Act. Looking back over the eight-year struggle, it is easy to understand why 1988 was the low point in the FMLA's development. It had been stalled in both houses for three years and the incoming president not only campaigned against it, but promised to veto the bill if Congress passed it.

During the next four years, several important events occurred that had a major impact on the outcome of the FMLA. First, by 1990, the Democrats succeeded in pushing through a child-care bill that George Bush reluctantly signed. Although it was watered down significantly and limited to lower income families, its passage was particularly relevant to FMLA advocates because child-care and family-leave proponents would no longer have to divide their time fighting battles on two fronts.

Second, the Democrats were successful in persuading high-ranking Republicans to cross over and support the FMLA. For example, in the House, Illinois Republican Henry Hyde, a strong pro-life advocate and an early opponent of family leave, spoke in favor of the bill after he was persuaded that the FMLA would help lower the abortion rate. If women wanted to maintain their careers, a leave policy would allow them to have children and still work. Aborting a fetus in order to save one's job could be avoided, thanks to the FMLA. Such logic also appealed to Republican Christopher Smith of New Jersey who also "moved to the other side." In the Senate, Kit Bond (R-MO) stands as an example of a Republican who crossed over. Such actions provided the necessary political cover other legislators needed to avoid jeopardizing their seats if they voted "yea" on family leave.

And third, as the compromises on each of the bills attracted more legislators to move to the other side, the votes in favor of the proposal began to increase, both in committee actions and on the floor of the House and Senate. By 1990, the Democratic leaders in both houses were convinced they had enough votes to pass the leave bill, but not enough to override an expected Bush veto, particularly in the House. If nothing else, the bill was at least "veto bait" that could be used against the Republicans in the 1990 congressional elections. On the Republican side, however, Senate Minority Leader

Bob Dole (R-KS) saw things differently. By allowing the leave bill to move through both chambers and on to the White House, it would give George Bush the opportunity to have one more of his vetoes sustained. By this time he had vetoed twelve pieces of legislation without being overridden once by Congress (Elving 1995; Jacobs and Davies 1994). Besides, Bush signed the child-care bill, a civil rights law, and the Americans with Disabilities Act in 1990. He believed he could afford a veto of family leave without appearing to abandon the "kinder, gentler America" pledge he made during his acceptance speech at his party's nominating convention two years earlier.

After passing in the House by a vote of 237–187 and by a voice vote in the Senate, President Bush kept his promise and vetoed the measure in June 1990. And, as was predicted, the House failed to override it a month later, falling short of the necessary two-thirds majority by fifty-three votes. But if 1988 was the low point for the proponents of family leave, 1990 can be identified as the major turning point of the battle. Not only had the bill passed in both chambers for the first time, but George Bush's veto put the monkey on the back of the GOP forever (Elving 1995). Unbeknownst to many Republicans (and Democrats, too), "family values" would infiltrate the next two presidential campaigns and the family leave bill would play a special role in each. In a strategic move, the Democrats deliberately held back the FMLA in 1991 and waited patiently, with their political snare in place, for the next election.[4]

## Family Values, Family Leave, and the 1992 Election

Family values, as a campaign issue, was catapulted onto the 1992 presidential campaign by a rather convoluted assortment of characters and events that included Rodney King, a victim of police brutality; a riot in South Central Los Angeles that followed a controversial jury verdict; a fictitious TV character and single mom, Murphy Brown; a feisty vice president, Dan Quayle; a special speech on families delivered in Cleveland by candidate Bill Clinton; and a night devoted to "family values" at the Republican Party's nominating convention. The ultimate outcome was the election of a new president, a reassessment of how seemingly unrelated events can shape social policy in America, and the push to get more family-oriented issues onto the political agenda. How and why this has occurred deserves some explanation.

In the spring of 1992, several Los Angeles police officers who were accused of excessive force in the videotaped beating of Rodney King, an African-American male who was stopped for a traffic violation, were acquitted by an all-white jury in a conservative suburban community of Los Angeles. The verdict produced a riot in the predominantly black community of South

Central Los Angeles, resulting in numerous deaths and major losses of property. Several days later, Dan Quayle appeared on national television and blamed the L.A. riots on the deterioration of the American family. He also blamed Hollywood for its anti-family bias that produced such shows as *Murphy Brown*, in which the main character, a highly successful career woman, chose to have a child through artificial insemination and raise it without a father. This outburst by Quayle prompted a response from the Democratic Party's leading candidate for the presidential nomination.

In early May, approximately two weeks after Dan Quayle's attack on *Murphy Brown*, Bill Clinton delivered a speech in Cleveland, Ohio, in which he outlined his "eight-point plan on the American family." His proposal included an intense media campaign to combat teen pregnancy, an $800-per-child tax credit for preschool children, an expansion of the Earned Income Tax Credit, a greater emphasis on child support, a call for more child-sensitive divorce laws, more parental responsibility, greater emphasis placed on family preservation programs, and the adoption of a family-leave policy (Marshall and Schram 1993).

Two months later, the Republicans devoted an entire evening to "family values" at their nominating convention while a Democratic Congress sought to embarrass President Bush by pressuring him to sign the Family and Medical Leave Act. Beginning on the eve of the Republican National Convention, the Senate approved its version of the bill by a voice vote on August 11. Although Senator Dodd favored a roll-call vote, Republican leaders threatened to block it, thus preventing the bill from leaving the Senate before the August recess, scheduled to begin August 13.

Over several months, Republican Senators Kit Bond of Missouri and Dan Coats of Indiana, and Congressmen Tom Coleman of Missouri, Bill Young of Florida, and James Saxton of New Jersey, were recruited through a variety of Democratic concessions. But in spite of growing support from such conservative Republicans, the Bush administration continued to oppose the proposed legislation. "They were not willing to deal," stated Bond. "I think the president is just plain wrong on this . . . and . . . it is a failure to reinforce what is a very important part of his platform" (*Congressional Quarterly Almanac* 1992).

As the 1992 presidential campaign continued, the House passed the measure on September 10 by a 241–161 vote. The Republicans described the bill as an election-year ploy designed to embarrass Bush. On September 16, the President announced an alternative to the Democratic bill. Instead of government mandates, he argued, businesses should be offered tax incentives. That is, a refundable tax credit of 20 percent of compensation, from $100 a week to a maximum total of $1,200, would be available for all businesses with fewer than 500 employees if they provide at least twelve weeks of family leave. More important, argued the president, his proposal would have covered about 15 million more workers and twenty times the number of workplaces than the Democratic version.

The day after his announcement, Congress sent its bill to the White House for Bush's promised veto. For Roukema, a longtime supporter of family leave, Bush's alternative was "an interesting supplement to the basic bill. But it is no substitute. To use the tax incentives does not give the job guarantee," she said (*Congressional Quarterly Almanac* 1992). Republican Congressmen Dick Armey of Texas, who opposed family leave from its inception, described the timing of Bush's proposal as "unfortunate." "To the extent the President's proposal is political, it's in response to the timing of the Democrats," Armey continued. "They thought this is a great time to embarrass the President by sending him a family leave bill so close to the election" (*Congressional Quarterly Almanac* 1992).

With Congress ignoring his pleas, Bush vetoed the Family and Medical Leave Act for a second time on September 22. "I want to strongly reiterate that I have always supported employer policies to give time off for a child's birth or adoption or for family illness and believe it is important that employers offer these benefits," he stated in his veto message. "I object, however, to the federal government mandating leave policies for America's employers and work force" (U.S. Executive Office of the President 1992).

Two days later, and after four years and thirty-two vetoes from President Bush, the Senate finally produced enough votes to override his opposition to a bill. Voting 68–31, two votes more than the two-thirds necessary, the Senate refused to sustain the President's veto on September 24. Within a week, however, the House failed to override the veto. On September 30, by a vote of 258–169, the veto override attempt fell short by twenty-seven votes. Not to be overlooked is the fact that forty-two Democrats voted to sustain the President's position (Elving 1995). The bill was dead for the 102nd Congress.

In November, Bill Clinton became the first Democrat to be elected president in twelve years. With his victory, the 103rd Congress underwent a major transformation. The 1992 elections produced 110 new House members and thirteen new senators, including unprecedented numbers of women and minorities. In the Senate, the number of women increased from two to six; in the House the number of women grew from twenty-nine to forty-eight. But the newcomers did little to change the partisan composition of the two houses. The Democrats' fifty-seven to forty-three advantage in the Senate was identical to that of the 102nd Congress, and the 258 to 176 to 1 House edge represented a loss of only ten seats (Bernie Sanders of Vermont is the "one" independent in the House). In contrast to the Reagan-Bush era, there would be little discussion of the number of votes necessary to override presidential vetoes, at least among Democrats. Owing perhaps to the near doubling of females in Congress, family-oriented issues in general, and the family-leave bill in particular, received increased attention even before Bill Clinton was sworn into office.

Between Election Day and Inauguration Day, both the House (265–163) and the Senate (71–27) acted favorably on the Family and Medical Leave Act. Key players in the legislative debate assumed predictable positions on the political territory they had staked out as early as 1985. The National Federation of Independent Businesses, the National Association of Manufacturers, the U.S. Chamber of Commerce, and the Concerned Alliance of Responsible Employers argued against the bill. They were countered again by the American Association of Retired Persons, the Children's Defense Fund, the National Organization of Women, and the Women's Legal Defense Fund. Unlike the child-care coalition of the 1970s that weakened over an eight-year period, the FMLA coalition grew stronger by making the bill more appealing to the undecided and by slowly converting some old adversaries. "By making common cause with antiabortion conservatives, the basic core of feminists and liberals had performed the essential trick that turns ideas into laws. They surrounded the opposition and minimized it" (Elving 1995, 290).

In essence, the long battle drew to a close when Congressman Henry Hyde, the conservative Republican from Illinois, took the floor of the House just weeks before Clinton's inauguration and spoke in favor of the FMLA. It was Hyde, an influential figure among House Republicans, who was persuaded two years earlier to support the bill because it may reduce abortions. While this image may serve as a description of what happened in the end, an explanation of how it all came about might be found in the statement of two key antagonists. "It hurt us to see it referred to as 'watered down,' but it helped with the numbers," explained Donna Lenhoff of the Women's Legal Defense Fund (now the National Partnership for Women and Families), describing the proponents' legislative strategy to capture more votes (Elving 1995, 288). On the other side, Mary Tavenner of the Concerned Alliance of Responsible Employers said, "If we had not been there, family leave would have passed as written. We made them change it. The bill became more and more 'reasonable' until inevitably some businesses were neutralized" (Elving 1995, 290).

When Bill Clinton affixed his signature to the Family and Medical Leave Act in February 1993, it was the very first major piece of legislation signed by the new president. As a result, employees in companies with fifty or more workers have the right to twelve weeks of unpaid leave to care for a child, a spouse, an ailing parent, or themselves. The bill also guarantees job security and requires an employer to continue healthcare benefits during the leave of absence. Finally, the act permits a company to deny leave to a salaried employee who falls within the top 10 percent of its paid workforce. All told, it applies to about 6 percent of the nation's employers and roughly 60 percent of the American labor force.

Ironically, the bill that Clinton signed into law was, in essence, a Republican product. It was very similar to the proposal Marge Roukema (R-NJ) introduced in 1987. But such an outcome may say more about the location of the Democratic Party on the political spectrum in the 1990s than it does about the skill and ingenuity of Republican legislators. With the passage of the FMLA, however, at least three perplexing questions emerged. One, why did President Bush wait so long to offer an alternative to the Democrats' proposal, particularly if he believed the opposition party was deliberately out to embarrass him over the family-values issue? In short, why did he not put forth his tax incentive proposal sooner? Two, with Clinton riding high on a presidential victory that brought with it a Democratic-controlled Congress, why did he not seize the opportunity to push for a much stronger family-leave bill? Why, especially during the honeymoon phase of his administration when his political influence was probably at its zenith, did the newly elected president choose to settle for the minimum, and thus provide the nation with one more example of what some may label as symbolic politics? And three, because it is unpaid and applies to only 6 percent of the corporations and about 60 percent of workers, how effective can it be in addressing the caregiving needs of America's families?

**Family Values and Family Leave in the 1996 Election**

What worked for the Democrats in the 1992 election was employed again in 1996. Choosing "Families First" as their campaign theme, the Democrats captured, at least temporarily, what Steiner (1981) refers to as "the higher moral ground" on family values. Bill Clinton reminded voters that the Family and Medical Leave Act was the first bill he ever signed as president and that his opponent, Bob Dole, had voted against it twice and repeatedly organized Republican efforts to kill the initiative on the Senate floor.

Most blatantly, perhaps, the Democrats selected September 24, 1996, as "Family Leave Day" to remind voters that on that date four years earlier, Bob Dole had voted to uphold George Bush's veto of the bill. Family advocates, business leaders, and key legislators across the country held special news events in forty-four states not only to highlight the success of President Clinton's Family and Medical leave Act, but to bash Bob Dole in the process. This approach was similar to Clinton's campaign efforts in forty-six states on September 18, which drew attention to the administration's anti-crime record. That event alone generated more than 500 local television news stories (Clinton-Gore Press Office 1996).

Family Leave Day was developed by Ann F. Lewis, the deputy campaign manager for communications. She was assisted by Stephanie Foster, manager of the campaign's women's outreach initiatives; Stacie Spector, the deputy communications director for field communications; and Donna Lenhoff, the author of the very first family-leave bill and a volunteer on leave from the Women's Legal Defense Fund. President Clinton, Vice President Gore, First Lady Hillary Rodham Clinton, and Tipper Gore kicked off the nationwide events in New Jersey, Louisiana, Connecticut, and Tennessee, respectively (Clinton-Gore Press Office 1996).

In a brief twenty-three minute talk in front of a Freehold, New Jersey, Revolutionary War monument, President Clinton reminded his audience that it was his administration that enacted the Family and Medical leave Act. "You hear people talking all the time about family values. Well, if we're going to talk about family values, shouldn't we value families?" the president asked. "I never go anywhere in America—never—that I don't meet families who have at least one or two examples in their own lives where they have felt the wrenching conflict between their responsibilities to their children or their parents, and their responsibilities at work" (*Home News Tribune* 1996). Standing by his side were David Del Vecchio, a candidate for the 12th District, and Congressman Bob Torricelli, the candidate who was seeking to capture the U.S. Senate seat vacated by fellow Democrat Bill Bradley.

Campaigning in Southern states where Republicans had strong support, Vice President Gore appealed to moderate voters by pushing the president's proposal to expand the existing Family and Medical Leave Act to cover short periods of unpaid time off for medical appointments and PTA meetings. Speaking in Shreveport, Louisiana, the vice president also took a swipe at Bob Dole for his position on family leave. "Again, if we're going to say we value strong families . . . then we've got to be willing to put our laws where our political rhetoric is" (Associated Press News Service 1996, 2). Mary Landrieu, Louisiana's Democratic candidate for the U.S. Senate, was standing by the vice president's side. "Guess who voted against it?" Landrieu asked the crowd of supporters. "Bob Dole, six times" (Associated Press News Service 1996, 2).

Hillary Rodham Clinton, speaking at Connecticut College in New London, Connecticut, on September 24, reminded the audience that it was her husband who signed the FMLA and that it was Bob Dole who opposed it. She emphasized again that "while Republicans talk about family values, Democrats prove that they value families" (*Connecticut Post* 1981, A-1). Representatives from two families that used family leave in the past appeared on stage with the First Lady and thanked the Clinton White House for signing the bill. Her visit also aimed to boost Congressman Sam Gejdenson's reelection bid. Just two years earlier he had defeated his opponent by only twenty-one votes.

Appearing at several rallies in Tennessee on September 24, Tipper Gore also highlighted the virtues of family leave while reminding voters that Bob Dole's labeling of Bill Clinton as a liberal was a distortion. "When I think of this administration, 'liberal' does not come to mind. We're very much middle of the road. The Democratic campaign's emphasis on family issues and values could be labeled conservative," she said (*Johnson City Press* 1996, A-1). Mrs. Gore appeared with Tennessee politicians who had supported the FMLA and several families who had benefited from it. She visited the Johnson City Medical Center Children's Hospital and participated in a round-table discussion at the Ronald McDonald House nearby. She later joined another round-table discussion on the attributes of the FMLA at a private home in Clarksville.

Concurrently, similar events were being held across the country. Department of Labor Secretary Robert Reich participated in radio interviews in Boston and Worcester, Massachusetts. In Florida, Governor Lawton Chiles held a news conference at Wackenhutt Security Firm in West Palm Beach. In Atlanta, at a Ben and Jerry's ice cream shop, Vicki and George Yandle, who participated in the White House signing ceremony in 1993, held a news conference and described the benefits of the FMLA. In Indianapolis, Indiana, Governor Evan Bayh sponsored a workshop on father-friendly workplaces. Of all the Family Leave Day events organized in forty-four states, very few did not include politicians who were competing for office. Clearly, the Family and Medical Leave Act had become valuable political currency for Democrats in the 1996 campaign.

But while the Democrats continued to hit Bob Dole over the head with the family-leave issue in 1996 as they had done with George Bush four years earlier, the Republican response was ineffective. Candidate Dole continued to emphasize that he had opposed the bill in 1992 and that he would do so again if he were still in the Senate and it came to the floor for a vote.[5] Instead of taking family leave head-on, Bob Dole and the Republicans attempted to corner Bill Clinton on family values by forcing two pieces of controversial legislation onto the president's desk in the summer before the election: the Welfare Reform Act of 1996 and the Defense of Marriage Act.

With respect to the former act, Clinton disarmed the Republicans by stating that he would sign what many considered to be a harsh bill. Viewing it as "veto bait" that could be used against him later in the campaign, as the family-leave bill was used against Bush in 1992, the president alienated many loyalists and lost some key White House staffers when he placed his signature on the legislation in August. However, his opponent could not accuse him of being soft on welfare during the campaign.[6]

With respect to the Defense of Marriage Act (DOMA), Clinton found himself negotiating a political minefield that was saturated with family values.

Following a December 1995 court ruling in Hawaii that legalized same-sex marriages (it was eventually defused via a state referendum opposing such marriages), state legislatures and members of Congress moved quickly to inoculate themselves against the recognition of such marital unions in other states or by the federal government. The passage of DOMA, clearly earmarked as veto bait by White House insiders, was part of a Republican strategy to embarrass the same president who spoke out strongly for gay rights in the military early in his first term. A veto of the bill would jump-start a lethargic, if not dead, Dole camp just in time for the home-stretch of the campaign.

Instead, President Clinton heeded the words of his trusted adviser, Dick Morris, and practiced triangulation. It was the same strategy Clinton had applied to the Welfare Reform Act.[7] Unlike the Family and Medical Leave Act signed by Clinton with much fanfare in the White House Rose Garden on February 5, 1993, the Defense of Marriage Act was signed at 12:50 A.M. on the morning of September 21, 1996, just six weeks before the election, by a president sitting alone in the Oval Office. When he refused to bend to gay activists who demanded that he pull Democratic campaign spots on Christian radio stations that praised him for signing DOMA, the president was then heeding the advice offered by Robert Byrd on the floor of the U.S. Senate during a heated debate over the bill. "At some point," stated the West Virginia Democrat, "a line must be drawn by rational men and women who are willing to say 'Enough'" (United States Senate 1996).

Bob Dole also had had enough. Efforts to attack Bill Clinton on family values had failed miserably. Even worse, from his perspective, decisions made by the former senator four years earlier had been used to inflict serious damage on him during a campaign that would have had to have been run flawlessly for him to at least have a chance of winning. With a strong economy staring him in the face, combined with failed attempts to corner the incumbent president on family values, Dole was politically finished. Consequently, although the Republicans would win both houses again, they would once again miss the opportunity to take the White House and have it all.

As the words from Bill Clinton's inaugural address drifted out over the nation on January 20, 1997, a soft echo from the not-too-distant past could be heard. Six and a half years earlier, on July 25, 1990, the White House was celebrating another failed override vote by Congress as the family leave bill went down to another defeat. During a TV interview on that same July evening, David Gergen, a former Reagan communications director, criticized George Bush in general and the Republican Party in particular for missing the boat on family leave. "The issue was a winner for the Democrats," Gergen stated, "because the Republicans were making it one" (Elving 1995, 198). The issue would keep returning again and again, he warned in 1990, and it would be bigger every time it came back.[8]

In retrospect, one should not conclude that the FMLA was the key to the Democratic victories in 1992 and 1996. It was simply one campaign strategy among many that was used to put the Republicans on the defensive. A weak economy in 1992 and a strong one in 1996 probably had more to do with Clinton's back-to-back victories than anything else. But although the Democrats used the Family and Medical Leave Act effectively in 1992 and 1996 by incorporating the bill into its family-values strategy, they also abused it shamelessly by portraying it as something much more than it actually was. For in the end, the FMLA provided no paid leave and applied to only 6 percent of corporations and 60 percent of the workforce. However, it did provide that rapidly growing confederacy of cynics with what many would consider to be one more excellent example of symbolic politics. And meanwhile, as will be discussed in chapter 9, the United States remains far behind other industrialized countries in addressing work and family issues.

## Notes

1. Connecticut was the first state to pass a family-leave bill. Concerned about the issue of cost if paid leave were to be proposed, the General Assembly chose the incremental approach. Therefore, the first bill in 1987 applied to the public sector only. A representative from the private sector (Southern New England Telephone) even spoke in favor of the bill, provided it was unpaid. Two years later, a second bill was passed that applied to the private sector. Neither bill provided paid leave.

2. Marian Wright Edelman, founder and director of the Children's Defense Fund, was particularly concerned about the family-leave lobby cutting into her child-care coalition. Whatever conflict may have existed between the Children's Defense Fund and the American Association of Retired Persons (AARP) was defused in the late 1980s when the two groups became cosponsors of Generations United, a Washington-based organization that was formed to address the "coming generational war." Today, Generations United suggests legislation and offers various community programs designed to bring generations together. See Wisensale's "Grappling with the Generational Equity Debate: An Ongoing Challenge for the Public Administrator" (1999b) in *Public Integrity*, Winter, 1–19.

3. The U.S. General Accounting Office (GAO) report proved to be instrumental in neutralizing the business community's claim that an unpaid family-leave bill would be too costly. The GAO estimated the costs to be relatively insignificant ($188 to $236 million) and confined mostly to the cost of maintaining employees' health insurance. For an interesting and thought-provoking analysis of the cost issue, see Spalter-Roth and Hartmann's *Unnecessary Losses: Costs to Americans of the Lack of Family and Medical Leave* (1990) and Spalter-Roth and Hartmann's "Science and Politics and the 'Dual Vision' of Feminist Policy Research: The Example of Family and Medical Leave" in Hyde and Essex's *Parental Leave and Child Care: Setting a Research and Policy Agenda* (1991). For example, Spalter-Roth and Hartmann concluded in 1991 that it costs American women more than $31 billion in earnings losses annually to have the next generation of workers and citizens. Also, refer to pages 86–90 in Elving's *Conflict and Compromise: How Congress Makes the Law* (1995).

4. Acording to William Safire's *Dictionary of American Politics* (1995), the use of the term "family values" began in 1976 with its inclusion in the Republican platform. "Divorce rates, threatened neighborhoods, and schools and public scandal all create a hostile atmosphere that erodes family structures and family values." Eight years later New York Governor Mario Cuomo referred to "family" and "values" separately in his 1984 speech before the Democratic National Convention. But the term stuck during the 1992 presidential campaign and has been with us ever since.

More recently, at least one scholar has explored the concept of "family values" through the prism of the U.S. Constitution, and the post–Civil War amendments in particular. See Peggy Cooper Davis's *Neglected Stories: The Constitution and Family Values* (1997).

5. The FMLA was not the key to Clinton's election in 1992; the economy was. But had Bush been reelected in 1992 and/or had the bill still been under debate during the 104th Congress, it probably never would have passed. The Congress that was elected with Clinton was no more "veto proof" than the two that convened under George Bush.

6. Two key White House aides who resigned in protest over Clinton's signing of the Welfare Reform Act of 1996 were David Ellwood and Peter Edelman. Edelman offers his explanation for his decision to resign in a March 1997 issue of *The Atlantic Monthly*. Particularly troubling to Edelman was Clinton's statement that he should be reelected in 1996 because only he could be trusted to fix the flaws in the legislation. This prompted political correspondent David Broder to write in the *Washington Post* that reelecting the president based on his promise to fix the law would be like giving Jack the Ripper a scholarship to medical school. Edelman, who is married to Marian Wright Edelman, head of the Children's Defense Fund, was the assistant secretary for planning and evaluation at the Department of Health and Human Services before he resigned in 1996.

7. There are numerous books on the Clinton presidency that explain his political motivations. Highly recommended is Caplan and Feffer's *State of the Union 1994: The Clinton Administration and the Nation in Profile* (1994). More specifically, pages 20–28 describe the political climate of divisiveness within which Clinton had to operate during his years in the White House. This analysis helps explain some of Clinton's policy choices, including welfare reform and the Defense of Marriage Act.

8. Additional sources that cover the formulation of the Family and Medical Leave Act are Zigler, Kagen, and Hall's (eds.) *Children, Families and Government* (1996); Sonja Ellison's "The Family and Medical Leave Act of 1993" (1997) in the *Journal of Family Issues* 18, 1: 30–54; and Michelle Marks's "Party Politics and Family Politics: The Case of the Family and Medical Leave Act" (1997) in the *Journal of Family Issues* 18 1: 55–70.

# Chapter 7

# Implementation and Evaluation of the Family and Medical Leave Act

The FMLA, which went into effect on August 5, 1993, stipulated that an evaluation of the law's impact be completed by a bipartisan commission within three years of its implementation. The Commission on Leave, which formed in November 1993, was chaired by Senator Christopher Dodd (D-CT), the bill's key sponsor in the Senate, and co-chaired by Donna Lenhoff, one of the original architects of the law. It included congressional leaders from both parties, important lobbyists representing various viewpoints on the issue, and key cabinet members whose purview covered family and medical leave issues. The Commission's primary charge was to determine the new law's impact on costs, benefits, and productivity. In short, was the FMLA working as expected and who was it helping or hurting?

Between 1993 and 1995, two major research strategies were employed by the Commission to gather information. First, public hearings in three different sites across the country were held to solicit comments from a variety of people about the law's strengths and weaknesses. Second, in 1995, the Commission contracted with two research organizations, Westat, Inc. and the Institute for Social Research at the University of Michigan, to complete two major studies. One, the Employer Survey, was a national, random-sample

A portion of this chapter was published in *WorkingUSA: The Journal of Labor and Society.* It is reprinted here with permission. Steven K. Wisensale, 1999, "The Family and Medical Leave Act in Court: A Review of Key Appeals Court Cases Five Years After." *WorkingUSA: The Journal of Labor and Society* 3, 4: 96–119.

study of private-sector employers to gauge their experience with the FMLA during the first two years of the law's existence. And two, the Employee Survey, was the first national, random-sample survey on employee leave-taking in the nation's history. Completed in June 1995, the Survey produced important national estimates on the utilization of the FMLA—that is, who is most likely to need it and use it, and why.

On April 30, 1996 the Commission on Leave issued its final report, *A Workable Balance: Report to Congress on Family and Medical Leave Policies*. The 314-page document, which was issued by the U.S. Department of Labor, concluded that the FMLA had a positive impact on employees overall and was not the burden on businesses that some had predicted. Ninety percent of companies covered by the law reported no negative impact. "For most employers, compliance is easy, the costs are non-existent or small and the effects are minimal," stated the report. "Most periods of leave are short, most employees return to work, and reduced turnover seems to be a tangible positive effect" (Commission on Leave 1996, xxii).

It was also reported that 3.4 percent of employees who needed leave did not take it. And, of those, more than 60 percent indicated that the reason they did not use the FMLA was because they could not afford it (Commission on Leave 1996). This finding in particular was not emphasized by proponents in 1996, perhaps deliberately in order to prevent it from becoming a political lightning rod during the presidential campaign. Raising the issue of affordability would have probably spawned a debate over paid leave. Instead, the Democrats chose to weave the FMLA into their "family values" strategy, as was discussed in the previous chapter. However, affordability would be used repeatedly three years later when President Clinton called for paid leave; that topic is reserved for the next chapter.

But whatever access problems were associated with the new law, America's workers were still using it. Presented in Table 7.1 is a breakdown of the utilization of the FMLA by employees between 1993 and 1996. At least three facts in particular stand out. One, most leaves (40 percent) were short, ranging from one to seven days, and about two-thirds (62.4 percent) of all leaves taken were under twenty-eight days in length. Two, longer leaves, from twenty-eight to eighty-five days, were taken for maternity reasons or to care for a newborn or adopted child. This was, of course, the primary reason for which the FMLA was created in the first place. And three, relatively short leaves (one to seven days) were taken for the care of an ill child, spouse, or elderly parent. In short, it appears the FMLA was being used for the reasons it was created and there were no signs of abuse, at least by 1996. With the exception of maternity or newborn leaves, the average length of time off from work fell well below the maximum allocation of twelve weeks.[1]

Table 7.1

**Leave-Takers at FMLA-Covered Work Sites: Length of Leave by Reasons for Leave** (1996) (number and percentage of employees)

| | All | Length of leave | | | | |
|---|---|---|---|---|---|---|
| | | 1–7 Days | 8–14 Days | 15–28 Days | 29–84 Days | 85+ Days |
| All reasons n= | 14,820,000 | 5,964,209 | 2,486,777 | 1,311,014 | 3,196,064 | 1,857,375 |
| | 100.0% | 40.3% | 16.8% | 8.9% | 21.6% | 12.5% |
| Reason for leave | | | | | | |
| Own health | 100.0% | 34.4% | 17.2% | 10.8% | 24.0% | 13.6% |
| Maternity-disability | 100.0% | 10.4% | 7.3% | 5.7% | 34.2% | 42.4% |
| Care for newborn, adopted, or foster child | 100.0% | 23.7% | 17.1% | 7.0% | 36.0% | 16.2% |
| Care for ill child | 100.0% | 76.3% | 15.6% | 5.3% | 1.4% | 1.4% |
| Care for ill spouse | 100.0% | 65.5% | 16.1% | 2.7% | 7.9% | 7.9% |
| Care for ill parent | 100.0% | 56.3% | 24.6% | 8.4% | 8.3% | 2.4% |
| Care for ill relative or other | 100.0% | 100.0% | 0.0% | 0.0% | 0.0% | 0.0% |

*Source: A Workable Balance: Report to Congress on Family and Medical Leave*, Washington, DC: U.S. Department of Labor, 1996.

Of special interest to many was, of course, the issue of cost. Did the law have a negative financial impact on businesses? According to the Commission's survey results, 89.2 percent of covered employers reported either no increase or only a small increase in administrative costs. Over 90 percent of covered work sites indicated no or small cost increases due to the continuation of employee benefits; 95 percent of employers reported no or small increases in cost as a result of new hires and training. Independent studies by Bookman (1998), Brinkman (1999), Gerstel and McGonagle (1998), and Ross (1998) reached similar conclusions. And finally, 98.5 percent of companies surveyed cited either no or "very small" cost increases in "other areas" (Commission on Leave 1996, 125). These findings in particular, were later challenged by the business community.[2]

Within days of the report being issued, the response to it was as bipartisan as the Commission that produced it. The vice chair, Donna Lenhoff, acknowledged that the law did not go far enough. "Many people who need the act are not protected because the eligibility and coverage requirements are so strict, or because they cannot afford to lose wages during their leave," she said (Kellogg 1996, B9). Senator Dodd (D-CT) did not believe any effort to expand the law, including a wage replacement, would be supported by a conservative Congress. Instead, he likened the FMLA to a 911 call. "Thank God not everybody needs it, but thank God it's there," he stated (Kellogg 1996, B9). Even conservative Senator Larry Craig (R-ID), who was a member of the Commission, offered praise for the new law, but was reserved in his assessment. Although he continued to argue against the use of federal mandates in the workplace, he referred to the FMLA as a "good start" while encouraging employers to voluntarily adopt more family-friendly policies.

Not to be overlooked is the fact that the report was issued before, *not* after, the 1996 election. Thus, it became part of the arsenal that was used against Bob Dole and his position on family leave, a strategy that was described in some detail in the previous chapter. For not only had Dole opposed the FMLA, he opposed a law that was apparently working quite well. However, despite the fact that proponents knew many potential users of the leave law could not take advantage of it because of financial reasons, Clinton was not about to propose expanding it by recommending paid leave. That idea would surface during the third year of his last term in office, not on the eve of his reelection.

But the findings presented by the Commission in *A Workable Balance* only provide us with a quick snapshot of the effectiveness of a law during a limited time period. At least three other sources of information should be consulted to better understand how the FMLA has been implemented, and to what extent it has succeeded or failed. What follows is an overview of three sources of data in particular that deserve attention. First, independent studies on the FMLA by academics and interest groups will be reviewed. Second, findings from the ongoing monitoring process carried out by the Department of Labor will be summarized. And third, more than 200 federal appellate court decisions between 1994 and 1999 that concerned the FMLA will be categorized and discussed. Each of these is addressed below.

## Studies by Academic Researchers and Interest Groups

Prior to 1995, little had been written about the impact of the FMLA on employers and employees. Most studies focused on the law's limitations—that it applied to too few workers, was of relatively short duration, and was unpaid (Wisensale 1997, 1994; Kamerman and Kahn 1995; Waldfogel 1999; Trzcinski and Alpert 1994). Even organizations that would normally be critical of such legislation offered the FMLA a two-year honeymoon in which studies predicted the law would provide little if any negative impact. For example, within the first year of implementation, the International Foundation of Employee Benefit Plans reported that of almost 100 respondents, only 1 percent indicated that employees might have abused the Act. Similarly, Hewitt Associates, a large international corporate consulting firm, concluded that of 628 employers, only 18 percent were concerned about potential employee abuse (Flynn 1994). The issue of cost would not emerge until 1996, and would not be taken seriously until 1999, when the Clinton administration proposed to expand the FMLA by reducing the employee cutoff to twenty-five workers and providing some sort of wage replacement through Unemployment Insurance.

"The FMLA tends to be an underestimated law," wrote Gillian Flynn just one year after it went into effect. "Described by many as a 'feel-good' initiative, it's often pushed to the back of the compliance to-do list, shadowed by the toothier Americans with Disabilities Act (ADA)" (1994, 36). Writing in *Personnel Journal*, Flynn warned that the new employee-friendly bill may be misused and misunderstood. "What was intended to be a shield may become a sword, with the employer held as captive," she wrote (1994, 36). Within three years after the Commission on Leave issued its report that indicated the FMLA was having "a minimal impact at minimal cost," a variety of studies produced a somewhat different picture.

In an article published in the *Journal of Policy Analysis and Management* (1999), Jane Waldfogel reported on the impact of the FMLA on coverage, leave-taking, women's employment, and women's earnings. With respect to the first issue, coverage, Waldfogel concluded that the FMLA had two primary effects on coverage. First, as a result of the law's passage, more companies, most of which are probably located in states that had no leave laws prior to 1993, are offering job-protected leaves for the first time. And second, many companies that previously offered leave have expanded their coverage, by extending the length of leave and/or continuing health insurance benefits that were not provided prior to passage of the FMLA. Klerman and Leibowitz (1997) reached similar conclusions about coverage, although both Katz (1997) and Honig (1997) questioned their methods. An intangible factor difficult to measure, of course, is the extent to which national publicity about the FMLA may have contributed to changes in employer and employee attitudes about leave-taking in general.[3]

The second research question that Waldfogel explored focused on the utilization of leave benefits following the passage of the FMLA. After comparing states that had leave laws prior to 1993 with those that did not, and by comparing utilization rates in large firms (500 or more employees) to medium companies (100 to 499 employees), to small businesses (25 to 99 employees), she reached three important conclusions. One, the FMLA has had little effect on large firms, confirming previous findings by Zigler and Frank (1988) and Hyde and Essex (1991) that bigger companies are more likely to provide leave regardless of state or federal law. Two, medium-size firms apparently are more sensitive to such legislation as the FMLA, having witnessed significantly more leave-taking since 1993. And three, for small businesses, it appears that state leave laws have had a greater impact on them than the FMLA, particularly if the state statute applies to firms of fewer than fifty employees.

Concerning the effect the FMLA may have on women's employment, neither the topic nor the research questions are new. Early on, opponents of mandated leave laws argued that such measures would ultimately retard women's entry into the labor force, primarily because employers would be reluctant to hire those (meaning women) who may be more inclined to be absent from work. Proponents, on the other hand, argued that policies such as the FMLA would result in more women being attached to the labor force for a longer period of time. Although Waldfogel's study is a mere snapshot of women's employment patterns for one year, she did find a 7.6 percent increase in the employment of women with children under one year of age in 1995. This percentage is significantly greater than the increase in employment for any other group that year. Clearly, more research needs to be completed in this area in the future in order to filter out national employment trends during a booming economy; or, for that matter, to also isolate negative employment trends during economic downturns so that the impact of the FMLA can be measured more precisely.

The fourth question posed by Waldfogel concerned the effect the FMLA

has had on women's wages. This particular area of research has been dominated by two hypotheses. One is that employers will be inclined to pass
along the costs of a mandated benefit such as the FMLA to those likely to
benefit most from it: women of childbearing age (Burtless 1995). Put another way, depending on how important women consider the benefit to be,
they may or may not be willing to accept lower wages in return for the benefit. "Well, we can't pay you that much," says the boss during an interview
with a female applicant, "but we do offer good benefits here such as our
family-leave program." A second hypothesis runs counter to the first. That is,
women with young children in particular will see their wages rise because
family leave will allow them to take time off without sacrificing their jobs,
thus maintaining an income that coincides with the seniority they have
achieved. However, Waldfogel (1997) and Ruhm (1998) found little or no
wage effects as a result of the FMLA. Therefore, to summarize the effect of
the new law from the perspective of traditional academic research, the FMLA
has had a fairly positive, though minor, effect on coverage and utilization
rates, with each increasing slightly within isolated groups. With respect to
employment and wage impacts, there is some effect. That is, there are signs
of a small but positive net employment gain but it is offset by virtually no
wage gains (Waldfogel 1999). In short, more people get and keep their jobs
longer but they don't necessarily earn more because of the FMLA. But again,
we need to remind ourselves that the findings presented here are over the
short run, not the long haul.

Traditional academic research aside, there has also been a visible increase
in reports and articles generated by the pro-business community. Recently,
many of these reports have migrated into the mainstream media. Relatively
silent during the first two or three years of the FMLA's implementation period, opponents of mandated leave benefits began to stir after the 1996 election when Clinton hinted at expanding the law. They emerged in full battle
armor after his "toward paid leave" address at Grambling State University in
the spring of 1999. Leading the charge against the president's proposal were
such organizations as CORE, Inc., the Employment Policy Foundation, and
the National Center for Policy Analysis, not to mention traditional opponents such as the U.S. Chamber of Commerce, the National Association of
Manufacturers, and the National Federation of Independent Businesses.

Based in Irvine, California, CORE is the largest independent provider of
absence reporting and clinical management services for U.S. employers, covering 1.7 million employees nationwide. Among its clients are Apple Computer, Bristol-Myers Squibb Company, the Commonwealth of Virginia,
Daimler-Chrysler, and General Electric. On May 15, 2000, CORE issued a
press release that summarized a study of more than 400,000 Family and

Medical Leave transactions. "The complexity of the federal Family and Medical Leave Act and the added state provisions can be costly to employers of any size," stated Rebecca Auerbach, CORE's vice president of research. "The administrative burden and potential for overlap with other benefits can have a serious impact on workforce productivity" (CORE 2000, 1). The study found that 29 percent of all FMLA leaves were to care for aging parents and 62 percent of the intermittent FMLA leaves were for absences of eight hours or less, adding to the administrative burden on employers. Concerned about litigation costs, CORE cited the Department of Labor's statistic that awards for litigation have nearly doubled in recent years, and an employer can expect to spend at least $100,000 per case in legal fees (CORE 2000).

The Employment Policy Foundation (EPF), established in 1983 and based in Washington, DC, describes itself as a unique nonpartisan research and education foundation whose primary purpose is to inform and to shape sound employment policy in the United States. Concerned about President Clinton's desire to expand the FMLA, the EPF produced a special report in the spring of 2000 that argued strongly against the president's proposed use of Unemployment Insurance trust funds to provide paid leave. In *Paid Family Leave: At What Cost?* (2000), author Anita Hattiangadi concludes that similar government mandates in Europe have hindered job creation, contributed to a rise in unemployment, and retarded economic growth. Instead of financing paid family leave through Unemployment Insurance trust funds, the study recommends other, less costly alternatives. These include more flexible scheduling, the use of compressed work weeks, more telecommuting or "flexiplace" work arrangements, and the use of "paid time off banks," in which vacation, sick, and personal time are all "banked" each year and can be used for any reason. The EPF estimates that the costs of paid leave funded by Unemployment Insurance could range between $6 billion and $30 billion per year, depending on utilization rates and length of leave (Hattiangadi 2000). This particular cost issue is discussed in greater detail chapter 8.

The National Center for Policy Analysis (NCPA) has also raised concerns about the impact of the FMLA. Emphasizing that the original statute of 13 pages has mushroomed into more than 300 pages of Department of Labor regulations, the NCPA contends that businesses are greatly disrupted by the law, and matters will only get worse if it is expanded to include paid leave. Some employers complain that continuity in the workplace is disturbed by some employees who can take the twelve weeks allotted to them in small increments as tiny as six minutes, forcing non-leave-taking coworkers to pick up the slack of the absentees. According to the NCPA, Southwest Airlines reports that in any one month as many as 800 employees take family leave, and more than one-third of its employees have used it so far. Other companies have filed similar reports. AT&T, for example, claims that on any given day, between 10 and 15 percent of its workforce was out on FMLA leave. And, according to the Society for Human Research Management, 92 percent of companies respond to an employee's leave by assigning work to other workers, 71 percent say they must hire other workers, and 42 percent report delaying some work until an employee returns (National Center for Policy Analysis 2000).

Meanwhile, organizations in support of paid leave have presented their arguments as well, in the form of reports and studies. The National Partnership for Women and Families (NPWF) offers a special web page that is devoted almost entirely to expanding the FMLA. Referring to various cost studies of paid-leave proposals, the NPWF contends that the use of Unemployment Insurance trust funds and/or the Temporary Disability Insurance model would amount to less than a few dollars per worker per week. Similarly, the International Labor Organization, the Families and Work Institute, and the Institute for Women's Policy Research have also endorsed an expanded FMLA, arguing that the cost for paid leave would be reasonable if not minimal. Equally important, proponents of the law have contended that it has been helpful to families without being harmful to business. But beyond the work of traditional academic researchers and efforts put forth by various interest groups on both sides of the issue, there are two other sources of data that should be tapped in examining the implementation of the FMLA. These include complaints filed with the Department of Labor and legal cases handled by the federal appellate court system. Each is discussed below.

### Department of Labor as Monitor of the FMLA

When the Family and Medical Leave Act was passed in 1993, the responsibility for its implementation was placed in the hands of the Department of Labor (DOL). In that capacity, the DOL issues new regulations and revises old ones, offers administrative rulings, clarifies ambiguous wording, receives and resolves complaints, and awards cash settlements when appropriate. Between August 1993 and the end of 1999, about 24 million people used the FMLA for one reason or another. Today, according to the DOL's Bureau of Labor Statistics, the FMLA covers approximately 50 million workers or 60 percent of the labor force and 300,000 companies, or about 6 percent of the nation's businesses. In addition, another 15 million state and local government employees are covered by the law. Federal employees are covered under a separate law.[4]

Summarized in Table 7.2 are the FMLA complaints that were submitted to the Department of Labor between August 1993 and September 1999. Of the 16,509 complaints filed by employees, 7,537 (46 percent) concerned workers being refused the same or equivalent job upon returning to work. A total of 3,603 complaints—or 22 percent—were due to workers' being denied leave, and another 2,672 (16 percent) were filed under the general category of discrimination, which usually implied that an employee believed he or she was punished in some way for taking leave.

Not all complaints filed, however, were considered to be valid by the DOL. Of the 16,509 filed during the FMLA's first six years of existence, 6,661 (40 percent) were dismissed, leaving a total of 9,848 (60 percent) that were acted upon. All told, the DOL reports that 8,666 of 9,848 cases heard, or 88 percent, were successfully resolved. The remaining 1,182 cases, or 12 percent, were reviewed for potential litigation. Among those cases, thirty-two were filed in court and all but four were resolved by June 2000. Two other points need to be emphasized with respect to Table 7.2.

First, there has been a decrease in the number of complaints between 1997–98 and 1998–99 in all categories. This is probably due to a combination of factors, including the DOL's ongoing clarification of FMLA regulations. As more questions are asked, either through administrative rulings or appellate court rulings (to be discussed next), the zone of potential conflict tends to diminish in size.

The second point is that the total amount of damages awarded to employees under the FMLA by the Department of Labor has increased steadily. Although it took four years (1993–97) to award $8.6 million in damages, it took only one year (1997–98) to award half that amount ($4.5 million). And in the 1998–99 year, the awards increased again ($5.8 million) for a grand total of $19,057,815 awarded in damages in the first six years of the law's existence. This dichotomy of fewer cases but higher damage awards can perhaps be explained by the fact that the issues arising today may go beyond the mere clarification of the language of a new law. Cases now being heard may involve more complex problems and higher stakes. Therefore, such litigation drives up costs.

Table 7.3 offers yet another perspective for understanding the implementation of the FMLA. Included is data on the types of private firms from which employee complaints originated, and the percentage of firms of different sizes that violated the FMLA. As indicated in the table, 91 percent of all the complaints filed came from the private sector, with more than half of those coming from manufacturing companies (26 percent) and the service industry (25 percent). Also, based on the data provided in Table 7.3, there appears to be a correlation between the number of complaints and the size of the company. Over 60 percent originate in companies with fewer than 250 workers, with 30 percent from firms of ninety-nine employees or less, and an-

Table 7.2

**Summary of FMLA Complaints Filed with the Department of Labor**
(August 5, 1993 through September 30, 1999)

| Complaints | Aug 93/ Sept 97 | Oct 97/ Sept 98 | Oct 98/ Sept 99 | Total |
|---|---|---|---|---|
| **Total complaints** | 9, 802 | 3,795 | 2,912 | 16,509 |
| **Types** | | | | |
| Refusal to grant leave | 2,298 | 716 | 589 | 3,603 |
| Refused job or equivalent job | 4,191 | 1,841 | 1,505 | 7,537 |
| Health benefits denied | 345 | 91 | 49 | 485 |
| Discrimination | 1,199 | 849 | 624 | 2,672 |
| Other | 723 | 298 | 145 | 1,166 |
| Multiple reasons | 1,046 | NA | NA | 1,046 |
| **Status of compliance—** | | | | |
| no violations | 4,106 | 1,424 | 1,131 | 6,661 |
| Employer not covered | 280 | 70 | 53 | 403 |
| Employee not eligible | 650 | 201 | 139 | 909 |
| Complaint not valid | 2,727 | 774 | 713 | 4,214 |
| Other | 449 | 379 | 226 | 1,054 |
| **No violation** | | | | |
| **Total number of** employees | 5,696 | 2,371 | 1,781 | 9,848 |
| and total monetary damages | $8,685,704 | $4,520,649 | $5,851,462 | $19,057,815 |

*Source:* U.S. Department of Labor Wage and Hour Division, Washington, DC, 2000.

other 30 percent generated by companies of between 100 and 249 workers. The numbers tend to decline significantly in businesses that range in size from 250 to 1,000 workers. However, in larger firms with a thousand or more employees, it appears that complaints begin to rise again but not quite as high as in much smaller companies.

These findings by the DOL are not surprising in that smaller firms are particularly vulnerable in a highly competitive environment. Because many smaller companies might lack the financial resources to cover the costs while an employee is on leave, they may be inclined to challenge the FMLA's regulations more frequently than larger firms. After all, few if any small companies have ever made *Working Mother*'s "most family-friendly companies" list.

Clearly, the implementation of the FMLA has not been smooth, as is revealed in the Department of Labor's statistics presented in Tables 7.2 and 7.3. However, a methodological approach that remains relatively unexplored to date, seven years after the FMLA took effect, is legal research.[5] That is, to what extent has the FMLA become a focal point for court action, what issues have been raised in court, who has raised them, why, and how have the courts ruled?

Table 7.3

**Source of FMLA Complaints and Size of Firms** (August 5, 1993 through September 30, 1999)

|  | Percent |
|---|---|
| Origin of complaints by type of firm | |
| Type | |
| Manufacturing | 26 |
| Services | 25 |
| Retail | 17 |
| Other | 32 |
| Size of firms in violation | |
| Number of employees | |
| 50–99 | 30 |
| 100–249 | 33 |
| 250–499 | 13 |
| 500–599 | 7 |
| 1,000+ | 17 |

*Source:* U.S. Department of Labor, Employment Standards Division, Wage and Hour Division, Washington, DC, 2000.

## The Family and Medical Leave Act in Appellate Court Cases

An emerging database for identifying various implementation issues related to the FMLA is the growing body of court cases brought forth since the law took effect in 1993. Three primary sources for collecting such data are LEXIS; Westlaw, the computerized national data file of assorted legal documents and court cases; and the Thompson Publishing Group, a specialist in monitoring the implementation of labor-related legislation. Thompson publishes *The Family and Medical Leave Handbook* (1993), which includes monthly updates of all legal activity (primarily court cases) related to the administration of the Family and Medical Leave Act. See Appendix B for a list of resources related to work and family issues.

In 1999, this author conducted an exploratory review of court cases directly related to the FMLA. The research project was completed in four steps. First, five specific research questions were posed. One, what issues or questions were brought before the courts? Two, were the cases brought by the employee or employer? Three, in cases brought forth by employees, what was the breakdown by gender? Four, what were the rulings in the cases and how many were won by employers in comparison to employees? And five, for those employees who filed cases, what was the breakdown by gender in terms of court victories and defeats?

Second, through a combination of LEXIS and Westlaw searches, as well as a review of the *Family and Medical Leave Handbook* (1993), including its updated supplements, 206 appeals court rulings between December 1994 and October 1999 were identified. Of those, almost all of the cases were decided in U.S. District Courts; fewer were decided in the U.S. Courts of Appeals; and a state court heard only one case.

Third, based on a review of the 206 cases, and with particular attention devoted to the issue or issues being raised in each case, ten issue categories were created. Some of these categories were pulled directly from the key provisions of the 1993 Act. For example, job security (the guaranteed return to the same or comparable job) is one of the major pillars of the law. Isolating particular issues raised in the court cases and placing them in common categories generated other categories. The cases were then examined through this analytical prism, and the five research questions posed above were applied to each category and answered accordingly.

The ten issue categories employed include: (1) the question of job security (e.g., employee has the right to return to the same or comparable job after taking leave); (2) the seriousness of the employee's illness (e.g., is a sinus infection a serious enough ailment to warrant taking leave?); (3) the question of eligibility (e.g., does part-time work count toward FMLA eligibility?); (4) employee giving sufficient notification for taking leave (e.g., what if there is a family emergency?); (5) calculating time (e.g., can time spent in company workshops after hours count toward eligibility for FMLA leave?); (6) the seriousness of the illness of a family member (e.g., is a child's ear infection serious enough to warrant time off?); (7) information provided by the employer to the employee concerning FMLA rights (e.g., is the company handbook clear about the process of requesting leave?); (8) defining the employer (e.g., should the employee sue the supervisor or the company president?); (9) the FMLA and labor contracts (e.g., can employers require employees to go to arbitration over FMLA rights before going to court?); and (10) the use of the FMLA as a shield or protector (e.g., can an employee declare himself an alcoholic and therefore be able to take leave under the FMLA?).

The fourth and final step of the research project was to summarize the results of the study, draw particular conclusions from the findings, and put forth specific policy recommendations designed to improve the continuing process of implementing the Family and Medical Leave Act. What follows is a presentation of the research findings followed by a discussion of their policy implications.

The responses to the five research questions are presented under each of the ten issue categories identified above. Tables 7.4, 7.5, and 7.6 represent a summary of the research findings. Table 7.4 lists in descending order the number of cases heard under the ten issue categories. As indicated in the table, almost 60 percent (120 of 206) of the cases concern either the issue of job security for

Table 7.4

**FMLA Court Cases by Issue Category, Frequency, and Percentage**

| Issue category (n = 10) | Number of cases (n = 206) | Percentage |
|---|---|---|
| Job security | 69 | 34 |
| Seriousness of employee's illness | 51 | 25 |
| Eligibility for leave/miscellaneous | 17 | 8 |
| Employee not giving sufficient notification | 17 | 8 |
| Calculating time | 12 | 6 |
| Seriousness of illness of a family member | 12 | 6 |
| Information provided to employees by employers | 11 | 5 |
| The FMLA and labor contracts | 8 | 4 |
| Definition of employer | 7 | 3 |
| The FMLA used as a shield or protector | 2 | 1 |
| Totals | 206 | 100 |

employees or the definition of a serious health condition. The next tier in the frequency of cases includes eligibility issues (seventeen cases), sufficient notification time given by an employee (seventeen cases), and calculating time (twelve cases). The issue of calculating time can be particularly problematic, for example, when an employer and employee disagree over the use of vacation time to cover the employee's absence from work.

Only twelve cases were heard regarding the seriousness of the illness of a family member. For example, is a child's ear infection considered to be serious enough to warrant an employee's leave of absence under the FMLA? A relatively small number of cases (eleven) emerged that concerned the provision of information by employers to employees. Usually, such cases concerned an employee who believed he or she was not properly informed about the existing rules, guidelines, and employee rights under the FMLA. The three categories that generated the least amount of court activity were eight cases under "the FMLA and labor contracts" category (what if a collective bargaining agreement contradicts a specific provision in the FMLA?); seven cases under the "definition of employer" category (does the employee's supervisor or the company's president get sued?); and only two cases under the "use of the FMLA as a shield or protector" (is alcoholism an illness that is covered under the FMLA?). A potentially complicated legal question that has just begun to surface concerns the interaction between the Family and Medical Leave Act and the Americans with Disabilities Act. For example, what if someone hired under the ADA requests frequent intermittent leaves under the FMLA? Most likely, this will be a future battleground for the courts.

Table 7.5

**FMLA Court Cases by Gender of Employee Plaintiffs and Outcome**

Total Cases = 206
Employee plaintiffs by gender
  Female plaintiffs = 121 (59%)
  Male plaintiffs = 85 (41%)
Case outcomes
  Employer wins = 134 cases won (65%)
  Employee wins = 72 cases won (35%)
Outcomes by gender (when employee wins)
  When female wins case = 48 (40% of cases filed by females)
  When male wins = 24 (28% of cases filed by males)
Outcomes by gender (when employee loses)
  Female loses = 73 (60% of cases filed by females)
  Male loses = 61 (72% of cases filed by males)

Table 7.5 illustrates the number of cases that were heard, who filed the complaints by gender, and what were the final court rulings, also broken down by gender in terms of victories and defeats.

Of a total of 206 cases filed, 121 (59 percent) were female plaintiffs and 85 (41 percent) were male. In court rulings, the employers prevailed in 134 of the 206 cases, or 65 percent of the time. Employees, on the other hand, were only successful in slightly more than one-third (35 percent) of the cases, winning seventy-two in all. When viewed further from the perspective of gender differences, females won a higher percentage of the cases they filed than male plaintiffs. That is, females won 48 out of 121 cases they filed or 40 percent of their cases. Males, however, only won 28 percent of the cases they filed, winning only twenty-four of their eighty-five cases. And although the females lost 60 percent of their cases, the males were on the losing side 72 percent of the time.

Table 7.6 is more detailed and somewhat more complicated than Tables 7.4 and 7.5. Presented in Table 7.6 is the number of court cases heard under each of the ten issue categories, the breakdown by male and female plaintiffs, the outcome by employer and employee victories and defeats, and the outcome by male and female victories and defeats.

For example, under the category labeled "job security," the courts determined a total of sixty-nine cases. Employers won fifty-one cases or 74 percent, an extremely high winning percentage. Women only won nine of the forty-one cases they filed, or 22 percent. The success rate for men was slightly higher, as they won only nine of the twenty-eight cases they filed or 32 percent. With respect to the other large category, "seriousness of the employee's illness," the employer won thirty-five of the fifty-one cases heard, or almost

Table 7.6

**FMLA Court Cases by Categories, Filings, and Outcomes (n = 206)**

| Category | Filed by | | Won by | | Won by | | Lost by[c] | | Total | % |
|---|---|---|---|---|---|---|---|---|---|---|
| | M | F | Employer | Employee | M | F | M | F | | |
| Job security | 28 | 41 | 51 | 18 | 9 | 9 | 19 | 32 | 69 | 34 |
| Employees' illness[a] | 24 | 27 | 35 | 16 | 2 | 14 | 22 | 13 | 51 | 25 |
| Eligibility | 7 | 10 | 12 | 5 | 2 | 3 | 5 | 7 | 17 | 8 |
| Notification | 9 | 8 | 11 | 6 | 4 | 2 | 5 | 6 | 17 | 8 |
| Calculating time | 3 | 9 | 5 | 7 | 1 | 5 | 1 | 4 | 12 | 6 |
| Family illness[b] | 4 | 8 | 9 | 3 | 3 | 2 | 3 | 6 | 12 | 6 |
| Info provided by employer | 6 | 5 | 4 | 7 | 3 | 4 | 3 | 1 | 11 | 5 |
| FMLA and labor contracts | 3 | 5 | 3 | 5 | 1 | 4 | 2 | 1 | 8 | 4 |
| Definition of employer | 0 | 7 | 3 | 4 | 0 | 4 | 0 | 3 | 7 | 3 |
| FMLA as shield/protector | 1 | 1 | 1 | 1 | 0 | 1 | 1 | 0 | 2 | 1 |
| | | | | | | | | | | |
| Totals | 85 | 121 | 134 | 72 | 24 | 48 | 61 | 73 | 206 | |
| Percentages | 41 | 59 | 65 | 35 | 28 | 40 | 72 | 60 | | 100 |

[a]"Employees' illness" refers to whether or not the illness of an employee is serious enough to take leave under the FMLA.

[b]"Family illness" refers to whether or not the illness of an employee's family member is viewed as serious enough for the employee to be granted a leave under the FMLA.

[c]The percentages under "Won by M F" and "Lost by M F" represent the number of cases won or lost divided by the total number of cases filed by males (85) and females (121). For example, males won 24 of the 85 cases they filed or 28 percent. Females won 40 percent of the cases they filed.

70 percent of the cases. Although employees won a little less than a third of their cases (sixteen of fifty-one), females won more than half of the cases they filed under this category (fourteen of twenty-seven), or 52 percent. Males, however, only won two of the twenty-four cases they filed for a lowly winning percentage of 8 percent. In short, under the two most active categories in which court cases were fought, employers prevailed in 86 of the 120 cases heard. That is, they won 72 percent of the time! What follows is an analysis of the 206 court rulings as categorized under the ten issue categories identified in Tables 7.4 and 7.6 and discussed above. Appropriate cases have been selected from each category to serve as examples throughout the discussion.

### *Job Security*

A key provision of the 1993 Family and Medical Leave Act is that an employee has the right to assume his or her old job or an equivalent (comparable) position upon returning to work. This provision, however, has become quite contentious over the past six years. Of the 206 cases filed between 1994 and 1999, 69 of them—34 percent—concerned job security. Perhaps most important, employers won fifty-one of the sixty-nine cases or 74 percent. Selected cases under this category are discussed in greater detail below.

One of the first rulings on job security, *Lempres v. CBS Inc.*, concluded that the FMLA *does not* guarantee job security. That is, although one is assured of the same or comparable job upon returning to work, there is no guarantee that employment in that position will be long term. When Christina Lempres returned to work after her maternity leave, she was unconditionally offered her previous position. When she inquired about its permanence, however, she was informed that it was "as permanent as anything else in the news business" (1996 U.S. Dist. LEXIS 2324). In *Patterson v. Alltell Information Services Inc.*, *Day v. Excel*, and *Donnellan v. New York City Transit Authority*, Edward Patterson, Donald Day, and Ann Donnellan all lost their jobs when their employers downsized during their leaves of absence. Three separate U.S. District Courts ruled that such dismissals do not violate the FMLA if they are part of budgetary cutbacks.

Similarly, two other court rulings indicate that "job security" can be an extremely elusive term under the FMLA. In *Clay v. City of Chicago*, the U.S. District Court dismissed Dorothy Clay's claim that the city violated her FMLA rights when it dismissed her for "poor job performance" shortly after she returned to work following a leave of absence. In *Beckendorf v. Schwegmann Giant Super Markets Inc.*, it was ruled that the employer was not required to reinstate her in the same or comparable position if she was incapable of performing her job.

An even more troubling ruling for proponents of the FMLA was handed down in *Kephart v. Cherokee County, N.C.* The federal district court ruled that because Rex Kephart, a county employee, had been declared a "key employee" under the FMLA, he was not entitled to a ninety-day leave that was recommended by his physician. Kephart had been granted the ninety-day leave by his employer, the county government, but was informed that his job might not be available when he returned. When he was replaced and denied his previous job, he sued the county but eventually lost in court. Generally, a "key employee" under the FMLA is a worker who falls within the top 10 percent of a given employer's salary scale.

All seven of these cases raise interesting legal questions. Can corporate downsizing or reorganizing be used to undermine the FMLA, or at least provide a legal loophole for employers? Can an employee eventually be punished for taking leave and be dismissed, even though the employer initially met the FMLA requirements by reinstating the employee in an equivalent or comparable position? As was raised in the *Lempres* case, what is meant by "job security" in terms of time on the job after one returns to work? On the other hand, to what extent should incompetent employees be granted immunity from dismissal under the FMLA? And how often will the "key employee" clause of the FMLA be applied in the future?

Of those cases under the "job security" category in which the employees prevailed, one (*Patterson v. Slidell Memorial Hospital and Medical Center*) concluded that an employer cannot place a returning employee in a more demanding position than the one vacated for a leave of absence and then declare the new position "equivalent." Another ruling (*Fejes v. Gilpin Ventures Inc.*) concluded that an employer (a gambling casino) must grant an employee (a blackjack dealer) the opportunity to renew her license that expired while taking FMLA leave.

One of the most recent and more famous "job security" cases to emerge was *Knussman v. Maryland* in which a state trooper, who claimed sexual discrimination because he was denied family leave when his daughter was born, not only won his case, but was awarded $375,000 in damages. It was the first sexual discrimination case brought under the Family and Medical Leave Act during its short history. Knussman had requested four to eight weeks of FMLA leave for the birth of his daughter, but his request was denied and he was informed that he could have no more than two weeks off. The *Knussman* case was one of the first rulings in which a cash award was given to the plaintiff. An award of $120,000 was given to Michael Nero (*Nero v. Industrial Molding Corporation*) when he was not reinstated following a leave to recover from a heart attack. The company's argument, though it was denied by the fifth Circuit Court of Appeals, was that they had decided to fire Nero a few days before he suffered the heart attack anyway.

## *Seriousness of Employee's Illness*

Fifty-one cases were identified under this category in which questions were raised concerning the seriousness of the illness of the employee. That is, have courts determined what illnesses in particular should be recognized by employers, and how serious must they be in order for an employee to be granted a leave under the FMLA?

As presented in Table 7.6, of the fifty-one cases that fall within this category, an almost equal number of cases were filed by males and females. However, there is a striking difference in the outcomes, with females winning more than half their cases (52 percent), but males winning only 8 percent. As was the case under the "job security" category, the employer won an overwhelming majority of cases, almost 70 percent.

Four cases in particular serve as indicators of what the courts *do not* consider to be serious health conditions for employees. In *Oswalt v. Sara Lee Corp.*, for example, it was concluded that food poisoning was not a serious illness because it did not require inpatient care. Nor were occasional rectal bleeding (*Bauer v. Dayton-Walther Corp.*), sino-bronchitis (*Hott v. VDO Yazaki Corp.*), the normal conditions of pregnancy (*Gudenkauf v. Stauffer Communications Inc.*), or an ongoing arthritic condition (*Reich v. The Standard Register Co.*) considered serious enough to warrant time off from work under the FMLA.

The courts have been cautious, if not reluctant, to apply the FMLA to mental-health conditions. For example, bereavement is not considered a serious health condition. In *Fisher v. State Farm Mutual Automobile Insurance Co.*, an employee was denied leave for an adjustment disorder related to his father's death. Similarly, in *Lange v. Showbiz Pizza Time Inc.*, an employee was denied additional leave under the FMLA after his mother died. Nor have the courts viewed work-induced stress and anxiety as serious health conditions, as ruled in *Boyd v. State Farm Insurance Co.*

At least four types of employee illnesses were considered serious enough by the courts to be covered under the FMLA. Interestingly, all are related to childbirth. In *Reich v. Midwest Plastic Engineering Inc.*, the court concluded that a pregnant employee with chicken pox is guaranteed protection under the FMLA. *In George v. Associated Stationers Inc.*, the U.S. District Court took the Reich ruling one step further by concluding that an employee (in this case a male) with chicken pox (and obviously not pregnant) was entitled to time off under the FMLA. In *Murphy v. Cadillac Rubber & Plastics*, an employee's miscarriage was considered a serious illness. And, in *Atchley v. Nordam Group Inc.*, the court ruled that a woman, who was forced to leave work one month early because of a prenatal condition, had a serious health condition and was therefore covered under the FMLA.

In a more recent case concerning the "serious health condition" of an employee, the 8th U.S. Circuit Court of Appeals ruled that an ulcer was a "serious health condition." In *Thorson v. Gemini Inc.*, the Court relied on a recent Department of Labor administrative ruling which stated that conditions not ordinarily considered to be serious health conditions could be protected under the FMLA. Therefore, concluded the Court, Gemini's firing of Mary Thorson because she violated the company's absence policy ran counter to the intent of the FMLA. She was awarded $49,592 to cover back pay, projected earnings, and court fees (*Family and Medical Leave Handbook* 2000). With 120 of the 206 cases devoted to either job security or the seriousness of employees' health conditions, only eighty-six cases remain to be divided among the eight remaining issue categories.

### Eligibility Issues

Whether or not an employee is eligible for FMLA coverage is a question that has been asked more frequently in recent years. Through the first fifty cases, the issue only arose two times in court. However, since 1996 another fifteen cases have been heard. As presented in Table 7.6, the employer has won twelve of the seventeen cases filed. It was indicated by the courts early on that the burden is clearly on the employee to show that he or she is eligible for FMLA leave. In both *Spurlock v. Nynex* and *Wolke v. Dreadnought Marine, Inc.*, the first two cases to deal with eligibility issues, it was concluded that the plaintiffs were responsible for proving they were eligible for leave. Jeurena Campbell (*Campbell v. Pritchard Police Department*) learned that she was not eligible to take time off under the FMLA to care for her ill grandmother. The law allows leave to be taken to care for a spouse, child, or parent, but not a grandparent, nor a mother-in-law or father-in-law for that matter. However, when Dwayne Kelley (*Kelley v. Crosfield Catalysts*) sought leave to seek custody of his child, the 7th Circuit Court of Appeals ruled that he was eligible for FMLA coverage.

In two of the five cases won by employees, the courts ruled that eligibility for FMLA leave continues even after a company is sold and comes under new ownership. In *Vanderhoof v. Life Extension Institute* and *Barrilleaux v. Thayer Lodging Group Inc.*, the new owners were declared "successors in interests," and therefore could not deny leave to qualified employees "because they haven't been with the company long enough."

### Sufficient Notification Required of Employees

The Family and Medical Leave Act makes it quite clear that an employee must give his or her employer thirty days notice prior to taking leave. This can become particularly problematic when caring for a frail elderly parent whose health status is unpredictable. However, few, if any, such cases have emerged. As presented in Table 7.6, seventeen cases have been heard in appeals courts with corporations winning eleven of them. In *Brannon v. Oshkosh B'Gosh Inc.*, the court ruled that Penny Brannon could not be terminated for "excessive absenteeism" because she not only provided a doctor's certification for her illness, but she also gave her employer proper notice. In two other cases, however, employees were legally terminated by their employers because they failed to provide proper notice prior to taking leave (*Johnson v. Primerica* and *Kaylor v. Fannin Regional Hospital Inc.*). In other cases, having one's mother deliver a note indicating that her daughter will be absent that day from work (*Satterfield v. Wal-Mart Stores Inc.*) is not sufficient notice. However, if an employee has documented a history of recurring migraine headaches but then requests a leave on very short notice, he or she is protected under the FMLA and cannot be terminated (*Ware v. Stahl Specialty Co.*). In *Gibbs v. American Airlines Inc.*, a California court ruled against an employee with the flu who called her employer after being absent four days. While the flu is considered a "serious health condition" under the FMLA, as decided in *Miller v. AT&T*, the burden is on the employee to notify the employer within a reasonable period of time.

### Calculating Time

The issue of time was one of several political flash points that were visible during the congressional debates over family leave. That is, questions concerning the length of leave (twelve weeks), during what time span (one year), the recognition of part-time work (twenty-five hours per week), and notification requirements (thirty days) prior to taking leave all had to be resolved prior to passing the Act. However, between 1993 and 1999, only twelve cases have surfaced in federal appeals courts. Of these, the employees won seven and the employers won five. Several cases can be identified as examples of the types of questions that arise under this category. In two cases (*Mion v. Aftermarket Tool & Equipment* and *Clark v. Allegheny University Hospital*), employees were denied FMLA coverage because they failed to meet "the hours of service" requirement of at least 1,250 hours of work over a twelve-month period. However, employees who begin as temporary workers may become eligible for FMLA leave (*Salgado v. CDW Computer Centers Inc.* and *Miller v. Defiance Metal Products Inc.*). Other appropriate cases under this category are summarized below.

In *Fry v. First Fidelity Bancorporation*, Lisa Fry claimed that Fidelity had not informed her how it calculates time for the family-leave period and that the company's handbook on the FMLA was misleading. The court agreed with Ms. Fry, stating that the employer must inform the employee of possible termination of employment if a leave period exceeds twelve weeks. Fidelity failed to do so. In *Robbins v. Bureau of National Affairs*, the court ruled that the employer (BNA) did not have to grant maternity leave to an employee because she had just returned six months earlier from giving birth. Therefore, concluded the court, she had not accumulated enough hours after her return to become eligible for leave under the FMLA. One is entitled to only twelve weeks during any twelve-month period. Similarly, in *Rich v. Delta Air Lines, Inc.*, a flight attendant who had not worked 1,250 hours in a twelve-month period was not eligible under the FMLA. Rich argued unsuccessfully that Delta did not include time consumed by deplaning, briefing sessions, and company workshops.

### Seriousness of Illness of Family Member

One of the driving forces behind the passage of the Family and Medical Leave Act was the belief that employees are frequently called upon to assist family members who are experiencing health problems. However, relatively few court cases have surfaced under this category. As presented in Table 7.6, only twelve cases have been heard in federal appeals courts, with employers winning nine of them. In all the cases, the primary issue concerned the severity of the family member's illness and whether or not it warranted time off under the FMLA. In *Seidle v. Provident Mutual Life Insurance Co.*, it was ruled that a child's ear infection was not serious enough for a parent, in this case a mother, to request and be granted FMLA leave. In *Cianci v. Pettibone Corp.*, the court ruled that because a daughter never proved the seriousness of her elderly mother's health condition, the company was correct in denying her leave to visit her ill mother in Italy. And in *Sakellarion v. Judge & Dolph Ltd.*, a mother was not entitled to take leave under the FMLA because the court did not consider her daughter's asthma attacks serious enough. However, in *Bryant v. Delbar Products Inc.*, the court ruled that a mother's request for FMLA leave to care for her son who had advanced kidney failure was justified.

But in *Land v. Aeroglide Corp.*, the District Court ruled against employee Stephen Land, who requested time off under the FMLA to care for his eighteen-year-old stepson following major surgery in which his spleen was removed. Although the FMLA does allow time off to care for an adult child, the child must be incapable of caring for himself or herself. That is, the child must depend on assistance from others in dressing, bathing, eating, or in performing other similar activities of daily living. Because the stepson, though recovering from surgery, was not incapable of self-care, the FMLA did not apply.

## The Remaining Issues—7 Through 10

The number of cases within the four remaining issue categories totals only 28 of the 206 cases. Therefore, these will be summarized briefly. Regarding the issue of the employer providing adequate and accurate information to the employees, it is clear that courts have placed the burden of explaining the rights and responsibilities under the FMLA to employees on the shoulders of the employer. Although only eleven cases have been heard under this category, the employees have won seven of them. In *McKiernan v. Smith-Edwards-Dunlap Co.*, it was determined that it is the employer's responsibility to inform employees about the method for calculating leave taken during a twelve-month period. A similar ruling was handed down in *Henderson v. Whirlpool Corp.*, when the court concluded that vague statements in an employee handbook do not fulfill the employer's obligation of properly informing the employees about their rights under the FMLA.

Seven cases concerned questions related to how employers are defined under the FMLA. Perhaps of all the categories explored in this study, this one has produced the most contradictory rulings. For example, may a supervisor be held personally liable for violations of the FMLA? No, based on *Frizzell v. Southwest Motor Freight Inc.* However, this decision contradicted the ruling in *Freemon v. Foley*, in which the court concluded that the FMLA defined employer status as "any person who acts, directly or indirectly, in the interest of an employer or to any of the employees of such employer." *Freemon* was later confirmed by a similar ruling in *Mercer v. Borden*, in which the court ruled that an individual supervisor may be held liable under the FMLA. But confusion still reigns with respect to the legal status of human resource managers. In *Johnson v. A.P. Products Ltd.*, a federal district court ruled that a human resources manager did not have the power to be defined as an employer under the FMLA. However, a different court handed down an opposite ruling in *Carpenter v. Refrigerator Sales Corp.*, because the human resources specialist who administered the FMLA for RSC had talked to the employee about her condition, made the decision to fire her, and signed her termination letter. And to complicate matters further, the Eleventh Circuit Court of Appeals in *Wascura v. Carver* ruled that public officials cannot be held individually liable under the FMLA.

With respect to the FMLA and labor contracts produced through collective bargaining, at least one challenging legal question has arisen. Can a company's policy or a collective bargaining agreement abrogate an employee's FMLA rights? As was the case in the preceding category (defining the employer), the courts have generated a number of contradictory rulings. For example, can employees file claims under the FMLA if their company requires that all employee disputes must first be taken to arbitration? No, because in *Hoffman v. Aaron Kamhi Inc.*, the company failed to notify Hoffman that, under the arbitration clause, he was waiving his right to go to court. But this ruling was contradicted nearly eight months later in *Satarino v. A.G. Edwards & Sons Inc.*, in which the court ruled that FMLA claims are subject to compulsory arbitration if mandated by a collective bargaining agreement. Although this ruling was confirmed in a separate case (*O'Neil v. Hilton Head Hospital*) by the Fourth Circuit Court of Appeals, the Tenth Circuit Court somewhat neutralized the power of collective bargaining agreements in *Oklahoma Fixture Co. v. Local 942 International Brotherhood of Carpenters and Joiners of America*. In that case, it was ruled that a collective bargaining agreement that stipulated seniority rights were tied directly to the number of days on the job was in direct conflict with the mission and purpose of the FMLA.

And finally, the issue category with the fewest number of cases, the "FMLA as Shield and Protector," has also raised some very provocative legal questions. Can excessive absenteeism be covered under the FMLA? Can an employee simply declare himself an alcoholic and use that as a reason for his inconsistent and unreliable work pattern? Perhaps the one case that best set the legal tone for this issue was *McCown v. UOP Inc.*, in which a U.S. District Court concluded that "the FMLA is not a shield to protect employees from legitimate action by their employers if their performance is lacking in some manner unrelated to their FMLA leave." This ruling was in response to the firing of an employee because of excessive tardiness and unexcused absences from work

### Future Challenges

It is clear from the findings presented here that the implementation of the FMLA has been, and will most likely continue to be, a very dynamic and politically charged process. The cases ruled upon so far are reflective of many of the issues that were raised during the congressional debates and the formulation of the law. Two issues in particular have consumed almost 60 percent of all court cases so far: job security questions and determining the seriousness of an employee's illness.

With respect to job security, employees appear not to be immune from corporate downsizing or restructuring, and there is no guarantee that the return to one's previous job will be long term. Employers prevailed in fifty-one of the sixty-nine cases heard under this category. Policymakers and researchers need to converge on this issue more aggressively in order to uphold the original intent of the FMLA and prevent employers from circumventing the law. Related to this point, more research needs to be done on the use or misuse of collective bargaining agreements (e.g., forcing employees to go to arbitration before they go to court), as a means of bypassing the law.

An equally troubling issue for both employees and employers concerns the definition of a serious illness. Here again, the employers won an overwhelming majority of cases (thirty-five of fifty-one). Unless another means can be employed for defining serious illnesses, much money and energy will be spent in courtrooms slowly creating the FMLA's version of Diagnostic Related Groups (DRGs). DRGs are a very quantitative, detailed categorization and ranking process of various illnesses that are used by health professionals to define and reimburse specific illnesses under Medicare.

These two issues identified here, along with several other trouble zones, such as calculating time, employees giving sufficient notice, and employers providing adequate information to their employees about the FMLA, will need to be addressed if the Family and Medical Leave Act is to be expanded, as some advocacy groups are currently demanding. In the meantime, however, the implementation of the FMLA has been further complicated by a recent U.S. Supreme Court ruling. On June 23, 1999, the Court ruled 5–4 in *Alden v. Maine* that state government employees cannot sue their employers under the Fair Labor Standards Act (FLSA) in state court. Therefore, other than lawsuits that are initiated by the U.S. Department of Labor Wage and Hour Division, state employees will not be able to take legal action against their employers. Consequently, if a state employee believes he or she is being denied certain rights under the FMLA, the complaint will have to be filed with the federal DOL, not in state court. Not only will this slow down the litigation process for state workers, but the DOL may have to fortify its legal staff to handle more cases. This ruling, however, should have no effect on the private sector.

### Notes

1. For various reasons, it is difficult to gather utilization rates of family leave in the states. One exception is Connecticut. Dennis O'Connor found that most leaves taken were shorter than the maximum twelve weeks under the FMLA. In 1998, the average leave for birth or adoption in Connecticut was 8.2 weeks, for family leave it was 4.3 weeks, and for personal medical leave it was 6.4 weeks. These findings coincide with those reported by the Commission on Leave in 1996. See O'Connor's "A 1998 Family and Medical Leave Summary for Connecticut Employees" (2000).

2. In several congressional hearings between 1999 and 2000, many representatives of the business community denounced the Commission on Leave's *A Workable Balance*, stating the study was done prematurely and the FMLA did have a negative financial impact on companies.

3. A brief but informative article on the difficulty of measuring a policy's impact is Lawrence F. Katz's (1997) commentary on Klerman and Leibowitz's "Labor

Supply Effects of State Maternity Leave Legislation" (1997).

4. Federal employees are covered under the Family Friendly Leave Act (FFLA), which has been in effect since 1994. Initially, it allowed a federal employee to use at least forty hours (five days), or an additional sixty-four hours (eight days), of his/her sick leave to care for or attend to a family member who is ill or injured, or for purposes related to the death of a family member. However, on May 23, 1999, President Clinton issued a directive that allows federal employees to annually use up to twelve weeks of accrued sick leave to care for a spouse, son, daughter, or parent with a serious health condition. The president also directed the Office of Personnel Management (OPM) to establish an Interagency Family Friendly Workplace Working Group "to promote, evaluate, and exchange information on Federal family-friendly workplace initiatives." For more information about the federal law, see Barbara L. Schwemle's "Use of Sick Leave by Federal Employees to Care for Sick Family Members" (1999). Also see U.S. Office of Personnel Management, *A Review of Federal Family-Friendly Workplace Arrangements* (1998). Available on the Internet at http://www.opm.gov/wrkfam.

5. There are at least two works that have explored the FMLA in litigation. See Sharon M. Dietrich's "Recent Developments Under the Family and Medical Leave Act—The Courts Start to Speak" (1998), a paper published by the National Employment Law Project, Philadelphia, PA. Also see Mary K. O'Melveny's paper, "Representing the Injured Worker: Recent Developments Under the Americans with Disabilities Act and the Family and Medical Leave Act" (1996).

# Part III

**Toward the Future**

# Chapter 8

# Toward Paid Leave

Between 1993 and 1999, almost twenty initiatives were put forth by members of Congress to expand the Family and Medical Leave Act. Some wanted the law to apply to smaller companies, others wanted to include additional hours to address basic family needs, such as taking children to dental appointments or for attending parent-teacher meetings. Still others proposed that the coverage be expanded to include domestic partners, parents-in-law, and grandparents. Several proposals were extremely narrow in focus and specific in structure, such as allowing employees to take leave for literacy training, to make living organ donations, and to prevent employers from requiring employees to take FMLA disputes to arbitration instead of court. All legislative proposals failed, however (Gladstone 1999; Jordan 1999).

When President Clinton celebrated the fourth anniversary of the Family and Medical Leave Act during his weekly radio address on February 1, 1997, he reminded listeners that the FMLA was the first piece of legislation he signed. He also took the opportunity to praise the bill's success and called upon Congress to expand the law. Workers should be permitted to take up to twenty-four hours of unpaid leave a year to attend parent-teacher conferences or take a child to dental or medical appointments, he argued. "By expanding family leave we can enable millions more of our fellow Americans to meet their responsibilities both at home and at work," he stated. "Our society can never be stronger than the children we raise or the families in which we raise them" (Office of the Press Secretary 1997).

Congress did not respond to the president's proposal in 1997, nor did it respond two years later when he recommended that the law be expanded further. Beyond his recommendation that twenty-four hours be added to ad-

dress family obligations, Clinton also urged Congress to cover more workers. In his State of the Union address on January 19, 1999, the president
reminded Americans that the law was not only effective, but its impact on
business was minimal. "I think it's time, with all the evidence that it has been
so little burdensome to employers, to extend family leave to more Americans
working for smaller companies" (Office of the Press Secretary, 1999). Although bills to amend the law were introduced in both houses of the 106th
Congress, none moved beyond committee.

In the House, Representative William Clay (D-MO), sponsor of the original leave bill in 1985, introduced H.R. 91, the "Family and Medical Leave
Improvement Act." The bill reduced the employee cutoff requirement from
fifty workers to twenty-five and included elder care in the additional twenty-
four-hour provision that Clinton had proposed two years earlier. The decision to include elder care should not be ignored. After all, once the original
leave bill in the 1980s was expanded to include care of elderly parents, the
FMLA picked up more support. A similar strategy was employed in 1999, at
least in the House. In the Senate, a companion bill, the "Family and Medical
Leave Fairness Act" (S.201), was introduced by Chris Dodd (D-CT). However, unlike Clay's proposal, the Dodd bill did not include elder care, thus
following a pattern from the 1980s. That is, Dodd was hesitant about including elder care in the original FMLA but eventually changed his mind when
he needed more votes in the Senate.

Confronted with a Republican Congress in the second half of his final
term, the lame-duck and beleaguered president, who survived an impeachment trial in the Senate, realized that few of his legislative proposals would
succeed. To overcome this obstacle, the president followed a path not unfamiliar to his predecessors. He deliberately bypassed Congress by issuing
orders to his federal agencies. Frustrated over Congress's inability to expand
the FMLA, Clinton chose to change the venue of the debate in the spring of
1999 from Capitol Hill to the Department of Labor.

In his commencement address at Grambling State University in Louisiana on May 23, 1999, the president announced two new initiatives aimed at
the FMLA. First, he directed the Department of Labor to explore ways states
may use surplus unemployment insurance funds to subsidize parents who
use the FMLA to care for a newborn or newly adopted child. The second
initiative recommended that federal employees be permitted to use up to
twelve weeks of accrued sick leave to care for a seriously ill child, parent, or
spouse. Prior to 1999, federal workers could only use up to thirteen days of
accrued sick leave per year to care for seriously ill family members. "I believe it is imperative that your country give you the tools to succeed not only
in the workplace but also at home. If you or any American has to choose

between being a good parent and successful in your careers, you have paid a terrible price, and so has your country," he told the graduates (President's Commencement Address 1999).

The following day, Clinton issued an Executive Memorandum entitled "New Tools to Help Parents Balance Work and Family." In the memo, the president ordered the secretary of labor, Alexis Herman, to propose regulations that would allow states to use Unemployment Insurance (UI) funds to support parents on leave following the birth or adoption of a child. He also called upon the secretary to develop model legislation that states could adopt in following these new regulations (Presidential Memorandum 1999).

Under the president's proposal, states would be permitted to tap the surpluses of their Unemployment Insurance trust funds to cover twelve weeks of parental leave. In short, any employee leaving work under the FMLA for the birth or adoption of a child would be classified as temporarily laid off, and therefore declared eligible for unemployment compensation. The idea runs parallel to the use of Temporary Disability Insurance, which provides a wage replacement for new mothers in five states, a model that was previously discussed. It should be emphasized here, however, that Clinton's recommendation regarding the use of UI funds was a fairly incremental step in that it only applied to child care and not to the care needs of other family members. The proposal was also unique and controversial, forcing many to explore the original purpose and history of Unemployment Insurance and compare it to Temporary Disability Insurance.

### Unemployment Insurance

The Unemployment Insurance system, created in the depths of the Great Depression, is a joint federal-state program that is administered by each state but with oversight authority assigned to the U.S. Department of Labor. Its original purpose was twofold. One, from a micro perspective, it was designed to serve as a safety net for the male breadwinner under the traditional family wage system. Payments to laid-off workers guaranteed, for a limited period of time, access to basic necessities (food, shelter, and clothing) until a job was found. And two, from a macro perspective, its purpose was to prevent occasional recessions from growing into major depressions. In Fiscal Year 1997 alone, even during a booming economy, nearly 8 million people received $20.6 billion in UI benefits (U.S. Department of Labor 1999).

Established by the Social Security Act of 1935 and implemented through the Federal Unemployment Tax Act, it is a self-financing system that is funded entirely through employers' state and federal payroll taxes, although a few states require small employee payments. That is, tax money collected from employers is maintained in state trust funds during economic upswings and spent during recessions. Because federal law dictates that trust funds must be maintained at a specified level, a significant drop in reserve funds automatically demands an increase in taxes. Employees pay nothing into the program (except very small amounts in a few states), but receive a partial wage replacement for a limited period, initially ranging as high as twenty-six weeks with a possibility of extending it to a maximum of forty-six weeks, depending on state policy. In FY 1997, about 6.3 million employers paid $22.2 billion in state unemployment compensation taxes (U.S. Department of Labor 1999).

An obvious concern to policymakers is the solvency of state trust funds. Put in more technical terms, the Average High Cost Multiple (AHCM) is the Department of Labor's measure for determining the number of years a state can afford to pay UI benefits during periods of severe recessions. According to the DOL, the acceptable AHCM level is 1.0, meaning that a state's trust fund could be the source of unemployment benefits for one year during a major recession without having to raise taxes. Once funds diminish to a point below a preestablished threshold, taxes are increased. If funds are depleted entirely, however, states must then borrow from the federal government in order to provide income for the unemployed. During the 1980–82 recession, for example, thirty-three states had to borrow more than $20 billion from the federal government to replenish depleted reserves. In 1998, the DOL predicted that a recession comparable to those of the 1980s could create a borrowing frenzy among twenty-five to thirty states that may total $20–$25 billion (U.S. Department of Labor 1998).

But since the end of the last recession in 1992, the American economy has grown beyond expectations, resulting in an unemployment rate that reached its lowest point in three decades. When Clinton entered the White House in 1993, the Dow Jones average stood at 3,000. By mid-2000, it was hovering around 10,800. Similarly, between 1992 and 1998, state UI trust fund reserves increased by 85 percent, doubling from $26 billion to about $52 billion (National Employment Law Project 1999). By 1998, thirty-three states had exceeded the AHCM standard in spite of the DOL's report that 7,263,000 people received $19.3 billion in UI benefits that year. That converts to an average weekly benefit of about $200 nationwide (Hattiangadi 2000).

An expanding economy and several other developments drew attention to Unemployment Insurance as a possible means for providing paid leave. First, with women entering the job market in record numbers, concerns were raised that traditional caregivers would devote less time to family needs without some compensation. When the Commission on Leave reported in 1996 that nearly two-thirds of those who desired to take leave could not do so because of financial reasons, the search for a wage replacement began, though quietly at first. Surplus revenues in state unemployment trust funds were particularly appealing to advocacy groups and some politicians who were uneasy about raising taxes to support paid family leave.

Second, as corporations generated record profits during the 1990s, the business lobby succeeded in getting UI taxes reduced dramatically during the same time period. For example, UI tax cuts in Georgia in 1998 cost the trust fund $122 million. In Michigan, four straight years of UI tax cuts of 10 percent cost the trust fund more than $750 million. And, in South Carolina, a 50 percent tax cut in 1998 cost that UI trust fund $50 million. Overall, at least fifteen states significantly cut UI taxes in recent years and many other states introduced legislation designed to do the same. As a result, between 1993 and 1998, the average rate of employer contributions to the UI system, as a percentage of taxable wages, dropped from 2.5 percent to 1.92 percent (National Employment Law Project 1999). Therefore, argued proponents of Clinton's proposal, how can conservative politicians complain that paid family leave will deplete UI trust funds when the business lobby has already succeeded in reducing UI reserves through major tax cuts? If anyone should receive a break, they argued, it should be America's family caregivers, not wealthy corporations.

A third development was the ability of proponents of paid leave to stand a traditional conservative argument on its head. That is, they have framed it as a "states rights" issue. Recall that a key component of Reagan/Bush policy, and one that has never been denounced by Clinton, if not endorsed by him, was New Federalism. Today it is referred to as "devolution." In short, the more federal power that is shifted to the states, the better. Ironically, perhaps, Unemployment Insurance was originally designed as a federal-state partnership with much flexibility granted to the states. Consequently, a variety of policies have been implemented among a number of states that have been approved by the Department of Labor and coincide with arguments put forth by supporters of the Clinton proposal.

For example, in seven states, employers may temporarily lay off workers during economic downturns. If the employees are not available to work elsewhere, they will receive UI benefits until they are recalled within a specified time period. One-third of the states provide UI benefits if employees must vacate their jobs through circumstances beyond their control, such as a spouse being relocated. And several states allow benefits to be paid to workers who leave their positions for job-training programs approved by their employers. If employees can take time off under these conditions and still receive Unemployment Insurance, argue supporters of paid leave, why should not the demands of family care be viewed in the same light (National Employment Law Project 1999)?

But at least two questions continue to cloud the debate over the use of Unemployment Insurance trust funds to provide paid family leave. One concerns presidential power, the other revolves around the issue of cost. With respect to the former question, the nonpartisan Congressional Research Service (CRS) has challenged the president's action. According to the CRS, under federal law, any money withdrawn from the trust fund must be used exclusively for the payment of unemployment compensation. Although states may redefine unemployment compensation to include family leave, such a step would fly in the face of the legislative intent and historical interpretation of the original law (Pear 1999, 18A).

The U.S. Chamber of Commerce (COC) reached the same conclusion. On June 26, 2000, the Chamber sued the Department of Labor to prevent states from offering paid leave through Unemployment Insurance. The COC petitioned the U.S. District Court for the District of Columbia to grant an injunction blocking any state program enacted during judicial proceedings. The Chamber's major argument is based on its belief that the DOL's regulations violate federal laws, including one that reserves unemployment benefits only for those unsuccessfully seeking work. Two other business groups, LPA Inc. and the Society for Human Resource Management (SHRM), plus two companies, Counterpulsation Inc. of Framingham, Massachusetts, and Danneman's Auto Service Inc. of Laurel, Maryland, joined the Chamber in its lawsuit (Love 2000).

Concerning the second question, cost, it will be discussed in greater detail later in this chapter. However, to counter accusations that businesses are benefiting from UI tax cuts while simultaneously opposing alternative uses of surplus funds, the Employment Policy Foundation, a pro-business consulting firm, warns that the president's proposal will produce a financial disaster. The EPF predicts that the UI trust funds in forty-five states will be insolvent in three years if twelve weeks of paid leave are offered, and forty-nine states will be insolvent in three years if twenty-six weeks of paid leave are offered under the FMLA (Employment Policy Foundation 1999).

**Temporary Disability Insurance**

Though not included in the president's proposal, Temporary Disability Insurance (TDI), as was discussed in chapter 5, has been employed by five states to provide a wage replacement to women for the birth or adoption of a child. TDI states are required to offer paid leave to employed women who are having children, just as they are required to offer paid leave to other employees who need time off for medical reasons. In most cases, TDI is funded through joint employer-employee contributions, and both the utilization rate and the amount of wage replacement varies by state. For example, claims for pregnancy and childbirth account for between 12 and 22 percent of the total claims in the five TDI states, and the average length of pregnancy leave taken is less than twelve weeks, which is below the FMLA maximum allotment (Wever 1996). With respect to wage replacement, the amount ranges between 50 and 60 percent, depending on state policy.

Like all insurance programs, the success or failure of Temporary Disability Insurance depends on how frequently the event covered by insurance actually occurs. Ideally, of course, small premiums collected from a large number of subscribers will cover all claims and still generate a substantial profit. According to a recent study by Hartmann, Yoon, et al. (1995), no state with a TDI program has a claims rate that exceeds 101 per 1,000 covered employees, and some report a claims rate as low as 55 per 1,000 workers. By all actuarial standards, such a ratio is considered to be very healthy within the insurance industry.

Including an overview of Temporary Disability Insurance in a discussion about the feasibility of using Unemployment Insurance as a wage replacement under the FMLA is important for at least two reasons. One, the TDI model has been in effect in five states for three decades or more. Thus, there exists a longitudinal database on usage and costs that policy researchers could tap and apply to the UI model. And two, there is information already available on the TDI programs that may prove helpful in predicting the impact of a UI wage replacement system for family leave. For example, a 1995 study found that California's TDI law "had no effect on absenteeism, tardiness, morale, productivity, retention, hiring, public relations or supervisory and co-worker relationships" (Wever 1996, 15). A small minority of firms even reported that the mandated paid leave program had a positive effect on employee morale, hiring, and public relations. Five years earlier, in a similar study, Trzcinski and Albert (1991) reached the same conclusion and emphasized that paid family care decreases turnover and is less costly than hiring and training new workers.

But despite these findings, limited in number as they are, an important unknown continues to lurk in the dark. That is, neither proponents nor opponents know for sure what the impact may be in terms of use and cost if the TDI model were expanded to include family care. Researchers at the Institute of Women's Policy Research, who are studying the feasibility of expanding TDI coverage beyond child care, concede that insufficient data on the likely usage of paid leave for family matters creates a major obstacle for policymakers who want to move forward on this issue (Hartmann, Yoon, et al. 1995). Perhaps that reason alone, more than any other, explains Clinton's incremental step of limiting UI coverage to childbirth and adoption. But with baby boomers nearing retirement, challenges of future caregivers will extend well beyond meeting the demands of small children. The role of the family and to what extent it should be supported by public funds for providing less expensive long-term, noninstitutional care of the elderly will be one of the most important public-policy questions facing legislators for the next twenty-five years.

### Reactions to the President's Proposal

Senior Republicans in Congress, including Representative Bill Archer of Texas, chair of the powerful House Ways and Means Committee, and Representative Nancy Johnson of Connecticut, sent a letter to the White House criticizing the president's actions. Using Unemployment Insurance funds for family leave would pit out-of-work Americans against their neighbors who have jobs, they argued. Democratic Senator Chris Dodd of Connecticut defended the president's initiative and reminded critics that because leave was unpaid, many people who needed time off for family matters could not afford to take it. To show support for the president's bold proposal, less than two months after the president's Grambling address, Dodd called on Congress in mid-July of 1999 to provide up to $400 million in federal funding a year, for five years, to establish state demonstration projects in paid leave.

Reactions of interest groups were also predictable. The National Federation of Independent Businesses and the U.S. Chamber of Commerce immediately voiced their opposition to the proposal. Patrick J. Cleary, vice president of the National Association of Manufacturers, an organization that opposed the FMLA from its inception, referred to Clinton's plan as "the nuttiest idea we have seen in a long time" (Pear 1999, 18A). Maurice Emsellem, an attorney for the National Employment Law Project and a strong advocate for paid leave, countered opponents' arguments by insisting that states have been both permitted and even encouraged to experiment with their unemployment compensation system since the early years of the New Deal.[1] His sentiments were echoed by Donna Lehnoff of the National Partnership for Women and Families (Lenhoff 2000).

For Richard Hobbie, however, the issue was not so black and white. Representing the Interstate Conference of Employment Security Agencies, a national organization of state labor officials, Hobbie and his organization supported the concept of paid leave but opposed the use of Unemployment Insurance trust funds to finance it. "State officials would argue that workers on family leave ought to be able to get benefits under some other government program or from employers," stated Hobbie (Pear 1999, 18A). But at least one member of Hobbie's organization disagreed with that position.

Thomas S. Whitaker, deputy chairman of the North Carolina Employment Security Commission, said he liked Clinton's proposal because it empowered states to do what they felt was best for their citizens. "If states don't want to do it, they don't have to," Mr. Whitaker said. "I hope the Labor Department takes that approach on other issues" (Pear 1999, 18A).

The mainstream media, particularly major newspapers, tended to support the proposal. The *New York Times*, the *Washington Post*, the *Atlanta Journal Constitution*, the *Baltimore Sun*, the *Hartford Courant*, and the *New Jersey Star Ledger* all carried favorable editorials. *The Chicago Tribune* conducted a poll and found that 88 percent of Chicago-area chief executives believed that the FMLA had no effect on their businesses, and 5 percent stated that it helped their firms (Goozner 1999).[2] Ellen Goodman, the syndicated columnist, came out in support of the proposal but dismissed it as too little too late. Referring to Clinton as the "Commander in Chief of Incrementalism," Goodman considered the labeling of parental leave as "unemployment" was a mere sleight of hand by a crafty politician. "He takes one teeny step at a time, extending a bit of health coverage for kids here, a touch of child care there," she writes. "In return, the Democratic Party has been rewarded—over-rewarded—with the terminal gratitude of women and a reputation as the party that cares about working families" (Goodman 1999, 14).

In the midst of much criticism and controversy, the Department of Labor responded to the president's May directive by issuing its "proposed unemployment compensation/parental leave regulations" on December 3, 1999 (U.S. Department of Labor 1999). During a sixty-day comment period that ran from December 3 to February 2, the DOL received nearly 4,000 comments from representatives on both sides of the issue. Those arguing against the adoption of the regulations, mostly from the business community, submitted 1,840 letters stating their respective positions. Supporters of the proposal filed 1,619 letters with the agency. Another 300 submissions did not state a position either way (Personal Communication 2000). After the dust had settled, however, the statements for and against the president's proposal were both clear and predictable.

Proponents employed three major strategies in putting forth their arguments. First, they reminded DOL's Commissioner Herman that traditional caregivers, namely women, continue to enter the labor force on a massive scale. Therefore, the original purpose and design of the UI system needs to be revisited and changed in order to accommodate the demands of modern family life. Second, the idea of providing funds to workers on leave who do not vacate their jobs involuntarily is not a revolutionary policy proposal. As indicated in the preceding discussion, many states allow corporations to temporarily furlough workers during economic downturns, and permit employees to collect unemployment checks during job-training programs if they promise to return to work. Clinton's proposal is merely adding one more option to what some consider a fairly flexible menu of choices under the current UI program. And third, proponents also contend that generous tax cuts to corporations are as much a threat to the solvency of state UI trust funds as any paid family-leave program could possibly be. Therefore, why not use the funds to support America's families instead of lining the pockets of big business?

Opponents, on the other hand, have argued that the U.S. Department of Labor lacks the authority to enact the regulations proposed by Clinton and has underestimated the costs of such a program. Further, they contend that the use of UI surplus funds for voluntary leave was not the original intent of the law, that paid leave will drive up the utilization rate of unemployment compensation, which will in turn cause an increase in corporate taxes in order to keep state UI trust funds solvent. And also, because the UI program is supported entirely by corporate payroll taxes, big business will be harmed financially, and will find it increasingly difficult to compete in the global economy. This in turn will drive up consumer prices in the United States and potentially result in more worker layoffs. And finally, in an argument that is all too familiar to feminists, opponents of the president's plan argue that it will inhibit women's progress in the private sector because businesses will be inclined to avoid hiring them in the first place. As the primary caregivers, women will be more willing to leave work for family matters if a wage replacement is available. This practice of "planned absenteeism" will disrupt corporate culture, they contend (Employment Policy Foundation 1999). But meanwhile, as the debate ensued at the national level, state legislators were acting on Clinton's proposal.

## State Initiatives

In 1997, almost two years before the president's Grambling address, several states had already proposed using UI funds to provide paid family and medical leave. In Vermont, for example, the state AFL-CIO pushed legislators to tap surplus reserves in the UI fund. However, because skeptics raised legal issues with the Department of Labor, the Vermont bill was never considered by the legislature. In 1998, several interest groups, including the national AFL-CIO, the National Employment Law Project, and the National Partnership for Women and Families, collaborated on writing model legislation that addressed the legal questions raised by the DOL. By the close of the 1998 legislative session, four states (Vermont, Maryland, Massachusetts, and Washington) had introduced bills designed to cover paid leave through the use of UI funds. All four proposals addressed two questions raised by the DOL:

One, did workers leave their jobs for reasons permitted by the state? Or, in other words, did the state's labor law include a "voluntary quit provision?" And two, were workers who took family leave considered able and available for work after they started to receive benefits?

Although not one of the four bills passed in 1998, their very existence drew attention from the White House and inspired the president to include the UI proposal in his Grambling address. Spurred on by Clinton's initiative, thirteen states, between May 23, 1999 and July 2000, introduced legislation that included a provision for some type of paid family leave. These states included California, Connecticut, Georgia, Illinois, Indiana, Maine, Massachusetts, Maryland, Minnesota, New Hampshire, New Jersey, Vermont, and Washington. Two states, Iowa in 1998 and California in 1999, proposed bills to fund feasibility studies on paid family leave. Iowa explored the creation of a special care fund independent of Unemployment Insurance. California focused on the fiscal impact of expanding the TDI program to include family care.

Among the thirteen states, there was much variation in both the aim and structure of their bills. There was also much variation geographically, with states in the Northeast, the South, the Midwest, and the Pacific coast represented. All but one state (Indiana) had passed some form of family-leave law prior to the enactment of the federal FMLA in 1993. A summary of the particular proposals put forth by each of the thirteen states during the 1999–2000 legislative session is presented below, with state initiatives described in alphabetical order.

### California

Most of the legislative action in California concerning family leave took place during the 1999 legislative session. A law was enacted to fund a study on the cost of expanding the state's TDI program beyond childbirth or adoption to cover family leave. The weekly TDI benefit cap was also increased from $336 to $490. It was also in 1999 that California adopted a law mandating that employers who already provide paid sick leave permit their employees to use some of their leave to care for other family members, such as an ill spouse, child, or elderly parent.

On May 24, 2000, Democratic Governor Gray Davis vetoed a bill that would have expanded the state's family-leave law. The vetoed bill would have expanded the act to include caring for adult children, grandparents, domestic partners, or others who depend on the employee for support.[3] "This measure, while well-intentioned, extends that right far beyond what any other state has permitted to a relationship outside the family," Davis said in his veto message (*San Jose Mercury News* May 25, 2000, 1).

## Connecticut

The Connecticut legislature, in response to a report issued by a special Family Leave Task Force, considered but did not pass a bill that coincided with President Clinton's proposal. Somewhat of a hybrid version, Connecticut's proposed bill would have created a wage-replacement system for qualified employees who take leave to care for a newborn or a newly adopted child, or due to the employee's own illness or the illness of a family member. However, only UI funds would be used to cover the birth or adoption provision; other leaves would be funded through a new Medical Leave Insurance Fund to be created by the new law. The proposal was passed by the General Assembly's Labor and Public Employees Committee but was defeated by the Appropriations Committee. However, a separate bill was passed that assigned funds to the Office of Policy and Management to conduct a fiscal-impact study of using UI reserves to support paid leave. The report is due on July 1, 2001.

## Georgia

Georgia introduced one of the more unique proposals during the 2000 legislative session. Employing the UI model recommended by Clinton, it offered a wage replacement for workers on leave if they could prove the existence of an "undue family hardship." Included in this category are victims of domestic violence who need time to recover and parents who need to care for ill children or other seriously ill family members. But the unique feature of the bill was its coverage of domestic violence. None of the other states had included such a provision in their proposals. Nevertheless, Georgia's bill died in committee.

## Illinois

In February 2000, the Illinois legislature introduced a bill that coincided with the Clinton initiative. That is, based on the provisions of the FMLA, all employees would be eligible for twelve weeks of paid leave, funded by the state's UI reserves. Although the bill died by April, another proposal to create a special working group to study paid leave was acted upon favorably. A final report is to be completed and submitted to the legislature by December 1, 2000.

## Indiana

Similar to Illinois, the Indiana legislature introduced a bill in early January 2000 calling for twelve weeks of paid leave covered by UI funds to care for a newborn or newly adopted child. Although the bill passed by a 52–44 bipartisan vote in the Indiana House, it stalled in the Senate. However, it was the first wage-replacement bill under the FMLA to be passed by a legislative chamber (National Partnership for Women and Families 2000).

## Maryland

As California did in 1999, Maryland enacted a law that required employers that were already providing paid leave to workers to expand their coverage. Therefore, workers who received a corporate-funded wage replacement following the birth of a child were required to grant the same leave to employees for the adoption of a child. However, with respect to extending paid leave to employees under the FMLA, Maryland failed to enact such a measure. Despite heavy lobbying efforts by advocacy groups who supported the UI funding model, the House Committee on Economic Matters killed the bill in the spring of 2000.

## Massachusetts

Massachusetts, following a strategy similar to other states, introduced several bills during the 1999–2000 sessions that included paid leave. One called for using Unemployment Insurance trust funds to provide a wage replacement for employees who take family and medical leave. Another bill established a financing mechanism that would have created a "family employment security trust fund" that could be tapped by caregivers. And one other legislative proposal would have established a state-mandated Temporary Disability Insurance system similar to the five programs that exist in California, Hawaii, New Jersey, New York, and Rhode Island. Although the state legislature passed a bill in the summer of 2000 that would have used UI funds to provide paid leave, it was ultimately killed by Governor Paul Cellucci. But unlike most states that introduced legislation, Massachusetts sought to expand coverage under the FMLA so that paid care would extend beyond childbirth and adoption. It should also be noted that in the mid-1980s when a handful of states were seeking to adopt family leave, Massachusetts was the first to propose paid leave. In short, TDI coverage for pregnancy would have been extended to include paid leave for family care in general. However, the initiative never emerged from legislative committee (Wisensale 1991a).

## Minnesota

Two bills introduced during the 2000 legislative session included a wage replacement for workers taking leave to care for a newborn or newly adopted child. One would have tapped the state's UI trust funds to guarantee unemployment compensation to workers taking time off under the state's "birth and adoption leave." Minnesota had created a unique program two years earlier in which low-income parents receive a subsidy if they remain home from work to care for infants under the age of one. A second bill offered incentives to employers to provide partially paid parental (not family) leave by creating a state "match program." That is, Minnesota would match an employer's contribution to an employee's wage replacement while the worker is on leave to care for a newborn or newly adopted child.

## New Hampshire

New Hampshire was one of four states that displayed some interest in adopting paid family leave, but chose to postpone any legislative action until a feasibility study was completed. In April 2000, Governor Jeanne Shaheen signed a bill produced by the legislature that created a special study commission charged with exploring a variety of options for providing FMLA benefits, including a wage replacement. The deadline for completing the report is December 2000. The other three states that chose to study the issue before proceeding are Connecticut, Illinois, and New York. Also, near the close of its legislative session, Massachusetts was also considering the creation of a special study commission (National Partnership for Women and Families 2000).

## New Jersey

As one of the five TDI states, New Jersey is both familiar and comfortable with paid leave that is funded through an employee insurance program. However, typical of the TDI model, paid leave was available only for childbirth. During the 2000 legislative session, New Jersey introduced Assembly Bill 2037. It would make twelve weeks of benefits available for workers taking leave to care for ill family members ("family temporary disability" or "FTD" leave), or to care for children during the first twelve months after their birth or adoption ("birth and adoption" or "BAA" leave). FTD benefits would be paid from temporary disability insurance (TDI), while BAA benefits would be covered under unemployment insurance. Thus, paid leave would be available to those who care for a newborn or adopted child, an ill parent, spouse, or child. However, the bill was shelved pending the completion, release, and discussion of a detailed cost study.

## New York

New York, a TDI state, moved on two fronts with respect to paid family leave. First, choosing to bypass President Clinton's proposal, the legislature chose instead to focus on expanding the state's TDI program to include family leave. And second, New York was among four states to fund a study on the feasibility of providing paid family leave.

## Vermont

Two bills were introduced by the Vermont legislature during the 2000 legislative session that dealt with paid family leave. One proposal called for a wage replacement funded by general tax revenues. Apparently, some legislators in Vermont may have been inspired by President Clinton's initiative to provide paid family leave, but they chose not to adopt the model he proposed. Instead, some of Vermont's lawmakers opted for a funding mechanism that was not considered by any other state. Instead of tapping state UI funds to provide a wage replacement, a bipartisan bill introduced in 2000 called for a three-year pilot program in which employees would receive a wage replacement during leave to care for a newborn or newly adopted child. Its uniqueness can be found in its financing mechanism: general tax revenues. Other states proposed either the UI or TDI program as a funding source. But another bill in Vermont did employ the UI model, providing a wage replacement for twelve weeks of leave. It also experienced some legislative success in that it passed the Vermont Senate in May when the lieutenant governor broke a tie vote. However, it failed in the House.

### Washington

Of the thirteen states that introduced legislation to provide paid leave, Washington was perhaps the most conservative in terms of benefits. It did employ the UI model to fund paid leave, but unlike other states that maintained the FMLA's duration of twelve weeks, Washington limited its bill to just five weeks and the coverage to just birth or adoption; broader family care was not included. Fearing that a more ambitious approach, such as twenty-six weeks of leave to care for family members, would create a backlash, supporters chose the safer incremental route. Based on a fiscal impact study, business taxes would not have to be increased to support a five-week leave, but taxes would rise considerably if twelve weeks of paid leave were provided. Although the bill was acted upon favorably by the Senate Committee on Labor and Workforce Development, it passed neither house of the legislature.

So, by the close of the 1999–2000 legislative session, thirteen states had responded to Clinton's Grambling speech and introduced legislation designed to provide some sort of wage replacement for workers on leave. Although most of the states proposed using UI reserves to fund paid leave, several attempted to broaden their already existing TDI programs to offer a wage replacement. However, as of July 1, 2000, not one initiative succeeded. On the other hand, four states, cautious about cost estimates, chose to postpone action until fiscal impact studies could be completed. Provided the economy remains healthy and UI trust funds continue to increase, it is likely that similar bills will be introduced again in the states during the next legislative session. And, not unlike the 1999–2000 term, cost will be the focal point of the debate

### The Cost Issue

In discussing the matter of cost, it is important to keep in mind two very important facts related to the FMLA and the Clinton initiative to use UI funds to cover paid leave. First, under the president's proposal, which is also known as Birth and Adoption Unemployment Compensation (BAA-UC), "Baby UC," or "Baby UI," those who work for companies with *fewer* than fifty employees may be eligible to receive UI benefits, depending how a given state frames its particular law. So not only is Clinton bypassing Congress with his BAA-UC proposal, he is also circumventing his own FMLA which applies to companies of fifty or more employees. Therefore, the determining factor with respect to access may not be company size but worker eligibility under the existing UI system. As a result, the scope of coverage will be broadened and, it is assumed, more workers will use it than under the current system of unpaid leave. Second, however, the Clinton initiative is also limited in scope in that it only applies to birth or adoption, *not* to family leave, as was the original intent of the FMLA. Here again the president is bypassing the FMLA. Therefore, any concerns about potential "overuse" of the new benefit may be neutralized by the fact that fewer workers will be eligible to receive paid leave.

Obviously aware of these two facts, the U.S. Department of Labor began drafting regulations concerning the use of UI funds to cover paid leave. Meanwhile, as was discussed above, the thirteen states introduced legislation to either enact such a policy or consider others similar to it. From the very beginning, there was little doubt in anyone's mind that the focus of the legislative debates would be on cost. However, because of the uniqueness of Clinton's proposal, there was little information available that could inform policymakers about the fiscal impact such an initiative might have on their state. Estimates based on assumptions would have to be forged from data collected for reasons unrelated to family leave. To address concerns raised by both proponents and opponents about using UI reserves to fund paid leave, the DOL devised a methodology for estimating the costs of such a program. Four states—Maryland, Massachusetts, Vermont, and Washington—were used by the DOL to construct its model. All four maintained Average High Cost Multiples (AHCM) either at or above the U.S. average of 0.94 in 1998. As stated previously, the AHCM is the DOL's standard measure for UI trust-fund solvency.

States either adopted the DOL model or crafted their own with a few modifications to address their specific needs. But regardless of what particular model was used to estimate cost, the DOL and the four states all manipulated their data within the parameters of five important policy questions. One, what will be the "take-up rate" if a wage replacement is provided under the FMLA? In other words, how many employees covered by Unemployment Insurance will use the new benefit? Two, what is the best estimate that can be made in terms of the duration of the leave employees will take? Will they use the full twelve weeks under the FMLA, or follow the pattern of only seven to eight weeks as has been reported under the current system in which there is no wage replacement? Third, what is the average weekly benefit amount (AWBA) paid out by each state, and how much will this total be when multiplied by the "take-up rate" and duration? Fourth, what sort of fiscal impact will such a new law have on a state in terms of total costs, depletion of UI reserve funds, and the need for corporate tax increases to cover the program? And finally, what are the estimated administrative costs for such a new program, both in the first year of implementation and over the long haul?

With respect to the first question concerning "take-up rates," the DOL assumed that an overwhelming majority of leave-takers would be employed women up to age fifty who are UI eligible and have a child under the age of one. This assumption was based on an analysis of 1997–98 data from the Current Population Survey and the Commission on Leave's study, *A Workable Balance.* From this data, the DOL concluded that 98 percent of women and 5 percent of men covered by UI and with children under one year old would take leave. UI eligible workers who had some sort of private paid-leave coverage (full or partial) provided by their employers were then subtracted from the total estimate. Also excluded were self-employed women up to age fifty who were not covered by Unemployment Insurance. But even though the estimates take multiple factors into consideration, at least two significant unknowns will haunt state policymakers in the future. One, how many people will *actually* take leave? And two, for how long?

Concerning the second question, duration of leave, the DOL relied on previous research conducted by Paul T. Decker. He concluded that "the lengthening in average unemployment spells is likely to be in the range of 0.5 weeks to 1.5 weeks for every 10 percentage-point increase in wage replacement rates" (Decker 1997, 296). In short, the more generous the wage replacement, the more likely the leave taken will be longer. In developing its model, the DOL operated under two assumptions in addressing the issue of duration. First, it assumed that all UI eligible workers would use the maximum amount of leave permitted in each state. Because most state laws coincided with provisions under the federal FMLA, that meant a twelve-week leave period. And second, the DOL also assumed that partially paid workers in the private sector (those who receive some wage replacement from their employer) would have a UI duration period half that of unpaid leave-takers.

The third major factor to be considered by the DOL was the average weekly benefit amount (AWBA) in each state, and based on that, plus the average take-up rate and duration of leave, how much will be paid out in benefits? It is primarily at this point where states display much variation in reporting the estimated costs of their proposed programs, mainly because each state offers a different weekly UI benefit amount to its unemployed. It ranges from more than $300 a week in states such as California, Connecticut, New Jersey, and New York, to less than $200 a week in states like Arizona, Louisiana, Mississippi, and South Dakota. Among the thirteen states that have introduced legislation to provide paid leave, the range is from about $350 a week in Massachusetts to around $200 in Indiana. Because women tend to earn less than men, they will most likely receive less in UI benefits than their male counterparts. To address this discrepancy, the DOL adjusted the AWBA downward by 3 percent because women, historically the lower earners, are the primary caregivers who will request leave. The AWBA is then multiplied by the estimated number of leave-takers (the take-up rate) and by the number of benefit weeks consumed during leave to produce the overall cost estimate for a given state.

The fourth area of concern that the DOL addressed in its methodology was the fiscal impact a UI-funded leave policy would have on a state's economy in general and on the solvency of the UI trust fund in particular. If enacted, it is assumed that the cost of the new program will be shifted to employers in increased UI taxes, either through an automatic "triggering mechanism" that is employed when trust funds fall below a specified level, or through legislated tax increases to maintain acceptable AHCM levels. The DOL also assumes that any tax increase on corporations will eventually be shifted to consumers in the form of higher prices.

The final component to be considered in making cost estimates is administrative costs. However, the DOL chose not to include administrative costs in their model because it was assumed that ongoing expenses due to increased workloads would be funded through the normal contingency funding process, as are increased workloads due to any other cause. If a state enacts BAA-UC, it will have to adapt accordingly in order to cover any increase in administrative costs, perhaps by shifting resources from other areas. However, according to DOL estimates, initial implementation costs should not exceed $1 million per state. That amount should then decrease over the years as the administration of the program becomes more efficient.

In 1999, the National Partnership for Women and Families compiled cost estimates that were prepared for six of the thirteen states proposing paid-leave legislation. Depending on the particular state, each cost study was completed by either a government agency or a private organization. Three states—Massachusetts, Vermont, and Washington—prepared cost estimates if Clinton's UI proposal (BAA-UC) is adopted. They are summarized in Table 8.1. Three other states—New York, New Jersey, and California, which are presented in Table 8.2—completed cost studies on the assumption that their existing TDI programs would be expanded to cover family care.

As indicated in Table 8.1, there is much variation among the three BAA-UC states in estimated take-up rates, length of leave, average weekly benefits, and cost. Only one of the three states, Washington, offered two variations of its proposed model, with the primary difference being in the length of the leave (thirty weeks under one model, five weeks under the other). In comparing the three states, it is clear that Massachusetts and Washington are most similar. They each serve about the same number of people under their current UI programs (2.6 to 3.0 million) and spend about the same amount of money on their unemployed ($783.5 to $801 million). However, fairly large discrepancies emerge when these two states are compared in terms of cost estimates under the BAA-UC proposal. For example, even under Washington's most expansive model (thirty weeks), the estimated total annual cost of expanding UI is $27.5 million, compared to Massachusetts's estimate of $200 million (twelve weeks). With respect to the "new cost as a percentage of total program," there is a glaring difference between 3 percent in Washington and 20 percent in Massachusetts. And even more interesting is the differences between the two states in "average cost per covered worker," with only eighty-eight cents a month or twenty cents a week for Washington compared to $5.56 a month or $1.25 for Massachusetts.

One explanation for these discrepancies may be found in the fact that Massachusetts lacked information under two of the most important categories: estimated number of leave-takers and the estimated length of leave. But still, major differences such as those illustrated in Table 8.1 attract skeptics, critics, and opponents of the BAA-UC strategy. The conflicting results may also explain why at least four of the thirteen states chose to appropriate funds to conduct their own studies before moving forward with legislation.

In July 2000, the Massachusetts figures were updated following a study by Randy Albelda and Tiffany Manuel (2000) of the Labor Resource Center at the University of Massachusetts, Boston. Based on state statistics from 1998, the researchers estimated the use and cost of paid parental leave using unemployment insurance. They assumed that there would be 28,887 claimants at a total annual cost of $32.7 billion, and an annual cost per covered worker of $10.81. Note that the latter figure of $10.81 is well above the $1.25 figure in Table 8.1. The average weekly wage for employees covered by the UI system in Massachusetts was $261 in 1998. The authors of the study, "Filling the Work and Family Gap: Paid Parental Leave in Massachusetts," anticipate increased use by those not currently covered by any paid-leave program and those who desire to take longer leaves. But again, until the methodology is completely refined and tested properly, cost estimates will differ within and between states.

Table 8.1

**Cost Estimates for Expanding State Unemployment Insurance (UI) Programs to Cover Periods of Family and Medical Leave: Summary of Studies**

| States | Washington 1999 Equal Opportunity Institute Study | | Massachusetts Albelda preliminary analysis | Vermont 1999 Associated Press estimate |
| | Variation 1 | Variation 2 | | |
| --- | --- | --- | --- | --- |
| Annual benefits paid under current UI program | $783.5 million | $783.5 million | $801 million | $46 million |
| Number of employees covered by UI | 2.6 million | 2.6 million | 3 million | 274,000 |
| Eligibility requirements benefits | Same as UI | Same as UI | Same as UI | Must be eligible for both UI *and* Vermont's Family and Medical Leave Law |
| New benefits coverage | | | | |
| Length of absence covered | 30 weeks | 5 weeks | 12 weeks | 12 weeks |
| Purposes of absence covered | • Care for newborn or newly adopted children <br> • Care for ill parents, spouses, or children <br> • Care for own serious medical condition | • Care for newborn or newly adopted children | • Care for newborn or newly adopted children <br> • Care for ill spouses, parents, or children | • Care for newborn or newly adopted children <br> • Care for ill spouses, parents, or children <br> • Care for own serious medical condition |

| | | | | |
|---|---|---|---|---|
| Estimated number of leave-takers likely to use new benefits | 16,665 | 11,279 | Not available | Not available |
| Average weekly benefit | $220 | $264 | $278.09 | $207.29 |
| Estimated length of leave | 7.5 weeks | 5 weeks | Not available | Not available |
| Estimated total annual cost of expanding UI to include family (and medical) leave | $27.5 million | $14.2 million | $200 million | $8–9 million |
| New cost as a percentage of total program | 3 percent | 2 percent | 20 percent | 14–16 percent |
| Average cost per covered worker | $0.88/month $0.20/week | $0.46/month $0.11/week | $5.56/month $1.25/week | $2.43–2.73/month $0.56–63/week |

*Source:* National Partnership for Women and Families, Washington, DC, 1999. Reprinted with permission. *Note:* A detailed explanation of this data is available from the NPWF (www.nationalpartnership.org).

Table 8.2 offers a different perspective on the issue of paid leave in that it depicts three of the five states that have adopted Temporary Disability Insurance as a means of financially supporting parents of newborns or newly adopted children. In 1999, each state considered expanding its TDI program to include family care. Although the same categories as those presented in Table 8.1 were used in making cost estimates, there was much variation among New York, New Jersey, and California in the amount of benefits paid out under TDI, the number of employees covered under the system, and the estimated number of leave-takers. As was the case with Massachusetts and Washington, there are obvious differences among the three TDI states in the estimated cost of expanding their programs, in the new cost as a percentage of the total program, and in the average cost per covered worker. Again, these discrepancies can be explained through a number of factors, including administrative inefficiencies, economies of scale, and the use or misuse of the particular cost-estimate methodology being employed. Whatever the explanation, the door is left wide open for critics of the new proposal to blast paid-leave initiatives. But on the other hand, even the highest cost per week per worker seems reasonable when one considers the benefit from what appears to be a relatively small cost.

Similar to Massachusetts, New Jersey released a study in the summer of 2000 that estimated the costs of Assembly Bill 2037 that called for a wage replacement under both the UI and the TDI systems (New Jersey is one of the five TDI states). Senior Legislative Analyst Gregory Williams (2000) completed the detailed study. At least one significant outcome of the research was that an expansion of TDI to cover "family temporary disability" (or FTD) will not create any tax increases for employers, but will raise worker TDI taxes by up to $21 per year per worker to cover the FTD benefit costs. At first blush, and without exploring the report's methodology in detail, that appears to be an extremely reasonable investment for the benefit it may provide.

One of the most aggressive and vocal groups to go on the attack against the use of UI funds to cover paid leave was the Employment Policy Foundation. As discussed briefly before, EPF is a self-described nonpartisan research and education organization devoted to the development of sound employment policy. Within a few months after President Clinton's Grambling address, EDF published its response to the White House initiative. *Paid Family Leave: At What Cost?* was supported by a grant from the Society for Human Resources Management and was authored by Anita U. Hattiangadi (2000), an EDF economist and specialist in work and family issues. The ninety-one-page report argues that U.S. policymakers will make a grave mistake if they use European parental-leave policies as models for a paid-leave program in the United States. The cradle-to-grave mentality of Europe runs counter to the history of industrial relations in the United States, argues the EPF. Benefits have traditionally been negotiated at the bargaining table, not mandated by government.

The EPF also contends that there is a significant difference between the United States and European nations in their choice of funding mechanisms when it comes to paid leave. Most European policies are funded through traditional social insurance systems in which employers *and* employees make contributions, unlike the BAA-UC proposal in the United States in which the entire cost burden will fall directly on employers. But what troubles the EDF most is the cost, which they estimate may be as high as $28.4 billion, or nearly double the current annual UI payments. Such an expense will deplete the reserves in UI trust funds, force an increase in corporate UI taxes, and drive up the costs of consumer goods, concludes the EPF. Ultimately, continues EPF's reasoning, higher costs will be borne by workers who will lose their jobs due to necessary downsizing and by consumers who will have to pay more for the goods they desire. If all fifty states were to implement the BAA-UC initiative, the EDF estimates that thirty-three of them will see their UI trust funds fall below the solvency level by 2001. Eight of those states are among the thirteen that sought to adopt paid leave in the 1999–2000 legislative session. They are California, Illinois, Maryland, Massachusetts, Minnesota, New Jersey, New York, and Washington (Hattiangadi 2000).

As anticipated, most of the attention devoted to the report has focused on the issue of cost, particularly the range of $6.2 to $28.4 billion that is projected by EPF to annually cover BAA-UC, depending on take-up rates, length of leave, and other factors. But the range is great and it may be exaggerated, argue the supporters of Clinton's proposal. Simply put, critics of the EPF report contend that the methodology employed to generate cost estimates was either not explained clearly or, when it was, a sufficient number of flaws were detected in the research process to raise questions about the reliability of the findings.

In June 2000, the National Partnership for Women and Families (NPWF) issued a memo attacking EPF's methods and conclusions. "Recent estimates by the Employment Policy Foundation (EPF) of the cost of parental leave/unemployment insurance programs are severely flawed, because they rely on assumptions about leave-taking and parenting in the United States that are wildly inaccurate" (National Partnership for Women and Families Memo 2000, 1). The memo then identified five faulty assumptions upon which the Employment Policy Foundation based its research.

Table 8.2

**Cost Estimates for Expanding State Temporary Disability Insurance (TDI) Programs to Cover Periods of Family Leave: Summary of Studies**

| States | New York 1998 Fiscal Policy Institute | New Jersey 1998 Williams Study | California 1995 Institute for Women's Policy Study |
|---|---|---|---|
| Annual benefits paid under current TDI program | $562 million (actual 1990 expenditure) | $325 million (actual 1997 expenditure) | $1.7 billion (actual 1990 expenditure) |
| Number of employees covered by TDI | 6.3 million (3.3 million covered both by TDI and FMLA) | 2.5 million | 11.1 million (1989) |
| Eligibility requirements for new benefits | Employees must be eligible for both TDI *and* FMLA leave | Employees must be eligible for temporary disability insurance | Employees must be eligible for state disability insurance |
| New benefits coverage | | | |
| Length of absence covered | 12 weeks | 12 weeks | 12 weeks |
| Purposes of absence | • Care for newborn or newly adopted children <br> • Care for ill parents, children, or spouses | • Care for newborn or newly adopted children <br> • Care for ill parents, children, or spouses | • Care for newborn or adopted children <br> • Care for ill parents, children, or spouses |

| Estimated number of leave-takers likely to use new benefits | 28,797–62,208 | 65–69,100 | 619,250 |
|---|---|---|---|
| Average weekly benefit | $136/$284 | $185.70 | $102.82–193.57 |
| Estimated length of leave | 1–12 weeks | 6.1 weeks (average) | 5–10 weeks |
| Estimated total annual cost of expanding TDI to include family leave | $11.6–$36.2 million | $110–$116 million | $835 million |
| New cost as a percentage of total program | 6 percent | 25–27 percent | 34 percent |
| Average cost per covered worker | $0.29–91/month $0.07–0.21/week | $3.67–3.87/month $0.85–89/week | $6.27/month $1.45/week |

Source: National Partnership for Women and Families, Washington, DC. 1999. Reprinted with permission.
Note: A detailed explanation of this data is available from the NPWF (www.nationalpartnership.org).

First, not every state will adopt BAA-UC as EPF assumes. Certainly those with low trust funds will not consider doing so. Second, EPF's assumption that all states will provide either twenty-six or twelve weeks is flawed as well. A state can set whatever limit on weeks it wants. None of the thirteen states proposed providing more than twelve weeks of coverage, and one limited its leave to five weeks. A third assumption was that every leave-taking parent will take the full number of weeks provided (either twenty-six or twelve weeks, according to the EPF). However, counters the NPWF, history tells us that most families will take the minimum amount of leave they need. Few can afford to live on a partial wage replacement for an extended period of time. The Employment Policy Foundation's fourth assumption was that almost every new working mother and father will take leave to care for her or his newborn or newly adopted child. In reality, however, the NPWF contends it is unlikely than many men will take leave, and 20 percent of families with children under six are headed by women with no husband or father present. And finally, EPF assumes that all workers eligible for UI benefits will take leave and collect benefits. But overlooked is the fact that 55 percent of employees in medium and large firms offer some form of temporary disability insurance that covers periods (though sometimes limited) of maternity leave (National Partnership for Women and Families Memo, June 8, 2000).

## What Cost for Inaction?

Clearly, questions concerning the reliability of cost estimates will dominate any future debates related to the expansion of the FMLA. Until the methodology employed is acceptable to both sides, the controversy surrounding the fiscal impact of paid leave will surely continue. However, an area often overlooked by researchers, particularly economists, is the cost of inaction. That is, can the absence of a particular policy be measured in terms of "cost" or economic "loss"? At least two studies completed so far related to family care address this very question.

In their study *Unnecessary Losses: Costs to America for the Lack of Family and Medical Leave* (1990), Spalter-Roth and Hartmann concluded that employees, employers, and government all lose if family leave is either unavailable or unpaid. For example, women lacking maternity leave who returned to the job market after childbirth were unemployed longer and earned lower wages, amounting to a total of nearly $607 million in lost earnings in one year, compared to women who could take leave and return to their job. Employers also benefit from family leave through lower worker absenteeism, reduced turnover rates, enhanced productivity, higher morale, and greater company loyalty. And also, argue Spalter-Roth and Hartmann, government costs are reduced as well if a family-leave policy, preferably a paid one, is in place. Women who give birth, but cannot take leave (paid or unpaid), will require more income assistance in the form of government transfer payments. This is particularly true for lower-income workers. "At the lower end of the labor market social welfare policies to some extent operate as paid maternity leave," writes Kristen Wever (1996, 20).

Another study that examined the costs of family care was the "1999 MetLife Juggling Act Study," produced for the MetLife Mature Market Institute in conjunction with the National Alliance for Caregiving and the National Center for Women and Aging at Brandeis University. According to the findings, family care costs individuals as much as $659,000 over their lifetimes in lost wages, lost Social Security benefits, and pension contributions because they take leave, quit their jobs entirely, or pass up opportunities for training, promotions, and choice assignments. When the $659,000 figure is broken down further, the caregivers studied lost $566,500 in wages, $67,000 in retirement contributions, and $25,500 in Social Security benefits. Twenty-nine percent reported that they declined promotions. Twenty-five percent turned down transfer or relocation opportunities, and 22 percent claimed they missed out on opportunities to develop new job skills (MetLife 1999).

Two years earlier, MetLife (1997) completed a study on the financial impact of family care on business. In the "MetLife Study of Employer Costs for Working Caregivers," it was reported that lost productivity due to family care costs U.S. businesses between $11 billion and $29 billion annually. But the real challenge of family care may still be in front of us. In 2010, the 78 million baby boomers in the United States will begin to turn sixty-five. Multiple chronic illnesses will become commonplace among this population and their caregiving demands will increase as they age. This development will have a severe impact on families, companies, and government. The extent to which policies such as family leave can cushion this anticipated demographic earthquake remains to be seen. However, perhaps some lessons can be learned from leave policies in other industrialized countries, a topic to be explored in the next chapter.

## Notes

1. As states moved on Clintion's BAA-UC proposal, a Republican-controlled Congress raised several red flags. On March 9, 2000, the House Subcommittee on Human Resources, chaired by Nancy Johnson (R-CT), held a hearing on state initiatives to use UI benefits to fund paid leave. Representative Johnson questioned the Department of Labor's authority to enact the UI regulations and was supported by testimony from several business representatives. Advocates for the Clinton proposal also testified. The hearing is a good example of the arguments that are usually pre-

sented on both sides of this issue. A videotape of the hearing can be purchased from the C-SPAN archives (http://www.c-spanarchives.org) at Purdue University in West Lafayette, Indiana.

2. Polling related to the FMLA is an interesting topic. In February 1988, the National Partnership for Women and Families released the results of a poll conducted by Lake Sosin Snell Perry & Associates. It found that nearly 80 percent of those surveyed favored paid leave. However, for women under age forty-five, 89 percent of Democratic women and 91 percent of *Republican* women supported paid leave! However, what is not clear is whether or not the Clinton proposal in particular would be acceptable to these groups.

See National Partnership for Families, "Americans Support Family-Leave Insurance," *Family Matters: A National Survey of Women and Men* (1998). Internet link: http:www.nationalpartnership.org.

3. An effort to provide coverage under the FMLA for same-sex partners was defeated during legislative debate in 1992. To date, no state has included such coverage in their family-leave policies. However, this may change. In the spring of 2000, the Vermont legislature passed and the governor signed a state domestic partnership law. This grants same-sex partners essentially the same rights as married heterosexual couples.

# Chapter 9

# Lessons from Abroad: Leave Policy from an International Perspective

In the fall of 1999, Cherie Blair, wife of British Prime Minister Tony Blair, surprised her husband with the news that she was pregnant with the couple's fourth child. Six months later, she shocked her spouse again with a public announcement that she expected her husband to take paternity leave when the baby arrived. Speaking at a legal forum in London in March 2000, she stated that she was thrilled to be pregnant again at age forty-five and looked forward to using her position as a means to push the issue of parental leave to the forefront. Citing the example set by Finish Prime Minister Paavo Lipponen, who took a week's leave after his wife gave birth in early March, Mrs. Blair made it clear that she expected her husband to be her ally. "I, for one, am promoting the widespread adoption of this fine example," she said (Reid 2000, 2).

Mrs. Blair (Booth is her professional name), an employment-rights lawyer, earned $175,000 a year at the time, nearly three times the salary of her husband. As a strong advocate for parental leave, her comment inspired women's groups and thrust the issue of work and family onto the front pages of British tabloids. "We would like to see many, many more fathers take time off to be with newborns," stated Belinda Phipps, head of the National Childbirth Trust, a parental leave advocacy group. "But the timing in this case is absolutely brilliant, because Tony Blair could teach everyone about our new laws on the subject" (Reid 2000, 2).

The new law Ms. Phipps was referring to was a legal right established in January 2000 by Parliament that permits new fathers to take as much as thirteen weeks off work without compensation at any time during the child's first year. His job or a comparable one is guaranteed when he returns to work. Mothers, on the other hand, are allowed eighteen weeks off after childbirth and twenty-nine weeks if the woman has been on the job for more than a year. As is the case with fathers, the job is guaranteed and the leave is unpaid. But there is more to the story. Not only did the Blair case emerge as an international symbol in the ongoing conflict between work and family, it also called into question the role of fathers in raising children, and once again drew attention to the controversial issue of government's involvement in family matters. For many in Great Britain, the new thirteen-week paternity leave law referred to above was, in reality, a "forced adoption." That is, its implementation (done somewhat reluctantly) followed a directive issued by the European Union a few years earlier.

The fact that work and family has become an internationally familiar topic should not be surprising, in that many of the social trends familiar to policymakers in the United States are also afoot in other western industrialized nations, particularly in Europe and Scandinavia. More people are living longer, marrying later or not all, having fewer babies, getting divorced at higher rates, raising children alone, and struggling with personal financial challenges amidst volatile economies. Today there are more women in the paid labor force than at any time in the history of the world (Baker 1995). It is this latter trend, more than any other, that has generated so much interest in family-leave policy in recent years and produced so many personal stories similar to the Blairs'.[1] The primary objective of this chapter is to compare family-leave policy in the United States to other countries. However, it is important to remind ourselves that leave policy is usually an ingredient of family policy, which in turn is a component of social welfare policy. Because comparative analysis tends to be more informative when there are more similarities than differences among nations, the countries explored here will be other western industrialized states, such as those in Europe and Scandinavia, that have produced political and economic systems similar to that of the United States.

## Comparative Family Policy: Establishing a Framework

Conducting comparative policy analysis across nations is not easy. Focusing on family issues can complicate matters further. Definitions of terms, such as "family," "household," "marriage," and "cohabitation," may vary greatly from country to country. Although efforts have been made to standardize definitions and establish international databases, major cultural and political differences exist among nations and shape the policies they adopt. Therefore, it is understandable why a particular policy in one country may not be adopted so easily by another. However, the value in comparing national social policies may lie more in the journey undertaken than the destination reached. In other words, the process itself may create a fresh perspective for generating new ideas that address old problems.

One of the earliest comparative studies of family-oriented policies was produced by the League of Nations in its *Report on the Employment of Women and Children and the Berne Convention of 1906* (1919). This was followed by a series of reports by the International Labor Office between 1924 and 1939 that compared family allowances, welfare benefits, and the treatment of pregnant employees in European countries. In 1940, the U.S. Social Security Administration published *An Outline of Foreign Social Insurance and Assistance Laws.* More recent comparative works include Kamerman and Kahn's classic work, *Family Policy: Government and Families in Fourteen Countries* (1978), Baker's *Canadian Family Policies: Cross-National Comparisons* (1995), Gauthier's *The State and the Family: A Comparative Analysis of Family Policies in Industrialized Countries* (1996), Ginsburg's *Divisions of Welfare: A Critical Introduction to Comparative Social Policy* (1992), Kamerman and Kahn's *Family Change and Family Policies in Great Britain, Canada, New Zealand, and the United States* (1997), and the ongoing seven-volume study of family policies in western industrialized countries by the Mannheim Center for European Social Research in Germany.[2]

According to Gauthier (1996), and confirmed by the works of O'Hara (1998), Baker (1995), and Ginsburg (1992), there are four major models of family policy under which western industrialized countries can be categorized. First, there is the *profamily/pronatalist model*, under which countries such as France and the Canadian province of Quebec identify low fertility as a major concern and call for government intervention to correct it. With the objective to reduce existing obstacles to higher fertility rates, child allowances tend to be generous, particularly with the birth of the third child, and both parental leave and state-of-the-art child-care facilities are given top priority by policymakers. Working mothers are not only acceptable, but conditions should be created and maintained to accommodate them.

A second model of family policy is the *traditional breadwinner model*, under which the government supports families in a variety of ways, but encourages a continuation of the traditional male-breadwinner family. Reluctant to intervene, the government calls for self-sufficiency as well as family, community, and volunteer efforts to address social problems. Not necessarily tied to any pronatalist strategy, this approach, characterized by Germany, prefers a traditional pattern of gender differences. Therefore, there is a reluctance to adopt policies that encourage women to enter the workforce or support them if they are already there. Child-care programs are limited, but leave policies are looked upon more favorably because women will remain home with their children longer and assume the more traditional role of mother as caregiver.

A third example of family policy is the *egalitarian model*, in which gender equity is the primary objective of the policy and family-support programs serve as the vehicle to achieve it. This approach, which is quite the opposite of the traditional breadwinner model described above, endorses aggressive government action to correct inequalities between men and women in the workplace. Thus, child-care programs and parental leave policies are generous in permitting women to enter and remain attached to the labor force. Both Denmark and Sweden are usually identified with this approach. By emphasizing parental rather than maternal leave, efforts are made in both countries to encourage not only mothers, but also fathers to take time off to raise children. Such a strategy, it is believed, further reduces gender inequities.

And finally, a fourth type of family policy is the *pro-family but noninterventionist model*. Under this approach there is a general belief that the family is the cornerstone of a stable society, but intervention by government should be limited primarily to those families in need. While women entering the workforce may not be openly opposed by policymakers, the general belief is that it is not the role of government to support them through publicly funded child-care programs and parental-leave policies. Both the United States and the United Kingdom fall under this category. Whatever family-support policies emerge, they tend to come late in comparison to other countries, and they are also limited in scope. The United States, for example, did not adopt a national child-care policy or pass family-leave legislation until the 1990s and, in both cases, the policies were quite incremental. Similarly, Great Britain was the last member of the European Union to adopt a parental-leave policy.

It should be emphasized at this point that the history of family policy in Europe and Scandinavia differed significantly from that in the United States in three respects. First, family-oriented policies in Europe and Scandinavia were generated primarily by concerns over low fertility rates. Therefore, pronatalist policies, such as family allowances, child care, and parental leave, were designed to encourage more women to have children. This is in sharp contrast to the United States, in which the government did not respond as much to low fertility rates (the United States had a major baby boom without the assistance of pronatalist policies) as it did to the demands created by women entering the workforce. Second, interest in family policy came much later in the United States than it did in Europe and Scandinavia. If the entrance of more women into the labor force is recognized as one of the major forces driving U.S. family policy, then we should remind ourselves that it was not until the early 1980s when this phenomenon began to influence policymakers. And third, as was discussed in the previous chapter, the United States chose to adopt the broader "family leave" model rather than the European model of "parental leave," because the former approach proved instrumental in attracting more supporters for the passage of the legislation. Simply put, by covering more people (young and old), it brought more interest groups and legislators inside the political tent to lobby in support of the proposed legislation. But while the American model is more comprehensive in coverage than the typical European version, it provides no wage replacement. More specific differences in leave policy among the European Union nations and the United States are discussed below.

## Comparing Parental and Family Leave Policies Across Nations

In 1998, the International Labor Organization (ILO) announced that more than 120 nations provide paid maternity leave. Three prominent exceptions among western industrialized countries were Australia, New Zealand, and the United States. These exceptions stand in sharp contrast to some countries that have had leave policies in effect for more than 100 years. Germany adopted the first maternity-leave law in 1883, followed by Sweden in 1891 and France in 1928. But for most European countries, their maternity-leave policies are moored to ILO conventions that occurred over eighty years ago. In 1919, for example, thirty-three countries signed the Maternity Protection Convention that consisted of three major components: a designated leave period of twelve weeks, a cash benefit to be determined by individual countries, and job protection (Ruhm and Teague 1997). This was revised in 1952 when it was recommended that the level of the wage replacement during leave be at least 45 percent of the woman's salary when she left her job.

Not unlike the United States, the primary objective of early European maternity-leave policies was to protect the health of mothers and their infants. Although gender equity in the workplace did emerge later, the early initiatives emphasized "special treatment" rather than "equal treatment," as was the case in the United States. Therefore, leaves were mandatory and job security was not guaranteed (Moeller 1993). This was true in Denmark, France, the Netherlands, Japan, Greece, and Finland (Ruhm and Teague 1997). Following World War II, however, concerns over low fertility rates and gender equity in the workplace produced more leave laws that were designed to protect the rights of pregnant women and address the nurturing and healthcare needs of their newborns. Such concerns clashed with efforts to restore women to their "proper" place and guarantee their jobs back when they returned to work. As was the case with Rosie the Riveter in the United States, many women in European countries who had assumed jobs in defense plants and elsewhere during the war—jobs that were held previously by men—were pressured into returning to their homes (Frank and Lipner 1988).

However, with growing concerns after 1960 about declining fertility rates, combined with the increase in female labor-force participation, maternity- and parental-leave policies began to supplant family allowances as a means for state support of European families. As reported by Gauthier (1996), Moors and Palomba

217

(1995), and Kauffman, Kuijsten, et al. (1997), as family allowances stagnated during the 1975–90 period with many countries slipping into means-tested programs, leave policies were upgraded considerably, particularly during the 1970s. Among eighteen European and Scandinavian countries, the average duration of leave grew from 15.5 weeks in 1975 to 22.1 weeks in 1990. The largest increases were in Sweden by thirty-five weeks, Finland by eighteen weeks, Denmark by fourteen weeks, and Norway by ten weeks (Gauthier 1996). But in addition to expanding the duration of leave, the amount of wage replacements were also increased in many countries during the 1975–90 time frame.

Gauthier (1996) explained this dual increase of duration and wage replacement by creating an index that captured the number of weeks that were fully compensated for under leave policies in particular countries. By multiplying the number of weeks of leave by the percentage of salary received during the leave, she concluded that the countries with the most liberal leave policies in 1990 were Sweden, Finland, Norway, and Denmark. The four western industrialized countries that were the most conservative in granting compensated leave were Greece, Switzerland, United Kingdom, and Canada. The United States, New Zealand, and Australia were not included in the survey because they did not offer a wage replacement during leave. In 1990, in the United States, less than thirty states offered any type of leave. And, of course, with the exception of the five states that had applied their temporary disability insurance to childbirth, no leave was paid.

A review of leave policies in various countries that covers the post–World War II era to 1990 is both informative and important. But policy developments in this area during the past decade are even more significant for at least three reasons. First, the movement of women into the workplace has continued to rise and the issues of gender equity and family-friendly policies have climbed near the top of policy agendas in numerous countries. As we enter a new century, it is clear that women in both Europe and the United States are more likely to retain their jobs after having children than was the case two decades earlier (Hattiangadi 2000). Equally important, the increase in women entering the labor force during the 1970s came from those who had preschool-aged children; the increase in the 1980s and 1990s is among women who have infants (RAND 1995). Meanwhile, the amount of time between childbirth and the return to work has shortened and the demands for more liberal leave laws and child-care programs have increased worldwide.

As presented in Table 9.1, there is much variation across countries of women working full time, with the United States leading at 60 percent, followed by Portugal, Greece, and Ireland. Often overlooked is the fact that those countries with the most liberal parental leave laws (Sweden, Denmark, and Finland) also have the lowest percentages of women working full-time.

Table 9.1

**The Percentage of Women Working Full-Time by Country** (1996)

| Country | Percent of women working full-time |
|---|---|
| United States | 60 |
| Portugal | 38 |
| Greece | 34 |
| Ireland | 32 |
| United Kingdom | 19 |
| Italy | 18 |
| Spain | 16 |
| France | 11 |
| Austria | 9 |
| Finland | 8 |
| Belgium | 7 |
| Germany | 7 |
| Denmark | 7 |
| Luxembourg | 6 |
| Sweden | 5 |
| Netherlands | 3 |

*Source:* Compiled from data in *Key Indicators of the Labor Market Foundation*, International Labor Organization (ILO) (1999) and the Employment Policy Foundation (2000).

According to Hattiangadi (2000), this point, that more American women are working full-time compared to other countries, explains why there is a growing demand in the United States to adopt paid leave. Unlike their European counterparts, American mothers lack the flexibility to adjust their work schedules and "work around" their pregnancies and child-care demands. However, women employees in Europe, as is the case in the United States, still wrestle with the issue of gender equity. Because so many women in Europe and Scandinavia work part-time, they remain dependent on their husband's income. Consequently, argue Ostner and Lewis, European countries are ambivalent about "whether to promote equity for breadwinners or parity for caregivers" (1995, 185).

A second reason why it is important to explore leave policies abroad, particularly during the past decade, is because the European welfare state has been subjected to numerous challenges in recent years in the form of budget reductions and program cuts. Beginning with the Thatcher years in the 1980s in Great Britain, we have witnessed numerous attacks on government-sponsored social insurance programs that will, in all likelihood, continue well into the new century. How existing parental-leave programs fare abroad amidst a prolonged period of retrenchment may tell us something about the potential for success in expanding family-leave policy in the United States.[3]

A third reason it is imperative to examine parental-leave policy in Europe is the growing importance of the European Union (EU) in shaping social policy within its membership and influencing its development elsewhere. As one of the major events of the twentieth century, the creation of the EU changed the political, social, and economic contours of Western Europe's economic and political landscape (McCormick 1999). Its roots can be traced as far back as the signing of the Treaty of Paris in 1951, which created the European and Coal and Steel Community (EESC), and the 1957 Treaty of Rome, which created the European Economic Community (EEC). The EU is credited for creating and sustaining the longest period of peace in the region's history, for shifting the balance of power in Eastern Europe, and for taking the lead in shaping a new global economy. Growing from six to fifteen members, the EU includes 373 million people who speak eleven different languages but who are reasserting themselves as a unified body on the world stage. It has its own flag, a uniform passport, its own currency (the euro), and even has its own anthem, the "Ode to Joy" from Beethoven's Ninth Symphony. As the largest economic bloc in the world, the EU accounts for 37 percent of global exports and 28 percent of the global gross national product (GNP) (McCormick 1999).

With full economic integration being the primary objective of the EU (it was known as the European Economic Community prior to 1993), there is general agreement that such integration cannot be achieved without social cohesion. By the 1980s, the EEC began to address social issues more aggressively by devoting greater attention to working conditions, labor relations, education programs, skills training, health services, social security, and adequate housing. The initial attempt to achieve these goals came with the Single European Act (SEA) of 1987. It eliminated existing barriers to the migration of people, money, goods, and services among the member states. This was followed by a series of Social Action Programs (SAPs) that were designed to improve the living and working conditions within the European community, and the passage of the Social Charter of 1989 that was specifically designed to protect the rights of workers. But it was the signing of the Maastricht Agreement on Social Policy (ASP) in 1993 that created the European Union, as it is known today. That is, it established a single currency, recognized common citizenship, created a unified police force, and shifted some power over law and social policy away from member states and toward EU institutions. The 1998 Treaty of Amsterdam reinforced these policies by refining the powers of the institutions and preparing the EU for new members representing Eastern European countries.

An important offspring of both the Maastricht Treaty and the Treaty of Amsterdam was the EU Directive on Parental Leave that was adopted on

June 3, 1996. Not only was it the first social-policy initiative based on the Maastricht Agreement, it also represented the first law produced by the EU that was designed to address work and family life. Dating back to the early 1980s, the Directive on Parental Leave has had a stormy history. Strongly opposed by the Thatcher and Major administrations in Great Britain during the 1980s and early 1990s because they believed it would be too disruptive and expensive for business, the Directive was vetoed directly by the British, thus preventing it from being implemented in other member states. Consequently, its pattern of existence during the 1980s was not unlike the existence of the FMLA in the United States during the same time period. That is, although the leave proposal had supporters among EU members, their numbers were insufficient to override the opposition. This changed, however, after a more liberal Tony Blair became the prime minister of the United Kingdom and new procedures handed down by the Maastricht Agreement allowed supporters to bypass opponents who were in a clear minority (Schmidt 1998).

By June of 1996, the major provisions of the EU Directive on Parental Leave had been ironed out and the policy was implemented. It allows all workers, men or women, full time or part time, employed by any business of any size, three months of unpaid leave for the birth, adoption, or care of a child up to eight years of age. Both parents are allotted three months of leave and they may use it separately or simultaneously without fear of losing their job. Although the term "minimum standards" was deliberately not employed, at least two points should be emphasized regarding the adoption and implementation of the EU Parental Leave Directive. One, any country may establish a leave policy with provisions that exceed those created by the European Union, but no country may use the Directive to reduce the provisions in their existing parental-leave laws. And two, although countries such as Sweden and Denmark may view the Directive as weak and incremental compared to their more liberal policies, the fact remains that prior to 1996, no statutory right to parental leave existed at all in Belgium, Luxembourg, and Ireland.

Similar to the FMLA that permits states and private corporations some leeway in implementing the law, the EU Directive grants member states and labor/management agreements certain rights and privileges as well. For example, states can set length-of-service qualifications but such a requirement cannot exceed one year. Or, special notice periods can be established by member states and specific dates can be set for employees beginning and ending their leaves. And, it is also up to the member states whether or not they want to require employers to continue health insurance and social security entitlement contributions during a worker's leave of absence. Presented in Table 9.2 is a breakdown of parental/family-leave policies in the fifteen European Union countries.

| Parental leave[a] | Paid amount | Special benefit |
|---|---|---|
| Until child reaches 24 months | Flat daily rate | Extra 4 weeks for premature or multiple births; breast feeding work breaks |
| 3 months full-time, 6 months part-time until age 4 | Flat rate per month | Father allowed postnatal leave if mother dies or is seriously ill. Career breaks[b] |
| 10 weeks plus 13–26 weeks for childcare | 60% of unemployment compensation | Can also use for job trtaining, but no job guarantee |
| 26 weeks after maternity leave | Low flat rate that drops as child ages | The higher the earnings, the lower the percentage paid; extra time for fathers from parental leave if desired |
| Parents can share full-time leave until child is 3 | Small flat rate only after birth of second child | Extra time for multiple births; extra time if other children; breast feeding work breaks |
| Mother or father until child is 3 | Flat rate based on income until child is 2 | Extra 4 weeks for premature or multiple births |
| 3 months per parent until child is 3½ | None | Parental leave applies only to companies of 50+ employees |
| 14 weeks per parent until child is 5 | None | Optional unpaid 4 weeks extra |
| 10 months after maternity; 11 months if father takes 3 months or until child is 8 | 30% of earnings | First year after birth, full-time employees get 2 rest periods—one hour each; father entitled to leave and time off if mother dies or is severely disabled |

*(continued)*

223

Table 9.2 *(continued)*

| Country | Maternity leave | Paid amount | Paternity leave | Paid amount |
|---|---|---|---|---|
| Luxembourg | Follows parental leave policy | — | — | — |
| The Netherlands | 16 weeks, 4–6 pre, 10–12 post | 100% to maximum level | None | — |
| Portugal | 90 days, 60 post, 30 flexible | 100% | None | — |
| Spain | 16 weeks, 6 post, 10 flexible | 100 % to maximum level | 2 days | 100% |
| Sweden[i] | 12 weeks, 6 pre, 6 post | 80% | 2 weeks | 80% |
| United Kingdom | 18 weeks / 40 weeks | 90% 6 weeks, flat rate for 12 weeks | None | — |

*Source:* Table compiled from data provided in Peter Moss and Fred Deven's (eds.) *Parental Leave: Progress or Pitfall?* (1991). Brussels, BE: NIDI/CBGS Publications.
*Notes:*
[a] Parental leave is a family entitlement that parents can share between themselves, but time allocated to each parent is not transferable in all countries.
[b] "Career breaks" permit Belgian workers to take up to 6 years full-time leave for any reason with some pay. Women tend to use it most, usually after childbirth.
[c] Denmark's wage replacement during leave is about equal to its level of unemployment compensation.

As illustrated in the table, there is much variation among the countries in the length of leave, whether or not it applies to fathers, and the extent of the coverage. There is less variation, however, in the level of wage replacement provided by EU countries and in the types of funding mechanisms employed to support it. The countries with the most liberal paternal-leave policies when measured by duration, coverage, and wage replacement include Austria, France, Germany, Spain, and Sweden. Although the United States offers only

Table 9.2 *(continued)*

| Parental leave[a] | Paid amount | Special benefit |
|---|---|---|
| 6 months full-time, 12 months part-time until child is 5[d] | Flat rate[e] | — |
| 6 months until child is 8[f] | None | — |
| 6 months per parent until child is 3[g] | None | Fathers entitled to mother's benefit payment in event of death or disability; breast feeding work breaks |
| Each parent may take full-time leave for 1 year until child is 3[h] | None | 2 weeks extra for multiple birth after second child; 1 hour work absence for 9 months, time can be transferred to fathers— maximum 10 weeks |
| 18 months per parent, 30 days must be taken by father, until child is 8 | Covers 450 days, 80% for 360 days, flat rate for 90 days | — |
| 13 weeks per parent until child is 5 | None | Women employed with same employer for 1 year or move get 40 weeks |

[d] Parental leave in Luxembourg is an individual entitlement and not transferable between parents.
[e] A parent may choose a flat rate payment for 22 months but without a job guarantee, or take 6 months with a job guarantee.
[f] Leave is an individual entitlement not transferable between parents.
[g] Leave is an individual entitlement not transferable between parents.
[h] Employers' social security payments are reduced if they hire an unemployed substitute for an employee on maternity or parental leave.
[i] Paid leave in Sweden is a family entitlement with built-in incentives designed to encourage fathers to participate. Italy has a similar policy.

twelve weeks of leave, its coverage is more extensive in that it permits leave to be taken for more reasons than in many of the other countries. On the other hand, as emphasized before, it is one of only three countries that provide no wage replacement out of 120 nations that offer parental leave. The other two are Australia and New Zealand (Moss and Deven 1999).

A category that has attracted much interest recently, primarily due to the Tony Blair case, is the provision for paternity leave. Because this entitlement is often shared with the birth mother, the duration can vary greatly across nations. For example, this is the case in Finland, Italy, and Sweden. In other countries, such as the Netherlands, Greece, Italy, Ireland, and Portugal, child-care leaves are only available to one parent. In Luxembourg, paternity leave is available to fathers but it must be taken immediately after the mother's maternity leave concludes. In Spain, leave is only accessible if both parents work, and in Austria, men can take six months but, like Luxembourg, the leave must immediately follow the sixteen months taken by the mother (Hattiangadi 2000).

Concern over the underutilization of parental leave by fathers prompted Germany to revise its law in March 2000. Because only 1.5 percent of those taking parental leave in Germany were men, a new statute was adopted that permits both parents to take up to three years off when they have a child. Further, with their employer's approval, they may take off an additional year when their child is between three and eight years old. The German law also increased the amount of part-time work parents can engage in while on leave, ranging from nineteen to thirty hours a week, or a total of sixty hours for both parents combined. And finally, the amount of wage replacement was increased to $450 a month per child and capped, provided at least one of the parents is not working (Associated Press 2000). Sweden was also concerned about the low number of men who elected to take parental leave, and there-fore put in motion a similar policy several years ago in which a couple can receive more weeks of leave if the father takes a designated amount. If the father elects not to use the leave, the couple loses the extra weeks.[4]

Another category that generates interest is that of the economics of paren-tal leave. That is, to what extent do leave-takers receive cash benefits and how are programs in various countries funded? As presented in Table 9.2, more than half (eight) of the fifteen EU countries provide a 100-percent wage replacement. For the remaining seven member states, the lowest wage re-placement provided is Ireland's at 70 percent. It should be pointed out, how-ever, that all nations have a cap of some sort. Thus, a multimillionaire will not receive 100 percent of his or her salary while on leave. With respect to the funding mechanisms that are used to support parental leave in the Euro-pean Union, most states rely on the standard social-security model, in which both the employer and employee contribute to a joint fund. Italy and the United Kingdom are the only exceptions to this approach. All states, how-ever, with the exception of Sweden, rely on some level of general revenues to cover the costs (Moss and Deven 1999).

The United States, of course, has no funding mechanism, but the Clinton administration has proposed the use of Unemployment Insurance trust funds to pay for leave. Because the burden would be shouldered entirely by employer contributions, the Clinton model would not fall under either the "social insurance" category or "general revenues" approach.

Understandably, it is this latter category, that of cost and the funding mechanism, that often stirs the most interest, particularly among economists. As argued by Ruhm and Teague (1997), some economists tend to be very wary of mandated benefits such as parental leave because such measures interfere with the free-market economy. In the ideal world of economic theory, it is assumed (without government intervention) that employers and employees will *both* agree to adopt a company family-leave policy if the anticipated benefits exceed the costs. However, if the reverse is true, in which the costs exceed the benefits, then the employees may choose to abandon the family-leave benefit in favor of higher wages. Therefore, continues the reasoning, government interference in the form of legislated mandates may benefit one party at the expense of the other. And further, contend Becker (1971), Mitchell (1990), and Summers (1989), family-leave benefits may increase rather than decrease occupational segregation by increasing the costs of hiring women for certain jobs. In other words, because companies may fear women employees will use leave too frequently, they will be less inclined to hire them. Consequently, men may dominate the particular company or occupation and higher unemployment rates may occur among the very people who are most likely to use the benefit: women.

Supporters of parental leave, such as Kamerman (1991), Bravo (1991), and Gilliand (1989), offer different arguments, of course, contending that time off to bond with and care for children is important for the welfare of the young, and contributes to the general well-being of society as a whole. Proponents who are economists argue that mandates can indeed produce positive economic outcomes for companies and the women they hire (Ruhm and Teague 1997; Trzcinski 1991). Leave policies help maintain women's attachment to the labor force, which allows them to increase their wages over time. They can avoid reentering the labor market at lower wages and having to be retrained for a different job. Spalter-Roth and Hartmann (1990) concluded that the benefits of family leave outweigh the costs by six times because unemployment is reduced and a job is guaranteed upon their return to work. Waldfogel (1997) reached a similar conclusion.

In a more recent study of job retention after childbirth in the United States, Britain, and Japan, Waldfogel, et al. (1999) concluded that family-leave coverage increases the likelihood that a woman will return to her employer after childbirth in all three countries. Therefore, any efforts to expand coverage in any of these countries will likely result in increased employment of women after childbirth. Another outcome may be to create what economists refer to as "positive externalities." That is, children may receive better care, be happier and even healthier if one parent stays home from work under a parental- or family-leave program. Thus, the family may see lower healthcare costs as a result. A few researchers have begun to explore this particular scenario.

Christopher Ruhm, for example, arrived at a similar juncture in a paper he prepared for the National Bureau of Economic Research in 1998. In a study of the utilization of parental leave in nine European countries between 1969 and 1994, he found that the more generous the leave entitlements, the lower the death rates of infants and young children. "In particular," he writes, "there is a much stronger negative relationship between leave durations and post-neonatal mortality or fatalities between the first and fifth birthday than for perinatal mortality, neonatal deaths, or the incidence of low birth weight" (Ruhm 1998, 1). Therefore, such findings indicate that leave policies may be cost effective in improving the overall health of children. However, more research needs to be conducted on the impact leave policies have on children, and done so with the same amount of enthusiasm that has been directed toward the effects of child-care programs.

Recently, the International Labor Organization (ILO), an affiliate of the United Nations, predicted that by 2010 about 80 percent of all women in industrialized countries and 70 percent worldwide will be working outside the home during their child-bearing years. In a special report, *Maternity Protection at Work* (1998), the ILO identified 120 of the world's 152 nations that have established some form of leave policy. During a well-publicized news conference to announce the release of the report, the chief of the organization's Conditions of Work Branch, F.J. Dy-Hammar, made a statement that sounded very familiar to family-leave advocates in the United States. "In all parts of the world, working women who become pregnant are faced with the threat of job loss, suspended earnings and increased health risks due to inadequate safeguards for their employment" (*Christian Science Monitor* 1998, 2).

The report emphasized that in many countries a woman's income is vital for the survival of the family. According to the ILO study, women provide the primary source of income in 30 percent of all households worldwide. In Europe, 59 percent of women employed full time are responsible for half or more of their family's income. In the United States the percentage is slightly less at 55 percent. If the social trends commonly associated with the western industrialized nations—such as the increase in divorce and a rise in women entering the job market—continue in the years ahead, either existing social policies will have to be reformed or new ones adopted.

Very likely in the near future, two areas in particular, one geographical, the other topical, will demand more attention from researchers and policymakers. One, the geographical region, is Eastern Europe, where previously extensive maternity-leave benefits have been considerably reduced due to political and economic restructuring that followed the fall of the Berlin Wall (ILO 1998). And two, the topical area, concerns the shape that leave policies will assume within the broader context of family policy as it evolves in various countries. To explain this latter point further, parental leave in four countries will be discussed in detail. Each of the countries (France, Germany, Sweden, and Great Britain) represents a particular model of family policy that was previously discussed. By isolating these countries, and describing their parental-leave laws within the broader context of family policy, we may be able to predict the future course of the political debate on this topic in the United States.

## Applying the Family Policy Framework to Family Leave

### France: The Pronatalist Model

Maternity leave was first adopted in France in 1913. Parental leave, on the other hand, was not implemented until 1977 and fathers did not become eligible until 1984. To understand the French parental-leave system, it is best to place it within the context of other family-oriented policies, such as family allowances, tax deductions geared to the number of children born, child-care benefits, and publicly funded child-care programs (creches). According to Fagnani (1996, 1998), support for working mothers has become an integral component of French family policy. And two forces driving that policy have been a labor strategy designed to attract more females into the workforce during periods of severe labor shortages, and an emphasis on pronatalism as a means of addressing low fertility rates. Economic volatility has always been a part of French history. With respect to concerns over low fertility, they can be traced to the Napoleonic era in which the size of armies often determined the outcome of military engagements. In modern times, pronatalism has been supported by a fairly large and vocal Catholic population (Baker 1995).

It is difficult to identify a specific event that had the greatest impact on work and family life in France. However, decisions by a series of socialist governments in the 1980s to fund a national child-care program helped to facilitate the migration of mothers with young children into the labor force (Fagnani 1998). This development, in turn, spawned demands for the expansion of parental leave, a policy that had begun in 1977. But it was during 1980–81 that the French government implemented its "third-child package," which consisted of three major components. One, the duration of paid maternity leave, was increased from sixteen to twenty-six weeks for the third child and subsequent children. Two, the postnatal benefit for working mothers was increased from 260 percent of the base wage to 717 percent for the third child and additional children born later. And three, the old-age pension credit was extended to mothers of three children. In prior years, only mothers who had raised four children were entitled to pension credits (McIntosh 1983).

The current parental-leave entitlement program in France is complex, but can be better understood if it is divided into two distinct parts and explained separately. First, there is parental leave or CPE (Conge Parental d'Education). This policy only kicks in after sixteen weeks of maternity leave have been expended by the birth mother. Twelve weeks must be taken after the birth of the child and an additional ten weeks are allocated to a birth mother if it is her third child or more. Parental leave, on the other hand, applies to all salaried employees, regardless if they are male or female, and provided they have worked for at least one year for the company before the birth or adoption of the child. It is available to both parents during the first three years of the child's life, but the thirty-six months can be extended if the child is gravely ill or severely handicapped. The leave-taker continues to receive work-related social benefits such as health insurance, and half the time consumed by the leave is counted toward length of service for retirement benefits. All employees are guaranteed the same or a comparable job upon their return to work (Fagnani 1999).

Although a woman taking maternity leave receives an 84 percent wage replacement (nontaxable), parental leave (CPE) is not paid. However, the second part of France's leave policy is its Child Rearing Benefit or APE (Allocation, Parentale d'Education). This flat-rate benefit is awarded to the mother or father if they have at least two children and the youngest is under three years of age. Since 1994, it has been a flat-rate benefit that is not means tested nor is it taxable. In 1999, the amount was Fr 3,045 a month or about $420. It is available to parents until the child reaches age three, but only if one of them stops work completely or is employed part time. In the latter case, the benefit is then reduced. Consistent with its pronatalist strategy, the eligibility requirements to receive APE are more liberal for parents with three or more children; those with two or fewer children face more restrictive eligibility criteria (Moss and Deven 1999).

France's use of CPE and APE illustrates the nation's ongoing internal conflict between a labor-market strategy on one hand and family policy on the other. Therefore, argues Fagnani, "CPE and APE should be understood as two distinct measures. One (CPE) coming out of employment legislation, the other (APE) coming out of the family law" (Fagnani 1999, 72). Under such a system it is possible for a parent to be on leave (CPE) without receiving APE, or for the parent to be receiving APE without being on leave (CPE).

And, of course, it is possible, and very likely, for parents to take CPE and receive APE simultaneously.

Two areas that continue to draw attention to France and its parental-leave policy are its funding mechanisms and its utilization rates. With respect to the former issue, parental-leave benefits are funded primarily through a social insurance program in which employees contribute about 7 percent of their total earnings annually, and employers contribute 12.6 percent of their total payroll per year. Other funding sources that are earmarked for parental leave include a 12 percent surcharge on automobile insurance premiums and taxes on advertising for drugs, alcohol, and tobacco (Baker 1995).

Concerning the utilization or "take-up" rates of parental leave, the information available is somewhat limited because employers in France are not required to report the use of CPE by their employees. A 1993 study based on 1992 data revealed that the CPE program was underutilized, and when it was employed, it was used almost exclusively by women (98 to 99 percent) and/or by those who were in high to middle management. However, with the expansion of APE in 1994 to include parents with two children as well as three, it is likely that the take-up rates for CPE have increased and will continue to rise, as will the take-up rates of APE. In fact, estimates are that between 1994 and 1997, about 110,00 working mothers with two children voluntarily left work under the APE program at a total cost of Fr 18 billion or $2.5 billion (Fagnani 1999).

But France, like other countries, is concerned about two problems in particular: One, will the overutilization of leave policies by women and the underutilization by men result in an increase instead of a decrease in existing gender inequalities, both at home and at work? And two, how should the costs to society for parental leave be weighed against the benefits it brings to families?

### Germany: The Traditional Breadwinner Model

The social insurance system that was created under Bismarck in 1883 has served as a model for numerous countries around the world. It both funds and covers sickness and maternity benefits for Germany's employed, unemployed, and self-employed. But Germany's approach to the issue of work and family, and the emergence of leave policy in particular, needs to be placed in its proper context. That is, following World War II, the nation was divided into East and West and was not reunified until 1990. Consequently, two different political cultures emerged over a forty-five-year period that had to be fused into one. This became particularly problematic for the women of the German Democratic Republic (GDR) or the former East Germany (Trczinski 1998).

When the GDR formed in 1945 and adopted its constitution four years later, it was very similar to that of the Soviet Union's. That is, it established equality between the sexes and guaranteed women the right to work, get an education, and earn wages equal to men. By 1980, the GDR had the highest rate of female labor-force participation in the world (nearly 90 percent), ranked the highest in female literacy rates, and was listed as third in the world in the number of women in higher education, behind Canada and the United States (Baker 1995). The GDR's maternity-leave policy was equally impressive. Women were entitled to twenty-six weeks of leave with a 90 to 100 percent replacement rate, and in 1986, an additional seven months of paid leave was added (Weigl and Weber 1991). Women were also allotted one day of leave per month for housework, a reduced workweek for mothers of two or more children (clearly a pronatalist strategy), and additional weeks of leave to care for sick children (Goldberg 1991). Little effort was made by policymakers to encourage fathers to participate in child care or housework.

In West Germany (FRG), on the other hand, when reunification occurred in 1990, women's participation rate in the labor force was significantly less, by about 30 percent, compared to the GDR. Although the unemployment rates for women in West Germany have been consistently high, the government has been reluctant to support the desire of many females to enter the job market (Baker 1995). The preferred policy had been to reward the traditional male breadwinner-family by encouraging women to stay home while giving their working husbands generous tax allowances (Goldberg 1991). As part of the reunification agreement, those in the GDR would be absorbed under the West German, not the East German, constitution. And imbedded in that constitution is a family policy that both encourages and supports the traditional male breadwinner model.

In more specific terms, the major objective of Article 6 of the FRG constitution is to protect the family from government intervention and preserve the traditional structure of the family unit. Therefore, both the tax structure and the rights of individuals and family members are designed to promote the married-couple/nuclear-family type. With respect to the tax structure, the traditional two-parent, one-earner family is given the most generous tax benefits compared to other types. Even the child-rearing allowance, the means-tested (*Erziehungsgeld*) that covers the care needs of the first two years of a child's life, requires that one parent (almost always the mother) be designated the full-time caregiver (Trzcinski and Albert 1998). An illustration of how deeply embedded the gender issue is in Germany's social and political culture is its name law. All children born to German parents can only be given names that appear on the government's preapproved list. Gender neutral names are not permitted, and women who desire to hyphenate their last name and combine it with their husband's when they get married are denied such a request under German law.

With respect to parental leave, it was introduced in the 1980s as part of a strategy to appease the growing demands of working women for more child-care facilities. After all, the employment rate of mothers with children up to six years of age was increasing from about 30 percent in 1961, to 35 percent in 1986, to 47 percent by 1997. Contending that children's needs can be best met by their own parents (an argument not unfamiliar to Americans), the German government rejected demands for more child-care facilities, and adopted instead a parental-leave policy that initially covered only the first year of a child's life. The policy has since been expanded several times—from twelve to fifteen months, then to eighteen months, and, since 1992, it covers the first three years of a child's life. Although the means-tested benefit payment (*Erziehungsgeld*) was extended from eighteen to twenty-four months in 1993, it has not kept pace with inflation and the eligibility criteria have become more restrictive (Pettinger 1999). The full level of benefit is about DM 600 per month, or $300. However, relatively few families receive the maximum amount.

Statistics on the utilization of parental leave in Germany are elusive, as is the case in many countries. However, at least since 1993, when separate applications for parental leave were first required, it is clear that the take-up rate among mothers is extremely high (98 percent) compared to fathers (2 percent). According to Pettinger (1999), the primary reason for the large discrepancy between mothers and fathers in using parental leave is the father's loss of income. Equally interesting are recent research findings that indicate almost 50 percent of women in the former West Germany and about 40 percent in the former East Germany are electing not to return to work after their leave period expires (Pettinger 1999).

Although confronted with one of the lowest fertility rates in Europe, Germany, unlike France, has viewed parental leave within the context of a labor policy, not a population policy. Therefore, it has elected not to initiate a pronatalist strategy.[5] This reluctance to put forth policies specifically designed to increase population may be rooted in the German government's unpleasant memories of the Nazi population policy (Gauthier 1996). Meanwhile, a newly elected government in 1998 addressed the work and family issue by moving toward more flexible eligibility criteria. In an effort to encourage more men to use the benefit, a "joint time account" was created for both parents. Some German politicians have encouraged longer leave periods, as long as eight years, so that parents can have more flexibility in deciding when to spend more time with their children (Pettinger 1999).

## Sweden: The Pro-egalitarian Model

By the 1940s, the worldwide depression had produced what many considered to be dangerously low birth rates in most of Europe. Sweden, however, was especially concerned because it had the lowest birth rates of all (Hatje 1974; Kalvemark 1980). Responding to this crisis, Alva and Gunnar Myrdal published *Crisis in the Population Question* (1934), in which they urged government intervention to improve the general well-being of families so they would find childbearing more agreeable economically. Arguing that mothers would produce more children if government policies were designed to combine work and motherhood, the Myrdals' approach was unique in recommending that Sweden develop a pronatalist policy that called upon society as a whole, rather than individual women, to display a commitment to family life (Haas 1992).

What followed was the passage of various pieces of legislation that established a firm foundation upon which a comprehensive family policy would be structured. With the passage of a 1937 law that prohibited employers from dismissing female employees because of marriage or pregnancy, the first steps toward gender equity were taken. Another act passed in 1937 established the nation's first maternity-leave law. Mothers were granted three months of unpaid maternity leave, six weeks before and six weeks after giving birth, and were guaranteed job security. In 1939, the leave period was increased to four and a half months, in 1945 it was extended to six months, and in 1955, three of the six months were paid leave (Gustafsson 1983).

Other legislative initiatives designed to address a low fertility rate were adopted as well. Included was a maternity-relief law that gave a lump sum of money to low-income mothers at childbirth, marriage loans that encouraged more couples to marry younger, subsidized housing for families with three or more children, a universal child allowance policy, and a national health insurance program (Haas 1992). Rehabilitation of slum housing and increase of subsidies for the poor were increased, increase of jobs in the public sector, and the public ownership of certain industries were deliberate strategies by government to relieve families of the steadily rising costs of basic necessities.

But contrary to popular belief, the initiatives described above did not immediately reverse a low fertility rate, nor did they encourage hordes of women to enter the labor force. It was not until the early 1980s that significant improvement in the fertility rate was recognized, and by 1989, Sweden had one of the highest birth rates in Europe (Swedish Institute 1989). It was an economic boom in the 1960s and a male labor shortage that resulted in women entering the workforce in large numbers. When given the choice between more immigrants being permitted to enter the country on work permits or recruiting women to fill vacant jobs, Sweden chose the latter option (Adams and Winston 1980). It was after this point in time that both child care and parental-leave policy were given more attention.

Today, parental-leave policy in Sweden has three primary objectives: first to enhance the well-being of children. Children will be better off both economically and developmentally if they bond early with both parents in a family that is financially stable. Second, autonomy for women is encouraged through jobs and careers identical to those held by men. Unlike Germany's male-breadwinner model, Sweden's "dual-breadwinner" approach encourages and supports a long-term attachment to the workforce for both men and women, with pay equity being a major objective. In terms of comparable worth, Sweden maintains the smallest gap between male and female wages of any industrialized country, with women earning 94 cents on every dollar earned by men (Ginsburg 1992). In the United States, it is 73 cents on the dollar. And the third objective of Sweden's parental-leave policy is to encourage men's involvement in child care by granting them the same opportunity to take time off from work as women, and encouraging them to take advantage of it.

Isolating and describing the specific provisions of Sweden's parental-leave policy is not an easy task. The law is complex and the options available to parents are many. There is maternity leave, parental leave, a Parental Leave Allowance, and several provisions that are specifically directed to fathers. Under maternity leave, sixty days are available before birth for women who cannot continue in their present job, or would desire to be transferred to less strenuous duties. Under this provision, fifty days are covered by a maternity allowance while coverage for the other ten days must come out of the Parental Leave Allowance. Or, women may opt for sixty days of parental leave after birth with a wage replacement equal to 80 percent of earnings. But it should be emphasized that all women in Sweden are guaranteed six weeks leave before and after childbirth (Moss and Deven 1999).

The parental leave law was first introduced in 1974 and has been changed frequently since, with the latest reforms occurring in 1995. Under existing policy, each parent is entitled to eighteen months of full-time leave (Child Care Leave) that includes a benefit payment (Parental Allowance) that allocates 450 days to each family per birth. There is an 80 percent wage replacement for the first 360 days, with the remaining ninety days covered at a flat rate of SEK 60 or $7 per day. Adjustments are made for multiple births. However, there is a cap on the amount that can be allotted each year. In 1999, it was SEK 273,000 ($33,000) a year, or SEK 672 ($84) a day (Moss and Deven 1999).

But perhaps the most unique feature of Sweden's parental-leave policy is found in its strategy to engage fathers in child care. Under law, 30 of the 450 days must be taken by the father. These 30 days are not transferable to the mother and are lost if not used by the father. By making paid leave a family entitlement, Sweden offers a unique model for other countries to consider.

Perhaps another novel feature of Sweden's approach is the amount of flexibility built into its policy. For example, although leave must be taken before a child reaches the age of eight (or completes the first year of school), parents may select blocks of time to take off from work. Also, paid leave is offered on a part-time basis as well. That is, a parent may work half time or quarter time, spend time at home with a child, and receive either half or three-quarters of the amount that would be awarded during a full leave period (Moss and Deven 1999).

In their analysis of Sweden's parental leave system, Haas and Hwang (1999) identify four features that make it especially unique. One, it has existed for more than twenty-five years in which it has offered generous, comprehensive, and flexible benefits to working parents. Two, it specifically encourages fathers to take leave. Three, the roots of its existence are often viewed as contradictory in some societies. That is, the dual focus on children's well-being and gender equity is considered unusual. And four, it is so widely accepted that neither politics nor economic downturns have undermined its basic principles or significantly decreased the level of its benefits. At worse, it has experienced "temporary retrenchment rather than reform" (Palme and Wennemo 1998, 31). But that is not to say that Sweden's policy is without its drawbacks, however. Women still tend to take leave considerably more often than men, and therefore, work and family are still viewed as separate spheres. "Sweden's system of parental leave benefits has the potential to challenge gendered distinctions between reproduction and production in society, but it has heretofore not succeeded in eliminating them" write Haas and Hwang (1999, 45).

### Great Britain: The Pro-family but Noninterventionist Model

Britain, like the United States, does not support an interventionist family policy. Practicing what they refer to as "familism," the British adhere to four common principles in addressing family concerns. First, the privacy rights of the family are emphasized and often used by conservative administrations, such as Margaret Thatcher's and John Major's in the 1980s and 1990s, to argue against aggressive policy interventions by liberal politicians who seek to expand the role of the welfare state (Ginsburg 1992). Second, like Germany, British family policy favors the two-parent, married, heterosexual model of the family. Alternative lifestyles that run counter to the traditional male breadwinner household are not rewarded (New and David 1985). And third, public and private caregiver policies reinforce gender differences in the home and at work. That is, women are expected to be the informal unpaid caregivers of the young, old, and frail (Lewis 1989). And finally, argues

Ginsburg, "Britain has a long-established eugenicist, neo-Malthusian tradition" (Ginsburg 1992, 166). This explains a dual family-planning policy that encourages the white middle class to have more children, but calls upon the poor and working class to limit family size (New and David 1985).

As was the case in the United States during World War II, British women were encouraged to enter the workforce in support of the war effort. Within four years, over 1,600 local nurseries were created in industrial regions to support working mothers. But by war's end only a few nurseries remained and women returned to domestic duties in the home. A directive issued by the Ministry of Health in 1945 set forth a policy that has been deeply imbedded in British political culture ever since and helps explain the United Kingdom's reluctance to adopt family policies such as parental leave. "In the interest of the health and development of the child no less than for the benefit of the mother," stated the directive, "the proper place for a child under two is at home with his mother" (British Ministry of Health 1945). The directive went on to state that the proper policy to pursue would be to discourage women with children under two from entering the labor market.

The 1945 policy handed down by the Health Ministry was fortified later by additional circulars and reports, including then parliamentarian Margaret Thatcher's education policy White Paper, in which she opposed government-sponsored child care, among other things. But despite the fact that more women were gradually migrating into the workforce in the 1970s and 1980s, the Thatcher government reduced statutory maternity benefits in 1979 in a response to corporate demands for deregulation. Consequently, the time required on the job in order to be protected against unfair dismissal increased from six months to two years. Firms with fewer than six employees were permitted to deny requests for maternity leave if it was seen as impractical, and in 1986, the Thatcher government shifted the administration of parental-leave benefits from the public to the private sector (Baker 1995). In May 1990, Mrs. Thatcher dismissed the need for a national child-care policy, stating that it could lead to "a whole generation of creche children who never understood the security of home" (*The Guardian* 1990). John Major, then the Chancellor of the Exchequer and successor to Thatcher, echoed the prime minister's words. "It is not for the government to encourage or discourage women with children from going out to work," he stated (Ginsburg 1992, 173).

Similar to the United States, Great Britain, especially since Thatcher's impact, emphasizes personal responsibility, self-reliance, and individualism in its social policies. The arguments against parental-leave policy are familiar. It will increase employers' costs, retard their competitiveness in the global economy, harm women who may be discriminated against in the hiring process because their leaves of absence may be disruptive to the company, and ultimately prove detrimental to children whose home life will be destabilized.

Considering the political culture of Great Britain, it is not surprising that it has one of the lowest rates of working women with young children in the European Union. Nor is it surprising that it was the last of the EU countries to adopt parental-leave policy under the Maastricht Treaty. The British policy is divided into two parts: Maternity and Parental Leave.

Beginning in May 2000, all pregnant employees became eligible for eighteen weeks of leave under a flat-rate payment system, but the duration may vary depending on the length of employment. Thus, women who work for at least one year for the same employer are entitled to forty weeks of leave, eleven weeks before the birth and twenty-nine afterwards. A wage replacement of 90 percent of earnings is guaranteed for six weeks, after which a flat-rate payment covers the following twelve weeks. Initially, paid leave only covered those workers earning £66 ($100) a week or more, but as of August 2000, it covers employees who earn at least £30 ($45). Tying eligibility for paid leave to income levels is unique in the EU, but it fits with Britain's emphasis on class differences. As stated previously, lower-income people in particular are discouraged from having more children (Ginsburg 1992).

Both Baker (1995) and Moss (1991) have identified at least four weaknesses of Britain's maternity-leave policy. First, because the wage replacement is low, most women return to work before the end of their entitled leave. Second, because the policy is based on male work patterns, many women do not create an employment history that qualifies them for the benefit to begin with. Third, although jobs are guaranteed for returning female workers, many women find it difficult to return to their original job because of a lack of adequate child-care facilities. And finally, there is no maternity leave for adoptive mothers.

Concerning parental leave, it became a statutory entitlement in Great Britain at the end of 1999. Under the law, each parent is entitled to thirteen weeks of full-time leave per child until the child is five years old. However, the policy is quite limited in that only four weeks can be taken in any one year. Therefore, a parent who desires to take a full thirteen weeks will have to spread it out over three years, or four weeks per year for three years and an additional week during the fourth year. The policy is also limited in that parental leave is unpaid.

Clearly, of the four countries profiled here, Great Britain is the most restrictive in addressing the issue of work and family. It was the last of the EU countries to adopt parental leave and, like the United States, is a laggard in this sphere of social policy. Its political history and culture can explain much about the design of its family policy in general and parental-leave policy in particular. The focus on self-reliance and individualism, combined with concerns about government intervention in private matters, has produced an outcome that is quite similar to the United States. That is, leave is available but limited.

## The Canadian Approach

Because Canada funds its paid parental-leave program through unemployment insurance trust funds, it is often looked upon favorably by advocates in the United States, who frequently refer to it as a successful model of paid family leave. This was further magnified following Clinton's Grambling speech in which he called for UI-funded parental leave. Policymakers in the United States looked northward with questions in search of answers. Therefore, though not a member of the European Union, Canada deserves some comment here.

Since 1969, a woman's job has been protected if she chooses to take parental leave, which has been paid since 1979. Beginning in January 1997, Canada's unemployment insurance system has provided leave-takers with a wage replacement. That amounts to about 55 percent of their average insured earnings. That converts to a maximum amount of approximately U.S.$275 a week, with low-income workers usually receiving slightly higher benefits. Under the Canadian program, either parent may take parental leave for seventeen weeks, of which fifteen are paid. And, with respect to the funding mechanism that is employed, both employers and employees contribute to the trust fund. For example, employees pay premiums up to a set amount (approximately U.S.$26,000) through deductions of about U.S.$2.55 for every $100 of the annual salary until the $26,000 has been reached. After that, workers no longer pay any premiums.

Perhaps most important, initial reports on the overall costs of paid parental leave in Canada appear to be reasonable, an encouraging assessment for those who advocate such a funding mechanism. A forthcoming work by Trzinski and Albert (2000) is expected to shed more light on the Canadian experience with paid leave.

Meanwhile, when compared to other countries, the United States continues to be a laggard with respect to leave policy. We were the last industrialized nation to adopt such a policy and remain one of three major nations that have not implemented paid leave. The recent proposal from the White House to fund a wage replacement during time off from work for family reasons produced much legislative activity in thirteen states, but it also served as an appealing lightning rod for those who oppose government mandates. But knowing where we are at this point is one thing. Trying to determine where to go next is quite another matter. That topic is reserved for the final chapter.

## Notes

1. Prime Minister Blair ultimately opted not to use parental leave. Interestingly, several months after making his highly publicized decision, Mr. Blair was embarrassed by a confidential memorandum he wrote that someone apparently leaked to the press. In the memo he raised concerns that his government "was losing touch with ordinary voters and was failing to convince them that it shared their worries over crime, the *family*, defense and patriotism." See the *New York Times*, "One More Leaked Memo on Party's Woes Embarrasses Blair," July 20, 2000, 9.

2. The Mannheim Center for European Social Research, based in Mannheim, Germany, has produced a seven-volume set on cross-national family policy, focusing primarily on European nations. Its web address is http://www.mzes.uni-mannheim.de/. Two other international centers that specialize in family policy are the Vanier Institute of Family Studies (http://www.vifamily.ca/), which is based in Canada, and the Australian Institute of Family Studies, which can be accessed at http://www.aifs.org.au/.

3. Two excellent and very recent studies that address the issue of retrenchment of social welfare policies in European nations are Paul Hirst's "Can the European Welfare State Survive Globalization? Sweden, Denmark, and the Netherlands in a Comparative Perspective" (1999), and Kamerman and Kahn's "Child and Family Policies in an Era of Social Policy Retrenchment and Restructuring" (1999).

4. Unlike Sweden and other countries, the United States has no built-in incentives in its family leave law to encourage more fathers to use it. It is estimated that half a million men take some sort of parental leave each year to care for a newborn or young child under the FMLA, compared to 1.4 million women. Some companies do encourage fathers to take parental leaves and more men are doing so. AT&T offers new parents up to a year unpaid, with a job guarantee. About one man takes advantage of the program for every eighteen women, but that's an increase from the 1 to 400 ratio a decade ago. See "Law or No Law, Dads Find It Hard to Ask for Parental Leave," CNN Interactive, February 9, 1999 (http://cnn.com). Also, at least one private nonprofit organization (The Family Leave Project) has begun a campaign to encourage more men to use the FMLA in order to bond with their children. Internet link: http://www.brigadoon.com/~menrghts/famlvpr.htm.

5. Both Germany and Japan have alarmingly low fertility rates, but unlike Sweden and France, neither country has elected to include a pronatalist component in its family-leave policy. Whatever efforts are made to increase the birthrate, they are incremental, to say the least. A few years ago, a story surfaced about a mayor in a small German town awarding $900 to parents of newborns in an effort to encourage more couples to have children. Japan's approach so far appears to be confined to the private sector. In May 2000, the Bandai Corporation, a Japanese toy maker, announced that it will pay employees one million yen, or $10,000, for every baby they have after their second child. See the *New York Times* on the web, "Japan's Employers are Giving Bonuses for Having Babies," May 30, 2000, http://www.nytimes.com/library/world/asia/053000japan-birthrate.html.

# Chapter 10

# Conclusions and Recommendations

While writing this book I attended a full-day workshop in the winter of 1999 on implementing the FMLA in the workplace. Sponsored by a major university's division of labor and industrial relations, the workshop was geared toward human resource professionals in the private sector. Of the thirty or so attendees, I was the only academic, and perhaps one of only three or four workshop participants who were not in the corporate world. My primary reason for enrolling in the course was to acquire a better understanding of the implementation process at ground zero, or where the rubber meets the road, so to speak. I was curious about the kinds of problems and questions that were surfacing among private-sector administrators six years after the bill was enacted, and as it turned out, about four months before Clinton's Grambling speech.

Perhaps it was sometime after the mid-morning coffee break that I began to feel a bit uncomfortable. This unexpected unease became my unwanted companion for the remainder of the day. What I sensed early on, and confirmed hours later, was that the primary lesson to be taught that day was to view the FMLA as one more regulatory obstacle confronting employers that will be abused by employees. Consequently, the human-resource specialists were to look upon themselves not as facilitators who are in a position to assist their employees, but as some sort of human firewall to protect their particular companies from major financial damage. In short, by operating from this very adversarial perspective, employees were not to be viewed as resources, but as threats.

As I returned home that evening, most of my thoughts were confined to the workshop I attended earlier, and how, in an almost eerie way, it was a microcosm of this nation's experience with family-leave policy. Deep feelings of resentment of the law by the private sector, as conveyed by the workshop leader, were fused with suggested strategies for circumventing it. I could not help but wonder how the day may have been different had Tom Peters been in charge of the workshop. Well known for his occasional shows on public television in which he praises companies that maintain worker-friendly policies, Peters is clearly someone who views employees as resources rather than threats, and encourages corporate heads to do the same.

But with respect to the antagonism toward the law that was displayed by the workshop leader, a similar scenario would apply to the law's formulation. That is, deep feelings of resentment of the law by a conservative Congress generated compromise strategies that produced a fairly weak bill—a bill that owed its birth to the election of a new president. Perhaps we should remind ourselves that the Congress that assumed office with Bill Clinton in January 1993 was not veto proof. A Bush victory would have probably postponed the FMLA's enactment for at least another four years or possibly longer.

I also thought about that portion of the corporate sector that elected to provide leave policies, some paid, to their employees even prior to the passage of the 1993 law. They obviously must benefit from such a policy in terms of worker loyalty, lower turnover rates, and higher productivity. Otherwise, they would not offer it. However, such firms are few in number and employ an extremely small percentage of the nation's workers. Because American labor history tells us that some sort of government intervention is frequently necessary to induce the private sector to move in a particular direction, we should accept the fact that most corporations, particularly mid-size or small firms, are unlikely to provide leave benefits without government mandates.

That said, and considering the fact that our political culture is dominated by ongoing struggles between individualism and collectivism, states' rights and federal authority, and family privacy and government responsibility, we find ourselves revisiting the deceptively simple question posed by George Lakoff in the opening paragraph of this book. That is, do we pick up the baby if it cries in the dead of night? My personal knee-jerk response is "yes," but I hasten to add that I understand the confusion such a query produces, as I can picture a pair of frustrated parents arguing in the hallway about the most appropriate action to take. And if I may venture a guess, I think the roots of the confusion and frustration can be traced to at least two factors. One, the information the parents have may not be sufficient. And two, the options they are considering may not be exhaustive. With that as a backdrop, I would like to make four strong recommendations with respect to future policy direction, and then discuss the role that both researchers and policymakers can play in the years ahead related to family policy in general, and family-leave policy in particular.

## Recommendations

My initial recommendation is clear and simple. Make family leave paid leave and do it now! As argued throughout this book, but particularly in the discussion in chapter 3 on household income, dual-earner couples and single parents are especially burdened financially, even during the recent economic boom. Of the three industrialized nations in the world without paid leave, the United States is the richest and the strongest of all. It has taken us much too long as a nation to recognize and respect housework and caregiving responsibilities as *work*. Therefore, it is time for such activities to be compensated. Caregivers will remain attached to the labor force and corporations, families, and society in general will be better for it. Besides, as argued in chapter 8 on paid leave, two major studies have reported on the drastic financial consequences for individuals, corporations, and society at large of *not* providing leave for employees. In other words, can we afford not to act?

Two, in pushing for paid leave, let us not sacrifice the family for the baby. That is, in 1985, when legislative strategists deliberately expanded the original bill to include family care, they did so for two reasons. First, they were fostering "equal treatment" (family care) over "special treatment" (maternity leave). And second, a broader-based bill that extended beyond maternity leave attracted more votes in the House and Senate, giving a shot in the arm to a fledgling coalition that was dividing its time between lobbying for child care on one hand and family leave on the other. It does not necessarily follow that advocates should now shrink the benefit by confining it only to care of newborns in order to appease opponents and attract political support. But the "Baby UI" does that very thing!

Even if the political strategy is correct, the timing is off. Like it or not, the year 2000 is upon us and we are about to witness the retirement of massive numbers of baby boomers. The state will depend on informal family care to help cushion the costs of what certainly will be an astronomically expensive long-term care system. Requests for intermittent leave to care for an elderly parent will increase substantially. Furthermore, by maintaining *family* in the policy and not specifically targeting childbirth, the growing backlash among childless workers is more likely to be defused. After all, at some point they too will need time off to care for a spouse, a parent, or themselves. And besides, by offering paid leave only under circumstances associated with childbirth, are we not trading in "equal treatment" for "special treatment" and revisiting a familiar battleground from years past?

Three, family leave should apply to more companies and be available to more workers. The fifty-worker threshold should immediately be reduced to at least twenty-five, and lowered continuously over time so that more employees in smaller companies are covered under the law. As presented earlier, those in higher-income brackets who work for larger firms are more likely to take leave than are lower-income employees in smaller companies. Most of the potential caregivers are women (much more needs to be done by men) who work for lower wages in smaller businesses. Not only do they deserve the same level of benefits as those who earn more in bigger companies, but it is also in society's best interest that they be rewarded. They will remain attached to the workforce and provide an important service (caregiving) at a very reasonable cost, while saving taxpayers a bundle in the process by either preventing or postponing formalized, institutionalized care.

And four, the law should be further expanded in another way. As currently written, grandparent care, in-law care, and the care provided by partners in a committed, domestic-partnership type of relationship are not covered. A few states have addressed several of these shortcomings, but other states and the federal government should follow. As presented in chapter 1, the family has changed and continues to do so. Meanwhile, too many policymakers in particular are dreaming 1950s dreams while sleeping in 1990s beds. We need to recognize and value families more for the functions they perform rather than for the form they take.

## Suggestions for Future Research

Seven years have passed since the Family and Medical Leave Act was implemented. At least one major evaluation (Commission on Leave's *A Workable Balance)* was completed at the three-year mark and funds have been set aside for another review in the near future. Independent studies have focused on the law's formulation and implementation, its effect on the labor participation rates of women, and how the law has fared in appellate court decisions. Following legislative initiatives in thirteen states to provide some sort of wage replacement, using either Unemployment Insurance or Temporary Disability Insurance, important cost studies have either emerged or have been budgeted in an effort to better inform legislators about the costs and benefits of paid leave. However, the research terrain has not been fully explored and much more needs to be done to assist policymakers as they wrestle with this complicated issue. I count at least six areas that remain wide open for future research.

First, we need to know more about the utilization of the law, at both the state and federal level. Who takes leave for how long and for what reason?

Appropriate data-collecting systems and monitoring mechanisms need to be established in order to annually track utilization so that adjustments can be made accordingly. In my research on the thirteen states that sought to provide paid leave, I was both surprised and disappointed in the lack of information on state utilization rates under some of the states' leave policies. Much more needs to be done in this area.

Second, we need to know more about the effect the FMLA and state leave laws have on children. Although much research has been completed on the impact child care has on kids, we know relatively little about how leave policies in particular affect the bonding process of parent and child, or the healing process of adults who are ill. With respect to children in particular, this area of research appears to be especially ripe for attachment theorists, and more of them should be encouraged to pursue it. Their findings may help to inform policymakers as they seek to amend the law over time.

Third, and related to the second point above, we need to figure out how to involve more men, fathers especially, in the nurturing and caregiving process. How can policies be designed not only to encourage men to provide more family care and nurture newborns, but to do so without fears of retaliation by their employer? Sweden and several other European Union countries are experimenting with incentives geared specifically to fathers, in an effort to encourage them to bond with their children early in their development. While the early returns on these incentives are mixed, we need to monitor such programs closely and determine what may work best in the United States.

Fourth, we need to know more about what is being taught in business schools concerning work and family issues, and whether or not the training of our MBAs is in step with the shifting sands of social change. In my very limited and unscientific survey of the nation's top schools, I was surprised at the absence of "work and family" in the business school curriculum. It also appears that relatively few faculty members include this topic in their research agendas. Nor can one find many institutes or centers embedded in business schools that address work/life problems. In short, with managers confronted with this issue everyday, why are they not better prepared to deal with it? And what can and should be done to fill this void?

A fifth area that demands more attention from researchers is the interaction between the Family and Medical Leave Act (FMLA) and the Americans with Disabilities Act (ADA). Enacted just three years apart, several court cases have already surfaced in which the two laws were intertwined. For example, is a particular illness identified under the ADA's eligibility criteria considered a "serious illness" under the FMLA's definition? More research needs to be completed in this area to better inform human resource managers as they attempt to cope with the ever-increasing complexity associated with this interaction.

And last but not least, we also need to know more about the interaction between the FMLA and welfare reform. Both policies have at least one objective in common: to maintain worker attachment to the labor force. Yet few studies have explored this area to determine whether or not "welfare-to-work" employees utilize the FMLA to any significant extent. And if they do, why are they using it and for how long? And most important perhaps, can we determine if the FMLA is playing a positive role in maintaining an attachment to the job market within a population that lacks a consistent work pattern?

## Options for Policymakers

By the time the state legislative sessions ended in early to mid-summer 2000, thirteen states had introduced legislation aimed at providing some form of wage replacement for employees taking family leave. Two models in particular were under consideration and both have already been discussed in some detail in chapter 8. One calls for the use of Unemployment Insurance for birth or adoption ("Baby UI"), and the other recommends that the Temporary Disability Insurance model be expanded to cover family care. As of January 2001, no state was successful in its effort to pass either of these models. However, several states appropriated funds to study the feasibility of paid leave, and it is therefore likely that by the summer of 2001, several states will have adopted such a measure.

Because both of these models, and particularly the UI approach, dominated the discussion on paid leave during the 1999–2000 legislative sessions, very few other options were even considered during the debate. For example, one means for funding paid leave is simply raising taxes and designating a specified amount to be used to cover periods of paid leave. However, as was previously discussed in this volume, the current political climate is not conducive to a tax hike. In fact, it is the politicians' deliberate avoidance of this strategy that has steered the debate toward the use of surplus unemployment funds. Therefore, because the use of general tax revenues for funding paid leave appears to be out of the question at this time, advocates should direct their energy elsewhere.

Another option that emerged in at least two states (Connecticut and Washington) was the creation of a special "dependent-care fund," to which both employer and employee would contribute and those taking leave would benefit. However, although neither state succeeded in adopting such a policy, it does not necessarily mean the concept is without merit. In fact, it may become more appealing to legislators if it were framed as a "private-public partnership" and shaped like a triangle. That is, the state (through a small tax increase), the employer, and the employee would all contribute to a trust fund for family caregivers that could be tapped by eligible workers. A similar model (Self-Sufficiency Trust) was created in Illinois about ten years ago to address the needs of the mentally disabled who are dependent on their parents but have outlived them. The state, families of the mentally disabled, and private contributors pay into a trust fund that guarantees the long-term care of the adult-but-dependent child in a preapproved shelter after the death of his or her parents.

Although the dependent-care fund sounds appealing, it would most likely require a financial jump-start by the state legislature, which would require a substantial tax increase to cover it. Perhaps it was for this reason (a tax increase), more than any other, that the use of general revenues or the creation of a dependent-care fund, which also requires a tax increase, did not advance legislatively. New Jersey's proposal (see chapter 8) to provide paid leave under UI and expand paid family care under TDI is enticing and should be monitored closely.

Left with Unemployment Insurance and Temporary Disability Insurance as their choices for covering paid leave, most of the thirteen states selected the former option, the use of surplus UI trust funds, primarily because they provided political cover from the White House. However, this approach clearly has its drawbacks. For example, because it is funded solely through an employer tax, it is susceptible to attacks from the business community on the grounds that it is unfair. And also, it is a proposal that is directly linked to the rise and fall of the economy. It is not a coincidence that its appeal today is related to a booming economy that has produced surplus reserves in the UI trust funds of most states. But will a paid-leave program survive a recession that drains UI reserves? And what happens after the moving van pulls out of the White House driveway? There is no guarantee that succeeding presidents will support such a strategy. During the 2000 presidential campaign Al Gore was on record for supporting the use of UI funds for paid leave, while George Bush opposed it. However, although both candidates talked in terms of helping America's working families, neither raised the issue of paid leave during the election.

As a member of the Connecticut State Task Force on Family Leave during the 1999–2000 legislative session, I endorsed our task force's recommendation that the legislature adopt the UI model. I testified at one legislative hearing in support of the proposal, and wrote three opinion pieces in major newspapers endorsing this approach. Aware of the conservative political climate both in Washington and Connecticut, I knew it was unrealistic to expect paid family leave to be supported through general tax revenues. With the 2000 elections approaching, no politician at the state or federal level would be willing to endorse a new program that costs taxpayers money. I didn't particularly like President Clinton's back-door approach of using Unemployment Insurance to fund paid leave, but I admired him for his creative thinking in trying to address a growing problem. In short, the UI model is not the best approach, in my mind, but it is far superior to what currently exists with respect to paid leave: nothing.

So, of the two options presently on the table, UI and TDI, I would prefer the latter. But unfortunately, Connecticut is not a TDI state, which means a TDI law similar to those passed in New York, Hawaii, Rhode Island, New Jersey, and California would have to be passed by my legislature prior to moving forward on paid leave. However, I still believe the TDI model is the best vehicle available for offering paid leave, for the following reasons. First, employers and employees in most of the five TDI states fund it through joint contributions, unlike the UI model in which the burden of support falls entirely on the backs of employers. Second, eligibility for collecting benefits under the TDI program is completely unrelated to the size of the company for which one works. Thus, employees at all salary levels, and regardless of professional skill, position in the firm, or socioeconomic class, would be covered under TDI. And three, the TDI system is not as susceptible to economic fluctuations as is the case with Unemployment Insurance. If New Jersey's estimate is correct, that to expand its TDI program to include family care would not cost employers a cent but would increase employee contributions by only $21 annually, then it appears a major benefit can be obtained at a relatively small cost.

So for the reasons stated above, I would support the UI model but would greatly prefer the TDI approach. However, I am assuming that both models include coverage for *family* matters, not just for childbirth and adoption. Therefore, the five states currently using the TDI model for paid leave for childbirth should consider expanding their provisions to include broader family coverage. Not only will such action set us apart from Europe and Scandinavia in that we provide "family coverage" (we already have that distinction), but we will finally join them and other industrialized societies in offering paid leave. We are long overdue and so much more work still needs to be done. But we should at least rejoice over the fact that an important issue has been placed on the political agenda in thirteen states and the debate has begun. It is within this context that I hope this book provides one more informative point of reference in a continuing dialogue about an important issue.

# *Appendix A*

## *Working Mother*'s Top 100 Companies for 1999 (alphabetically)

AARP
Aetna Inc.
Allstate Insurance
American Express
American Home Products
Ameritech
Arthur Anderson LLP
AT&T
Autodesk Inc.
Bank of America
Bank One
Baptist Health Systems
Bayfront/St. Anthony's Health
Bell Atlantic
Benjamin Group
Beth Israel Decaness
   Medical Center
Bon Secours Richmond Health
Booz-Allen & Hamilton
Bristol-Meyers Squibb Co.
Calvert Group
Chase Manhattan Corp.
Cigna Corporation
Cinergy
Liz Claiborne
Corning, Inc.
Daimler Chrysler
Dayton Hudson
Deloitte and Touche
Deutsche Bank

DuPont
Eastman Chemical
Eastman Kodak
Ernst & Young LLP
Fannie Mae
First Tennessee Bank
First Union
Fleet Financial Group
Ford Motor Co.
Gannett Co., Inc.
Gen America
Genentech, Inc.
General Motors
Glaxco Wellcome, Inc.
GTE Corporation
Gymboree Corporation

Hoffman-La Roche
Household Interior
IBM
Imation
JFK Medical Center
Johnson & Johnson
S.C. Johnson & Son
Edward Jones
Lancaster Laboratories
Life Technologies, Inc.
Eli Lilly and Company
Lincoln Financial
Lotus Development

Lucent Technologies
Marriott International
Mattell, Inc.
MBNA America Bank
Mentor Graffics Corp.
Merck & Company, Inc.
Merrill Lynch & Co.
Metlife
Monsanto Company
J.P. Morgan
Morrison & Foerster
Motorola, Inc.
Mutual of Omaha
Nordstrom
Novartis Pharm.

Patagonia, Inc.
Pfizer
Phoenix Home Life
Pricewaterhouse
Procter & Gamble
Prudential
Rex Healthcare
Ridgeview, Inc.
Rockwell
St. Raphael Health
Sara Lee Corp.
Seagrams & Sons
Sears, Roebuck
Seattle Times Co

Security Benefit
Sequent Computer
St. Paul Companies
Stride Rite Company
Texas Instruments

Tom's of Maine
TRW, Inc.
Universal Studios
U.S. West, Inc.
Valassis Communications

Warner-Lambert
West Group
Xerox

# Appendix B

---

# Chronology of Leave Policy in the United States

**1867**  Wisconsin passed the first state policy related to maternity and employment by restricting the hours on the job for women.

**1905**  *Lochner v. New York.* In a 5–4 decision, the U.S. Supreme Court struck down New York's ten-hour day/sixty-hour workweek on the grounds that it violated the contract between labor and management.

**1908**  *Muller v. Oregon.* Unanimous U.S. Supreme Court decision upholds Oregon's ten-hour workday on the grounds that "excess work can harm women."

**1942**  Rhode Island is the first state to offer paid leave under its Temporary Disability Insurance (TDI) program. Four states follow between 1946 and 1948: CA, NJ, NY, HI.

**1964**  Civil Rights Act passed by U.S. Congress. Prohibits discrimination based on race, sex, or ethnic group.

**1972**  Equal Employment Opportunity Commission (EEOC) rules that employment policies that exclude women are in violation of Title VII of the 1964 Civil Rights Act.

**1976**   *General Electric v. Gilbert.* U.S. Supreme Court denounced 1972 EEOC ruling and concluded that pregnancy was an "additional risk unique to women."

**1978**   Pregnancy Discrimination Act passed by Congress. Stipulated that "women affected by pregnancy, childbirth, or related medical conditions shall be treated the same for all employment-related purposes."

**1985**   First leave bill is introduced at the federal level. On April 4, 1985, Patricia Schroeder (D-CO) introduced the Parental and Disability Act. It stalled in committee.

**1986**   Parental and Medical Leave Act is introduced but it is stalled in congressional committee.

**1987**   *California Federal Savings and Loan (Cal Fed) vs. Guerra* (the Garland case). U.S. Supreme Court in a 6 to 3 decision upholds California law that protected employment rights of women workers who become pregnant.

**1987**   Twenty-eight states introduce parental/family-leave bills. Four states pass legislation: CT, MN, OR, and RI.

**1987**   Given its new name, the Family and Medical Leave Act is introduced in the U.S. House of Representatives but is unsuccessful.

**1990**   The FMLA passes in the U.S. House and Senate but is vetoed by President Bush. The House fell short by fifty-three votes to override the presidential veto.

**1992**   The FMLA is passed again by Congress but vetoed for the second time by President Bush, seven weeks before he lost the election to Bill Clinton.

**1993**   The FMLA passes in the House and Senate by clear majority votes and is signed into law by President Clinton on February 5, 1993. Thirty-two states had passed leave legislation between 1987 and 1993.

**1996**   President Clinton and the Democrats use Bob Dole's anti-family-leave record against him during the 1996 presidential campaign. With "Families First" as their campaign slogan, the Democrats designated

September 24, 1996, "Family Leave Day " to remind voters that on that date four years earlier, Bob Dole voted to sustain George Bush's second veto of the FMLA. Clinton becomes the first Democratic president to be elected to a second term since Franklin Roosevelt.

**1999**    On May 23, 1999, President Clinton delivers the commencement address at Grambling State University in which he recommends that the Department of Labor assist states to provide paid leave through the use of Unemployment Insurance trust funds. Thirteen states introduce "paid-leave legislation" in 1999–2000 but not one bill succeds.

**1999**    December 3, 1999, Alexis Herman, secretary of labor, announces that proposed regulations concerning the use of UI trust funds to cover paid leave are available for comment. Approximately sixty days later, the regulations are approved.

**2000**    June 10, 2000, President Clinton officially announces the publication of the Department of Labor's Regulations permitting states to use Unemployment Insurance funds to provide paid leave.

**2000**    June 26, 2000, the U.S. Chamber of Commerce sues the Department of Labor in an effort to prevent states from tapping UI trust funds to cover paid leave.

**2000**    July 31, 2000. The Massachusetts legislature is the first in the nation to pass a paid family-leave bill but it is killed by Republican Governor Paul Cellucci on August 10.

# Appendix C

# Resources for Researchers, Educators, Administrators, and Policymakers

There are numerous advocacy groups, professional organizations, and publications that address the issue of work and family. The list that follows is inconclusive, but many of the web sites have multiple links to other sites. Perhaps the best web site that contains the most relevant links to work and family issues is Penn State's *Work and Family Links* at http://www.la.psu.edu/lsir/workfam/links.html.

## Research

Boston College Center for Work and Family. Specializes in research, workplace partnerships, and communication and information services. http://www.bc.edu/bc_org/avp/csom/cwf/center/overview.html

Center for Research on Women at Wellesley College. http://www.wellesley.edu/WCW/crwsub.html

The Centre for Families, Work and Well-Being at the University of Guelph, Canada. http://www.uoguelph.ca/cfww

Center for the Ethnography of Everyday Life at the University of Michigan. http://www.ethno.isr.umich.edu

Center for Working Families. Located at the University of California, Berkeley. Offers fellowships for visiting scholars to conduct research on work and family issues. http://workingfamilies.berkeley.edu

Cornell Employment and Family Careers Institute. http://www.blcc.cornell.edu/cci

Families and Work Institute. Includes numerous publications on work-life research and is also the home of The Fatherhood Project. http://www.familiesandwork.org

Gender, Work and Family Project. Focuses on pay equity issues and poverty among women workers. http://www.genderwork.org

Institute for Women's Policy Research. Publishes numerous papers, research briefs, and books on work and family issues. http://www.iwpr.org

Labor Project for Working Families. Located at the Institute of Industrial Relations, University of California, Berkeley. http://laborproject.berkeley.edu

National Partnership for Women and Families. Very informative site that monitors FMLA and state initiatives among other issues, including women's health. http://nationalpartnership.org. The NPWF offers in hard copy its *Guide to the Family and Medical Leave Act: Questions and Answers*.

Parents, Children and Work. An Alfred P. Sloan Family Center at the University of Chicago and the National Opinion Research Center. http://www.src.uchicago.edu/orgs/sloan

Radcliffe Public Policy Center. Based at Radcliffe College, Harvard University. Conducts much research on women's issues and work and family integration, and offers research fellowships. http://www.radcliffe.edu/pubpol

W.E. Upjohn Institute for Employment Research. Research includes family and labor issues and unemployment insurance. http://www.upjohninst.org

**Government Agencies**

Administration for Children and Families—U.S. Department of Health and Human Services. http://www.acf.dhhs.gov/programs/acyf

U.S. Department of Labor. Employment Standards Administration Wage and Hour Division. FMLA Compliance Guide. http://www.dol

**Business Organizations**

Conference Board. A resource center and clearinghouse for businesses, the CB has shown an interest in work/life issues for at least a decade. They continue to work closely with the Families and Work Institute. http://www.conference-board.org

Employment Policy Foundation. Conducts research on employment policy with a particular focus on the effect of government regulations on businesses. www.epf.org

National Association of Manufacturers. http:///www.nam.org

National Federation of Independent Business. The largest advocacy group in the country representing small and independent businesses. Particularly concerned about the FMLA's impact on small firms. http://www.nfib.com

Society for Human Resources Management. The major professional organization representing human resource managers and other personnel specialists responsible for implementing the FMLA at the work site. http://www.shrm.org

U.S. Chamber of Commerce. A long-time opponent of government-mandated family leave. In 2000, the Chamber sued the U.S. Department of Labor to prevent it from adjusting regulations to provide paid leave under unemployment insurance. http://www.uschamber.org

**Advocacy Groups**

AFL-CIO's Working Families Agenda. An informational bank on work and family issues and strategies to incorporate worker-friendly policies in labor contracts. http://www.aflcio.org/front/wfa.htm

Alliance for a Caring Economy. Promotes social and economic policies that recognize and reward caring work. http://www.globalfutures.org/ace

Alliance for Work/Life Professionals. Professionals in business, academia, and the public sector who promote a healthier balance between work and family. http://www.awlp.org

Center on Budget and Policy Priorities. Concentrates on fiscal policy issues affecting low-and moderate-income families. Monitors the Earned Income Tax Credit (EITC), among other things. http://www.cbpp.org

College and University Work/Family Association. Provides information on work and family issues within higher education. http://www.cuwfa.org/main.html

Critical Path. A site dedicated to the concerns of isolated workers worldwide and their rights on the job. http://www.criticalpath.co.uk

Mothers and More. Supports "sequencing women"—mothers who have altered their career paths in order to care for their children at home. http://www.mothersandmore.org

9 to 5 National Association of Working Women. A national grassroots membership organization that strengthens women's ability to work for economic justice. http://www.9to5.org

**Consultants on Work and Family Issues**

Dependent Care Connection. Assists companies and employees in addressing family needs of workers. http://www.lifecare.com

Hewitt Associates. An international consulting firm specializing in personnel matters. http://www.hewitt.com:80/hewitt

Great Place to Work Institute. Based in San Francisco, the Institute consults with corporations concerning human resources management. Each year it publishes its own "Top 100 Best Companies to Work for in America." http://www.greatplacetowork.com/

The Impact Group—Work/Life Resource and Referral. Hired by companies to assist their employees in locating child-care programs, adult/elder care, and special needs, among other services. http://www.the-impact-group.com/corp/worklife.htm

Thompson Publishing Group. Monitors implementation of laws related to work and family issues. Offers regular updates on court decisions related to the FMLA. http://www.thompson.com

Tom Peters. Consultant and inspirational speaker. Critical of poor personnel management but profiles and praises companies "who treat their workers right." http://www.tompeters.com

Work and Family Directions. Offers a variety of services under the heading of "work/life." http://www.wfd.com

Work and Family Benefits, Inc. An employee benefits company dedicated to making child- and elder-care benefits available to working people. http://www.wfbenefits.com

## Publications

*Community, Work and Family.* A professional journal devoted to theory, research policy, and practice related to work and family issues in particular. http://www.carfax.co.uk/cwf_ad.htm

*National Report on Work and Family.* Published twice monthly, it provides updates on legislative initiatives, human resource strategies, and other areas related to work and family. http://www.bpinews.com

*The Sandwich Generation.* An online site that includes a regular column on aging and elder/parent-care issues for those who are working, raising children, and caring for an aging parent. http://www.globesyndicate.com

*Work and Family Connection.* Publishes the Work and Family Newsbriefs. Up-to-date information on work/family issues and access to a clearinghouse of information. http://workfamily.com

*Wall Street Journal.* Sue Shellenberger produces a regular column on work and family issues. http://www.workfamily.com

## Managing the FMLA at the Work Site

FMLA Tracker Software and the FMLA Compliance Guide assist managers in complying with the FMLA and tracks the utilization of family leave within a company. http://www.intellisysinc.com

*Managing Employees under FMLA and ADA* is a six-page, biweekly newsletter written in layman's language to assist human resource manages and others through the legal maze of the FMLA and ADA. http://www.employmentpractices.com/epfmla.htm.

*Reference Guide to the Family and Medical Leave Act of 1993.* Produced by Michigan State University, the online information bank is presented in a question-and-answer format for those seeking information about implementing the law. Updated regularly. http://www.hr.msu.edu/web/FMLAGuide.asp

**Other Relevant Links**

American Association of Retired Persons. http://www.aarp.org

Children's Defense Fund. http://www.childrensdefense.org

Generations United. A non-profit organization based in Washington that develops strategies and programs to bring generations together. http://www.gu.org

National Organization for Women (NOW). http://www.now.org

# References

Aaron, Henry. 1987. "The Impossible Dream Comes True." *Brookings Review* 5, 1: 3–10.

Adams, Carolyn, and Kathryn Winston. 1980. *Mothers at Work—Public Policies in the United States, Sweden, and China.* New York: Longman.

AFL-CIO. 1992. *Putting Families First: AFL-CIO Working Family Resource.* Washington, DC: AFL-CIO.

————. 2000. "Ask a Working Woman Survey." Washington, DC: AFL-CIO. March 9.

Albelda, Randy, and Tiffany Manuel. 2000. *Filling the Work and Family Gap: Paid Parental Leave in Massachusetts.* Boston, MA: Labor Resource Center, University of Massachusetts.

Anderson, Elaine, and Richard Hula, eds. 1991. *The Reconstruction of Family Policy.* Westport, CT: Greenwood Press.

Anderson, Karen. 1981. *Wartime Women: Sex Roles, Family Relations and the Status of Women During World War II.* Westport CT: Greenwood Press.

Anderson, Lisa, and Sheila Tobias. 1974. "What Really Happened to Rosie the Riveter? Demobilization and the Female Labor Force, 1944–47." New York: MSS Modular Publications.

Anderson, Mary. 1951. *Women at Work: The Autiobiography of Mary Anderson as Told to Mary N. Winslow.* Minneapolis, MN: University of Minnesota Press.

Associated Press News Service. 1996. "Gore Touts Family Leave to Louisiana Moderates." September 25: 1–2.

————. 2000. "German Parents Get Parental Leave." March 29: 1.

Auerbach, Judith D. 1988. *In the Business of Child Care: Employer Initiatives and Working Women.* New York: Praeger.

Babcock, Barbara. 1978. *Sex Discrimination and the Law: Causes and Remedies.* New York: Aspen.

Bailyn, Lotte. 1996. *Beyond Work and Family: Adventures on the Fault Line.* Cambridge, MA: Radcliffe Public Policy Institute, Radcliffe College.

Baker, Maureen. 1995. *Canadian Family Policies: Cross-National Comparisons.* Toronto: University of Toronto Press.

Bane, Mary Jo. 1980. "Toward a Description and Evaluation of United States Family Policy." In *The Politics and Programs of Family Policy,* eds. J. Aldous and W. Dumon with K. Johnson, 155–190. Notre Dame, IN: University of Notre Dame and Leuven University Press.

Barilleaux, Ryan, and Mary E. Stuckey, eds. 1992. *Leadership and the Bush Presidency.* Hanover, NH: The University Press of New England.

Barlett, Donald L., and James B. Steele. 1994. *America: Who Really Pays the Taxes?* New York: Simon and Schuster.

Bauer, Gary. 1996. *Our Hopes Our Dreams: A Vision for America.* Colorado Springs: CO: Focus on the Family Publishing.

Becker, Gary S. 1957. *The Economics of Discrimination*, 1st ed. (2nd ed., 1971). Chicago, IL: University of Chicago Press.

———. 1960. "An Economic Analysis of Fertility." In *Demographic and Economic Change in Developed Countries.* A conference of the Universities National Bureau Committee for Economic Research. Princeton, NJ: Princeton University Press, for the National Bureau of Economic Research.

———. 1964. *Human Capital*, 1st ed. (2nd ed., 1975). New York: Columbia University Press.

———. 1965. "A Theory of the Allocation of Time." *Economic Journal* 75:493–517.

———. 1971. *The Economics of Discrimination.* 2nd ed. Chicago, IL: University of Chicago Press.

———. 1973. "A Theory of Marriage: Part I." *Journal of Political Economy* 81, 4: 813–846.

———. 1974. "A Theory of Marriage: Part II." *Journal of Political Economy* 82, 2, 11–26.

———. 1977. "An Economic Analysis of Marital Instability." *Journal of Political Economy* 85, 6: 1141–1187.

———. 1981. *A Treatise on the Family.* Cambridge, MA: Harvard University Press.

———. 1985. "Human Capital, Effort, and the Sexual Division of Labor." *Journal of Labor Economics* 3, 1: 33–58.

———. 1988."The Family and the State." *Journal of Law and Economics* 31, 1: 1–18.

———. 1993. "The Nobel Lecture: The Economic Way of Looking at Behavior." *Journal of Political Economy*, 101, 3: 385–409.

Becker, Gary S., and W.M. Landes, eds. 1974. *Essays in the Economics of Crime and Punishment.* New York: Columbia University Press for the National Bureau of Economic Research.

Becker, Gary S., and Nigel Tomes. 1986. "Human Capital and the Rise and Fall of Families." *Journal of Labor Economics* 4, 3: 1–39.

Becker, Gary S., and Guity Nashat Becker. 1997. *The Economics of Life: From Baseball to Affirmative Action to Immigration, How Real-World Issues Affect Our Everyday Life.* New York: McGraw-Hill.

Bellah, Robert. 1996. *Habits of the Heart: Individualism and Commitment in American Life.* Berkeley, CA: University of California Press.

Belsky, Jay. 1988. "The Effects of Infant Care Reconsidered." *Early Childhood Research Quarterly* 3: 235–272.

Belsky, Jay, and David Eggebeen. 1991. "Early and Extensive Maternal Employment and Young Children's Socioemotional Development: Children of the National Longitudinal Survey of Youth." *Journal of Marriage and the Family*, November: 204–210.

Bennett, William J. 1994. *The Index of Leading Cultural Indicators.* New York: Simon & Schuster.

———. 1998. *The Death of Outrage: Bill Clinton and the Assault on American Ideals.* New York: The Free Press.

Bergmann, Barbra R. 1987. "The Task of a Feminist Economics: A More Equitable

Future." In *The Impact of Feminist Research in the Academy*, ed. Christie Farnham, 131–147. Bloomington, IN: Indiana University Press.

————. 1995. "Becker's Theory of the Family: Preposterous Conclusions." *Feminist Economics* 1, 1: 141–150.

Berlau, John. 1998. "Will the Payroll Tax Ever Be Cut?" *Investors Business Daily*, May 19: 14–16.

Bernstein, Anya. 1997. "Inside or Outside? The Politics of Family and Medical Leave." *Policy Studies Journal* 25, 1: 87–99.

Berry, Marilyn. 1993. *The Politics of Parenthood: Child Care, Women's Rights, and the Myth of the Good Mother*. New York: Viking Press.

Birnbaum, Jeffrey, and Alan Murray. 1987. *Showdown at Gucci Gulch: Lawmakers, Lobbyists, and the Unlikely Triumph of Tax Reform*. New York: Random House.

Bittker, Boris J. 1975. "Federal Income Taxation and the Family." *Stanford Law Review* 27: 1389–1463.

Blankenhorn, David. 1995. *Fatherless America: Confronting Our Most Urgent Social Problem*. Lanham, MD: Rowman & Littlefield.

Blankenhorn, David, Stephen Bayme, and Jean Bethe Elshtain, eds. 1990. *Rebuilding the Nest: A New Commitment to the American Family*. Milwaukee, WI: FamilyService America.

Bogenschneider, Karen, Jonathan Olson, Kirsten D. Linney and Jessica Mills. 2000. "Connecting Research and Policymaking: Implications for Theory and Practice from the Family Impact Seminars." *Family Relations* 49, 3: 327–339.

Bookman, Ann. 1998. "Reshaping the Social Contract Between Employers and Families: The Case of Family and Medical Leave Policies." A paper presented at the Annual Meeting of the Association for Public Policy Analysis and Management, Washington, DC, October 29, 1998.

Bork, Robert, H. 1996. *Slouching Toward Gomorrah: Modern Liberalism and American Decline*. New York: Regan Books.

Boskin, Michael J., and Eytan Sheshinski. 1983. "Optimal Tax Treatment of the Family: Married Couples." *Journal of Public Economics* 20: 281–97.

Bowen, Gary. 1995. "Corporate Supports for the Family Lives of Employees: A Conceptual Model for Program Planning and Evaluation." In *The Work and Family Interface: Toward a Contextual Effects Perspective*, eds. Gary L. Bowen and Joe F. Pittman, 422–429. Minneapolis, MN: National Council on Family Relations.

Bowen, Gary L., and Joe F. Pittman, eds. 1995. *The Work and Family Interface: Toward a Contextual Effects Perspective*. Minneapolis, MN: National Council on Family Relations.

Brandeis, Louis D., and Josephine Goldmark. 1908. *Women in Industry.* Introduction by Leon Stein and Philip Taft (1969 reprint). New York: Arno Press.

Bravo, Ellen. 1991. "Family Leave: The Need for a New Minimum Standard." In *Parental Leave and Child Care: Setting a Research and Policy Agenda,* Janet Hyde and Marilyn Essex, eds. 163–175. Philadelphia, PA: Temple University Press.

Brinkman, April B. 1999. "Family and Medical Leave: Interest Group Politics and Leaving Well Enough Alone." A paper presented at the Annual Meeting of the American Political Science Association, Atlanta, GA, September 2–5, 1999.

British Ministry of Health. 1945. "Ministry of Health Circular 221/45." London: British Ministry of Health.

Brownmiller, Susan. 1975. *Against Our Will: Men, Women, and Rape*. New York: Simon and Schuster.

Burggraph, Shirley. 1997. *The Feminine Economy and Economic Man*. Reading, MA: Addison-Wesley.

Burke, J. Vincent, and Vee Burke. 1974. *Nixon's Good Deed*. New York: Columbia University Press.

Burkett, Elinor. 2000. *The Baby Boon: How Family-Friendly America Cheats the Childless*. New York: The Free Press.

Burns, James MacGregor, and Georgia J. Sorenson. 1999. *Dead Center: Clinton-Gore Leadership and the Perils of Moderation*. New York: Scribner.

Burtless, Gary. 1995. "Costs and Benefits of the Family and Medical Leave Act from the Perspective of Employers: Comments on the Employer and Employee Surveys." Washington, DC: Brookings Institution.

*Business Week*. 1996. "Grading Family Friendliness." September 16: 18–23.

Buss, David, M. 1975. "Human Mate Selection." *American Scientist* 73: 47–51.

Cable News Network, May 28, 1998.

*California Federal Savings and Loan Association v. Guerra*. 1987. United States Supreme Court, 479, U.S. 272, No. 85–194.

Campbell, Colin, and Bert Rockman. 1996. *The Clinton Presidency: First Appraisals*. Chatham, NJ: Chatham House.

Caplan, Richard, and John Feffer. 1994. *State of the Union 1994: The Clinton Administration and the Nation in Profile*. Boulder, CO: Westview Press.

Card, David, and Alan Kreuger. 1998. *Myth and Measurement: The New Economics of the Minimum Wage*. Princeton, NJ: Princeton University Press.

Carlson, Allan. 1986. "What Happened to the Family Wage?" *The Public Interest* 83: 3–17.

Carter, Jimmy. 1976. "The American Family: A Campaign Statement in Manchester, New Hampshire." August 3, 1976. Washington, DC: U.S. Government Printing Office.

Center on Budget and Policy Priorities. 1999. "Another Tax Benefit for Families! The Child and Dependent Care Credit." Washington, DC: Center on Budget and Policy Priorities.

Chadwick, Bruce A., and Tim B. Heaton. 1999. *Statistical Handbook on the American Family*. Phoenix, AZ: Oryx Press.

Chafe, William. 1972. *The American Woman: Her Changing Social, Economic and Political Roles, 1920–1970*. New York: Oxford University Press.

Cherlin, Andrew. 1983. "Family Policy: The Conservative Challenge and the Progressive Response." *Journal of Family Issues* 4: 427–439.

———. 1988. *The Changing American Family and Public Policy*. Washington, DC: The Urban Institute.

———. 1992. *Marriage, Divorce, and Remarriage*. 2nd ed. Cambridge, MA: Harvard University Press.

———. 1996. *Public and Private Families*. New York: McGraw-Hill, Inc.

Chiappori, Pierre-Andres. 1992. "Collective Labor Supply and Welfare." *Journal of Political Economy* 100: 437–467.

*Christian Science Monitor*. 1998. "Why Do Americans Get Short-Changed on Maternity Leave." February 18: 1–2.

Citizens for Tax Justice. 1998. "'97 Tax Act Gives Zero to Most Families This April." Washington, DC: Citizens for Tax Justice, March 31 press release.

Clarke-Stewart, K. Alison. 1991. "A Home Is Not a School: The Effects of Child Care on Children's Development." *Journal of Social Issues* 47, 2: 215–225.

Clinton-Gore Press Office. 1996. "Forty-four States to Hold Family and Medical Leave

Day News Events to Highlight the Impact of President Clinton's Law." Washington, DC: National Deputy Press Secretary, Clinton-Gore Campaign, September 24.

Clinton, Hillary. 1996. *It Takes a Village: And Other Lessons Children Teach Us.* New York: Simon and Schuster.

CNN (1998). "Decline of Traditional American Family Slows in 90s." Atlanta, GA: Cable News Network .Cable News Network, May 28, 1998.

CNN Interactive. 1999. "Law or No Law, Dads Find It Hard to Ask for Parental Leave." Web posted on February 5. Internet link: http://cnn.com.

Coalition of Labor Union Women. 1991. *Bargaining for Family Benefits: A Union Member's Guide.* New York: Coalition for Labor Union Women.

Cohen, D. 1989. "Bush and Congress: The Honeymoon Is Over." *National Journal,* October 14: 2508–2512.

Cohen, Susan, and Mary Fainsod Katzenstein. 1988. "The War Over the Family Is not Over the Family." In *Feminism, Children and the New Families,* eds. Sandford M. Dornbusch and Myra H. Strober, 25–46. New York: The Guilford Press.

Colker, Ruth. 1998. *American Law in the Age of Hypercapitalism: The Worker, the Family, and the State.* New York: New York University Press.

Collins, Chuck, Chris Hartman, and Holly Sklar. 1999. "Economic Disparity at the Century's Turn." Boston, MA: United for a Fair Economy.

Collins, Chuck, Betsy Lonegar-Wright, and Holly Sklar. 1999. *Shifting Fortunes: The Perils of the Growing American Wealth Gap.* Boston, MA: United for a Fair Economy.

Commission on Leave. 1996. *A Workable Balance: Report to Congress on Family and Medical Leave Policies.* Washington, DC: U.S. Department of Labor.

*Congressional Quarterly Almanac.* 1992. Washington, DC: *The Congressional Quarterly.*

———. 1994. Washington, DC: *The Congressional Quarterly.*

Congressional Research Service. 1987. *Parental Leave Legislation in the 100th Congress.* No. 1B86132. Washington, DC: The Library of Congress.

*Connecticut Post.* 1996. "Hillary Pushes a New Family Leave Plan: Time Is Set Aside for School Events." September 25, A-1.

Coontz, Stephanie. 1992. *The Way We Never Were: American Families and the Nostalgia Trap.* New York: Basic Books.

CORE, Inc. 2000. "Complex Family and Medical Leave Act Regulations Could Pose Serious Burdens to Employers." Irvine, CA: CORE, Inc.

Council of Economic Advisers. 1999. *Families and the Labor Market, 1969–1999: Analyzing the Time Crunch.* Washington, DC: Council of Economic Advisers.

Cox, W. Michael, and Richard Alm. 1999. *Myths of Rich and Poor: Why We're Better Off Than We Think.* New York: Basic Books.

———. 1996. "The Family Has Always Been Vulnerable to Social Change." *Modern Maturity,* May/June: 38–43.

C-SPAN Archives. 1999. *Family and Medical Leave Signing Ceremony,* White House Rose Garden, February 5, 1993. West Lafayette, IN: C-SPAN Archives. ID: 37753.

Davis, Peggy Cooper. 1997. *Neglected Stories: The Constitution and Family Values.* New York: Hill and Wang.

Decker, Paul D. 1997. "Work Incentives Disincentives." In *Unemployment Insurance in the United States,* eds. Christopher O'Leary and Stephen Wandner, 285–320. Kalamazoo, MI: W.E. Upjohn Institute.

Del Boca, Daniel. 1997. "Intrahousehold Distribution of Resources and Labor Market Participation Decisions." In *Economics of the Family and Family Policies*, eds., Inga Persson and Christina Jonung, 65–83. London and New York: Routledge.

Demos, John. 1970. *A Little Commonwealth: Family Life in Plymouth Colony*. Oxford: Oxford University Press.

Dempsey, John J. 1981. *The Family and Public Policy*. Baltimore, MD: Brookes.

Diamond, Irene. 1983. *Families, Politics, and Public Policy: A Feminist Dialogue on Women and the State*. New York: Longman.

Dietrich, Sharon M. 1998. "Recent Developments Under the Family and Medical Leave Act: The Courts Start to Speak." Philadelphia, PA: National Employment Law Project.

Domestic Policy Council. 1986. *The Family: Preserving America's Future*. Executive Office of the President. Washington, DC: The White House.

Dratch, Howard. 1974. "The Politics of Child Care in the 1940s." *Science and Society* 38, 3: 167–204.

Droege, Kristin. 1995. "Child Care: An Educational Perspective." *Jobs & Capital*, Winter: 124–132.

Dychtwald, Ken. 1999. *Age Power: How the 21st Century Will Be Ruled by the New Old*. New York. Putnam.

Easterlin, Richard. 1991. "The Economic Impact of Prospective Population Changes in Advanced Industrial Countries: A Historical Perspective." *Journal of Gerontology: Social Sciences* 40, 6: 299–309.

Economic Policy Institute. 1999. "Family Income Finally Regains 1989 Level." *Snapshot*, February 3, 2.

Edelman, Marian Wright. 1987. *Families in Peril: An Agenda for Social Change*. Cambridge, MA: Harvard University Press.

Edelman, Peter. 1997. "The Worst Thing Bill Clinton Has Done." *The Atlantic Monthly*, March: 43–58.

Ehrenreich, Barbara, and Deirdre English. 1989. "Blowing the Whistle on the 'Mommy Track.' " *Ms.* 18, 1: 96–99.

Eisenstein, Zillah. 1983. "The State, the Patriarchal Family, and Working Mothers." In *Families, Politics, and Public Policy: A Feminist Dialogue on Women and the State*, ed. Irene Diamond. New York: Longman.

Elazar, Daniel. 1984. *American Federalism: A View from the States*. New York: Harper and Row.

Ellison, Sonja K. 1997. "The Family and Medical Leave Act of 1993." *Journal of Family Issues* 18, 1: 30–54.

Ellwood, David. 1988. *Poor Support: Poverty and the American Family*. New York: Basic Books.

———. 1996. "Welfare Reform as I Knew It: When Bad Things Happen to Good Policies." *The American Prospect*, May–June: 1–15.

Elshtain, Jean Bethke. 1999. "A Call to Civil Society." *Society* 36, 4: 11–19.

Elving, Ronald. 1995. *Conflict and Compromise: How Congress Makes the Law*. New York: Simon and Schuster.

Employment Policy Foundation. 1999. "Using Unemployment Insurance to Fund Parental Leave Could Have Unintended Consequences." *Economic Bytes*, June 16. 1–2, Washington, DC.

Engels, Friedrich. 1972. *The Origin of Family, Private Property, and the State*. New York: International Publishers. Reprinted from original publication.

Erickson, Nancy. 1982. "Historical Background of Protective Labor Legislation: *Muller v. Oregon*." In *Women and the Law: A Social Historical Perspective*, vol. 2, ed. D. Kelley Weisberg, 160–174. Cambridge, MA: Schenkman.

Fagnani, Jeanne. 1996. "Family Policies and Working Mothers: A Comparison of France and West Germany." In *Women of the European Union: The Politics of Work and Daily Life*, eds. D. Garcia-Ramon and J. Monk, 121–138. London: Routledge.

———. 1998. "Recent Changes in Family Policy in France: Political Trade-offs and Economic Constraints." In *Women, Work and the Family in Europe*, eds. Eileen Drew, Ruth Emerek, and Evelyn Mahon, 78–104. London: Routledge.

———. 1999. "Parental Leave in France." In *Parental Leave: Progress or Pitfall? Research and Policy Issues in Europe*, eds. Peter Moss and Fred Deven, 69–83. The Hague/Brussels: NIDI CBGS Publications.

Families and Work Institute. 1991. *Corporate Reference Guide for Work-Family Programs*. New York: Family and Work Institute.

———. 1997. *The 1997 National Study of the Changing Workforce*. New York: Families and Work Institute.

*Family and Medical Leave Handbook*. 2000.Washington, DC: Thompson Publishing Group.

Farnham, Rebecca. 1939. *Women at Work: A Century of Industrial Change*. U.S. Department of Labor, Women's Bureau, Bulletin 161. Washington, DC: U.S. Government Printing Office.

Ferber, Marianne A., and Brigid O'Farrell. 1991. *Work and Family: Policies for a Changing Work Force*. Washington, DC: National Academy Press.

Firestone, Shulamith. 1971. *The Dialectic of Sex: The Case for Feminist Revolution*. New York: Bantam.

Flax, Jane. 1983. "Contemporary American Families: Decline or Transformation?" In *Families, Politics, and Public Policy: A Feminist Dialogue on Women and the State*, ed. Irene Diamond, 21–40. New York: Longman.

Fleenor, Patrick. 1999. *The Price of Civilized Society*. Washington, DC: Tax Foundation.

Flesch, Rudolf F. 1955. *Why Johnny Can't Read and What You Can Do About It*. New York: Harper.

Flynn, Gillian. 1994. "HR Must Take Proactive Steps to Curb FMLA Misuse." *Personnel Journal* 73, 9: 36–37.

Foner, Philip S. 1979. *Women and the American Labor Movement. Vol. I*. New York: The Free Press.

———. 1982. *History of the Labor Movement in the United States. Vol. 6: On the Eve of America's Entrance into World War I, 1915–1916*. New York: International Publishers.

*Fortune*. 1999. "The 100 Best Companies to Work For." *Fortune*, January 11: 118–142.

Frank, Meryl, and Robyn Lipner. 1988. "History of Maternity Leave in Europe and the United States." In *The Parental Leave Crisis: Toward a National Policy*, eds. Edward F. Zigler and Meryl Frank, 3–22. New Haven, CT: Yale University Press.

Fried, Mindy. 1998. *Taking Time: Parental Leave Policy and Corporate Culture*. Philadelphia, PA: Temple University Press.

Friedan, Betty. 1963. *The Feminine Mystique*. New York: Dell.

Furstenburg, Frank F., Jr. 1999. "Is the Modern Family a Threat to Children's Health?" *Society* 36, 4: 31–37.

Galinsky, Ellen, James Bond, and Dana Friedman. 1993. *Highlights: The National Study of the Changing Workforce.* New York: Families and Work Institute.

Galinsky, Ellen, and James Bond. 1998. *The 1998 Business Work-Life Study: A Sourcebook.* New York: Families and Work Institute.

———. 1999. *Ask the Children: What America's Children Really Think About Working Parents.* New York: William Morrow.

Gallagher, Maggie. 1996. *The Abolition of Marriage: How We Destroy Lasting Love.* Washington, DC: Regnery Publishing.

———. 1999. *The Age of Unwed Mothers.* New York: Institute for American Values.

Gardlund, T. 1990. *The Life of Knut Wicksell.* Cambridge, UK: Edward Elgar.

Garey, Anita I. 1999. *Weaving Work and Motherhood.* Philadelphia, PA: Temple University Press.

Gauthier, Anne Hélène. 1996. *The State and the Family: A Comparative Analysis of Family Policies in Industrialized Countries.* Oxford: Clarendon Press.

*General Electric v. Gilbert.* 1976. U.S. Supreme Court, 429 U.S. 125, No. 74–1589.

Genovese, R. 1984. *Social Needs and Public Policies.* New York: Praeger.

Gerstel, Naomi, and Katherine McGonagle. 1998. "Taking Time Off: Job Leaves, the Family and Medical Leave Act, and Gender." A paper presented at the Institute for Women's Policy Research Fifth Women's Conference. Washington, DC, June 12.

Giele, Janet A. 2000. "Decline of the Family: Conservative, Liberal, and Feminist Views." In *Public and Private Families: A Reader,* ed. Andrew J. Cherlin. New York: McGraw-Hill.

Giles, Nell. 1944. "What About the Women: Do They Want to Keep Their Factory Jobs When the War's Over?" *Ladies Home Journal,* June.

Gill, Richard T. 1997. *Posterity Lost: Progress, Ideology, and the Decline of the American Family.* Lanham, MD: Rowman & Littlefield.

Gilliand, Pierre. 1989. "Evolution of Family Policy in the Light of Demographic Development in West European Countries." *International Social Security Review* 42, 4: 395–426.

Ginsburg, Norman. 1992. *Divisions of Welfare: A Critical Introduction to Comparative Social Policy.* Newbury Park, CA: Sage.

Gladstone, Leslie W. 1999. "The Family and Medical Leave Act: Proposed Amendments." Order code: 97017. Washington, DC: Congressional Research Service

Gladstone, Leslie W., J. Williams, and R. Belous, 1985. *Maternity and Parental Leave Policies: A Comparative Analysis.* Washington, DC: Congressional Research Service Report, no. 85–148.

Glass Ceiling Commission. 1995. *A Solid Investment: Making Full Use of the Nation's Human Capital.* Washington, DC: U.S. Government Printing Office.

———. 1995. *Good For Business: Making Full Use of the Nation's Human Capital.* Washington, DC: U.S. Government Printing Office.

Glenn, Norval D. 1997. *Closed Hearts, Closed Minds: The Textbook Story of Marriage.* New York: Institute for American Values.

Gluck, Sherna B. 1987. *Rosie the Riveter Revisited: Women, the War, and Social Change.* Boston, MA: Twayne.

Goettsch, S. 1986. "The New Christian Right and the Social Sciences: A Response to McNamara." *Journal of Marriage and the Family* 48: 447–453.

Goldberg, G. 1991. "Women on the Verge: Winners and Losers in German Unification." *Social Policy* 34, 2: 35–44.

Goldin, Claudia. 1990. *Understanding the Gender Gap: An Economic History of American Women.* New York: Oxford University Press.

Goode, William. 1963. *World Revolution and Family Patterns.* New York: The Free Press.

Goodman, Ellen. 1999. "Caretaking Requires Real Solution, Not Baby Steps." *Hartford Courant*, November 16: 14.

Googins, Bradley. 1991. *Work/Family Conflicts: Private Lives—Public Responses.* New York: Auburn House.

Goozner, Merrill. 1999. "Limits of Family Leave." *Chicago Tribune*, May 4, 1999.

Greenberg, Stanley, B. 1995. *Middle Class Dreams: The Politics and Power of the New American Majority.* New York: Random House.

Greenhouse, Steven. 1999. "So Much Work, So Little Time." *New York Times*, September 15: A-1.

Greer, Germaine. 1971. *The Female Eunuch.* New York: McGraw-Hill.

Gregory, Chester. W. 1974. *Women in Defense Work During World War II: An Analysis of the Labor Problem and Women's Rights.* New York: Exposition Press.

Gronau, R. 1973. "The Intrafamily Allocation of Time." *American Economic Review* 63: 634–51.

Grossbard-Schectman, Shoshana, and Mathew Neideffer. 1997. "Women's Hours of Work and Marriage Market Imbalances." In *Economics of the Family and Family Policies*, eds. Inga Persson and Christina Jonung, 100–18. London and New York: Routledge.

Grossman, Laurie. 1993. "What About Us? Family-Support Programs May Have a Side Effect: Resentment Among Childless Workers." *Wall Street Journal*, June 21: 14.

Grundy, Lea, and Netsy Firestein. 1997. *Work, Family, and the Labor Movement.* Cambridge, MA: Radcliffe Public Policy Institute, Radcliffe College.

*Guardian.* 1990. "Thatcher Opposes National Child Care." May 18:2

*Guidelines on Discrimination Because of Sex.* 1972. Federal Register 6836, 29 C.F.R., 1604. Washington, DC: U.S. Government Printing Office.

Gustafsson. 1983. "Equal Employment Policies in Sweden." Stockholm: Center for Working Life.

Haas, Linda. 1992. *Equal Parenthood and Social Policy: A Study of Parental Leave in Sweden.* Albany, NY: State University of New York Press.

Haas, Linda, and Philip Hwang. 1999. "Parental Leave in Sweden." In *Parental Leave: Progress or Pitfall? Research and Policy Issues in Europe*, eds. Peter Moss and Fred Deven, 45–68. The Hague/Brussels: NIDI CBGS Publications.

Hadden, Jefferey. 1983. "Televangelism and the Mobilization of a New Christian Right in Family Policy." In *Families and Religions: Conflict and Change in Modern Society*, eds. William D'Antonio and Joan Aldous, 247–266. Newbury Park, CA: Sage.

Hapke, Laura. 1995. *Daughters of the Great Depression: Women, Work, and Fiction in the American 1930s.* Athens, GA: University of Georgia Press.

Harker, Susan. 1996. "The Family-Friendly Employer in Europe." In *The Work-Family Challenge: Rethinking Employment*, eds. Suzan Lewis and Jeremy Lewis, 48–62. Newbury Park, CA: Sage.

Hartmann, Heidi, Young-Hee Yoon, Roberta Spalter-Roth, and Lois Shaw. 1995. "Temporary Disability Insurance: A Model to Provide Income Security for Women Over the Life Cycle." A paper presented at the Annual Meeting of the American Economics Association. Washington, DC: January 8.

Hartman, Susan. 1982. *The Home Front and Beyond: American Women in the 1940s.* Boston, MA: Twayne.

Harvard Business School Press. 2000. *Harvard Business Review on Work and Life Balance*. Boston, MA: Harvard Business School Publishing.

Hatje, Ann-Katrin. 1974. *The Population Question and Welfare*. Stockholm: Allmanna Forlaget.

Hattiangadi, Anita U. 2000. *Paid Family Leave: At What Cost?* Washington, DC: Employment Policy Foundation.

Hefferen, C. 1982. "Federal Income Taxation and the Two-Earner Couple." *Family Economics Review* 2: 3–10.

Hewlett, Sylvia Ann, and Cornel West. 1998. *The War Against Parents: What Can We Do for America's Beleaguered Moms and Dads?* Boston, MA: Houghton Mifflin.

Himmelfarb, Gertrude. 1999. *One Nation, Two Cultures*. New York: Alfred A. Knopf.

Hirst, Paul. 1999. "Can the European Welfare State Survive Globalization? Sweden, Denmark, and the Netherlands in Comparative Perspective." A paper prepared by Paul Hirst, Birkbeck College, University of London.

Hochschild, Arlie R. 1989. *The Second Shift: Working Parents and the Revolution at Home*. New York: Viking Press.

———. 1997. *The Time Bind: When Work Becomes Home and Home Becomes Work*. New York: Holt.

Hoge, Warren. 2000. "One More Leaked Memo on Party's Woes Embarrasses Blair." *New York Times*, July 20: A-9.

Holcomb, Betty. 2000. "Family Friendly for Whose Family?" *Ms.*, April/May: 40–45.

Holmes, Stephen A. *New York Times*. 1996. "Traditional Family Stabilized in 90s, New Study Suggests." March 7: A1.

———. 1999a. "What's the Problem?" *Week in Review* section, August 4: A-4.

———. 1999. "Household Incomes Rise, 4th Straight Year." September 30: A1.

Holt, Helle, and Ivan Thaulow. 1996. "Formal and Informal Flexibility in the Workplace." In *The Work-Family Challenge: Rethinking Employment*, eds. Suzan Lewis and Jeremy Lewis, 79–92. Newbury Park, CA: Sage.

*Home News Tribune*. 1996. "Family Gets Focus: Clinton Emphasizes Values in Speech at Freehold." September 25: A1.

Honey, Maureen. 1984. *Creating Rosie the Riveter: Class, Gender, and Propaganda During World War II*. Amherst, MA: University of Massachusetts Press.

Honig, Marjorie. 1997. "Commentary on Chapter Three." In *Gender and Family Issues in the Workplace*, eds. Francine D. Blau and Ronald G. Ehrenberg, 89–91. New York: Russell Sage Foundation.

Howe, Neil, and Bill Strauss. 1993. *13th Gen: Abort, Retry, Ignore, Fail?* New York: Vintage Books.

Hudson, Robert B., ed. 1997. *The Future of Age-Based Public Policy*. Baltimore, MD: Johns Hopkins University Press.

Humphries, Jane. 1977. "Class Struggle and the Persistence of the Working Class Family." *Cambridge Journal of Economics* 1: 3.

Hyde, Janet, and Marilyn Essex. 1991. *Parental Leave and Child Care: Setting a Research and Policy Agenda*. Philadelphia, PA: Temple University Press.

ILO Report. 1999. *Key Indicators of the Labor Market*. Geneva: International Labor Organization.

Institute for Women's Policy Research. 1988. *Unnecessary Losses: Costs to Americans for the Lack of Family and Medical Leave*. Washington, DC: Institute for Women's Policy Research.

———. 1996. *The Status of Women in the States: Politics, Economics, Health,* *Demographics.* Washington, DC: Institute for Women's Policy Research.

———. 1999. *Equal Pay for Working Families.* Washington, DC: Institute for Wom Policy Research.

Jacobs, Francine, and Margery Davies, eds. 1994. *More Than Kissing Babies? C rent Child and Family Policy in the United States.* Westport, CT: Greenwood Pre

Johnson, Arthur. 1987. "The Family: The Need for Sound Policy, Not Rhetoric a Ideology." *Public Administration Review* 47, 3: 280–84.

Johnson, Julie. 1989. "Child Care Has No Shortage of Proposals: A Push by Conse vatives as Well as Liberals." *New York Times*, March 26: E-5.

*Johnson City Press.* 1996. "Mrs. Gore Promotes Family Leave." September 25: A-1

Jordan, Laura. 1999. "FMLA Proposals." Office of Legislative Research. Hartford CT: Connecticut General Assembly.

Kalvemark, Ann-Sofie. 1980. *More Children of Better Quality?—Aspects of Swedish Population in the 1930s.* Stockholm: Almqvist and Wiksell International.

Kamerman, Sheila, and Alfred Kahn. 1978. *Family Policy: Government and Families in Fourteen Countries.* New York: Columbia University Press.

———. 1991. "Child Care Policies and Programs: An International Overview." *Journal of Social Issues* 47, 2: 179–196.

———. 1995. *Starting Right: How America Neglects Its Youngest Children and What We Can Do about It.* New York: Oxford University Press.

———. 1997. *Family Change and Family Policies in Great Britain, Canada, New Zealand, and the United States.* Oxford: Clarendon Press.

———. 1999. "Child and Family Policies in an Era of Social Policy Retrenchment and Restructuring." A paper prepared for presentation at the annual conference of the Association of Public Policy Analysis and Management. Washington, DC: November 4–6.

Kamerman, Sheila, Alfred Kahn, and Paul Kingston, eds. 1983. *Maternity Policies and Working Women.* New York: Columbia University Press.

Kantrowitz, B., and P. Wingert. 1986. "Parental Leave Cries to Be Born." *Newsweek*, June 5: 64.

Katz, Lawrence. 1997. "Commentary on Chapter Three." In *Gender and Family Issues in the Workplace*, eds. Francine D. Blau and Ronald G. Ehrenberg, 86–88. New York: Russell Sage Foundation.

Kaufmann, Franz-Xaver, Anton Kuijsten, Hans-Joachim Schulze, and Klaus Peter Strohmeier. 1997. *Family Life and Family Policies in Europe.* Oxford: Clarendon Press.

Kellogg, Anne. 1996. "Family Leave Found Benign to Business." *Hartford Courant* May 2: 89.

Kesselman, Amy. 1990. *Fleeting Opportunities: Women Shipyard Workers in Por land and Vancouver During World War II and Reconversion.* Albany, NY: Sta University of New York Press.

Killingworth, Mark, and James J. Heckman. 1986. "Female Labor Supply: A S vey." In *Handbook of Labor Economics*, vol. 1, eds. Orley Ashenfelter and Ri ard Leyard, 103–204. Amsterdam: Elsevier Science Publishers.

Kismaric, Carole, and Marvin Heiferman. 1996. *Growing Up with Dick and J* San Francisco, CA: Collins.

Klerman, Jacob A. and Arleen Leibowitz. 1997. "Labor Supply Effects of S Maternity Leave Legislation." *Gender and Family Issues in the Workplace*,

Francine D. Blau and Ronald C. Ehrenberg, 65–84. New York: Russell Sage Foundation.

Kolb, C. 1994. *White House Daze: The Unmaking of Domestic Policy During the Bush Years.* New York: The Free Press.

Koziara, Karen S., Michael H. Moskow, and Lucretia D. Tanner. 1987. *Working Women: Past, Present, and Future.* Washington, DC: The Bureau of National Affairs.

Labor Project for Working Families. 1996. *Work and Family Bill of Rights.* Berkeley CA: Institute for Industrial Relations, University of California.

Lakoff, George. 1996. *Moral Politics: What Conservatives Know that Liberals Don't.* Chicago, IL: University of Chicago Press.

Lammers, William W., and Michael Genovese. 2000. *The Presidency and Domestic Policy: Comparing Leadership Styles, FDR to Clinton.* Washington, DC: Congressional Quarterly Press.

Lantz, Herman R. 1976. *Marital Incompatibility and Social Change in Early America.* Newbury Park, CA: Sage.

Larossa, Ralph, Charles Jaret, Malati Gadgil, and G. Robert Wynn. 2000. "The Changing Culture of Fatherhood in Comic Strip Families: A Six-Decade Analysis." *Journal of Marriage and the Family* 62, 2: 375–387.

Lasch, Christopher. 1995. *Haven in a Heartless World: The Family Besieged.* New York: Norton.

League of Nations. 1919. *Report on the Employment of Women and Children and the Berne Convention of 1906.* London: Harrison and Sons.

Lenhoff, Donna. 2000. "Pro and Con: Americans Need Affordable Family Leave." *IntellectualCapital.com*, February 3. Internet link: http://www.intellectualcapital.com/issues

Levitan, Sar A., Richard Bellous, and Frank Gallo. 1998. *What's Happening to the American Family?* Baltimore, MD: Johns Hopkins University Press.

Levy, David. 1945. "The War and Family Life." *The American Journal of Orthopsychiatry* 15, 2: 140–153.

Levy, Frank. 1999. "Rhetoric and Reality: Making Sense of the Income Gap Debate." *Harvard Business Review*, September–October: 163–70.

———. 1998. *The New Dollars and Dreams.* New York: Russell Sage Foundation.

Levy, Frank, and Richard Michel. 1991. *The Economic Future of American Families.* Washington, DC: The Urban Institute Press.

Lewis, J. 1989. "It All Really Starts in the Family: Community Care in the 1980s." *Journal of Law and Society* 16: 1.

Lichter, Daniel T., Felicia B. LeClere, and Diane K. McLaughlin. 1991. "Local Marriage Markets and the Marital Behavior of Black and White Women." *American Journal of Sociology* 96: 843–867.

*Lochner v. New York.* 1905. United States Supreme Court, 198 U.S. 45, no. 292.

Long, Clarence. 1958. *The Labor Force Under Changing Income and Employment.* Princeton, NJ: Princeton University Press, for the National Bureau of Economic Research.

Longman, Philip. 1987. *Born to Pay: The New Politics of Aging America.* Boston, MA: Houghton-Mifflin.

Love, Alice A. 2000. "Labor Department Sued Over Paid Leave." Associated Press, June 26.

Lowi, Theodore. 1969. *The End of Liberalism, Ideology, Policy and the Crisis of Public Authority.* New York: Norton.

Mack, Dana. 1997. *The Assault on Parenthood: How Our Culture Undermines the Family.* New York: Simon and Schuster.

Manser, Marilyn, and Murray Brown. 1980. "Marriage and Household Decision-Making: A Bargaining Approach." *International Economic Review* 34: 334–75.

Manton, Kenneth G., and Eric Stallard. 1994. "Interaction of Disability Dynamics and Mortality." In *Demography of Aging,* eds. Linda G. Martin and Samuel H. Preston, 217–278. Committee on Population, National Research Council. Washington, DC: National Academy Press.

Marshall, Ray, and Beth Paulin. 1987. "Employment and Earnings of Women: Historical Perspective." In *Working Women: Past, Present, Future,* eds. Karen Shallcross Koziara, Michael H. Moskow, and Lucretia Dewey Tanner, Washington, DC: The Bureau of National Affairs.

Marshall, Will, and Martin Schram. 1993. *Mandate for Change.* New York: Berkley Books.

Marks, Michelle. 1997. "Party Politics and Family Politics: The Case of the Family and Medical Leave Act." *Journal of Family Issues* 18,1: 55–70.

Maternal and Child Health Bureau. 1998. *Child Health USA 1998.* Washington, DC: United States Department of Health and Human Services.

Mattox, William R. Jr. 1998. "Government Tax Policy and the Family." In *The Family, Civil Society, and the State,* ed. Christopher Wolfe, 193–198. Boulder, CO: Rowman and Littlefield.

McCaffery, Edward J. 1997. *Taxing Women.* Chicago, IL: University of Chicago Press.

McCormick, John. 1999. *The European Union: Politics and Policies.* Boulder, CO: Westview Press.

McDaniel, A., and E. Thomas. 1991. "Bush's No-Risk Policy." *Newsweek,* June 24: 20.

McElroy, Marjorie, and Maureen Honey. 1981. "Models of Household Decisions." *International Economic Review* 22: 333–349.

McIntosh, C. Allison. 1983. *Population Policy in Western Europe: Responses to Low Fertility in France, Sweden and West Germany.* Armonk, NY: M.E. Sharpe.

McLanahan, Sara, and Gary Sandefur. 1994. *Growing Up with a Single Parent: What Hurts, What Helps.* Cambridge, MA: Harvard University Press.

McNamara, Patrick. 1985. "The New Christian Right's View of the Family and its Social Science Critics: A Study in Differing Presuppositions." *Journal of Marriage and the Family* 47: 449–458.

McNeely, R.L., and Barbe A. Fogarty. 1995. "Balancing Parenthood and Employment: Factors Affecting Company Receptiveness to Family-Related Innovations in the Workplace." In *The Work and Family Interface: Toward a Contextual Effects Perspective,* eds. Gary L. Bowen and Joe F. Pittman, 430–438. Minneapolis, MN: National Council on Family Relations.

MetLife. 1997. "MetLife Study of Employer Costs for Working Caregivers." Westport, CT: MetLife Mature Market Institute.

———. 1999. "MetLife Juggling Act Study." Westport, CT: MetLife Mature Market Institute.

Meyer, Stephen J. 1984. *The Five-Dollar Day.* Albany, NY: State University of New York Press.

Meyers, Michael. 1995. "Taking Pregnancy Leaves." Minneapolis: *Star Tribune,* February 6: A1.

Millett, Kate. 1970. *Sexual Politics.* Garden City, NY: Doubleday.

Mincer, Jacob. 1962. "Labor Force Participation of Women." In *Aspects of Labor Economics*, a conference of the Universities—National Bureau Committee for Economic Research. Princeton, NJ: Princeton University Press, for the National Bureau of Economic Research.

Miringoff, Marc, and Marque-Luisa Miringoff. 1999. *The Social Health of the Nation: How America Is Really Doing*. New York/Oxford: Oxford University Press.

Mishel, Lawrence, Jared Bernstein, and John Schmitt. 1999. *The State of Working America: 1998–99*. Ithaca, NY: Cornell University Press.

Mitchell, Olivia. 1990. "The Effect of Mandatory Benefit Packages." In *Research in Labor Economics*, vol. 11, eds. L. Bassi, D. Crawford, and R. Ehrenberg. Greenwich, CT: JAI Press.

Moeller, Robert G. 1993. *Protecting Motherhood: Women and the Family in the Politics of Postwar West Germany*. Berkeley, CA: University of California Press.

Monica, Mary. 1993. "The Real Victims of the Nine-to-Five Dilemma." *Fidelity*, July/August: 114–23.

Moody, Harry. 1992. *Ethics in an Aging Society*. Baltimore, MD: Johns Hopkins University Press.

Moody, J. Scott. 1999. *State and Local Property Tax Collections*. Washington, DC: Tax Foundation.

Moors, Hein, and Rossella Palomba. 1995. *Population, Family, and Welfare: A Comparative Survey of European Attitudes*. Vol. I. Oxford: Clarendon Press.

Morehouse, M. 1988. "Senate Democrats Are Stymied on So-called Family Issues." *Congressional Quarterly*, October 8: 59.

Moss, Peter. 1991. "Day Care for Young Children in the United Kingdom." In *Day Care for Young Children: International Perspectives*, eds. E.C. Melhuish and P. Moss, London: Routledge.

Moss, Peter, and Fred Deven, eds. 1999. *Parental Leave: Progress or Pitfall? Research and Policy Issues in Europe*. The Hague/Brussels: NIDI CBGS Publications.

Moynihan, Daniel Patrick. 1965. *The Negro Family: The Case for National Action*. Department of Labor, Office of Policy Planning and Research. Washington, DC: U.S. Government Printing Office.

———. 1986. *Family and Nation*. New York: Harcourt, Brace, and Jovanovich.

*Muller v. State of Oregon*. 1908. U.S. Supreme Court, 208 U.S. 412, No. 107.

Murray, Charles A. 1984. *Losing Ground: American Social Policy—1950–1980*. New York: Basic Books.

Myrdal, Alva, and Gunnar Myrdal. 1934. *Crisis in the Population Question*. Stockholm: Albert Fonnier Forlag.

National Alliance for Caregiving and American Association for Retired Persons (AARP). 1997. *Family Caregiving in the U.S.* Washington, DC: National Alliance for Caregiving.

National Center for Policy Analysis. 2000. "Family Care Leave Proposal Would Be Costly and Abused." Washington, DC: National Center for Policy Analysis.

National Employment Law Project.1999. "Unemployment Insurance Tax Cuts on the Rise: A Summary of Recent State Experiences." New York: National Employment Law Project.

National Marriage Project. 1999. *The State of Our Unions: The Social Health of Marriage in America*. New Brunswick, NJ: Rutgers University Press.

*National NOW Times*. 1987. "Family and Medical Leave Compromise Stirs Controversy among Supporters." September/October/November: 8.

National Opinion Research Center. 1999. *The Emerging 21st-Century American Family.* Chicago, IL: National Opinion Research Center.

National Partnership for Women and Families. 1998. "Americans Support Family Leave Insurance. Findings from *Family Matters: A National Survey of Women and Men.*" Conducted for the National Partnership for Women and Families by Lake, Sosin, Snell, Perry & Associates. Washington, DC: National Partnership for Women and Families.

————. 1999. "State Family Leave Laws that are More Expansive than the Federal Family and Medical Leave Act." Washington, DC: National Partnership for Women and Families. Internet link: http:// www.nationalpartnership.org.

————. 2000. "State Family—Leave Income Initiatives: Making Family Leave More Affordable." Washington, DC: National Partnership for Women and Families. Internet link: http://www.nationalpartnership.org/workandfamily/fmleave/flinsur.htm.

National Partnership for Women and Families Memo. 2000. "Overestimating the Costs of Parental Leave: Fundamental Flaws in the Employment Policy Foundation's Cost Assessments of Birth and Adoption Unemployment Compensation Programs." June 8, 2000. Washington, DC: National Partnership for Women and Families. Internet link: http://www.nationalpartnership.org.

Navarro, Peter. 1993. *Bill Clinton's Agenda for America.* Portland, OR: Williams.

New, C., and M. David. 1985. *For the Children's Sake: Making Child Care More Than Women's Business.* Hamondsworth, UK: Penguin.

*New York Times* on the Web. 2000. "Japan's Employers are Giving Bonuses for Having Babies." Posted on the Web, May 30. Internet link: http://www.nytimes.com.

*New York Times.* 1999a. "What's the Problem?" Week in Review, August 9: 4.

————. 1999b. "Household Incomes Rise, 4th Straight Year." September 30: A-1

Nock, Steven L. 1999. "The Problem with Marriage." *Society* 36, 4: 20–27.

Norton, Arthur J., and Louisa F. Miller. 1992. *Marriage, Divorce, and Remarriage in the 1990s.* United States Bureau of the Census, Current Population Reports, Series P23–180. Washington, DC: U.S. Government Printing Office.

O'Connor, Dennis 2000. "A 1998 Family and Medical Leave Summary for Connecticut Employees." An unpublished manuscript. Storrs, CT: University of Connecticut Institute of Public Affairs.

Office of the Press Secretary. 1997. The President's Weekly Radio Address. February 1, 1997. Washington, DC: The White House.

————. 1999. The President of the United States, State of the Union Message, January 19. Washington, DC: The White House.

————. 2000. The President of the United States, State of the Union Message, January 27. Washington, DC: The White House.

————. 2000. The President's Weekly Radio Address, February 12, 2000. Washington, DC: The White House.

O'Hara, Kathy. 1998. *Comparative Family Policy: Eight Countries' Stories.* Ottawa: CA: Renouf.

O'Melveny, Mary, K. 1996. "Representing the Injured Worker: Recent Developments Under the Americans with Disabilities Act and the Family and Medical Leave Act." The Labor Law Exchange, No. 16. Washington, DC: AFL-CIO Lawyers Coordinating Committee.

Orthner, Dennis, K., and Joe F. Pittman. 1995. "Family Contributions to Work Commitment." In *The Work and Family Interface: Toward a Contextual Effects Perspective,* eds. Gary L. Bowen and Joe F. Pittman, 439–446. Minneapolis, MN: National Council on Family Relations.

Osborne, David. 1988. *Laboratories of Democracy.* Boston, MA: Harvard Business School Press.

Ostner, Ilona, and Jane Lewis. 1995. "Gender and the Evolution of European Social Policies." In *European Social Policy: Between Fragmentation and Integration,* eds. Stephan Leibfried and Paul Pierson, 159–193. Washington, DC: The Brookings Institution.

Palley, Thomas. I. 1998. *Plenty of Nothing: The Downsizing of the American Dream and the Case for Structural Keynesianism.* Princeton, NJ: Princeton University Press.

Palme, J., and I. Wennemo. 1998. *Swedish Social Security in the 1990s: Reform and Retrenchment.* Stockholm, Sweden: The Printing Office of the Cabinet Ministries.

Pankhurst J., and S. Houseknecht. 1983. "The Family, Politics, and Religion in the 1980s: In Fear of the New Individualism." *Journal of Family Issues* 4: 5–34.

Pear, Robert. 1999. "Dispute Over Plan to Use Jobless Aid for Parental Leave." *New York Times,* November 8: A18.

Peden, Joseph, and Fred. Glahe. 1986. *The American Family and the State.* San Francisco, CA: The Pacific Institute for Public Policy Research.

Personal communication. 2000. Donna Lehnoff and Sandhya Subramanian of the National Partnership for Women and Families, March 8.

Persson, Inga, and Christina Jonung, eds. 1997. *Economics of the Family and Family Policies.* London and New York: Routledge:

Pettinger, Rudolf. 1999. "Parental Leave in Germany." In *Parental Leave: Progress or Pitfall? Research and Policy Issues in Europe,* eds. Peter Moss and Fred Deven, 123–140. The Hague/Brussels: NIDI CBGS Publications.

Philips, Kevin. 1990. *The Politics of Rich and Poor.* New York: Random House.

———. 1993. *Boiling Point: Democrats, Republicans and the Decline of Middle Class Prosperity.* New York: Harper Collins Publishers.

Piccirillo, Mary. 1988. "The Legal Background of a Parental Leave Policy and Its Implications." In *The Parental Leave Crisis: Toward a National Policy,* eds. Edward F. Zigler and Meryl Frank, 293–314. New Haven, CT: Yale University Press.

Pidgeon, Mary, E. 1954. *Changes in Women's Occupations: 1940–1950.* U.S. Department of Labor, Women's Bureau, Bulletin 253. Washington, DC: U.S. Government Printing Office.

Pleck, Joseph H. 1993. "Are 'Family-Supportive' Employer Policies Relevant to Men?" In *Men, Work and Family,* ed. Jane C. Hood, 217–237. Thousand Oaks, CA: Sage.

Poirer, John. 1999. "Senate Republicans Block Minimum Wage Increase." Washington, DC: Reuters. September 22, 1999.

Popenoe, David. 1988. *Disturbing the Nest: Family Change and Decline in Modern Societies.* New York: A. de Gruyter.

———. 1993. "Scholars Should Worry About the Disintegration of the American Family." *Chronicle of Higher Education,* April 14: A-60.

———. 1999. "Can the Nuclear Family be Revived?" *Society* 36, 4: 28–30.

Population Reference Bureau. 1996. *The United States at Mid-decade.* Population Bulletin 50, 4: March 1996. Washington, DC: Population Reference Bureau.

President's Commencement Address. 1999. Grambling State University, Grambling, LA, May 23. Washington, DC: The White House.

Presidential Memorandum. 1999. "Memorandum for the Heads of Executive Departments and Agencies, New Tools to Help Parents Balance Work and Family." May 24. Washington, DC: The White House.

Presser, Harriet B. 2000. "Nonstandard Work Schedules and Marital Instability." *Journal of Marriage and the Family* 62, 1:93–110.

Quirk, Paul J., and Joseph Hinchliffe. 1996. "Domestic Policy: The Trials of a Centrist Democrat." In *The Clinton Presidency: First Appraisals*, eds. Colin Campbell and Bert A. Rockman, 262–289. Chatam, NJ: Chatham House.

Radigan, Anne. 1988. *Concept and Compromise: The Evolution of Family Leave Legislation in the U.S. Congress.* Washington, DC: Women's Research and Education Institute.

Rainwater, Lee, and W. Yancey. 1967. *The Moynihan Report and the Politics of Controversy.* Cambridge, MA: MIT Press.

Raisan, John. 1996. In the foreword to *The Economic way of Looking at Behavior.* Palo Alto, CA: Hoover Institution, Stanford University.

RAND. 1995. " '93 Time Out for New Mothers: Some Issues for Maternity-Leave Policy," *Labor and Population Program Research Brief*, December. Santa Monica, CA: RAND.

Reid, T.R. 2000. "Paternity Leave for Blair? He's Thinking About It." *Washington Post Service*, March 29: 2.

Rimer, Sara. 1999. "Caring for Elderly Kin Is Costly, Study Finds." *New York Times*, November 27: A-1.

Roberts, Sam. 1993. *Who We Are: A Portrait of America.* New York: Times Books.

Robertson, Brian C. 2000. *There's No Place Like Work: How Business, Government, and Our Obsession with Work Have Driven Parents from the Home.* Dallas, TX: Spence.

Robinson, John. 1988. "Who's Doing the Housework?" *American Demographics* 10, 12: 24–25.

Robinson, John, and Geoffrey Godbey. 1997. *Time for Life: The Surprising Ways Americans Use Their Time.* State College, PA: Pennsylvania State University Press.

Rosen, Harry S. 1987. "The Marriage Tax Is Down But Not Out." *National Tax Journal* 40: 567–575.

———. 1992. *Public Finance.* 3rd ed. Homewood, IL: Irwin.

Ross, Katherin. 1998. "Maternity Leave Law Has Limited Impact." *Population Today* 26 5: 5–6.

Rothman, S. 1978. *Woman's Proper Place.* New York: Basic Books.

Rovner, Julie. 1987. "Revised Family-Leave Measure OK'd by Divided House Panel." *Congressional Quarterly*, November 21: 280–284.

Rubin, Rose M., and Bobye J. Riney. 1995. *Working Wives and Dual-Earner Families.* Westport, CT: Praeger

Ruhm, Christopher J. 1998. "The Economic Consequences of Parental Leave Mandates: Lessons from Europe." *Quarterly Journal of Economics* 113, 1: 258—318.

Ruhm, Christopher J., and Jackqueline L. Teague. 1997. "Parental Leave Policies in Europe and North America." In *Gender and Family Issues in the Workplace*, eds. Francine D. Blau and Ronald G. Ehrenber, 133–156. New York: Russell Sage Foundation.

Rupp, Leila. 1978. *Mobilizing Women for the War: German and American Propaganda, 1939–1945.* Princeton, NJ: Princeton University Press.

Ryscavage, Paul. 1998. *Income Inequality in America.* Armonk, NY: M.E. Sharpe.

Safire, William. 1995. *The Dictionary of American Politics.* New York: Simon and Schuster.

*San Jose Mercury News.* 2000. "Davis Vetoes Expanded Family Leave Bill." May 25: 1.

Scanzoni, John. 1991. "Balancing the Policy Interests of Children and Adults." In *The Reconstruction of Family Policy*, eds. Elaine Anderson and Richard Hula, 11–22. Westport, CT: Greenwood Press.

Schlotterbeck, Karl T. 1943. *Postwar Employment: The Magnitude of the Problem.* Pamphlet No. 54. Washington, DC: The Brookings Institution.

Schmidt, M. 1998. "The EC-Directive on Parental Leave." In *Labour Law and Industrial Relations in the European Union*, ed. R. Blanpain, 181–192. London: Kluwer International.

Schorr, Juliet B. 1993. *The Overworked American: The Unexpected Decline of Leisure.* New York: Basic Books.

Schwartz, Felice N. 1989. "Management Women and the New Facts of Life." *Harvard Business Review*, January–February: 78–84.

Schwemle, Barbara L. 1999. "Use of Sick Leave by Federal Employees to Care for Sick Family Members." *Congressional Research Service Report for Congress*, RL30259. Washington, DC: Congressional Research Service.

Sharp, Elaine B. 1999. *Culture Wars and Local Politics.* Lawrence, KS: University Press of Kansas.

Singh, Gopal. 1994. "Annual Summary of Births, Marriages, Divorces, and Deaths: United States, 1994. *Monthly Annual Statistics Report* 43, 13: October 23. Washington, DC: United States Bureau of the Census.

Skocpol, Theda. 1992. *Protecting Mothers and Soldiers: The Political Origins of Social Policy in the United States.* Cambridge, MA: The Belknap Press of Harvard University.

———. 1996. "Delivering for Young Families: The Resonance of the GI Bill." *The American Prospect* 28: 66–72.

———. 2000. *The Missing Middle: Working Families and the Future of American Social Policy.* New York: W.W. Norton.

Skolnick, Arlene. 1991. *Embattled Paradise: The American Family in an Age of Uncertainty.* New York: Basic Books.

Smith, Adam. 1981. [1776]. *An Inquiry into the Nature and Causes of the Wealth of Nations.* 2 vols., eds. R.H. Campbell and A.S. Skinner. Reprint, Indianapolis, IN: Liberty Classics.

Soldo, Beth J., and Vicki A. Freedman. 1994. "Care of the Elderly: Division of Labor Among the Family, Market, and State." In *Demography of Aging*, eds. Linda G.Martin and Samuel H. Preston, Committee on Population, National Research Council.Washington, DC: National Academy Press

Spalter-Roth, Roberta M., and Heidi I. Hartmann. 1991. "Science and Politics and the 'Dual Vision' of Feminist Policy Research: The Example of Family and Medical Leave." In *Parental Leave and Child Care: Setting a Research and Policy Agenda*, eds. Janet Shibley Hyde and Marilyn J. Essex, 41–65. Philadelphia, PA: Temple University Press.

———. 1990. *Unnecessary Losses: Costs to Americans of the Lack of Family and Medical Leave.* Washington, DC: Institute for Women's Policy Research.

Stacey, Judith. 1990. *Brave New Families: Stories of Domestic Upheaval in Late Twentieth Century America.* New York: Basic Books.

———. 1996. *In the Name of the Family: Rethinking Family Values in the Postmodern Age.* Boston, MA: Beacon Press.

Steinem, Gloria. 1983. *Outrageous Acts and Everyday Rebellions.* New York: Holt, Rinehart and Winston.

Steiner, Gilbert. 1981. *The Futility of Family Policy.* Washington, DC: Brookings Institution.

Steuerle, Eugene, C. 1995. "The True Tax Rate Structure." *Tax Notes* 69: 371–372.

Stevenson, Richard. 2000. "The Fight over Tax Changes: The Marriage Penalty and More." *New York Times*, July 23: A-14.

Stoesz, David. 1996. *Small Change: Domestic Policy Under the Clinton Presidency.* White Plains, NY: Longman.

Strum, Philippa. 1984. *Louis D. Brandeis: Justice for the People.* Cambridge, MA: Harvard University Press.

Summers, Lawrence. 1989. "Some Simple Economics of Mandated Benefits." *American Economic Review* 79, 2: 177–183.

Swedish Institute. 1989. "Equality Between Men and Women in Sweden." *Fact Sheets on Sweden.* Stockholm: Swedish Institute.

Sweet, James A., and Larry L. Bumpass. 1987. *American Families and Households.* New York: Russell Sage Foundation.

Tauber, Cynthia. 1996. *Statistical Handbook on Women in America.* Phoenix, AZ: The Oryx Press.

Thompson, Richard, and Charles Scavo. 1992. "The Home Front: Domestic Policy in the Bush Years." In *Leadership and the Bush Presidency,* eds. Ryan J. Barilleaux and Mary E. Stuckey, 149–164. Hanover, NH: The University Press of New England.

*Time.* 1991. "A Tale of Two Bushes." January 17: 18–20.

Tolnay, Stewart E., and Scott J. South. 1992. *The Changing American Family: Sociological and Demographic Perspectives.* Boulder, CO: Westview Press.

Townsend, Bickley, and Kathleen O'Neil. 1990. "American Women Get Mad." *American Demographics* 12, 10: 17–19.

Triest, Robert K. 1990. "The Effect of Income Taxation on Labor Supply in the United States." *Journal of Human Resources* 25: 491–515.

Trzcinski, Eileen. 1991. "Employers' Parental Leave Policies: Does the Labor Market Provide Parental Leave?" In *Parental Leave and Child Care,* eds. Janet Hyde and Marilyn Essex, 209–228. Philadelphia, PA: Temple University Press.

Trzcinski, Eileen, and William T. Albert. 1991. "Handling Work During Leave: Strategies and Costs." *Journal of Managerial Issues* 3: 403–426.

———. 1994. "Pregnancy and Parental Leave in the United States and Canada." *Journal of Human Resources* 29, 2: 535–554.

———. 1998. "Gender and German Unifcation." AFFILIA 13, 1: 69–101.

United for a Fair Economy. 1999. "Dangerous Inequalities: The Widening Gap Between the Rich and Everyone Else and What it Means." Washington, DC: United for a Fair Economy.

United States Bureau of the Census. 1990. *Who's Minding the Kids? Child Care Arrangements.* Current Population Reports (Winter 1987–88): Series, P-70, No. 20. Washington, DC: U.S. Government Printing Office.

———. 1996. *65+ in the United States.* Current Population Reports, Special Studies, P23–190. Washington, DC: United States Bureau of the Census.

———. 1997. *Statistical Abstract of the United States*: 1997. No. 66, No. 75, No. 145, No. 150 (117th Edition). Washington, DC: United States Bureau of the Census.

———. 1998. *Marital Status and Living Arrangements.* March 1997. Washington, DC: United States Bureau of the Census.

United States Bureau of Labor Statistics. 1948. *Handbook of Facts on Women Workers.* Bulletin 225. Washington, DC: United States Bureau of Labor Statistics.

———. 1998. "Employment Characteristics of Families in 1997." *Bureau of Labor Statistics News.* USDL98–6378, May 21, 1998. Washington, DC: United States Bureau of Labor Statistics.

United States Department of Labor. 1992. Bureau of Labor-Management Relations and Cooperative Programs. *Work and Family Provisions in Major Collective Bargaining Agreements*. Washington, DC: United States Department of Labor.

———. 1998. *A Dialogue: Unemployment Insurance and Employment Service Programs*. Washington, DC: U.S. Department of Labor. Internet link: http://www.doleta.gov/dialogue/master.htm.

———. 1999. Employment and Training Administration Fact Sheet. Washington, DC: United States Department of Labor. Internet link: http://www.wdsc.org/layoff/ui.htm.

———. 2000. Employment Standards Division, Wage and Hour Division, *FMLA Complaints Filed with the Department of Labor*. Washington: United States Department of Labor.

United States Executive Office of the President. 1992. "The President's Veto Message on the Family and Medical Leave Bill." Washington, DC: The White House, September 22.

United States General Accounting Office. 1988. *Parental Leave: Estimated Cost of Revised Parental and Medical Leave Act Proposal*. HRD-88–132. Washington, DC: U.S. Government Printing Office.

———. 1999. DOL Federal Regulation 67972, December 3, 1999. Washington, DC: United States Government Printing Office.

United States Government Printing Office. 1978. "A Statement in New Hampshire." *The Presidential Campaign, 1976, Jimmy Carter.* Washington, DC: United States Government Printing Office.

U.S. Office of Personnel Management. 1998. *A Review of Federal Family-Friendly Workplace Arrangements*. Washington, DC: U.S. Office of Personnel Management.

United States Senate. 1996. Proceedings and Debates of the 104th Congress, Second Session. *The Defense of Marriage Act*. Washington, DC: U.S. Government Printing Office, September 10: S. 10109.

United States Social Security Administration. 1940. *An Outline of Foreign Social Insurance and Assistance Laws*. Washington, DC: U.S. Social Security Administration.

United States Supreme Court Reports. 1986. *California Federal Savings & Loan Association, et al., Petitioners v. Mark Guerra, Director, Department of Fair Employment and Housing, et al.* October Term, vol. 479. Rochester, NY: The Lawyers' Cooperative Publishing Co.

Verhovek, Sam H. 1993. "At Issue: Hold a Baby or Hold That Line." *New York Times*, October 20: A-1.

Vitz, Paul, C. 1998. *The Course of True Love: Marriage in High School Textbooks.* New York: Institute for American Values.

Waldfogel, Jane. 1997. "Working Mothers Then and Now: A Cross-Cohort Analysis of the Effects of Maternity Leave on Women's Pay." In *Gender and Family Issues in the Workplace,* eds. Francine D. Blau and Ronald C. Ehrenberg, 92–126. New York: Russell Sage Foundation.

———. 1999. "The Impact of the Family and Medical Leave Act." *Journal of Policy Analysis and Management* 18, 2: 281–302.

Waldfogel, Jane, Yoshio Higuchi, and Masahiro Abe. 1999. "Family Leave Policies and Women's Retention after Childbirth: Evidence from the United States, Britain, and Japan." *Journal of Population Economics* 12: 523–545.

Weigl, I., and C. Weber. 1991. "Day Care for Young Children in the German Democratic Republic." In *Day Care for Young Children: International Perspectives*, eds. E.C. Mehhuish and P. Moss, 41–63. London: Routledge.

Wever, Kristin. 1996. *The Family and Medical Leave Act.* Cambridge, MA: Radcliffe Public Policy Institute. Radcliffe College.

White House. 1998. "The Balanced Budget Delivers a Mainstream Middle Class Tax Cut." Washington, DC: Office of the President, the White House.

———. 1999. News Conference. President Clinton authorizes states to pay unemployment benefits to parents who take leave for newborns. Washington, DC: Office of the President, the White House, November 30.

Wicksell, Nordquist L. 1985. *Anna Bugge Wicksell: A Woman Before Her Time.* Lund, Sweden: Liber.

Will, George. 1993. "As the Family Disintegrates, So Does Our Society." *Norwich Bulletin*, December 16: 17.

———. 1997. "Echoes of the GI Bill." *Newsweek*, October 27: 82.

Williams, Gregory. 2000. "Estimate of Utilization and Cost of Family Leave Benefits under Assembly Bill No. 2037." Trenton, NJ: Office of Legislative Analysis, General Assembly of New Jersey.

Williams, W. 1984. "Pregnancy: Special Treatment vs. Equal Treatment." *Responses: New York University Review of Law and Social Change* 13: 407–410.

Williamson, John, Diane M. Watts-Roy, and Eric R. Kingson, eds. 1999. *The Generational Equity Debate.* New York: Columbia University Press.

Wilson, James Q. 1993. *The Moral Sense.* New York: Free Press.

Wilson, William J. 1987. *The Truly Disadvantaged.* Chicago, IL: University of Chicago Press.

———. 1996. "When Work Disappears." *New York Times Magazine*, August 18: 27–53.

Wisensale, Steven K. 1988. "Implementing Family Leave Policy in the Public Sector: An Analysis of Four States." *Journal of Management Science and Policy Analysis* 6, 1: 27–36.

———. 1989a. "Family Policy in the State Legislature: The Connecticut Agenda." *Policy Studies Review* 8, 3: 146–154.

———. 1989b. "Family Leave Legislation: State and Federal Initiatives." *Family Relations* 38: 182–218.

———. 1990. "Approaches to Family Policy in State Government: A Report on Five States." *Family Relations* 39, 2: 136–140.

———. 1991a. "An Intergenerational Policy Proposal for the 1990s: Applying the Temporary Disability Insurance Model to Family Caregiving." *Journal of Aging and Social Policy* 3, 2: 163–183.

———. 1991b. "The Family in the Think Tank." *Family Relations* 40, 2: 199–207.

———. 1994. "Family Leave Policy in the United States." *Social Policy and Administration* 28, 2: 128–138.

———. 1997. "The White House and Congress on Child Care and Family Leave Policy: From Carter to Clinton." *Policy Studies Journal* 25, 1: 75–86.

———. 1999a. "Partnering with the State Legislature: The Connecticut Family Impact Seminar." In *Serving Children and Families Through Community-University Partnerships: Success Stories*, eds. Tom Chibucos and Richard Learner, 43–46. Newbury Park, CA: Sage.

———. 1999b. "Grappling with the Generational Equity Debate: An Ongoing Challenge for the Public Administrator." *Public Integrity*, Winter: 1–19.

———. 1999c. "Family Values and Presidential Elections: The Use and Abuse of the Family and Medical Leave Act in the 1992 and 1996 Campaigns." *New England Journal of Public Policy* 15, 1: 35–50.

————. 1999d. "The Family and Medical Leave Act in Court: A Review of Key Appeals Court Cases Five Years Later." *WorkingUSA: The Journal of Labor and Society* 3, 4: 96–119.

Wolf, Douglas. 1994. "The Elderly and Their Kin." In *Demography of Aging*, eds. Linda G. Martin and Samuel H. Preston. Committee on Population, National Research Council. Washington, DC: National Academy Press.

Wolfe, Christopher, ed. 1998. *The Family, Civil Society and the State.* Lanham, MD: Rowman and Littlefield.

Wolff, Michael, Peter Rutten, and Albert F. Bayers III. 1992. *Where We Stand: Can America Make It in the Global Race for Wealth, Health, and Happiness?* New York: Bantam Books.

Woloch, Nancy. 1996. *Muller v. Oregon: A Brief History with Documents.* Boston, MA: Bedford Books.

*Working Mother.* 1999. "Working Mother's Top 100 Companies." *Working Mother*, September. Web site: www.workingmother.com.

Zaretsky, Eli. 1986. *Capitalism, the Family, and Personal Life.* New York: Perennial Library.

Zigler, Edward F., and Meryl Frank, eds. 1998. *The Parental Leave Crisis: Toward a National Policy.* New Haven: Yale University Press.

Zigler, Edward F. Sharon Lynn Kagan, and Nancy W. Hall, eds. 1996. *Children, Families, and Government.* Cambridge, MA: Cambridge University Press.

Zimmerman, Shirley. 1988. *Understanding Family Policy: Theoretical Approaches.* Newbury Park, CA: Sage

————. 1992. *Family Policies and Family Well-being: The Role of Political Culture.* Newbury Park, CA: Sage.

## Selected Cases by Issue Category by Order of Appearance in Chapter 7

### *Job Security*

*Lempres v. CBS Inc.* D.D.C. Civil action 95–451 (RMU), Feb. 16, 1996 (1996 U.S. Dist. LEXIS 2324).

*Patterson v. Alltel Information Services Inc.* D.Me., Civil No. 95–188-P-C, March 15, 1996 (1996 U.S. Dist. LEXIS 5253).

*Day v. Excel* D. Kan., No. 94–1439-JTM, May 17, 1996 (1996 U.S. Dist. LEXIS 8269).

*Donnellan v. New York City Transit Authority* S.D.N.Y., 98 Cov/1096(BSJ), July 22, 1999.

*Peterson v. Slidell Memorial Hospital and Medical Center* E.D. La., Civil Action No. 96–2487, Section "G," Dec. 16, 1996.

*Clay v. City of Chicago* N.D. Ill., No. 96 C 3684, April 8, 1997.

*Beckendorf v. Schwegmann Giant Super Markets Inc.* E.D. La., No. 95–3822, Section "K" (3), April 21, 1997.

*Kephart v. Cherokee County N.C.* W.D.N.C., 52F. Supp. 2d 607, May 12, 1999.

*Fejes v. Gilpin Ventures Inc.* D. Colo., Civil Action No. 95-B-1765, April 25, 1997.

*Knussman v. Maryland* D. Md. 16F Supp. 2d 601, Aug. 13, 1998.

*Nero v. Industrial Molding Corp.* 5th Cir., 167 F.3d 921, March 2, 1999.

## Seriousness of Employee's Illness

*Oswalt v. Sara Lee Corp.* N.D. Miss., 889 F. Supp. 253, June 20, 1995 (1995 U.S. Dist. LEXIS 8844).

*Bauer v. Dayton-Walther Corp.* E.D. KY., Civ. No. 94–101, Jan. 5, 1996 (1996 U.S. Dist. LEXIS 193).

*Hott v. VDO Yazaki Corp.* W.D. VA., Civil Action No. 94–00064-H, March 8, 1996 (1996 U.S. Dist. LEXIS 3447).

*Gudenkauf v. Stauffer Communications Inc.* D. Kan. No. 94–4228-SAC, Feb. 13, 1996 (1996 U.S. Dist. LEXIS 4387).

*Reich v. The Standard Register Co.* W.D. Val, No. 96–0284-R, Feb. 17, 1997.

*Fisher v. State Farm Mutual Automobile Insurance Co.* E.D. Tex., 999 F. Supp. 866, March 23, 1998.

*Lange v. Showbiz Pizza Time Inc.* D. Kan., 12 F. Supp. 2d 1150, May 8, 1998.

*Boyd v. State Farm Insurance Co.* 5th Cir., 158 F.3d 326, Nov. 3, 1998.

*Reich v. Midwest Plastic Engineering Inc.* W.D. Mich., Case No. 1: 94-CV-525, June 6, 1995 (1995 U.S. Dist. LEXIS 8772).

*George v. Associated Stationers Inc.* N.D. Ohio, 932 F. Supp. 1012, June 3, 1996 (1996 U.S. Dist. LEXIS 14670).

*Murphy v. Cadillac Rubber & Plastics Inc.* W.D. N.Y., 95-CV-422H, Nov. 21, 1996.

*Atchley v. Nordam Group Inc.* 10th Cir., No. 98–5006, 98–5020, 98–5087, 98–5125, June 4, 1999.

*Thorson v. Gemini Inc.* 8th Cir., No. 99–1656/99—112059, No. 99—1708, March 3, 2000.

## Eligibility Issues

*Spurlock v. Nynex* W.D. N.Y., 96-CV-0098C(F), Dec. 6, 1996.

*Wolke v. Dreadnought Marine, Inc.* E.D. Va., Civil Action No. 2: 96cv843, Feb. 19, 1997.

*Campbell v. Pritchard Police Department* S.D. Ala., Civ. No. 97–0496-AH-C, Nov. 19, 1997.

*Kelley v. Crosfield Catalysts* 7th Cir., No. 97–1643, Feb. 9, 1998.

*Vanderhoof v. Life Extension Institute* D.NJ., Civil Action No. 96–3335 (NHP), Dec. 19, 1997.

*Barrilleaux v. Thayer Lodging Group Inc.* E.D. La., Civil Action No. 97–3252, March 12, 1999.

## Sufficient Notification Required of Employees

*Brannon v. Oshkosh B'Gosh Inc.* M.D. Tenn., No. 2: 94–0090, Aug. 9, 1995 (1995 U.S. Dist. LEXIS 12805).

*Johnson v. Primerica* S.D. N.Y., 94 Civ. 4869 (MBM) (RLE), Jan. 30, 1996 (1996 U.S. Dist. LEXIS 869).

*Kaylor v. Fanin Regional Hospital Inc.* N.D. Ga., Civil No. 2: 95-CV-0067-WCO, Oct. 22, 1996.

*Satterfield v. Wal-Mart Stores Inc.* 5th Cir. 135F.3d 973, Feb. 25, 1998, cert. Denied 119 S. Ct. 72 (Oct. 5, 1998).

*Ware v. Stahl Specialty Co.* W.D. Mo., No. 97–0436-CV-W-6, April 9, 1998.
*Gibbs v. American Airlines Inc.* Cal. Ct. APP., 74 Cal. App. 4th 1, Aug. 10, 1999.
*Miller v. AT&T.* S.D. W.Va., 60F. Supp. 2d 574, Aug. 9, 1999.

### Calculating Time

*Mion v. Aftermarket Tool & Equipment* W.D. Mich., Case No. 4: 97-CV-25, Nov. 4, 1997.
*Clark v. Allegheny University Hospital* E.D. Pa., No. 97–6113, March 4, 1998.
*Salgado v. CDW Computer Centers Inc.* N.D. Ill., No. 97 C 1975, Feb. 5, 1998.
*Miller v. Defiance Metal Products Inc.* N.D. Ohio, 989F Supp. 945, Dec. 12, 1997.
*Fry v. First Fidelity Bancorporation* E.D. Pa., Civil Action No. 95–6019, Jan. 30, 1996 (1996 U.S. Dist. LEXIS 875).
*Robbins v. Bureau of National Affairs* D.D.C., Civil Action no. 95–685 (JHG), Aug. 12, 1995 (1995 U.S. Dist. LEXIS 11889).
*Rich v. Delta Airlines* N.D. Ga. CA No. 1: 94-CV-2847-RLV, Feb. 7, 1996 (1996 U.S. Dist. LEXIS 3750).

### Seriousness of Family Member's Illness

*Seidle v. Provident Mutual Life Insurance Co.* E.D. Pa., Civil Action No. 94–3306, Dec. 19, 1994 (1994 U.S. Dist. LEXIS 18281).
*Cianci v. Pettibone Corp.* N.D. Ill., No. 95 C 4906, April 8, 1997.
*Sakellarion v. Judge & Dolph Ltd.* N.D. Ill., 893 F. Supp. 800, July 19, 1995.
*Bryant v. Delbar Products Inc.* M.D. Tenn., 18F. Supp. 2d 799, Aug. 27, 1998.
*Land v. Aeroglide Corp.* E.D.N.C., No. 5: 98—CV—437—H(2), May 13, 1999.

### Information Provided by Employers to Employees

*McKiernan v. Smith-Edwards-Dunlap Co.* E.D. Pa., Civil Action No. 95–1175, May 17, 1995 (1995 U.S. Dist. LEXIS 6822).
*Henderson v. Whirlpool Corp.* N.D. Okla., 17F. Supp. 2d 1238, Aug. 13, 1998.

### Definition of Employer

*Frizzell v. Southwest Motor Freight Inc.* E.D. Tenn. No. 1: 95-CV-275, Nov. 20, 1995 (1995 U.S. Dist. LEXIS 18582).
*Freemon v. Foley* N.D. Ill., No. 95 C 209, Nov. 7, 1995 (1995 U.S. Dist. LEXIS 16574).
*Mercer v. Borden* C.D. Cal., 11F. Supp. 2d 1190, July 24, 1998.
*Johnson v. A.P. Products Ltd.* S.D.NY., 96 CV 0838 (BDP), Aug. 6, 1996 (1996 U.S. Dist. LEXIS 11593).
*Carpenter v. Refrigeration Sales Corp.* N.D. Ohio, 1: 98-CV-940, May 5, 1999.
*Wascura v. Carver* 11th Cir., 169 F. 3d 683, March 9, 1999.

### The FMLA and Labor Contracts

*Hoffman v. Aaron Kamhi Inc.* S.D. N.Y., No. 95-Civ. 2752 (DC), March 27, 1996.

*Satarino v. A.G. Edwards & Sons Inc.* N.D. Texas, 3: 96-CV-1587-D, Oct. 23, 1996.
*O'Neil v. Hilton Head Hospital* 4th Cir., No. 96–2460, June 13, 1997.
*Oklahoma Fixture Co. v. Local 942 International Brotherhood of Carpenters and Joiners of America* 10th Cir., No. 97–5009, June 11, 1997.
*Alden v. Maine*, 119, U.S. Supreme Court 2240, June 23, 1999.

## The FMLA as Shield and Protector

*McCown v. UOP Inc.* N.D. Ill. No. 94 C2179, Aug. 29, 1995 (1995 U.S. dist. LEXIS 1265).

# Index

# About the Author

**Steven K. Wisensale** is an associate professor of public policy in the School of Family Studies at the University of Connecticut, where he teaches courses in family policy, law, comparative family policy, human-services management, and aging policy. Much of his research has focused on family leave policy and aging issues, with a particular interest in the allocation of resources across generations. He is a recipient of the University of Connecticut's Excellence in Teaching Award and the Northeastern Gerontological Association's Research Award. He has been a consultant to the United Nations and the state of Connecticut where, in 1999–2000, he served on the State Task Force on Family and Medical Leave. Professor Wisensale holds a Ph.D. in social welfare policy from the Heller School at Brandeis University.